Edexcel GCSE (9-1) 1DT0 Design and Technology

M.J. Ross

E. Arnold

E. Berry

Published by
PG Online Limited
The Old Coach House
35 Main Road
Tolpuddle
Dorset
DT2 7EW
United Kingdom
sales@pgonline.co.uk
www.pgonline.co.uk

2019

PG ONLINE

Acknowledgements

The answers in the Teacher's Supplement are the sole responsibility of the authors and have neither been provided nor approved by the examination board.

Every effort has been made to trace and acknowledge ownership of copyright. The publishers will be happy to make any future amendments with copyright owners that it has not been possible to contact. The authors and publisher would like to thank the following companies and individuals who granted permission for the use of their images in this textbook.

Cover
Cover picture © 'Stop Static (Before It Stops You)'
Acrylic on canvas 76cm x 61cm 2014
Reproduced with the kind permission of Grant Wiggins
www.grantwiggins.com

Section 1
Fruit packing: © ArtistGND / Shutterstock.com
Lunatik watch: © MINIMAL
Fairtrade Bananas: © Thinglass / Shutterstock.com
Hyderabad: © SNEHIT / Shutterstock.com
Pippy oak dining table courtesy of Jim Tory Furniture www.jimtoryfurniture.co.uk
Key turner: courtesy of OTS Ltd
Easi-Grip Trowel with Arm Support courtesy of Peta (UK) Limited
The Lionmark © British Toy & Hobby Association

Section 2
Vertu phones: © Hadrian / Shutterstock.com
Crossrail tunnel: © Paul Daniels / Shutterstock.com
Tesla car: © RossHelen / Shutterstock.com
Child labourer: © StevenK / Shutterstock.com
Dutch floating house: © Alamy

Section 3
Turanor solar boat: © Igor Karasi / Shutterstock.com
Construction of concrete columns: © Aisyaqilumaranas / Shutterstock.com
Thermochromic sheet: © SFXC Good Life Innovations Ltd
Conductive thread courtesy of SparkFun Electronics
Common input components courtesy of RS Components Limited
Circuit Wizard screenshot: © New Wave Concepts
WaterLily turbine © WaterLily / Seaformatics Systems Inc.
Electric paint © Bare Conductive

Section 5
Zaha Hadid aquatics centre © Ron Ellis / Shutterstock.com
Buzz Lightyear figurine © Nicescene / Shutterstock.com
Tesla car © franz12 / Shutterstock.com
Adidas X Parley Shoe made using Parley Ocean Plastic™
Anna G Corkscrew, Designer Alessandro Mendini: © Alessi, S.p.a., Crusinallo, Italy
Designer's sketch: © Robert Bronwasser (2007)
Fashion sketch courtesy of Leonora Sheppard
Plopp chocolate: Cloetta AB
The New Fiver: © Bank of England
Joe Casely-Hayford © Casely-Hayford
Greyhound bus: © Chris Jenner / Shutterstock.com

Section 6-1
Tommy Alven © / Shutterstock.com
FSC logo: © The Forest Stewardship Council
PEFC logo: © PEFC UK Ltd
Quality Control go / no go gauge: © Yorkshire Precision Gauges Ltd

Section 6-2
Transrapid SMT maglev train: © Pavel L Photo and Video / Shutterstock.com
Apple Watch Sport © Alexey Boldin / Shutterstock.com
Maserati factory: © MikeDotta / Shutterstock.com
MacBook Pro: © Peter Kotoff / Shutterstock.com
Metal bandsaw courtesy of Axminster Tool Centre Ltd

Section 6-3
Traditional papercutting: © chinahbzyg / Shutterstock.com
Paper detail: © Phenom-World
Maun safety rule: Maun Industries Ltd, Axminster Tool Centre Ltd
Maun safety rule with cutting mat courtesy of Axminster Tool Centre Ltd
Paper Shears: © Dahle
Tamper proof sticker courtesy of StickerYou Inc.
Metal band saw courtesy of Axminster Tool Centre Ltd
Creasing machine: © Punchbind - UK Distributors of Cyklos Creasing Machines
PCB Scrub block courtesy of RS Components Limited
Rotary cutting tool courtesy of Olfa

Section 6-4
Apple Watch: © charnsitr / Shutterstock.com
Oil spill in Thailand: © kajornyot wildlife photography / Shutterstock.com
Group of Tanzanian women: © Rashad Mammadov / Shutterstock.com
Laser cutter: © Shutter B Photo / Shutterstock.com

Section 6-5
Jiujiang factory: © humphery / Shutterstock.com
Copper Clad circuit board: © Yoonseo Kang, OpenStax CNX
Common input components courtesy of RS Components Limited

Section 6-6
Harris Tweed label: © Stephen Plaster / Shutterstock.com
Rana Plaza disaster: © Sk Hasan Ali / Shutterstock.com
Samburu warriors: © Dietmar Temps / Shutterstock.com
Rotary cutting tool courtesy of Olfa
Flame resistant fabric: © Finlam Technical

All Sections
Photographic images: © Shutterstock

Preface

This is a brand new book that provides comprehensive yet concise coverage of all the topics covered in the new Edexcel 1DT0 Design and Technology (9-1) specification, written and presented in a way that is accessible to teenagers and easy to teach from. It can be used both as a course text and as a revision guide for students nearing the end of their course.

Each chapter contains exercises and questions, written in an examination style. Answers to all of these are available to teachers only in a Teacher's Supplement which can be ordered from our website **www.pgonline.co.uk**.

Pearson endorsement statement

In order to ensure that this resource offers high-quality support for the associated Pearson qualification, it has been through a review process by the awarding body. This process confirms that this resource fully covers the teaching and learning content of the specification or part of a specification at which it is aimed. It also confirms that it demonstrates an appropriate balance between the development of subject skills, knowledge and understanding, in addition to preparation for assessment.

Endorsement does not cover any guidance on assessment activities or processes (e.g. practice questions or advice on how to answer assessment questions), included in the resource nor does it prescribe any particular approach to the teaching or delivery of a related course.

While the publishers have made every attempt to ensure that advice on the qualification and its assessment is accurate, the official specification and associated assessment guidance materials are the only authoritative source of information and should always be referred to for definitive guidance.

Pearson examiners have not contributed to any sections in this resource relevant to examination papers for which they have responsibility.

Examiners will not use endorsed resources as a source of material for any assessment set by Pearson.

Endorsement of a resource does not mean that the resource is required to achieve this Pearson qualification, nor does it mean that it is the only suitable material available to support the qualification, and any resource lists produced by the awarding body shall include this and other appropriate resources.

First edition 2019

A catalogue entry for this book is available from the British Library

ISBN: 978-1-910523-13-1

Copyright © M J Ross, E Arnold and E Berry 2019

All rights reserved

No part of this publication may be reproduced, stored in a retrieval system, or transmitted in any form or by any means without the prior written permission of the copyright owner.

Printed on FSC® certified paper
Printed and bound in Great Britain by Bell & Bain Limited

Contents

Core sections 1–5

Section 1 New and emerging technologies — 1
- **Chapter** 1 Industry and enterprise — 2
- 2 Sustainability and the environment — 7
- 3 People, culture and society — 13
- 4 Production techniques and systems — 19

Section 2 Informing design decisions — 25
- **Chapter** 5 Critical evaluation of technologies — 26
- 6 Contemporary and future scenarios — 29
- 7 Ethical and environmental perspectives — 32

Section 3 Energy, materials, devices and systems — 38
- **Chapter** 8 Energy generation — 39
- 9 Powering systems — 44
- 10 Modern materials and smart materials — 48
- 11 Composite materials — 52
- 12 Technical textiles — 55
- 13 Mechanical devices — 59
- 14 Electronic systems — 67
- 15 Programmable components — 70

Section 4 Material types, properties and structure — 77
- **Chapter** 16 Ferrous and non-ferrous metals — 80
- 17 Papers and boards — 83
- 18 Polymers — 85
- 19 Textiles — 88
- 20 Natural and manufactured timbers — 93

Section 5 Designing principles — 99
- **Chapter** 21 Social and economic challenges — 100
- 22 The work of others — 105
- 23 Avoiding design fixation — 109
- 24 Developing design ideas — 112

Specialist sections

Section 6–1 Timbers — 121
- Chapter 25 Sources, origins and sustainability — 122
- 26 Physical and working properties — 126
- 27 Selection of materials and stock forms — 129
- 28 Planning and production methods — 136
- 29 Material processing and joining — 141
- 30 Material treatments and finishes — 148

Section 6–2 Metals — 152
- Chapter 31 Sources, origins and sustainability — 153
- 32 Physical and working properties — 157
- 33 Selection of materials and stock forms — 160
- 34 Planning and production methods — 166
- 35 Material processing — 170
- 36 Finishing — 180

Section 6–3 Papers and boards — 185
- Chapter 37 Sources, origins and sustainability — 186
- 38 Physical and working properties — 190
- 39 Selection of materials and stock forms — 192
- 40 Planning and production methods — 200
- 41 Material processing — 208
- 42 Finishing — 213

Section 6–4 Polymers — 218
- Chapter 43 Sources, origins and sustainability — 219
- 44 Physical and working properties — 223
- 45 Selection of materials and stock forms — 227
- 46 Planning and production methods — 235
- 47 Material processing — 242
- 48 Finishing — 249

Section 6–5 Systems — 251

Chapter 49 Sources, origins and sustainability — 252
50 Physical and working properties — 257
51 Selection of materials and stock forms — 263
52 Planning and production methods — 268
53 Material processing — 277
54 Finishing — 283

Section 6–6 Textiles — 287

Chapter 55 Sources, origins and sustainability — 288
56 Physical and working properties — 295
57 Selection of materials — 300
58 Stock forms, planning and production methods — 304
59 Material processing — 309
60 Surface treatments and finishing — 316

Index — 322

Section 1
New and emerging technologies

In this section:

Chapter 1	Industry and enterprise	2
Chapter 2	Sustainability and the environment	7
Chapter 3	People, culture and society	13
Chapter 4	Production techniques and systems	19
Exercises		24

Chapter 1 – Industry and enterprise

Objectives

- Apply a breadth of technical knowledge and understanding of the characteristics, advantages and disadvantages of:
    - Industry, including unemployment, workforce skill set, demographic movement, and science and technology parks
    - Enterprise, including privately-owned business, crowd funding, government funding for new business start-ups, and not-for-profit organisations

New and emerging technologies

Design technologists have always looked very closely at the world of science in order to utilise new discoveries. They turn these discoveries into new ideas, materials and products that fulfil a human need.

Design and technology is often thought of as the practical application of science; some would say it is the point at which science meets art. The role of a technologist is to embrace change and to turn inspired ideas into reality. This is done by exploring, creating and refining – making lots of mistakes along the way. The ability to take risks and experiment, and then learn from the issues that arise, is an essential quality of a good design technologist.

It is human instinct to strive for a better and easier life. This is the driving force behind new inventions. From early man using simple tools to help hunt and farm, to astronauts exploring space; it is the risk takers, inventors and creators who have helped shape the modern world.

To stay at the cutting edge, designers and manufacturers have to keep up-to-date with the latest inventions and ideas in areas such as materials development, electronics and design.

The industrial revolution, which began around 1760, was assisted by the discovery of how to harness water power to drive machinery. The invention of the steam engine then led to greater automation. Since then, an ever-increasing number of new technologies has helped shape the way we live. Think of the discovery of electricity, and the invention of the light bulb, the telephone, the internal combustion engine, the computer and the Internet.

The first personal computer was built more than 40 years ago in 1975, but it was not until the mid-1990s that a significant number of people had access to one on a regular basis. The last 20 years have seen a massive change in how computers have been integrated into our lives, not least with the introduction of the smartphone. People in the developed world use computers in so many aspects of their daily lives that it is almost impossible to imagine how our society could exist without them.

Q1 Which inventions do you feel have significantly changed the way we live our lives? Justify your response and compare with other students.

Industry

Before the industrial revolution, most people lived in the countryside outside cities and towns, working on the land. As automation led to larger workshops, mills and factories, more people moved away from the countryside to find work. Towns and cities grew up around areas of manufacturing, and flourished. Output increased, prices fell and generally quality improved. Gradually, a society based on consumerism and enterprise developed. People now had money to buy goods and services and manufacturing boomed. This same society exists today, although there have been a number of changes along the way.

Q2 Which technological developments in agriculture have led to fewer people being needed to work the land to produce food?

Unemployment and workforce skill set

Historically, greater technical advances have signalled that the type of employment available and the skills required are likely to change. As villagers and country folk came into towns and cities, they had to learn new skills to find work. It is similar today and failure to move with the times, develop and updatie one's personal **workforce skill set**, could leave you redundant or unemployed.

There has always been fear within the workforce that new technologies result in **unemployment**. The truth is actually much more complicated. Greater demand for products originally created jobs as machines needed manual labourers, machine operators and engineers to keep them running. More recently, with the introduction of intelligent machines and robotic production lines, many of these jobs have been lost. The latest fully automated production lines only require a few highly skilled engineers to ensure that smooth running is maintained. Additionally, automation leads to high levels of safety and quality products.

Q3 How might automation have affected unemployment in industrialised areas?

Unemployment in the UK had rarely been lower than it was in early 2019, having hit a 44-year low, despite high levels of automation in manufacturing, logistics and business amongst other sectors. The argument that new technologies create overall unemployment are unfounded, however it is true to say that job roles change and some people do lose their job to automation.

The way in which designers, architects and engineers work has dramatically altered since the introduction of computers and specialist software. Although sketching initial ideas and designs is often considered the best way to get thoughts onto a page, the development of designs almost always involves the use of **computer aided design** (CAD), using specialist software packages. Detailed analysis and manipulation of the designs can be achieved quickly and accurately, saving valuable time and money.

Demographic movement

To ensure people can find work, they may need to travel very large distances. They may even have to move to another country. This is call **economic migration**. This can happen if large industries shut down, such as the closing of nearly all coal mines across the UK. With the European Union having an open border policy for economic migration, we have seen a much more diverse workforce in many sectors of the UK economy over the last few decades. There are fears that a deterioration in the relationship between Britain and the EU may result in an insufficient supply of workers for some sectors, especially in the medical profession and for seasonal work.

Demographic movement balances labour shortages for low-paid low-skilled jobs as well as the high-paid and highly-skilled professional market. Migrant workers can earn more and send money home if needed. It boosts cultural diversity but can cause issues with language and culture.

Science and technology parks

Since the 1950s, likeminded entrepreneurs, leading businesses and educational establishments have tended to cluster together to become centres of excellence. The best-known example of this is Silicon Valley in California, where a very large number of computer and Internet based companies have their head offices. In the UK, we have a number of similar, albeit smaller, centres. These are often near reputable universities and training providers such as the Cambridge Science Park, which benefits from talent being fostered at Cambridge University.

Healthy competition and cross-pollination of ideas and research make science and technology parks important in the development of world-leading technological advances. With so many of the best companies and research establishments in one area, it can mean that relocation is essential if someone wants to succeed in a certain field.

Enterprise

New and emerging technologies are routinely used by creative people to produce innovative ideas. These ideas, if nurtured sufficiently, go on to become viable products and businesses. **Enterprise** is a word that encompasses many meanings, but in relation to design, it means that an idea is cultivated into a business proposal that has commercial viability as a product.

There are many opportunities for creative people to get their ideas noticed by potential investors; the Internet and the boom in social media sites allow creative people access to very large audiences. These have provided a platform for designers to attract attention more readily than by the traditional methods of sending proposals to existing companies or visiting their bank manager for approval.

Privately owned businesses

Privately owned businesses are the economic backbone of the UK economy. In 2017 83% of all employment was created in the private sector with small businesses accounting for over half of those jobs.

Small and medium sized businesses have the flexibility to adapt quickly to fluctuations in the market, to changes in fashion and buying trends and to the availability of new and emerging technologies. However, they may not be financially robust enough to see off competition, invest in the latest equipment or to get through long downturns in the market. Larger companies may be more resilient but they are slower to respond to change and can find themselves left behind. The boom in using the Internet as a selling platform has left many large retailers losing ground to newer, more versatile companies.

Crowdfunding

Crowdfunding has become a popular way for designers and creative entrepreneurs to raise enough money to enable the manufacture of their products. Crowdfunding is usually an Internet-based way to gain small contributions from many investors who believe the product or idea has a future. www.kickstarter.com is a crowdfunding site for design and technology based ideas.

Case study: TikTok + LunaTik Multi-Touch Watch Kits

On November 17th 2010 Scott Wilson used kickstarter.com to launch his idea of converting old Apple iPod nanos into multi-touch watches.

He needed to raise $15,000 to get production of the concept underway but astonishingly, raised nearly $1million in one month.

He has gone on to make other innovative products and the business is thriving.

Q4 Which low-cost methods of self-promotion and advertising could young designers use to get their ideas noticed?

Government funding for new businesses and start-ups

There are a growing number of agencies looking for **start-up businesses** to invest in. A start-up company is usually one that has come up with an idea that has the potential to grow into a profit-making business.

One of the biggest growth areas is in **app design and development** for smart devices. Computer software has made development of apps more accessible and as a result, more people are able to see their ideas come to life. The most important aspect is the idea itself.

The UK Government support new businesses and start-ups through offering direct loans and grants to the businesses and by offering tax relief to business investors. Many fledgling companies don't make it but those that do can offer a very high level of return, therefore this type of investment is risky but has potentially big rewards. The government can afford to back these schemes as the tax that is paid by the businesses and their employees eventually filters back to the treasury. They also provide a boost to the economy and help to raise employment levels.

Not-for-profit organisations

Companies, charities and conscientious organisations that reinvest all of their profits back into the business for the betterment of the people, animals or country are classed as not-for-profit. Amnesty International is perhaps one of the most highly regarded organisations, supporting human rights across the world.

Forest Stewardship Council (FSC) is a global not-for-profit organisation that strives to reduce the amount of illegal and unsustainable logging to protect the world's forests. They ensure that all the timber baring their logo is sustainably sourced and traceable. This also extends to certifying the timber, paper, board and even some textile-based products that use FSC timber.

FSC also offer support to all those connected to their timber supply chain. This includes protecting the rights of the indigenous people that rely on forests for their homes and livelihood, and ensuring that forest workers are protected through appropriate health and safety provision with good working and living conditions. Above all, the FSC help protect the ecosystems surrounding the forests that they support, meaning that the flora and fauna are left intact and have all that is needed to flourish, saving and protecting many species of plants and animals.

It is an alternative approach to business that is run entirely by its members. The organisations involved, such as the forestry companies, environmental groups and retailers, and the individual members, including students, academics and activists, all have a say in the FSC's procedures and policies.

As of 2019 the FSC are active in 84 countries and have issued over 1,500 certificates protecting nearly 200 million hectares of forest. This sustainable timber is supplied to 124 countries through over 36,000 certified custodians.

Illegal logging in the Brazillian Amazon rainforest

Chapter 2 – Sustainability and the environment

Objectives

- Understand that new and emerging technologies need to be developed in a sustainable way
- Consider the following with regards to sustainability:
    - Transportation costs, pollution, the demand on natural resources and the waste generated
- Understand the positive and negative impacts that new products can have on the environment including:
    - Pollution, waste disposal, materials separation, the transportation of goods around the world and the packaging of goods

Sustainability

Our planet has to provide all of our basic human needs, such as food, shelter and warmth. Humans have learned to use and manipulate many of earth's natural resources to help provide these essentials and increasingly, many non-essential products as well. The long-term sustainability of the planet's resources is very much in the forefront of responsible designers' minds when new and emerging technologies are invented or discovered.

Designers now have a much better understanding of which materials are sustainable and which are not, and the effect that overharvesting and overconsumption has on the planet. Each of the specialist material sections in this book covers the sustainability of specific materials used in that area of technology.

The general principle is that resources fall into two categories:

Finite resources are ones which are in limited supply or that cannot be reproduced. Use of these should be avoided where possible or used only in small amounts if essential where an alternative cannot be used.

Non-finite resources are those which are in abundant supply and are unlikely ever to be exhausted, or those that can be grown and replaced, at least, at the same rate that they are being used.

> **Q1** Give **two** examples of finite resources, and **two** examples of non-finite resources.

The impact that the use of resources has on the planet, both in terms of the environment and its inhabitants can be measured in many different ways. These include the following:

- CO_2 emissions - energy required to produce materials and whilst products are in use
- Transportation methods and the distance travelled
- Impact on the environment through mining or harvesting
- Impact on availability or scarcity
- Maintenance and repair costs, appropriate use of material
- Welfare of workers in the supply of the material, e.g. Fairtrade
- Ethical and moral issues

Environment

There has been a population explosion since the beginning of the 20th century which has led to accelerated use of all types of natural resources. In 1920, just a century ago, the planet's population was less than two billion, having taken well over 100 years to grow by one billion. It currently takes just 12 years for the global population to increase by a billion. In spring 2019, the world's population was over 7.7 billion.

The consequences of such a large population are that resources are being used up at a very fast rate, and the impact on the environment is becoming increasingly noticeable. Some new technologies are being developed to try to reduce this negative impact and are being adopted by forward-thinking designers and manufacturers.

Technologies that have a positive impact often involve the following:

- using only renewable materials from managed sources
- using renewable energy to power the production of products
- using recycled and recyclable materials
- designing products to be repairable, reusable and fully recyclable
- producing products with low power consumption
- designing products with fewer components and less weight
- designing products that are upgradeable so their life is extended
- creating products that are sourced, produced and sold locally

Technologies that have a **negative impact** tend to rely on the following:

- overuse of finite and non-recycled materials
- use of many components that are hard to repair or recycle
- fossil fuels to power manufacture
- high power consumption on standby and in use
- products that have **built-in obsolescence** that are not designed to be upgradable
- component parts of the product which travel long distances and are shipped globally

Q2 Explain how a rapidly growing population affects or influences the demand on natural resources.

Demand on natural resources

Ever since our early ancestors used simple tools to help feed, clothe and shelter themselves, humans have placed a demand on the earth's natural resources in order to develop a modern lifestyle. Until the industrial revolution, this demand was quite limited and was not considered to severely affect the environment. However, in some parts of the world, historians have found evidence that excessive use of wood for boat building and house construction caused localised **deforestation**.

Much of the power generated to run our homes and our economy comes from burning fossil fuels. Unfortunately, this releases CO_2 and contributes to **global warming**, however there are alternatives in the form of renewable energy sources such as wind, solar and tidal power.

Manufacturing uses finite and non-finite resources. Finite resources include oil, gas and coal and any materials derived from these such as petrochemicals and most polymers. All metals are finite but fully recyclable. Some metals come from ores that are very abundant, such as bauxite from which aluminium is made, although many are becoming increasingly difficult to find and mine, which increases the price. Wherever possible, renewable and non-finite resources should be considered over finite so that remaining resources will last longer.

Q3 What natural resources have you consumed in the last 24 hours? Consider your journeys, your meals and any purchases.

Transportation

Costs

A significant part of the cost of most products is the cost of transportation. The cost is not just monetary but also environmental as most forms of transport use a significant amount of energy. Although many forms of transportation are becoming more efficient and logistics companies are using efficient route planning, steps taken to reduce actual **product miles** travelled are the most effective.

The whole supply chain is energy hungry and companies can reduce the environmental impact and transportation costs by taking action that includes:

- Sourcing materials near to the manufacturing centre
- Manufacturing products near to their largest markets
- Reducing the size and weight of products and the packaging
- Using the shortest and quietest routes to reduce energy consumption
- Moving to energy efficient vehicles, such as electric vehicles and avoiding air travel
- Using existing transport infrastructure

Transportation of goods around the world

A product is normally a collection of materials and components. Each element may have taken a very different journey on its way to being part of a product. For example, a garden bench may have steel legs that came from China, teak wood slats from Africa, nuts and bolts from Italy and might be assembled in the UK. By adding up all the miles that individual parts have travelled and considering the weight of each component, you can work out the CO_2 emissions that have been produced in transportation alone to obtain the materials for the product.

The next part of the journey is the distribution to the specific country or the location of the wholesaler or shop. Then the product travels to the consumer. Eventually it will be disposed of, and the product makes its final journey to a tip or recycling plant, which may also be several thousand miles away.

There is a growing movement among British consumers to buy local and British products whenever possible. This helps to reduce product miles and CO_2 emissions. When ordering products, it is worth finding out where they will be dispatched from to avoid excessive miles. The transportation of products overland or by sea is much better for the environment than by air. Buying locally also helps to support jobs and increases investment in the local economy.

Waste and pollution

Waste generated

We are now living in a society where everybody should take responsibility for reducing waste and recycling when possible. This is to ensure that the resources we have will last as long as possible and that landfill sites do not fill up too quickly. Manufacturing companies are also required to recycle as much as possible, and in many areas of manufacturing strict targets are set by national and international organisations. Areas such as consumer electronics and the automotive industry have very rigid requirements.

Careful planning of waste reduction and disposal within a company can have many positive effects including the following:

- Less raw material is required so demand is **reduced**
- Waste materials are **reused** internally for alternative parts and products
- Some of the cost of materials is recouped through the sale of **recyclable** waste
- Energy to heat and power a business may be generated through **recovery**

Most businesses are charged additional fees to dispose of waste materials. Any form of reduction in waste generated is likely to save a company money, meaning that the products can be manufactured more cheaply. A reduced unit cost makes a company more competitive and profitable.

Waste disposal

When products come to the end of their useful life they are generally disposed of in landfill sites or they are recycled. Better options are to repair or reuse, however this is not always an option. Businesses have many regulations to adhere to regarding waste disposal and heavy fines are given to companies who ignore these rules. Waste reduction strategies need to be implemented by all companies.

The WEEE directive (Waste Electrical and Electronics Equipment recycling) came into force in 2006 and was updated in 2013. It governs the recycling of the estimated two million tonnes of electrical items that UK companies and households dispose of each year

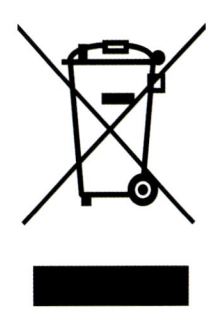

The WEEE symbol

Q4 What might constitute WEEE waste from a company and from a household?

Q5 Explain why you should never throw used batteries in the bin.

Pollution

It is almost impossible to make a product without causing some form of **pollution**. It may be created directly through processing materials or indirectly through energy consumption in manufacture or during the product's use. A business has an obligation to reduce the levels of pollution caused by the manufacture of a product. By conducting a **Life Cycle Analysis (LCA)**, a company will find out how much pollution is being created by their activities and therefore enable them to plan a reduction strategy accordingly. Common ways to reduce pollution are to move to using renewable energy and recycled or recyclable materials when manufacturing. There are many regulations restricting the amount of CO_2 and other harmful pollutants created during manufacture.

The environmental consequences of pollution can be seen in many ways. Oceanic and atmospheric pollution are both rising and are having a negative effect on global flora and fauna. It has been reported that microscopic pieces of plastic which are too small to be effectively filtered out, have been found in bottled water. Fish and birds have been found with large quantities of plastic in their stomachs and it is also regularly reported that it is found in our food chain.

The air we breathe has an impact on our health and every year levels of pollutants in many cities in developed countries far exceed recommended levels. Much of this is due to transportation and our demand for energy to power our new technologies. People, businesses and governments need to consider ways to reduce pollution by moving away from wasteful and harmful technologies and embracing cleaner, greener and more efficient options.

Material separation

To make recycling more efficient, designers and manufacturers need to consider how easy it is to separate products into their component materials. By avoiding permanent bonding techniques of different material types, separation for reusing or recycling is much easier.

Case study:

In the town of Kamikatsu in Japan the 1700 residents separate their waste into 34 different categories and have a 'zero waste' ethos. They work together to reduce the impact that the town has on the environment. They hope to recycle 100% of their waste by 2020.

Packaging of goods

Packaging is becoming a very hot topic with environmentalists and governments around the world. Packaging is essential to protect products and in many cases, it can prolong the life of the contents; perishable items and food stuffs in particular. Where possible, packaging should be kept to a minimum and made from renewable materials that are recyclable or biodegradable.

Designers and manufacturers need to consider the environment when designing packaging, as additional materials create extra weight and bulk which needs to be transported along with the product. It also means more to dispose of or recycle when it reaches the consumer.

Chapter 3 – People, culture and society

Objectives

- Understand how new and emerging technologies impact the workforce, with regard to:
    - Highly-skilled staff, wage levels and apprenticeships
    - Consumers, children and people with disabilities
- Understand how population movement within the EU and social segregation is influenced by technologies
- Be aware of changes in society and how they affect designers and manufacturers, including:
    - Changes in working hours and shift patterns, the Internet of Things (IoT), remote working and the use of video conferencing

People

Developing a detailed understanding of the market place in order to launch new technologies is not easy for designers and manufacturers. Many aspects need to be taken into consideration when launching a product and many companies now employ specialist management consultants who analyse data to see which products would be successful in which areas.

People across the world can have very different needs and tastes, and products successfully launched in one country can be a complete failure in another.

Workforce and highly-skilled staff

The global workforce has always had to adapt. Farmers and villagers moved towards towns and cities as the industrial revolution grew. Machines are designed to make our lives easier and make things accurately, quickly and efficiently. It is inevitable that they take over many mechanical and repetitive jobs. The latest developments in robotics and artificial intelligence are set to take over many jobs that were once considered 'safe'. With the development of autonomous vehicles, driving is one area that will likely be affected over the coming years.

It is often said that universities are training minds to do jobs that haven't been invented yet. It is the adaptability of a workforce to learn new skills that is perhaps the most important factor in our modern society. Problem solving and analytical skills are most sought after as physical labour is slowly becoming less needed. There is a general move from 'brawn to brain' with fewer mid-skilled positions available but a greater need for highly-skilled workers such as engineers, technicians, programmers, scientists and project managers.

Apprenticeships

An apprenticeship is an excellent way to learn a new trade from a skilled employer. Traditionally found in practical and vocational roles such as mechanical engineering, carpentry, tailoring, printing and electrical engineering, apprenticeships offer 'on the job' training whilst earning a small wage. Apprentices have the opportunity to attend a college or university for day-release training so they achieve a formal qualification whilst they work and train. New technologies have created a demand for higher-skilled workers and apprenticeship places have begun to increase in recent years. They offer an affordable and reliable workforce to the employer in return for time allowance and funding to attend an appropriate course.

> **Q1** Why might an apprenticeship be better for skills-based jobs than attending a college or university course full-time?

Wage levels

New and emerging technologies have had a varied effect on wages. There has been an increase in highly-skilled jobs, such as technicians, engineers, computer programmers and project managers and therefore the higher demand has led to higher wages. If companies want to recruit a highly-skilled workforce they need to pay a competitive wage to attract and keep them. On the other hand, some of the low- and many mid-skilled jobs have been automated meaning that fewer people are needed. Wages in these areas have remained stagnant as there are many people going after a limited number of positions.

Consumers

We live in a consumer society and new technologies and scientific advances are discovered or invented constantly. It is not long before these are available for us to purchase either as a necessity or a luxury. Consumerism drives the economy, which drives the research and development of new technologies.

The way we buy our products is changing. The high-street is seeing a slump in sales in many sectors and Internet sales continue to rise. This is due to lower prices and the convenience of having products delivered.

> **Q2** A growing number of consumer products are home delivered. Discuss the impact of these deliveries on the environment compared to collecting goods from a store.

Children

Children's lives have changed considerably over the last thirty years due to the rapid increase in the use of computers. Their education and recreational time is now punctuated with time using a computer of some sort. This can be a very positive change if managed well, however there are many reports that too long on a digital device, especially if not being used for personal development, can lead to stress, unhappiness and reduced social interaction.

The CE Mark, Lion Mark, Age warning label

Toys, clothing and bedding for children have very strict guidelines governing their manufacture and use. This is particularly the case in the UK and the European Union but not in many other parts of the world. There have been many cases of poorly made products harming young people. It is always worth avoiding cheap imports and looking out for symbols on labels that inform the user as to the appropriate standards that the product has been made to. The Lion Mark indicates a toy has been made to a code of practice which includes rules covering the ethical and safe manufacture of toys. The CE mark signifies that products sold in Europe have been assessed to meet high safety, health, and environmental protection requirements.

People with disabilities

Most developed and developing countries are striving to become more inclusive, catering for the disabled and the elderly. New and emerging technologies have allowed designers and manufacturers to create products and designs ranging from simple tools and household gadgets, to transportation methods and access to buildings, that dramatically improve the lives of many.

Inclusive design is important for any new product. A designer should maximise the number of people a product will appeal to, whilst being aware of whom it may exclude and whether any design modifications can be made to make it accessible for all.

Modification of products is an area that offers inclusivity, as specialist equipment and adaptations can be made to help those who find themselves outside the normal range of ability.

Modern technologies play an important role in this field of design, making products lighter, tougher and more adaptable than ever before. The use of carbon fibre and other light modern materials has allowed disabled people to take part in all sorts of activities that would have been virtually impossible before their discovery and invention. For example, equipment for Paralympians is frequently at the cutting edge of inclusive design and utilises many of the most up-to-date materials.

The world's population is becoming increasingly elderly as advances in medicine lead to people living longer. Unfortunately, not all who live longer are as healthy or as strong as younger people, and therefore any products that address particular difficulties or offer a better quality of life will find an increasingly profitable market.

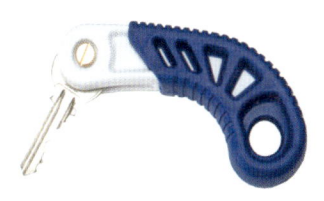

> **Q3** How are pavements, crossings and street furniture, such as benches, designed to avoid a negative impact on elderly or disabled users?

Culture

Culture is an amalgamation of the ideas, beliefs, customs and social behaviours of a society or group of people. It often manifests itself through ritual, art and fashion. It is important for designers to be aware of the society around them and to try to understand the different cultures that exist within it.

Some parts of the world are still dominated by one type of culture, especially where a government or a particular religious belief has a very powerful influence over the population. Designing products for these countries may be considered easier, as there is less diversity and the majority of people have similar lifestyles. The downside of this, from a manufacturer's point of view, is that customers may require a limited range of products.

In the United Kingdom, and especially in large cities, there is a very diverse mix of cultures. Selling a product to this type of market can be quite challenging as so many factors need to be considered.

> **Q4** How are colours, icons and text displayed or interpreted differently across different cultures?

Population movement within the European Union

People have always travelled long distances to find work and a better life. When the move is permanent it is known as **migration**. The EU has had open borders for many years, meaning that its members are free to move around and settle wherever they want in the EU. This has allowed workers to find jobs that suit them in the country of their choice.

In Britain we employ many EU workers from other countries in many technological sectors. The wider choice of potential employees allows employers to look at diversity of skills and culture as well as expertise and innovation.

Social segregation and clustering within ethnic minorities

It is only natural for people from the same countries and cultures, who speak the same language, to want to live close to each other and form social communities. This clustering, within ethnic minorities, is normal and happens all across the globe, including large numbers of Brits living on the coast of Spain amongst other places. It only becomes a problem when people from within the minority community fail to mix with the locals, learn the language and integrate with local people and culture. Technologies are beginning to help with some of these issues, such as language translation apps to help communication between cultures.

Social segregation occurs when large groups of an ethnic minority become self-sufficient within their own micro-society living in another country and culture. This can result in resentment by the local community for not participating in local culture and activities or for failing to integrate with the local society and traditions. Sometimes whole areas within a town or city can be monopolised by one foreign culture and the locals start to feel displaced or unwelcome. This can lead to unrest and cultural conflicts and disputes can occur. Luckily, many parts of the UK have very well integrated societies incorporating many cultures, many of whom live in large groups but happily accept British culture as well as respecting and being true to their own culture and heritage.

Society

At the forefront of responsible design are companies that use new and emerging technologies to consider the environment and their impact on society before profit. The areas of design that are considered to be socially and environmentally responsible include one or more of the following:

- Products that are produced by carbon neutral means
- Products that are made from renewable materials
- Products that reduce carbon emissions and/or other greenhouse gases in use
- Products that reuse existing materials or use recycled materials
- Products designed to be 100% recyclable
- Products that are designed to help or ease suffering or that promote fair trade
- Products that are made and sold locally to avoid transportation costs and associated pollution
- Organisations that are not-for-profit and where all money is reinvested to support good causes

Many forward-thinking companies try to achieve one or more of these targets and as a result they are considered to be more 'eco-friendly' or more responsible than some of their competitors.

This may give them an advantage over their competitors, as some consumers will usually take the greener option as long as they feel the additional cost of the goods or service is worth it. Unfortunately, if the greener option is too expensive, then the advantage is easily lost.

Changes to working hours and shift patterns

The traditional 9 to 5 working day is becoming less common, as an ever-increasing amount of people are asked to, or prefer to do shift work. There are many reasons why this is the case, but one is that more factories are set up to work 24/7, in three eight-hour shifts. Increased levels of automation have led to this happening and the workers are there to assist the machinery in producing goods around the clock. It has led to efficiencies and cheaper products, but this comes at a price, as many people are required to rotate through the shifts, occasionally working through the night.

Remote working

The Internet and improved digital connectivity have allowed people to work remotely, often from home or in transit, enabling more relaxed and flexible access to the office. This has helped many working parents who can work around their commitments and reduce the need for expensive childcare. This flexibility increases workers' morale and in many cases, improves productivity.

Further advances in technology allow teams of people to be connected, working on the same projects from different parts of the world, in different time zones. This form of global remote working is set to increase as better connectivity and cloud-based storage solutions become increasingly reliable.

The benefits include reduced travel and therefore a saving on time and fuel, and the ability to work flexible hours with potentially fewer distractions than working in a busy office environment. Some downsides may be an irregular work pattern that might not suit all and reduced contact with colleagues. This results in less social interaction or the ability to bounce ideas around. It may also become difficult to maintain a work-life balance if trying to hit targets and stay competitive.

The Internet of Things (IoT)

More of the products that we use in our lives are becoming connected to the Internet. This technology is known as the **Internet of Things**.

The ability to turn your central heating on 30 minutes before arriving home can lead to energy savings and greater convenience. Being able to access security cameras around a home can offer peace of mind; and having a fridge order food and drink automatically for a regular delivery can save hours of tedious shopping. There is a drawback to all of this connectivity beyond the cost of purchasing the technology in the first place, and that is personal security. All of these devices are logging and storing data about your habits and your lifestyle. If that data was to fall into the wrong hands through hacking, then personal security is at risk. There are many news stories about data breaches which need to be considered when connecting important parts of our lives to the Internet.

Use of video conference meetings

Technological advancements in Internet speeds and communications software such as Skype and Facetime have allowed social communication to join the video conferencing platform that used to be only available for business users. Being able to conduct meetings with multiple contributors is a real bonus for business.

Video conferencing reduces the need for time consuming and expensive travel and it enables whole multi-disciplinary teams to meet to discuss strategies in an organised and efficient way. It can be used for training purposes as well as for making design decisions as you are able to see ideas, prototypes and products and ask pertinent questions. The drawbacks include a reliance on a high-quality, reliable data connection with a software package and the need for all attendees to be available at the same time no matter which time-zone they live in. Some non-verbal communication does not translate well through video, especially if there is a slight time-delay and some people become camera shy and don't perform at their best. Additionally, the set-up costs for some high-quality systems can be very expensive. These costs, however, are usually offset very quickly by the savings in travel and time.

Chapter 4 – Production techniques and systems

Objectives

- Understand the advantages and disadvantages of standardised design and components
- Understand how Just In Time (JIT) and lean manufacturing contribute to manufacturing efficiencies
- Understand how products are produced in different volumes
- Explain when and why different manufacturing methods are used for different production volumes

Production techniques and systems

The use of computers in industry has grown enormously over the last 30 years and as a result, the way products are designed and manufactured has become increasingly automated. Computers are now used in all areas of design and manufacture; this chapter looks at how computers and digital integration have changed production lines and working practices.

Standardised design and components

To make it possible for certain components, parts and products to be used nationally and internationally there are a series of standards that manufacturers work to. Metric and imperial measurements are perhaps the most well-known standards, however in electronics, textiles and all other material areas there are standardised sets of weights, sizes, thread pitches, component values and other measurements that make interchangeability and adaptability possible.

> **Q1** In your chosen specialism name **two** standard components, material sizes or thicknesses.

Having standardised design and components speeds up production time as manufacturers are not having to come up with their own solutions each time. They simply use readily available stock forms and components that are made in bulk by other manufacturers. It is much easier for designers, manufacturers and consumers to work with and use standard components and sizes. Consider battery or shoe sizes for example. The only downside is when a standard component doesn't fit your requirements and a bespoke one is needed, as this can cost extra time and money to make it from scratch.

Lean manufacturing and Just-in-time (JIT)

Lean manufacturing is based on an ethos of eliminating waste in manufacture, overburden and bottlenecks. A growing number of responsible manufacturers now adopt this principle to save money and resources. It was first witnessed in Japan during the 1990s and has grown in popularity as manufacturers across the world are cutting down on the waste that they produce. To do this, they have had to change the way they operate.

By using **Just In Time (JIT)** production methods, manufacturers are able to respond to customer demands more effectively. JIT manufacturing ensures that customers get the right product, at the right time, at the right price. A customer's order triggers the production process and the manufacturer makes the product specifically to meet the order.

Many companies now seek to make constant improvements to their systems and they reward employees if they find ways to cut waste even further.

Advantages of just in time:

- Products are made to order, so no products need storing whilst waiting to be sold, thus saving on storage costs
- Money is not tied up in unsold stock
- Orders are often secured on a deposit or full payment, so money is in the bank before outlay is needed on materials and production costs
- Materials and components are supplied just when needed, saving financial outlay on unused materials and additional storage (very low stock levels are maintained)
- Improved competitiveness results from minimal waste of materials and time
- Stock does not become old, out of date or obsolete
- High reliance on making sure products are 'right first time' means less time is spent correcting mistakes, or money wasted on faulty products
- Almost all waste is reused or recycled, meaning there is little or no landfill waste produced

Disadvantages of just in time:

- Relies on a high quality, fast and reliable supply chain for raw materials and components
- All production could stop if the supply chain breaks down
- Stock is not ready to be purchased off the shelf; some consumers prefer not to wait at all and sales could be lost
- Usually a deposit or the whole cost of the product needs to be paid upfront which could be off-putting for some consumers
- Discounts from suppliers for bulk purchasing of materials may be not available

Scales of production

The number of products being made determines the level of production required. There are no definitive quantities that make an item suitable for one type of production rather than another, but there are a few principles that make selecting the appropriate production method easier to understand.

The four scales of production are one-off, batch, mass and continuous production.

Bespoke elliptical Pippy Oak dining table with steam bent legs

One-off production

Bespoke items that are designed for, or commissioned by, individual clients are classed as **one-off** products. They might be made to perform a specific task and cannot be bought off the shelf. The name suggests that only one item is made and this is generally true, although if a dining room table and set of six chairs were made, this would still be classified as one-off production.

When products are being developed, designers will make a prototype. These are one-off versions and are used to test out ideas and to receive feedback from user groups and potential clients.

Many products made for theatre and television are one-off products, as are personalised and hand-made wedding dresses and wedding cakes, pieces of art and some jewellery. A GCSE project will be a prototype and hence a one-off product.

With the introduction of digital techniques such as 3D and digital printing, a number of products that are customised and personalised for consumers blur the lines between one-off and other levels of production. Having your name engraved on something does not make the product a one-off. One-off products are not available for anyone other than the original client or purchaser.

One-off production is very labour intensive and products are frequently handmade by a specialist. Designers and manufacturers may work closely with their clients to deliver the desired outcome. This process means the products can be very expensive and can take a long time to create.

> **Q2** One-off products are usually much more expensive than mass-produced goods. Using an example of a particular item, suggest reasons why a customer might ask a manufacturer to create a one-off product for them.

Batch production

This method of production is used when a certain number of identical products are required. This is known as a **batch**, as they will all have been produced together. One batch could contain a large or small number of products.

Batch production methods tend to use a higher level of automation than one-off production. Machines may be specifically set up to perform certain tasks and **templates**, **jigs**, **patterns**, **moulds** and **formers** are used to save time and ensure parts are identical. Usually, once a batch has been produced some or all of the processes will be altered to produce the next batch. This may be as simple as changing the colour or size of a product for the next batch, or it may involve making a totally different product.

Batch production still uses some highly skilled labour. However, as some of the tasks are more repetitive, small production lines and semi-skilled workers may be employed. Expensive specialist tools and equipment are frequently needed to produce batches of products, and initial set-up costs can be high. The more products being made, the cheaper the overall unit cost of each item.

With batch production, there is often quite a short **lead time** to get products to market, meaning that manufacturers can respond quickly to changes in market trends and fluctuations in order levels. The short lead time is made possible by using adaptable machinery and staff. Typical batch produced goods include surfboards and kayaks, some furniture, clothing and food items.

Q3 Explain what is meant by **lead time**.

Mass production

Mass-produced products tend to be items that are in constant use and where the design does not change significantly. Drinks and food containers, electronic products such as mobile phones and even large assembled products such as cars and motorbikes are typical examples.

When large numbers of products are required, the best way to produce them is to set up a dedicated production line that does not need to change. This way their manufacture can be highly automated and use as little skilled labour as possible. Where manual workers are needed, the tasks tend to be simple and repetitive. Production lines need to have some highly skilled technicians to keep them running efficiently, as any downtime could be very costly.

The high volume of goods being produced means that the very high set-up costs of specialised production line equipment and tooling can be quickly recovered, and the unit price can be kept low.

Continuous production

Continuous production is very similar to mass production although the products tend to be made to create stock or standard material forms (primary processing) before final processing or assembling elsewhere. The factory will operate up to 24 hours a day 7 days a week. Staff are mainly low-skilled and operate the factory in shifts. The products made rely on high levels of automation and this type of factory normally makes a very limited range of products. This saves any potential changes to the production line, avoiding any downtime.

Q4 What type of production would be suitable for a shoe manufacturer making a range of very popular trainers? Give reasons for your answer.

Q5 Continuous production is usually used for simple products.
(a) Give **three** products that are made on a continuous production line.
(b) What makes these products suitable for this type of manufacture?

Exercises

1. Describe what a 'not-for-profit' organisation does. [2]

2. Explain what is meant by the term 'crowdfunding'. [2]

3. Some new and emerging technologies can have a negative environmental impact. Give **two** ways that a new technology may negatively impact the environment. [2]

4. Study the images below.

   The CE Mark   *The Lion Mark*

   Explain how either of the symbols pictured can represent the protection of child consumers if they appear on a toy or its packaging. [2]

5. Explain the differences between finite and non-finite resources. [2]

6. Explain what is meant by an apprenticeship. [2]

7. Give **two** advantages and **one** disadvantage of a manufacturer using the just-in-time (JIT) production system. [3]

8. Study the image below of a Wi-Fi enabled door lock.

   Evaluate the advantages and disadvantages of 'the Internet of Things'. [9]

Section 2
Informing design decisions

In this section:

Chapter 5	Critical evaluation of technologies	26
Chapter 6	Contemporary and future scenarios	29
Chapter 7	Ethical and environmental perspectives	32
Exercises		37

Chapter 5 – Critical evaluation of technologies

Objectives

- Understand how to critically evaluate new and emerging technologies that inform design decisions with reference to:
  - Budget constraints
  - Timescale
  - Who the product is for
  - The materials used
  - Manufacturing capabilities

Evaluating a design proposal

To ensure that the design of a new product is as good as it can be, designers take ideas from existing products to determine where improvements or savings can be made. Factors that influence the evaluation or existing products include:

- The form and function of the product
- The user profile and their requirements of the product, including the problem that the product is designed to solve
- The performance requirements of the product and to what extent the product has been over- or under-engineered
- The materials used
- The scale of production, manufacturing techniques and likely cost of manufacture
- The sustainability and environmental impact of the product

Q1 Study the child's toy shown above. Using one or more of the criteria given, evaluate the suitability of the product for young children.

Informing design decisions

Once a thorough evaluation has been completed, the details and conclusion gathered can be used to inform future design decisions for a new product or new version. You may ask, for example, "What works well?", "What didn't work so well, and why?" or "Can new technology offer any additional benefits to the product?".

Making design decisions

Critical evaluations of new and emerging technologies inform design decisions for new or upgraded versions of products.

Budget constraints

The **budget** available to spend on the design and development of a product will affect the quality of the end result. It is also likely to affect, or be determined by, the sale price. A high-end luxury product will command a high price tag and will therefore be expected to have been made to a very high standard. Conversely, a low-cost product will have been made on a tight budget and consumers cannot expect as high a standard of quality in the build or the design.

Most products have a ceiling price, above which, companies are unlikely to sell anything. This price will fluctuate with the market over time. This tends to be different when new technologies hit the market for the first time. For example, the first CD players retailed at around £1,000 in 1982 and their price steadily declined; new portable sets can now be bought for under £10.

> **Q2** What is the maximum price you would be prepared to pay for a new set of headphones? What features would you expect of these headphones at your maximum budget?

Case study: Vertu

Vertu was a luxury smart phone manufacturer established in 1998. Despite establishing a customer base of several hundred thousand individuals, the company finally went bankrupt in 2017.

Its range of phones started at £11,000 with their top model, made from red gold, retailing for close to £40,000. Much like very expensive watches, each phone was handmade using materials such as ruby, sapphire crystal glass and titanium.

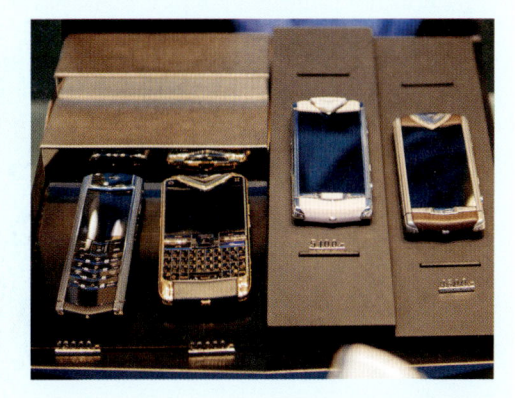

> **Q3** Should price dictate quality, or should quality dictate price? Explain your answer.

Timescale for manufacture

Many products are designed and manufactured to be available at a certain time. Sometimes this will coincide with particular events such as film releases or special times of year. Launching a new Christmas toy in January is unlikely to be as successful as a launch in early autumn for example. Companies need to ensure that any new technologies they are using are tried and tested well before the launch of a product otherwise it may be safer to use traditional materials and techniques that are known to work. The issues that can arise could cause delays and adversely affect a company's name.

In September 2015 Porsche announced 'Mission E', which was a commitment to create an all-electric sports car that would go for 500km (310 miles) on one charge and could recharge its batteries to 80% within 15 minutes. Mission E is due to hit the market in 2020. Only then, five years later, will they be judged on their commitment to the use of new and emerging technologies.

Research and development into using new technologies can absorb enormous amounts of time and money. Self-driving cars have been in development for well over a decade and are still not considered safe enough for use on UK streets. Waymo's fleet of driverless vehicles have driven over 10 million miles in testing. It can be a very costly and time-consuming process to get a new technology declared safe.

Knowing the market for a product

Careful consideration needs to be given to the potential market a new product is being aimed at. Questions should be asked such as "What features will customers look for in a new product?", "How long do they expect it to last?", "How will they use the product?", "What quality will be expected?" and "What price point should it be launched at?".

By asking these and many other questions, a manufacturer can determine the level of quality, materials and safety constraints that may impact **lead times** and budget.

Materials

Manufacturers are often keen to be among the first to use new and emerging technologies as they can provide an immediate competitive advantage. However, the costs of being the first can be high as all of the research and development needs to be borne by these innovators. The timescales involved in fully testing these products can be very long and safety testing processes can add even more time. This is particularly the case in medical trials. The effect on the body of using new technologies, for example nitinol stents, will often not be fully known for several years after initial clinical use.

Manufacturing capabilities

New technologies are not only changing the functionality of new products but are also used to manufacture new products. This allows manufacturers to create products in ways that have not previously been possible. This may increase the ability to create more intricately shaped parts from a single piece of material avoiding weaknesses in joins. It may allow us to create one-off items more quickly or more cheaply, or to reduce lead times through more efficient and automated processes.

3D metal printing is beginning to revolutionise what is possible to manufacture. In the long term, this will affect the costs of prototyping, tooling and the testing of parts. 3D printing techniques are being used with **generative design** which is a form of CAD that finds the most efficient way to make components using the data gathered from simulation and testing software. The results produce incredibly strong yet weight efficient designs.

Chapter 6 – Contemporary and future scenarios

Objectives

- Consider contemporary and future scenarios in making design decisions
- Critically evaluate the use of new and emerging technologies in these scenarios, including:
    - Natural disaster alerts, defence and recovery
    - Medical advances
    - Travel
    - Global warming
    - Communication

Future scenarios for design decisions

What the future will bring is unknown, but we can be sure that many new and emerging technologies we can't even dream of today will continue to be discovered and developed, and these are likely to have a huge impact in many areas of our lives in the future.

Natural disaster alerts, defence and recovery

The frequency of natural disasters across the globe is steadily increasing as the world continues to warm up. **Global warming** affects sea and air temperatures, atmospheric pressure, air and sea currents and sea levels. These in turn affect weather systems and create dramatic and often catastrophic weather events such as extended droughts, extreme changes in temperature and ferocious storms and sea surges.

Floods and the devastation and disease that follow are one of the biggest killers globally and companies are constantly innovating to find solutions to cope with rising tides and the ever-changing distribution of water around the planet. A Dutch company Dura Vermeer has manufactured 'amphibious' homes that float on water. These are built on foundations manufactured from multiple layers of plastic foam and a hollow concrete base that can support the entire structure above water.

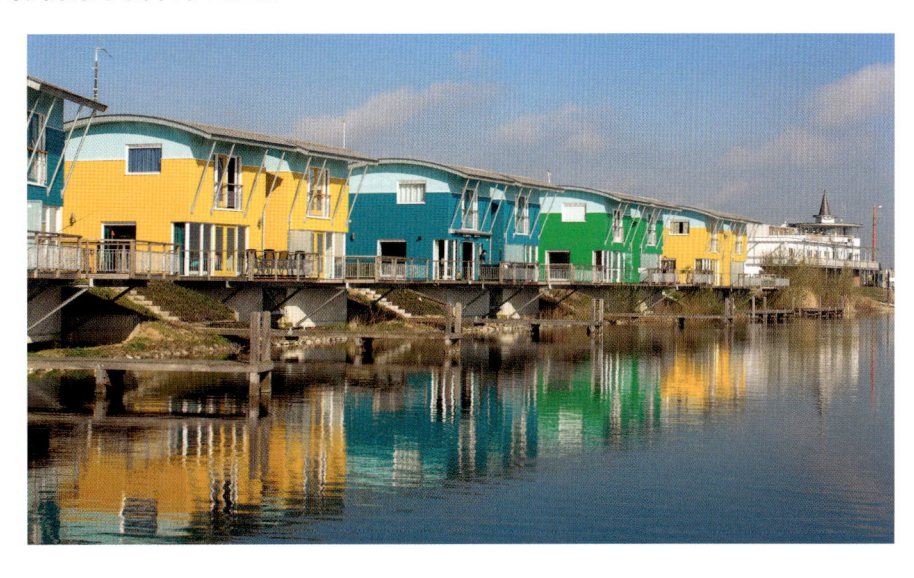

Mobile devices are beginning to play a greater role in warning the public about impending natural disasters. People in some areas at risk of earthquakes and tsunamis can sign up to public alert and warning systems where the collective data available from smartphone users can be used in a variety of effective ways to predict and warn of potentially disastrous natural events.

> **Q1** This is an accelerometer gyroscope chip similar to that used in most modern smartphones. It is so sensitive that it can sense extremely small vibrations produced by early earthquake tremors. Explain how this technology could be used to warn communities living in earthquake or tsunami prone areas.

Medical advances

Medicine is an area where there is constant development in the use of new and emerging technologies. Smart polymers, for example, can react to their surroundings. Stimuli-sensitive polymer implants or hydrogels can administer targeted drugs precisely when and where required. Ultra-high performance polymers are also being developed for use as implants. These are inert with a very low water absorption capability and can be manufactured using injection moulding or extrusion techniques to create implants for spinal discs for example.

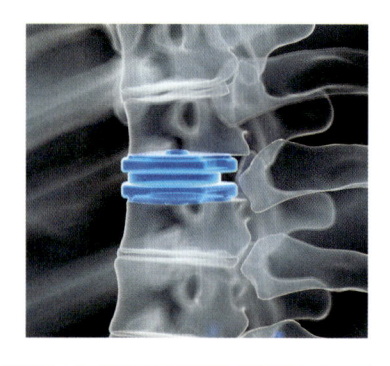

> **Q2** New technologies including advanced robotics control, high-speed fibre optic communication and augmented reality are being used by surgeons to control robots that can then operate on patients remotely.
>
> Evaluate the use of this technology in providing access to surgical experience and streamlining healthcare.

Travel

London's Crossrail project has been one of the greatest UK infrastructure engineering ventures for decades with over 400 innovations adopted by the project to improve safety and efficiency. Low-carbon concrete has also been tested in part of the build to reduce the carbon footprint of the project since cement manufacture is one of the largest contributors to CO_2 emissions.

London's Crossrail tunnel experimenting with low-carbon concrete

The electric vehicle revolution is gathering more and more momentum as battery technology continues to improve, now providing a single-charge distance almost equivalent to that of a small petrol or diesel vehicle. Charging points are becoming more available and the time taken to charge a flat battery is reducing.

Global warming

Due to the worldwide population explosion since the industrial revolution, mixed with the boom in global manufacturing, unprecedented levels of carbon dioxide (CO_2) and other greenhouse gases such as methane (CH_4) and nitrous oxide (N_2O) have been released into the atmosphere. Many scientists attribute these, and other factors driven by human activity, as the main causes of a gradual rise in the average temperature of Earth's atmosphere and oceans.

Global warming is becoming increasingly hard for sceptics to deny, as according to the National Centre for Environmental Information in 2018, fifteen of the last sixteen warmest years on record have occurred since 2000.

> **Q3** The Paris agreement in December 2015 was the first global climate agreement involving 195 countries. Find out the main aim of the agreement.

New technologies are helping to reverse and stabilise the effects of global warming. These include:

- Battery farms
- Renewable energy sources including developments in solar, wind, tidal and geothermal technologies
- Energy usage monitoring equipment
- Electric vehicles

Communication

Our insatiable appetite for convenient access to information and data has created many innovative global technological solutions. Communication is narrowing the digital divide. Africa and large parts of Asia and South America have never had terrestrial communication networks, thus creating huge problems for developing nations. Mobile technology has helped to connect these areas without constructing physical communication lines and the supporting infrastructure.

Bluetooth technologies and optic fibre have enabled extremely fast or wireless communication between an ever-growing number of devices. Vehicles are increasingly becoming Wi-Fi enabled and with the combination of self-driving vehicles, technology may soon enable one vehicle to talk to another to make journeys easier, safer and road networks more efficient.

Chapter 7 – Ethical and environmental perspectives

Objectives

- Consider ethical perspectives when evaluating new and emerging technologies referencing:
    - Where a product was made and who by
    - Who it will benefit
    - Fair trade products
- Consider environmental perspectives including:
    - The use of materials
    - Carbon footprint
    - Energy usage and consumption
    - Life cycle analysis (LCA)

Product origin

Provenance is a word that that is being used more and more by consumers and hence retailers, designers and manufacturers. It means to know the origin or the source of something, but when relating to products it can mean knowing how and where a product's raw materials were sourced, how and where it was manufactured and what method of shipping was used. Knowing the provenance of a product, especially when utilising new and emerging technologies, allows consumers to make environmental and ethical decisions about the products they purchase.

Product labour

Knowing where a product comes from can tell a consumer a number of things about it. Firstly, if it was made and sold in the UK then it is not likely to have travelled too far compared to being made in China, for example. This means a reduced **carbon footprint** for the product and that local business and the UK economy will have benefitted from the sale. Secondly, workers' rights, pay and working conditions vary dramatically between countries. In the UK, high standards of welfare and health and safety conditions are set, a minimum wage is paid and child labour is banned. Unfortunately, this is not the case in all countries.

Beneficiaries of a product

When a product is bought by a consumer, the money paid for it represents all the many stages that its component parts have been through. In the example of an item of high-tech protective clothing, the designer may have been British, the main fabric may be Kevlar, which could have been sourced from the USA and dyed in India. The lining may be silk from Sri Lanka, the polymer thread from Germany and the whole garment might be assembled in Vietnam. It may then be sold all over the world. At every stage of the product's life, farmers, designers, manufacturers and their workers, drivers, shopkeepers and many others are linked through its sale and will have benefitted in some way or another, not least the end user. Not everyone may be getting a fair amount for their input, but it creates employment and keeps the various economies productive.

> **Q1** Who benefits from someone sending a birthday card to a friend?

Fair trade

Fair trade supports the development of thriving farming and worker communities that have more control over their futures and protecting the environment in which they live and work.

It is a different approach that is based on partnership; one between those who grow food and those who consume it. When you buy products with the Fairtrade Mark, it means that the Fairtrade ingredients in the product have been produced by small-scale farmer organisations or plantations that meet Fairtrade social, economic and environmental standards. The standards include protection of workers' rights and the environment, payment of the Fairtrade Minimum Price and an additional Fairtrade Premium to invest in business or community projects. More than 1.65 million farmers and workers in 74 countries benefit from having Fairtrade certification for their products.

> **Q2** What products are commonly sold under the Fairtrade label?

Environmental perspectives

The environmental impact that the production of a product or its individual components may have is increasingly affecting design decisions. Producing eco-friendly products should benefit all stakeholders, however there are sometimes monetary costs involved in swapping from a polluting technology to a greener one. In this case investors and board members may resist change for fear of losing profits.

The use of materials

Moving to low carbon manufacturing is a slow process. When new 'greener' materials are discovered there is always a 'settling in' phase where prices are high, and demand is low. As people trust the product more and it is proven to work, costs start to decline and demand increases.

Reducing the amount of material in a product is a designer's responsibility, avoiding waste through clever and **responsible design**. Good products are made to last, made from sustainable materials and are fully recyclable. To aid this, they will have parts that are easily separable into their component materials at the end of life. Although this all sounds easy, it can in fact be very difficult to achieve whilst keeping prices competitive.

Carbon footprint

Carbon is produced during the manufacture of products. The amount of carbon-dioxide (CO_2) emitted during a process (for example, designing and making a product) is known as its **carbon footprint**. In fact, there are six so-called 'greenhouse gases' which are damaging to the atmosphere to various degrees, and each of them can be measured in terms of the damage they cause, and quantified in terms of a single measure, kilogrammes of 'carbon dioxide equivalent' (**CO_2e**). Calculating a **carbon footprint** is a way of estimating greenhouse gas emissions caused by a product, process, person, event or organisation.

> **Activity: What is your carbon footprint?**
>
> There are many carbon footprint calculators available online and take only a few minutes to complete. They give you a detailed analysis of particular human activities and lifestyles. Try http://footprint.wwf.org.uk. The calculation takes into consideration such factors as:
>
> - how you heat your home
> - the temperature that your thermostat is set to at home
> - how much you recycle
> - whether you are a meat eater, vegetarian or vegan
> - what type of transport you usually take

Most western lifestyles result in too much CO_2 being produced, and are considered to be unsustainable. It is widely believed that changes to the way we produce and use energy are essential to ensure the planet will cope with a growing population.

Energy usage and consumption

The last decade has seen a drive to reduce energy consumption in industry and manufacturing. Manufacturers have been challenged with making lower-powered appliances and less-polluting vehicles as well as re-evaluating the energy they use to create products and supply services.

Transportation is a huge factor as most goods need to be shipped and delivered. Congestion charges exist in many cities and a ban on the sale of all new petrol and diesel cars will take effect from 2040 in the UK. This is a very long way off, but it means that the whole transport industry will now be investing in alternative fuel technologies which will be beneficial to the planet in many ways.

Responsible companies like to be seen as having 'green' credentials and are making efforts to reduce their energy consumption (and costs) as well as saving precious natural resources and reducing waste where possible.

Carbon offsetting

It is very unlikely that goods being produced will have no negative impact on the environment. However, companies are able to consider their products sustainable and environmentally friendly by offsetting their negative impact through investment in positive activities that reduce carbon emissions. A product is considered to be carbon neutral if it produces zero net emissions when a **Life Cycle Analysis** has taken all actions into consideration.

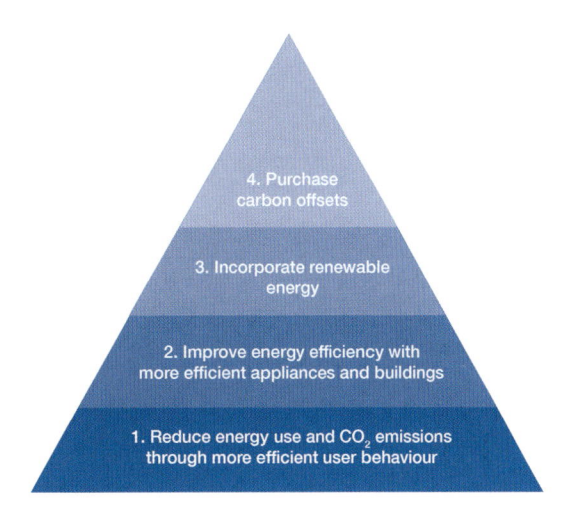

Pyramid diagram:
- 4. Purchase carbon offsets
- 3. Incorporate renewable energy
- 2. Improve energy efficiency with more efficient appliances and buildings
- 1. Reduce energy use and CO_2 emissions through more efficient user behaviour

The pyramid above shows what steps can be taken to reduce carbon emissions by companies and consumers. When all reasonable steps have been taken, there may still be a carbon deficit and the purchasing of carbon credits may be the only way to achieve zero net emissions.

A number of organisations sell carbon credits to companies and consumers to help them reduce their carbon footprint. The money raised is invested in carbon-reducing activities such as the mass planting of trees and forest regeneration, the development and production of renewable energy and the conservation of finite resources.

Q3 Wind-up radios and torches have had a very positive influence in developing countries. What factors do you feel make wind-up products of this type sustainable and environmentally friendly?

Q4 Explain how carbon offsetting helps to reduce the overall CO_2 emissions of a company.

Life Cycle Analysis (LCA)

Conducting a **Life Cycle Analysis (LCA)** is a way for companies to assess the environmental impact of a product during the different stages of the product's life. The LCA will investigate the whole life of the product from 'cradle to grave'.

Although a major part of the investigation looks at the amount of energy used, measured by CO_2 emissions, the LCA can also be used to inform the ethics and provenance of the product.

There are five main stages to an LCA:

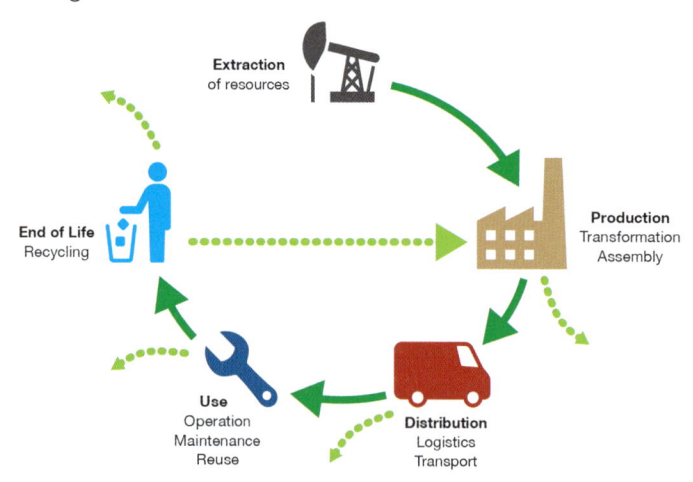

Extraction and processing: The amount of energy used to extract raw material from the earth, or to produce it through farming or other methods, and process it ready for manufacturing

Manufacturing and production: The energy required to manipulate the raw and refined materials into a product ready for sale

Distribution: The packaging and transportation of the product to the end user

Use: The energy that the product and any related consumables used during its working life or useful lifetime

End of life: The energy that is required to recycle the product and/or dispose of any waste.

The LCA can highlight a number of ethical questions to be considered by a company such as:

- where can energy be saved?
- where can working conditions be improved?
- where can emissions be reduced?
- where can material be saved or recycled?
- do our actions have a negative effect on communities or natural environments?

Responsible companies can then decide how to neutralise any negative effects by taking positive action to counteract them, for example by planting trees or choosing more environmentally friendly versions of a material.

> **Q5** What can a company learn by carrying out a life cycle analysis?

> **Q6** In pairs, learn and test yourselves on the five stages of the life cycle analysis.

Exercises

1. Explain why new and emerging technologies are often very expensive when first released to market, yet the price falls the longer it is produced. [2]

2. It is estimated that the waste produced per person rose from 403kg in 2017 to 413kg in 2018.
   Calculate the percentage increase of waste produced per person from 2017 to 2018 giving your answer to 1 decimal place. [2]

3. State the meaning of the word 'provenance' in relation to a product. [1]

4. Explain what is meant by the term 'carbon footprint'. [2]

5. Name the **five** stages of a life cycle analysis. [5]

6. Discuss the benefits of fair trade organisations to the farmers and producers of fairly traded products and goods. [6]

7. Study the image below.

   Discuss how global warming may create a greater need for flood defences in certain parts of the world. [6]

Section 3

Energy, materials, devices and systems

In this section:

Chapter 8	Energy generation	39
Chapter 9	Powering systems	44
Chapter 10	Modern and smart materials	48
Chapter 11	Composite materials	52
Chapter 12	Technical textiles	55
Chapter 13	Mechanical devices	59
Chapter 14	Electronic systems	67
Chapter 15	Programmable components	70
Exercises		75

Chapter 8 – Energy generation

Objectives

- Understand how energy is generated from fossil fuels and renewable sources
- Understand how power is stored
- Understand how systems are powered by different forms of generated energy
- Know how to choose appropriate power sources when designing systems and products

Energy generation

There are many ways to convert energy, and these can be separated into two main categories; fossil fuels and renewables. Countries across the world are attempting to steer their economies to adopt as many renewable sources of energy production as possible, in order to help reduce the build-up of greenhouse gases, which are thought to be one of the main contributing factors of global warming.

Turbines and generators

Most forms of electricity production involve rotating a turbine which turns a generator. Fossil fuels are burned to create heat which in turn superheats water. The resulting steam is used to rotate turbines which are linked to a generator to provide us with a supply of electricity. Biofuels, which are renewable energy sources, use a similar process. In the case of wind, wave and hydroelectric energy production, the energy harnessed from the wind, waves or falling water is converted into mechanical energy which directly rotates the turbine. A generator then converts the mechanical energy from the turbine into electrical energy.

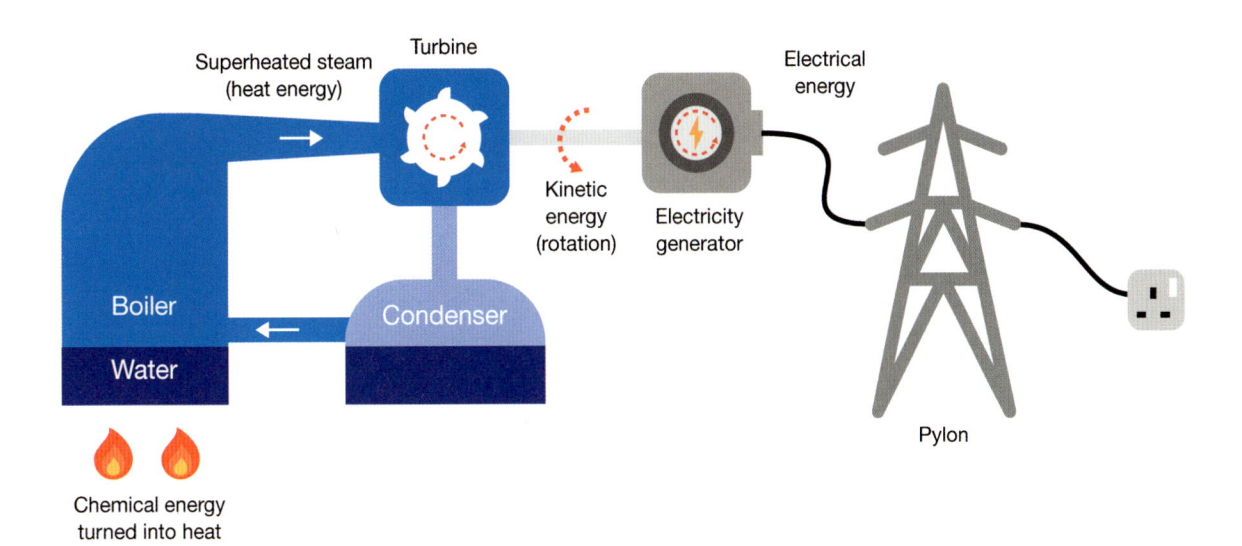

Q1 What are the main differences between fossil fuels and renewable fuels?

Q2 When fossil fuels are burned, what role does water play in producing the mechanical energy used by a generator to generate electricity?

Fossil fuels

Most of the heat that we use to generate electricity in the UK comes from burning fossil fuels such as **coal**, **gas** and **oil**. These are considered **finite** resources as they were formed over many millions of years and cannot be replaced as they run out. In 2017, coal- and gas-fired power stations accounted for just under 50% of the UK's electricity production. Oil, however, is mainly used for transportation and heating; only around 1% of our electricity is generated from oil.

When **fossil fuels** are burned, they produce CO_2 (carbon dioxide). Although some modern power stations can scrub the exhaust gas emissions by trapping the CO_2, it is still generally not considered to be an environmentally friendly or sustainable way of creating energy.

Renewable energy sources

Energy that comes from the planet's non-finite resources is considered to be **renewable**. This includes wind, wave and tidal, hydroelectric, geothermal, biofuels and solar energy. Although a continuing matter of debate, nuclear energy is also sometimes included in this category as the amount of uranium it uses is unlikely to run out in under 1000 years and may well last many times longer. It also produces very low levels of CO_2.

Nuclear energy accounts for about 21% of the UK's electricity. Other forms of renewable energy produced just over 29% in 2017, according to government statistics; up from 17.6% in 2014. Greener ways of producing electricity are on the rise, although it is proving more difficult to reduce our dependency on fossil fuels for heating and transportation.

> **Q3** For each of the energy sources listed above, explain the source of energy that justifies them being considered renewable.

Tidal energy

There are a few different varieties of tidal energy devices but they all use the same principle to generate electricity. They rely on the movement of water to turn turbines which drive the generators that produce electricity.

The benefit of tidal energy production over wind and solar is that it is more predictable and generally more consistent. The main difficulty is the environment in which the machinery needs to be located. Usually the conditions are harsh and some distance from land, making repair and maintenance more difficult. Tidal and wave energy is expensive to build, however investment is nevertheless increasing and large scale projects are beginning to be developed.

Wind turbines

Wind farms are becoming a common sight around the country. An increasing amount of our energy is being produced this way and it is a relatively cheap option.

Wind turbines produce more power in the winter months when the demand is higher, but they have some drawbacks. They do not produce power when it is not windy or when it is too windy, they can harm wildlife, especially birds, and they are considered an eyesore by many.

Most people agree that they are a good idea, although they would not like to have one situated near to where they live. The term 'nimby' stands for 'not in my back yard'. Nimbyism has stopped many proposed wind farms from being developed.

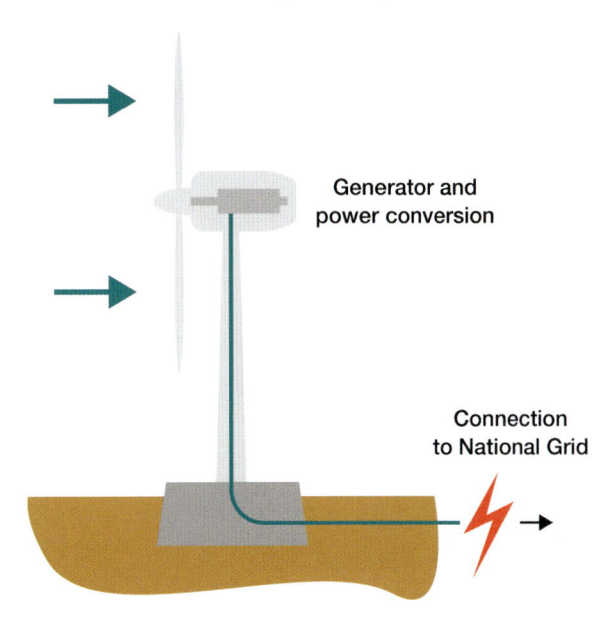

> **Q4** A local energy company is increasing its commitment to renewable energy in the area and would like to place a wind turbine on your school site, which is also very near your home. List your reasons for and against the proposal.

Solar energy

The photovoltaic effect involving the conversion of solar energy into electrical energy was discovered in 1839 by French physicist Alexandre-Edmond Becquerel, but it is only since the turn of this century that the price of producing photovoltaic cells has dropped enough for it to be a viable method for large scale energy production. **Solar** farms are now commonplace in the countryside and many private houses now have solar panels fitted.

The solar cell technology captures the sun's rays and converts them into electrical energy. The cells only produce energy during the daytime and production is less in the winter months, owing to the shorter daytime length and the reduced angle of the sun's rays.

Solar energy is also used to heat water, either in domestic systems where it provides hot water for the home or commercially, where water is superheated to turn turbines by directing the sun's rays at a large water tank using mirrors.

Hydroelectric power

Hydroelectric power (HEP) generation is a very reliable source of renewable energy. It has high initial set-up costs, both financially and environmentally, as vast areas of land need to be flooded to create a reservoir. However, the reservoirs usually mature into thriving leisure facilities such as boating lakes and nature reserves which can have a positive effect on the local area.

Power generation is more efficient during periods of heavy rainfall. At other times, water is pumped back up to the top of the reservoir when the demand for electricity is low. The flow of water through the turbine is easily controlled, making it simple to alter the power being produced depending on the demand at different times of the day.

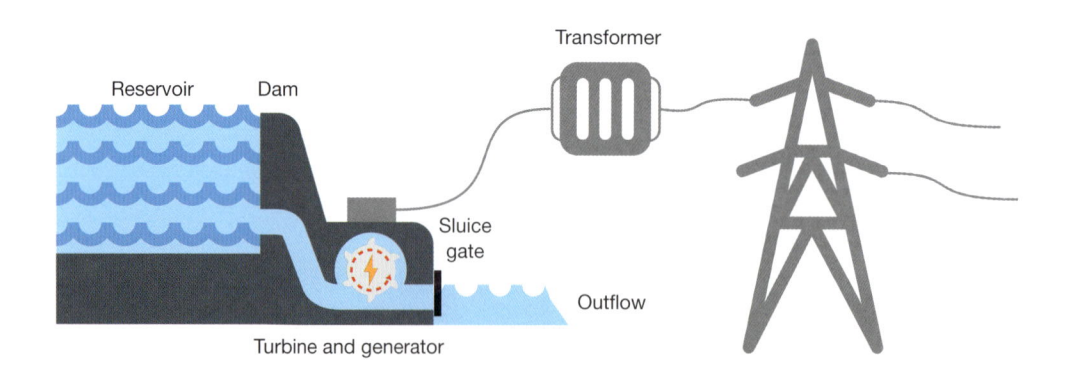

> **Q5** What might be the impact on the natural environment and wildlife of constructing a dam at the end of a valley and flooding the valley to create a reservoir for a hydroelectric power station?

Biofuels

The production of **biofuel** is becoming a viable way of producing energy for our transportation and heating needs. Oil- and starch-producing crops are grown, harvested and refined into a number of products, including **biodiesel** used in place of traditional petroleum-based diesel. The process is commonly known as **biomass** energy production. The term biomass can include other solid biofuels such as wood chips and farm waste. In 2017 biofuels produced nearly one third of all electricity generated by renewable sources in the UK.

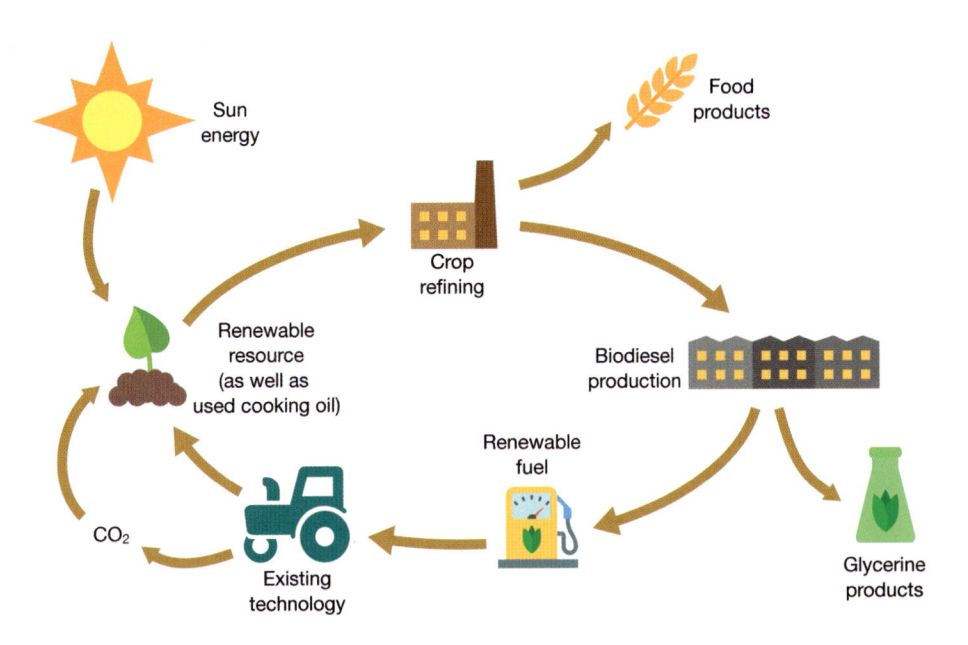

Q6
(a) Explain what happens to the CO_2 during the life cycle of biofuel production and use.
(b) If biofuel is so environmentally friendly, why do you think it is not more commonly used at present?

Chapter 9 – Powering systems

Objectives

- Be able to identify alternative ways to power systems
- Understand the use and limitations of mains power, batteries, solar cells and wind power
- Be aware of the financial cost and environmental impact of powering systems
- Understand how systems are connected and power can be portable

Powering systems

There are many different types of systems, from a small digital watch using a miniature battery to a fully automated car manufacturing plant operating 24/7. They both need a constant supply of energy to perform their task, however they vary dramatically in their level of demand.

The National Grid is a series of cables running the length and breadth of the country and supplies mains electricity to commercial businesses and domestic homes. Other options for powering mobile or remote systems may be to use **wind** or **solar** power. There is a huge growth in adopting solar, wind and rechargeable battery technology for systems as it is much more environmentally friendly and sustainable and can also result in financial saving in the long term.

MS Tûranor PlanetSolar - The world's largest solar-powered boat

Mains electricity

Electrical power is generated and supplied to the National Grid where it travels along a network of underground cables or overhead via pylons. When electricity enters a domestic home, it is supplied at 230V (voltage) and is an alternating current (AC). In the UK we usually use a three-pin plug to connect our appliances to the power sockets.

Batteries and cells

Electrical power can be stored in **batteries**. Batteries contain electrochemicals that react with each other to produce electricity. They come in many different shapes and sizes and provide an array of different voltage outputs and power levels. A battery contains one or more **cells**, with each cell typically providing 1.5V. Each cell has a positive side and a negative side.

Section 3 **Energy, materials, devices and systems**

Modern battery technology is rapidly improving. Older batteries, that a few years ago powered a mobile phone for only a few hours, have now been replaced with versions that last for days and are capable of powering many types of portable electronic devices.

Alongside improved battery technology, the power consumption of our modern electronic devices has decreased. This combination is helping to save valuable finite materials by **miniaturisation**, reducing the size of products.

> **Q1** A PP3 battery produces 9 volts. How many cells does it contain?

Alkaline cells

Alkaline batteries have a higher capacity for their size than traditional acid-based varieties, as the dense manganese oxide inside them uses less space to produce the same power, making them more efficient. Alkaline batteries tend to hold their charge well.

Rechargeable batteries

These are available in many different forms and are used in various products such as mobile and cordless phones, cordless headphones, portable speaker systems, portable power tools, laptops and tablets.

Rechargeable batteries are capable of being charged and discharged many hundreds, if not thousands of times. This reduces the quantity of resources needed to produce new disposable batteries and also reduces the number of batteries needing disposal. The time it takes for rechargeable batteries to reach full charge has improved in recent years, making their use in products far more convenient.

> **Q2** A single rechargeable battery cell is rated at 1.2V. Explain why rechargeable PP3 batteries provide 8.4V instead of the 9V provided by disposable versions.

Portability of a power source

Using power on the move or in remote places is becoming more widely possible and more in demand. People like to be constantly connected to their business, family and friends while on the move, therefore portability plays a major role in facilitating this connectivity. Battery technology is one part of the chain but recharging them is the tricky bit. There has been a surge in the number of products that support remote charging including compact, flexible solar cells and micro-wind turbine generators that can take advantage of flowing rivers as well as air streams. Home generators, including biomass versions, are becoming smaller and more efficient, meaning that power can be taken to more remote locations that are not connected to the National Grid.

Case study: WaterLily turbine

This advanced charging device works in both moving air and water. It can recharge devices using a USB or 12V charging cable delivering up to 15W of power to charge smartphones, battery packs, lights or speakers in areas without any standard power source.

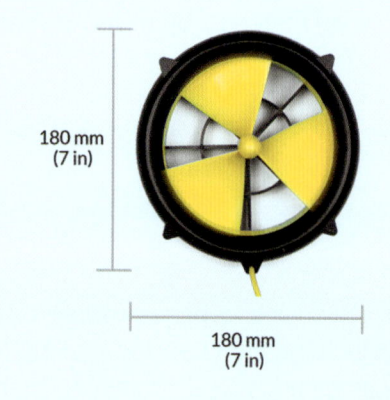

https://waterlilyturbine.com/products/waterlily-turbine

Environmental impact of power generation and storage

The environmental impact of some power generation is obvious, such as the smoke and CO_2 produced from burning fossil fuels, others are more subtle, such as the noise from wind farms and the potential harm to migrating birds colliding with turbine blades. The energy and natural resources needed to create these generators also needs to be considered, however, on balance, renewable energy sources have a much-reduced impact compared to fossil fuel powered systems.

> **Q3** Other than the CO_2 emissions from burning fuel to create electricity, what other environmental factors might affect people living near a fossil fuelled power station?

Disposal of batteries

Batteries need to be disposed of properly since they contain toxic electrochemicals and some metals that can be harmful to the environment. If a battery is disposed of in a landfill site, it will degrade over time and the chemicals and metals from which it is made can leach into the soil and eventually end up entering the water table and river systems. The result is that the increased levels of toxins and metals can cause serious harm to wildlife and potentially humans too.

> **Q4** Explain why rechargeable batteries are better for the environment.

Power output

Modern society has an insatiable demand for power, mainly in the form of electricity to power our homes and businesses but also in fossil fuel for transportation and heating. Modern electrical and electronic devices are becoming increasingly efficient, for example lighting in the form of LED bulbs. Many products must carry an energy rating and in some products, including hairdryers and vacuum cleaners, maximum power ratings have been placed on them. There is increasing pressure on manufacturers to make appliances and devices as economic as possible.

The amount of power needed nationally needs to be consistent and meet demand, however with increasing numbers of solar and wind farms, the unpredictability of supply increases. Nuclear, hydroelectric and gas powered stations are quick to respond to demands and help the National Grid maintain a balanced supply.

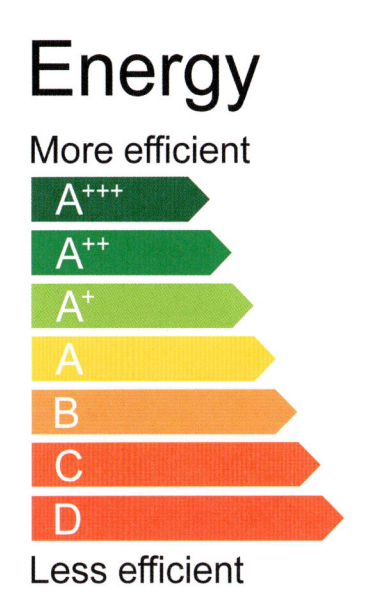

Energy

More efficient

- A^{+++}
- A^{++}
- A^{+}
- A
- B
- C
- D

Less efficient

Circuit and system connections

There are some international standards regarding how electrical and electronic systems are connected, however some manufacturers operate independently. A standard connection is better as it allows greater connectivity and creates less waste in both time and resources.

The British three-pin plug is an example where products need to be different for the UK domestic market. This is an added expense for global manufacturers having to supply two different models or at the very least two different leads or adapters. Computers are an example of a worldwide protocol being applied. The USB port and the mains socket are the same for every country, as are many of the internal connections on the motherboard and this standardisation is paramount for the ability of devices to share power sources and to be sold internationally.

Cost

When designing systems and products the potential cost of the energy source needs to be considered. The running costs of a product are important both financially and environmentally, and trade will be lost if it is too expensive or wasteful. Products that can take advantage of rechargeable and renewable energy can find that they have a competitive advantage in the market place.

> **Q5** Why are LED lightbulbs a more environmentally friendly option than traditional incandescent and halogen bulbs?

> **Q6** A rechargeable battery costs £4.75, a disposable battery costs £0.95. How many disposable batteries will be thrown away before the rechargeable battery becomes better value for money?

Chapter 9 **Powering systems**

Chapter 10 – Modern and smart materials

Objectives

- Be able to recognise and characterise a range of modern and smart materials
- Describe the advantages and disadvantages of using modern and smart materials for different applications

Modern and smart materials

This chapter covers a small selection of the many modern and smart materials available to designers. Technology is constantly progressing and new materials, as well as new ways of working with materials, continue to be developed. A good designer will utilise and exploit these materials where appropriate and keep up-to-date with the latest developments.

A **modern material** is a material or element that has been relatively recently discovered. It may also be used or combined in a way that is different from its normal function. It might be blended, coated, alloyed or treated to improve its functional or aesthetic properties.

A **smart material** is a material that reacts to an external **stimulus** by changing its characteristics and/or its properties. Common stimuli include light, heat, movement and electricity.

Shape memory alloys

Most materials have some form of memory, meaning that they will try to resist deformation or spring back to their original shape. **Shape memory alloys** (**SMA**) take this a step further; they can remember a preset shape and return to it despite being dramatically reshaped. The stimulus for returning to the preset shape is heat or electricity.

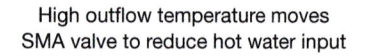

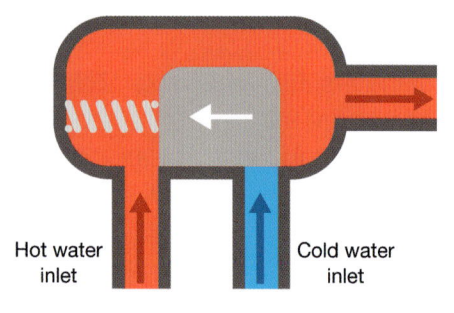

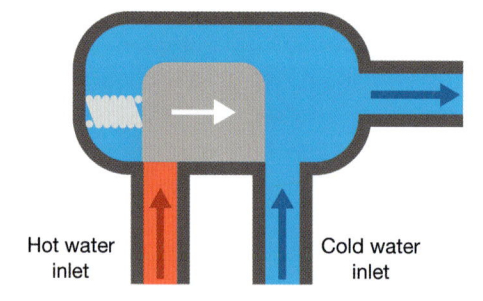

Nitinol, an alloy of nickel and titanium, is the most commonly used SMA. To program its shape memory, the nitinol must be held in the desired position and heated to around 540°C, then allowed to cool. It can then be deformed to a different shape. When it is heated to around 70°C, it will spring back to its programmed shape. This can also be achieved by passing an electric current through it. It can be re-programmed by reheating it to 540°C.

SMA used as a self-expanding surgical stent

Nitinol can also be used as muscle wire. The wire is first stretched and then, when an electrical current is passed through it, it will contract approximately 5% of its length. This is used in dental braces. Nitinol is often used for glasses frames as it can easily be straightened if they get bent out of shape.

> **Q1** Explain how a piece of shape memory alloy could be used in a fire detector controlling a sprinkler system.

Nanomaterials

In the field of **nanotechnology** there are several materials that are classed as nanomaterials. This means that the material is normally between 1 and 100 nanometres (but could be up to 1000 nanometres) in at least one dimension. Nanomaterials include carbon nanotubes, fullerene and quantum dots. These materials exist on an atomic or molecular scale and have potential benefits for scientific studies in the areas of electronics and engineering amongst others.

Their use in electronics has helped aid miniaturisation whilst improving conductivity. In the textiles industry, they have been used as protective coatings, films or particles to improve water resistance, as UV protection or as an anti-bacterial agent in footwear for example.

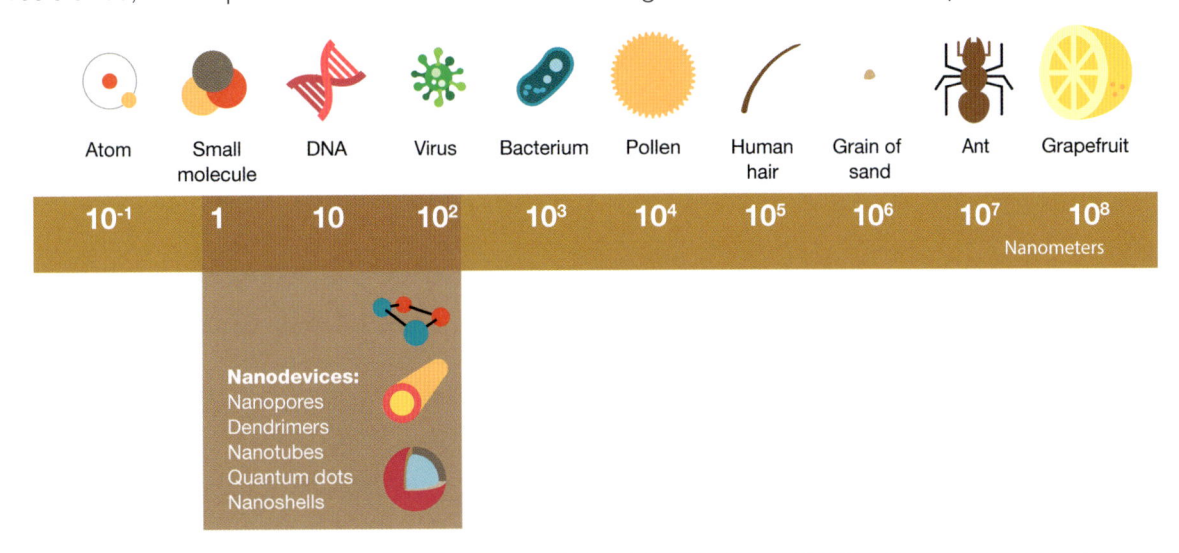

Atom	Small molecule	DNA	Virus	Bacterium	Pollen	Human hair	Grain of sand	Ant	Grapefruit
10^{-1}	1	10	10^2	10^3	10^4	10^5	10^6	10^7	10^8

Nanometers

Nanodevices:
Nanopores
Dendrimers
Nanotubes
Quantum dots
Nanoshells

> **Q2** According to the diagram above, how many times smaller is a bacterium than a grain of sand?

Reactive glass

There are three main different types of glass that can react to their environment. Reactive glass, smart glass and photochromic glass.

Reactive glass reacts to a bright light by darkening almost instantly. It is used in applications such as welding helmets and self-darkening mirrors. An LCD panel is used to control the darkening effect and is triggered using a **light dependent resistor** (**LDR**) as the input on an electronic control circuit. When the LCD panel is powered, it darkens and when no voltage is applied it becomes clear.

Smart glass is very similar to reactive glass as it uses an LCD screen to obscure the light passing through it. Smart glass is manually switched on to make it clear and is opaque when turned off. It is used for privacy in offices and homes without the need for blinds or curtains, however it is very expensive which restricts its use.

Photochromic glass uses photochromic particles called silver halides that react to UV light. The most common application is in sunglasses. The particles enable the treated lenses to darken when the user wears them in sunlight, and the same glasses will appear clear when they are worn inside, where there is little or no UV light.

One drawback with these lenses is that they take up to two minutes to fully darken and the same to become clear again. Another issue is that over time they lose the ability to return to a completely clear state, eventually staying dark.

> **Q3** How could the two minutes' delay in a pair of sunglasses darkening or lightening be an issue to the user?

> **Q4** How could a glass office building benefit from having its windows covered in photochromatic film?

Piezoelectric material

Although it is not a conductor, a **piezoelectric** material responds to movement, stress and electrical stimuli. It produces an electrical voltage when squeezed or put under pressure. It is commonly used in quartz clocks, inkjet printer heads and in gas lighters to create a spark that ignites the gas. **Quartz** is a natural piezoelectric material, and some polymers and ceramic materials have the same effect.

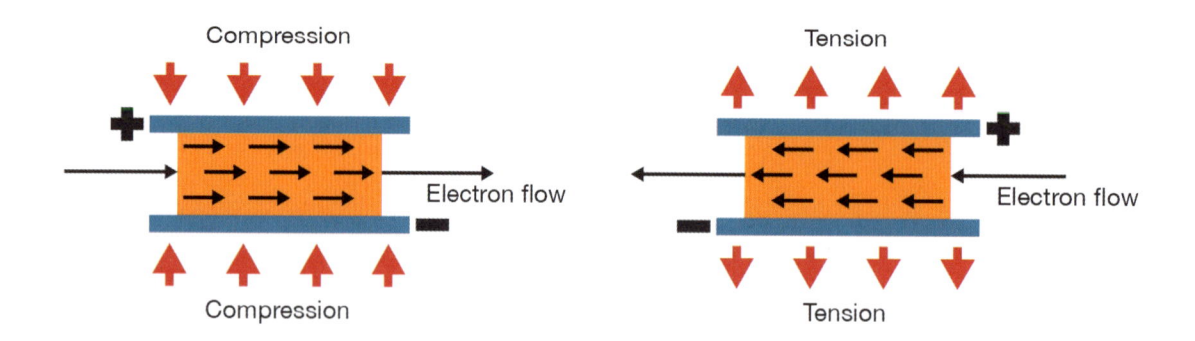

If a voltage is applied to the piezoelectric material it causes it to change shape. It is this principle that allows for its use in speakers and sounders. The electrical signal makes the metallic diaphragm move, which creates sound. A microphone receives soundwaves which move the diaphragm, creating an electrical signal.

> **Q5** How could piezoelectric material be used to detect vibrations in an alarm system?

Temperature responsive polymers

The most common type of heat responsive polymers contain **thermochromic pigments**, inks and dyes that react to heat by changing colour at specific temperatures. A colour change can indicate that a particular temperature has been reached. For example, a product could turn red when it becomes hot to signify danger or a need for caution. These pigments are used in applications such as room and paediatric thermometers, spray paints, novelty goods and children's cutlery.

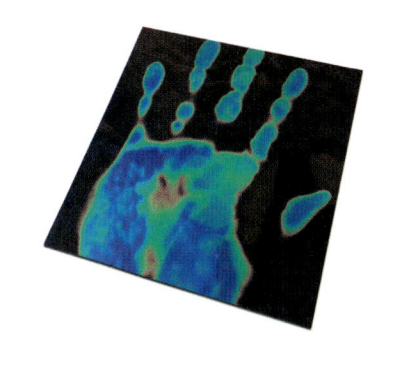

Irreversible versions of the pigment are available which can be used to indicate that a critical temperature has been reached. This is very useful to warn someone if heat sensitive products, such as medical supplies, have been poorly stored or transported.

Some special heat responsive polymers have the ability to be liquid at cool temperatures and solidify with a small rise in temperature. These have many medical and scientific uses are still being developed.

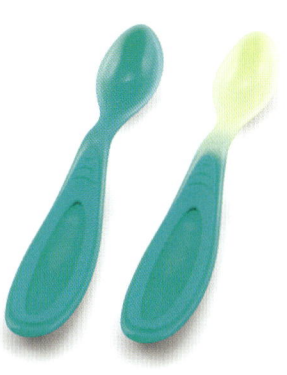

Q6 How could thermochromic pigments be used for packaging in the food industry?

Q7 Explain how thermochromic pigments can be used to indicate a fever in a young child.

Conductive inks

Conductive inks and paints contain conductive particles that enable circuits and connections to be drawn by hand, screen printed or printed digitally. It is available in pots or pens, is usually quick drying and works on most non-conductive surfaces. Non-toxic versions are available and can make for interesting experiments on skin.

Chapter 11 - Composite materials

Objectives

- Understand how material characteristics and properties can be enhanced by combining two or more materials
- Understand the advantages and disadvantages for a range of composite materials
- Have an awareness of the applications for a range of composite materials

Composite materials

Composite materials are formed when two or more distinctly different materials are combined together to create a new material with improved properties and functionality.

Concrete

Concrete has been used in construction for millennia in various forms. It is now a combination of various aggregates, water and cement. The ratio of parts varies depending on the intended use and the required strength. Concrete has good compressive strength but is weaker under tension. Reinforced concrete has steel rods or mesh embedded in the mixture which increases tensile strength and means that more complex architectural structures can be built.

Q1 Explain how the inclusion of steel mesh or rods in cement improves its tensile strength.

Plywood

Plywood is a very strong and stable manufactured board. It is made from an odd number of thin wood veneers bonded to each other, with one sheet perpendicular to the next. A strong adhesive is used to give strength and rigidity. Flexible versions are available made from especially thin veneers and are used for creating curves for projects such as furniture and interior design features. More expensive hardwood veneers are often used on the outer layers to give the impression of a solid hardwood. One drawback is that the edges can be hard to finish.

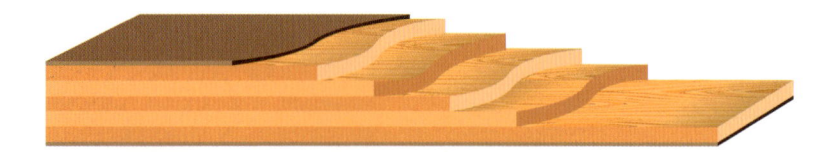

Q2 Why does plywood have an odd number of veneers?

Glass- and carbon-fibre

Glass and carbon-fibre reinforced plastics are two composite materials that are similar in the way they are manufactured. Both are based on a matted or woven material that is combined with a **thermosetting** plastic to produce very lightweight and very strong composites.

Although the processes do vary slightly from each other, the basic principles are the same:

1. Prepare a mould or former for the required shape
2. Apply release agent to the mould or former
3. Apply the first resin coat (or gel coat for GRP) to the mould or former
4. Apply the GRP matting or woven carbon fibre sheet on top of the first coat
5. Apply another coat of resin and work into the material
6. Repeat stages 4 and 5 until the required thickness of material is achieved
7. Seal the workpiece in a vacuum bag and place in an oven for the resin to cure. (The workpiece could alternatively be clamped and left to cure naturally in a workshop.)
8. Release the workpiece from the mould or former
9. Trim and finish the workpiece

Name	Appearance	Image	Characteristics	Uses
Glass reinforced plastic (GRP)	Glass fibre matting is covered with smooth plastic resin (gel coat) which sets hard with a high gloss finish. It is easily coloured and complex shapes can be formed		Lightweight, good strength-to-weight ratio, good corrosion chemical and heat resistance, waterproof, high VOCs / resins used. Can be trimmed with rotating blade. Labour-intensive to produce	Boat hulls, car and truck body parts, liquid storage tanks, pipes, helmets, seating
Carbon-fibre reinforced plastic (CRP)	Carbon-fibre is a cloth woven from individual strands, the interlacing provides an interesting and modern aesthetic, available in different patterns, can be coloured but frequently left natural, vinyl decals can be added for decoration		Very high strength-to-weight ratio, good tensile strength but not good compressive strength, stiff and rigid, very expensive, high VOCs / resins used, waterproof and resistant to chemicals. Manufacture is a labour-intensive and skilled process	Supercars and sports cars, top-end sports equipment, bespoke boats and musical instruments, increasingly developed for prosthetic uses

Reinforced polymers

This range of composite polymers uses a layer of fibres embedded into a polymer to strengthen it. They range from hosepipes with tough, integrated textile threads to industrial pipes with steel and aluminium wires adding support against fracture. The pipe pictured has a laminated metal layer to add thermal insulation as well as to offer protection from kinking when it is bent around corners. A common application is for connecting up a central heating system.

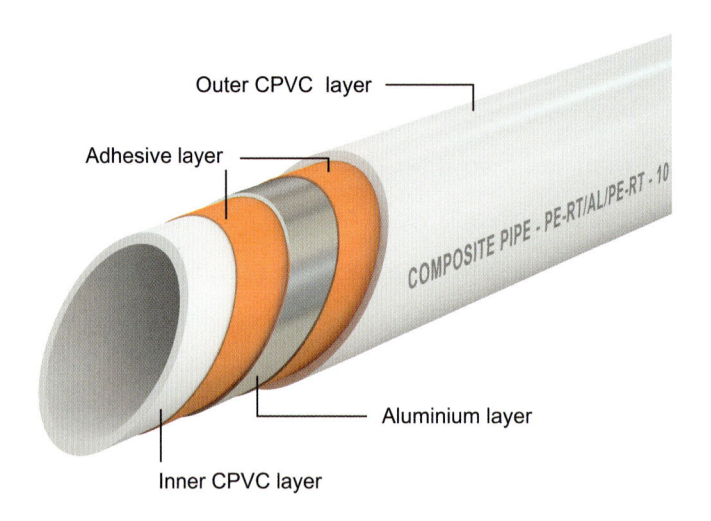

Outer CPVC layer
Adhesive layer
Aluminium layer
Inner CPVC layer

COMPOSITE PIPE - PE-RT/AL/PE-RT - 10

Q3 How does the embedded nylon thread in the hosepipe pictured reduce the chance of it splitting when filled with water under pressure?

Robotic materials

Robotic materials are a new and theoretical area of development where material scientists are attempting to get materials to 'think'. The theory is that materials will be able to sense, process and output data or responses. One area of this research is looking into biomimicry where a material might be able to camouflage itself like some sea creatures do.

Q4 Why is it difficult to recycle many composite materials?

Chapter 12 – Technical textiles

Objectives

- Be able to recognise and characterise a range of technical textiles in use
- Describe the advantages and disadvantages of using technical textiles for different applications

Technical textiles

A technical textile is one which has been developed with enhanced properties to withstand specific uses. The function is often vastly more important than the aesthetic qualities of the material. The following technical textiles perform specific roles, and because of the research and development involved in creating them, they can often be perceived as expensive.

Many technical textiles perform their function owing to the special way they have been manufactured and in many cases, the way they have been spun and woven.

Agro-textiles

Agro-textiles gather their name from their agricultural use. They come in a variety of forms for different use such as moisture retention, suppressing weeds and netting to protect crops from animals, birds, biological pest control as well as adverse weather, be it hail or extreme sunshine. They can be woven or non-woven but will normally have added protection against UV light which can prematurely age textiles if left untreated.

Construction textiles

These textiles have many similarities to agro-textiles but are used in the construction industry for various applications. Netting, attached to scaffolding, is used to protect workers onsite as well as the general public passing by below from flying debris. Non-woven construction textiles are used under roads and footpaths as weed suppressants and a special heavy-duty rubber waterproof membrane is used to line swimming pools, garden ponds and protect buildings that have eco-friendly green roofs.

Geo-textiles

Geo-textiles are used to hold sand, soil and other aggregates in place. Commonly seen in use as sandbags and to transport large amounts of building supplies around. They are used on a more industrial scale to protect eroding coastlines and to help prevent flooding in vulnerable areas. They can also be used to prevent the integration of different layers of aggregate in civil engineering projects such as urban landscaping.

> **Q1** Explain why agricultural netting can be bought with so many different sizes of holes.

> **Q2** Why are some non-woven technical textiles perforated?

Domestic textiles

Domestic textiles are common in the home and come in the form of cleaning cloths, padding for cushions and other home furnishings. They may be natural or synthetic, woven or non-woven. Fabrics range from cotton and linen to acrylic and PVC.

Microfibre is an incredibly popular domestic textile, however it is believed to be one of the largest contributors to plastic pollution in our rivers and oceans. When microfibres are washed, millions of tiny fibres are broken off and are flushed away with waste water. The fibres are so small that they pass through filters in water treatment plants and are washed into our waterways. Unfortunately, sea creatures and other animals digest these fibres which stay in their systems and, in many cases lead to ill health and death.

Environmentally friendly textiles

This eco-friendly group of textiles have no lasting impact of the environment and the earth's resources. They are made from natural and renewable resources such as plants and animals. These resources should be sustainably grown and managed using organic, rather than intensive, farming methods that will not affect natural habitat.

Wool and silk are two low-impact animal-based fibres that make quality textiles. Plant-based fibres are plentiful but not all are that environmentally friendly. Cotton is a very water hungry plant and should be avoided in arid parts of the world. Bamboo, coconut, linen and hemp are alternative natural fibres to consider. **Lyocell** is one of the most environmentally friendly fibres and is made from wood pulp. It is used for bedding supplies and other furnishings but is quite an expensive option.

Protective textiles

There is a wide range of protective textiles ranging from lightweight disposable non-woven textiles used by the medical profession for scrubs and dressings, to bullet proof and fire-resistant woven aramid fibres used by the emergency services and the armed forces. Even workmen, chefs and waiters wear protective textiles, often simple cotton fabric will suffice as it is hardwearing and can be treated to be fire and stain resistant.

Gore-Tex® fabric

A wide range of clothing products now come with a Gore-Tex® membrane sewn between layers of other fabrics. This creates a waterproof yet breathable garment which is commonly used in a variety of outdoor clothing including, jackets, gloves, walking boots and trainers. The specific benefit of Gore-Tex® over other waterproof materials is that it is breathable. This means that the Gore-Tex® layer not only stops water coming in, but also allows airborne moisture to escape.

This reduces the build-up of **condensation** inside a jacket or a pair of boots, making the wearer much more comfortable.

Gore-Tex® membrane has around 150 million pores per square centimetre and works because each pore is 20,000 times smaller than a water droplet, so the rain cannot get through. However, the damp moisture **vapour** being produced by the wearer can pass through the pores, keeping the wearer warm and dry.

Q3 Explain how a Gore-Tex® membrane stops water from getting in, yet lets water vapour out in both hot and cold environments.

Kevlar®

Kevlar® is a fibre developed by DuPont™ that has high tensile strength, has great heat resistance and is extremely hard-wearing and cut resistant. It is also non-flammable and resistant to most chemicals. It has a natural yellowish-gold tone but also comes dyed in many colours. Its woven texture varies from a very fine to a rather course weave.

Kevlar is a flexible and lightweight synthetic fibre from the class of fibres known as aramids which are modified polyamide (nylon) fibres. Kevlar® is used in many applications including body armour, personal protective equipment for use in hazardous situations and sports equipment. It has also been found to have useful acoustic properties and is used in the production of quality loudspeakers and some musical instruments.

Q4 How could Kevlar be used to protect students in a school workshop?

Fire resistant fabrics

Heat and flame resistant fabrics such as **Nomex**® and **Kevlar**® have been developed to withstand high temperatures and reduce combustion when exposed to a naked flame. There are many different brands of fabric that have differing levels of heat and flame protection. Most of these fabrics are based on a group of synthetic fibres known as **aramid** fibres. They are generally closely woven, very strong and heat-resistant. Applications include fire blankets, firefighting uniform, safety clothing such as gloves, aprons and boiler suits and protection for racing car drivers

Flame retardants are different and can be applied to a range of regular fabrics, in particular, curtains and sofa fabrics. They are designed to produce a chemical reaction that slows down and even stops ignition taking place.

> **Q5** For which activities in a school workshop would wearing fire resistant PPE be of benefit?

Sports textiles

Specialist sports fabrics have improved greatly in the last few decades becoming better at thermal insulation and protection from the weather. They have increased breathability (wicking fabrics) allowing perspiration and condensation to escape quickly, leaving the wearer dry and warm. Most sports textiles have high elasticity allowing the user to be comfortable and supported.

Many sports textiles need to be tough, impact resistant and hardwearing but some also require other properties such as UV resistance, anti-fungal and anti-bacterial properties. Take a shared football or hockey kit for example. **Microencapsulation** is used to embed various chemicals and compounds into the fibres of garments, such as mosquito repellent, anti-bacterial agents and deodorants.

Conductive fabrics

Also known as **e-textiles**, these highly conductive threads and fabrics allow an electrical signal to pass through them with very little resistance. The fabric can be used in strips so as to create paths for electricity to flow along, connecting components such as LEDs, headphones and microphones. It is even possible to remotely connect a smartphone, in an inside coat pocket, to controls on the cuff or a pair of gloves. Conductive thread is a single strand of silvery conductive material that can be sewn onto or into non-conductive fabrics.

Applications include connecting wearable inputs, processes and outputs such as switches, lights, Bluetooth connectivity and speakers in technical clothing, children's soft electronic toys, wearable electronic sports equipment and anti-static clothing.

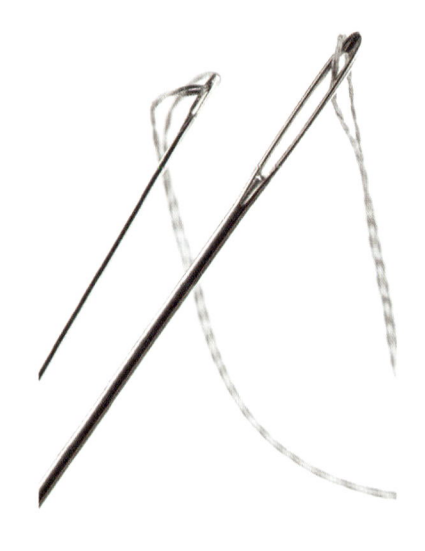

> **Q6** How could conductive thread and fabric be used to improve safety features for cyclists?

Chapter 13 – Mechanical devices

Objectives

- Understand the principles and performance of a range of mechanical devices
- Be able to apply the principles of different types of movement to influence changes in magnitude and direction through levers and rotary systems
- Be able to calculate mechanical advantage and velocity ratio for a range of mechanical devices

Mechanical devices

Mechanical devices are machines or tools that have one or more parts. They use and manipulate energy to perform tasks and specific actions.

Types of movement

Motion is the action or process of something being moved. Motion can take many different forms. The following examples are the most commonly found. Different motions can be added together and changed from one to another to suit certain tasks or applications.

Linear motion

Linear motion is movement in one direction along a straight line. An example of linear motion is a train travelling along a straight section of track, or a runner doing a 100-metre sprint.

Reciprocating motion

This is repetitive up-and-down or back-and-forth linear motion, such as a needle moving up and down in a sewing machine, or a piston moving back and forth in a cylinder.

Oscillating motion

This motion is similar to reciprocating motion, but the constant movement is from side to side along a curved path. Examples include a pendulum in a clock and windscreen wipers moving across a windscreen.

Rotary motion

Examples of rotary motion include a ball tied to a rope and being swung round in a circle, or a merry-go-round as it rotates around a fixed axis.

> **Q1** Which type(s) of motion are associated with:
> (a) a paper trimmer?
> (b) the hands of a clock?
> (c) a child's swing?

Classification of levers

A lever is a very simple way to gain **mechanical advantage** (**MA**), making lifting or moving something much easier or to exert greater pressure. Levers can also be used to apply pressure at a particular point. They have two parts; a bar and a pivot called a **fulcrum**. There are three elements to consider when using levers; the **effort** (input), the **load** (output) and the position of the fulcrum. Levers are chosen depending on the specific movement or mechanical advantage required to perform a task.

Classes of lever

A seesaw acts like a pair of balances or scales and is one type of lever. There are three different types of levers known as classes or orders. The same principles for calculating changes in magnitude and force apply to all classes of levers.

First order lever (Class 1) – This is most easily remembered as a seesaw action. The load and effort are on opposite sides of the fulcrum which can be positioned anywhere between them.

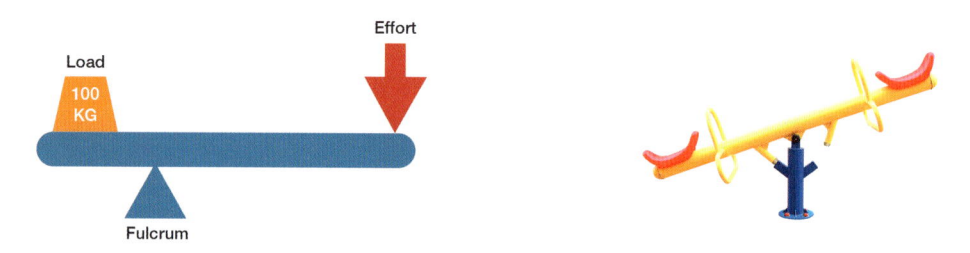

Second order lever (Class 2) – This is most easily remembered as a wheelbarrow action. The fulcrum is at one end with the effort at the opposite end and load is somewhere in the middle.

Third order lever (Class 3) – This is most easily remembered as a tweezer action. The fulcrum is at one end, the load at the opposite end and the effort is applied somewhere in the middle.

Class 3 levers have a MA of less than 1, meaning that the force taken to move them is greater than the force they apply.

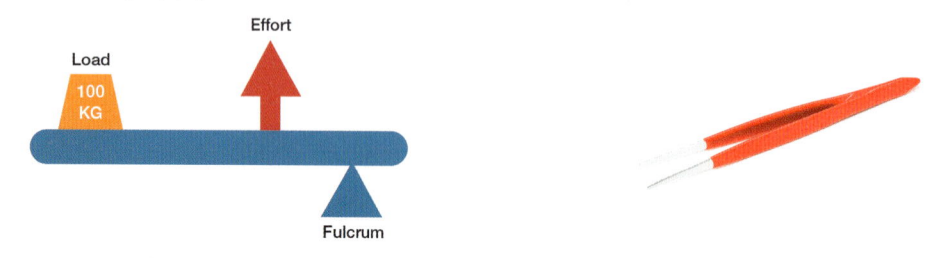

Q2 Which class of lever best describes:
(a) a pair of scissors?
(b) a stapler?
(c) a nut cracker?

Mechanical advantage (MA)

The mechanical advantage is defined as the amplification of the input achieved when compared to the output.

To calculate the MA of a mechanism, such as the wheelbarrow pictured, use the following formula:

$$MA = \frac{Load}{Effort} = \frac{300N}{100N} = \frac{3}{1}$$

Also written as 3:1 or just MA of 3

Using some types of lever can seem like you are gaining MA for nothing, but you are actually sacrificing the length of movement. When the handles of the wheelbarrow are lifted 300mm the actual load is only lifted 100mm, however it is three times easier to lift.

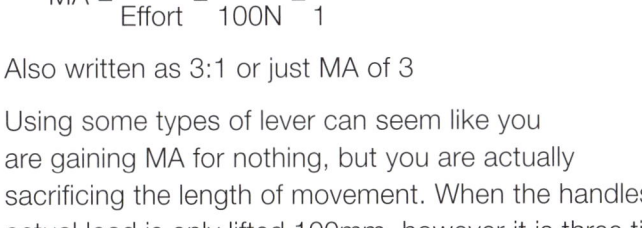

> **Q3** Calculate the mechanical advantage if the load was 875N and the effort was 125N. Express the answer as a ratio.

Velocity ratio (VR)

Velocity ratio is similar to mechanical advantage but measures the distance travelled as opposed to the effort required.

$$VR = \frac{Distance\ moved\ by\ effort}{Distance\ moved\ by\ load}$$

In this example $VR = \frac{400}{100} = \frac{4}{1}$

Or 4:1 as a ratio.

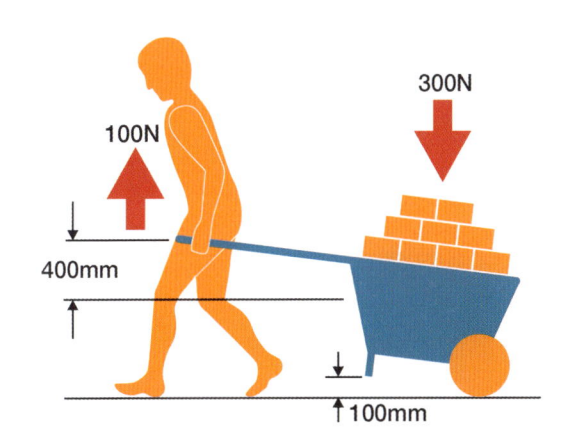

> **Q4** If a metalworker was cutting some aluminium plate with a guillotine which had a VR of 6:1 and the lever was moved 300mm, how much aluminium would be cut?

Efficiency

If every machine worked in a perfect environment with no friction then it would operate at 100% efficiency, however friction does exist and actual performance is reduced. Heat build-up, air resistance, vibrations, wear and tear and even noise cause inefficiencies.

To calculate the efficiency of a machine we used the following formula:

$$Efficiency = \frac{MA}{VR} \times 100\%$$

> **Q5** Calculate the efficiency of a machine that has a mechanical advantage of 5 and a velocity ratio of 6.

Linkages

Bell crank

The bell crank linkage changes the direction of the input motion through 90°. It can be used to change horizontal motion into vertical motion or vice versa. It uses a fixed pivot and two moving pivots.

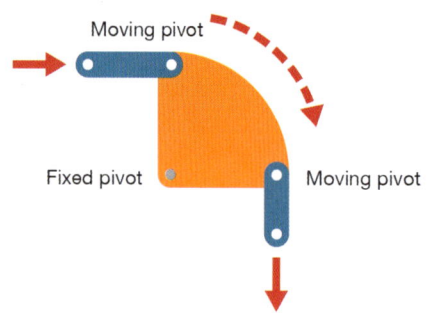

Reverse motion linkage

The reverse motion linkage changes the direction of the input motion so that the output travels in the opposite direction. If the input is pulled, the output pushes and vice versa. It uses a central bar held in position with a fixed pivot (fulcrum) that forces the change in direction and two moving pivots which are connected to the input and output bars.

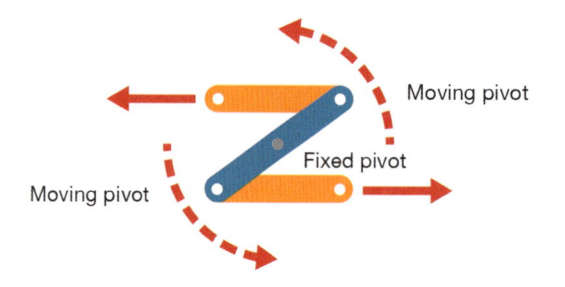

Q6 Which linkage changes the direction of motion through 90°?

Rotary systems

Rotary systems are used to drive mechanisms in equipment and machinery. They transfer the direction of force along different paths and through changes of angle and direction. They can also change one type of motion into another.

Cams and followers

A **cam** is a shaped piece of material, usually wood, metal or plastic, attached to a rotating shaft. The rotating rod is often known as a **camshaft** when used in an engine or other mechanical device. There are many different shaped cams which perform various jobs and create differing movements.

A cam is mainly used to change rotary motion into reciprocating motion through the use of a **follower**. A crank is used to rotate the shaft which rotates the cam, which in turn moves the follower up and down.

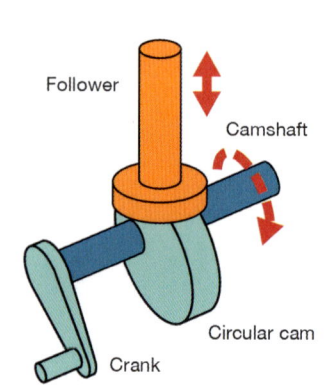

The movement of the follower is directly affected by the shape of the cam it follows.

The follower will rise and fall according to the cam shape. At times during a revolution the follower may be stationary; this is known as the **dwell**. A cam can be formed into any number of shapes but the following are the most commonly used varieties.

(a) **Eccentric or circular cam** – a simple round cam with the shaft position off centre – the follower has a steady rise and fall.

(b) **Pear cam** – a rapid rise and fall followed by a long dwell period.

(c) **Drop or snail cam** – a long dwell followed by a steady rise and a sudden drop – can only be used in one direction.

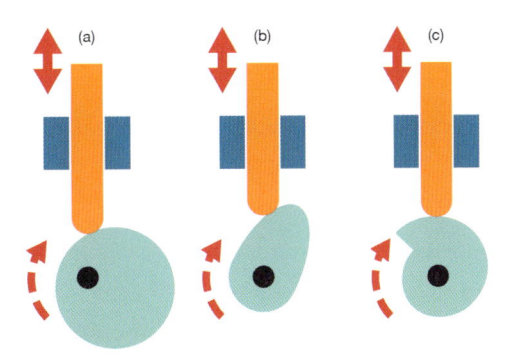

Q7 Which cam could be used on an automaton to create the motion of the jaw of an animal slowly opening then snapping shut?

Q8 Which cam could be used on an automaton to make a mouse slowly peek out of a hole and slowly retreat again?

Followers

Followers come in three main varieties and are used for different applications.

(a) **Flat follower** – This is not very accurate and has high levels of friction due to the surface area in contact with the cam. It can cope well under load.

(b) **Knife edged follower** – The fine edge tracks the movement of a cam very accurately. It has low friction although there can be a high level of wear due to the fine edge. It is not efficient under heavy load.

(c) **Roller follower** – A roller tracks the cam's movement with some accuracy. Friction is greatly reduced due to the rotation of the roller, which often has a bearing for smooth running and low wear. It is efficient under load.

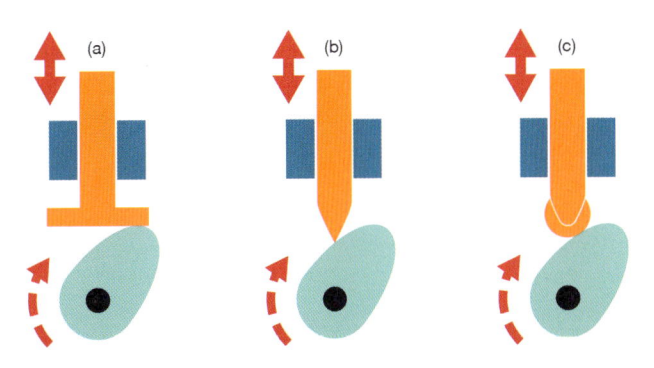

Crank and slider

The crank and slider linkage changes rotary motion into reciprocating motion or vice versa. It uses a crank which is held with a fixed pivot. A connecting rod uses two moving pivots to push and pull a slider along a set path.

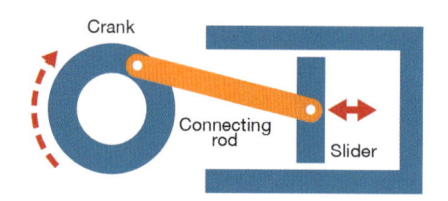

Pulleys and belts

A drive belt relies on friction to operate effectively and therefore is often made from rubber as it has the ability to grip effectively under appropriate tension. They can also be made from rope, cord and even steel cable as seen on ski lifts.

A pulley is a grooved rimmed wheel that is used in conjunction with a drive belt to transfer movement. Like a gear without teeth, the pulley is attached to an axle and rotates. The friction between the drive belt and the pulley allows them to rotate together. Pulleys have many uses including lifting equipment and transforming rotational motion into linear, for example, a winch.

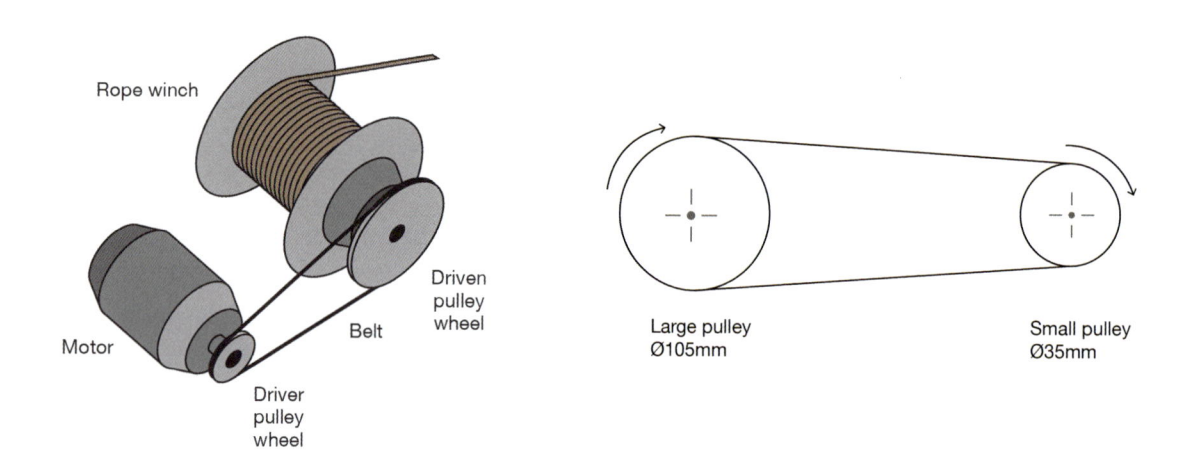

Pulley system calculations:

To calculate velocity ratio of a pulley system we use the following formulae:

$$VR = \frac{\text{Diameter of driven pulley}}{\text{Diameter of driver pulley}} = \frac{35}{105} = \frac{1}{3} = 1:3$$

To calculate the output speed of a pulley system we use the term revolutions per minute (rpm) for the output speed:

$$\text{Output speed} = \frac{\text{Input speed}}{\text{Velocity ratio}} = \frac{150}{1/3} = 150 \times 3 = 450 \text{rpm}$$

> **Q9** What is the VR of a pulley system with a driver pulley size of 100mm diameter and a driven pulley of 20mm diameter?

Gear types

Gears are similar to pulley systems but offer a direct drive where the teeth of the cogs interlock or 'mesh' together. Gear systems offer a more reliable drive and do not rely on a belt to transfer the drive, however this makes it more difficult to move the drive around a system.

Simple and compound gear train

A simple gear train consists of a drive cogwheel or drive 'gear' which in turn rotates the driven gear. The gear ratio is calculated by working out how many times the drive gear turns the driven gear per rotation. For example, if the drive gear has 40 teeth and the driven gear has 20 teeth, then for each rotation of the drive gear the driven gear would rotate twice. This can be expressed as a gear ratio of 2 which is known as gearing up.

If the cogs were the other way round, then the ratio would be 1:2 (or 0.5) and this is known as gearing down. One thing to note on a simple gear train is that the driven gear always rotates in the opposite direction to the drive gear.

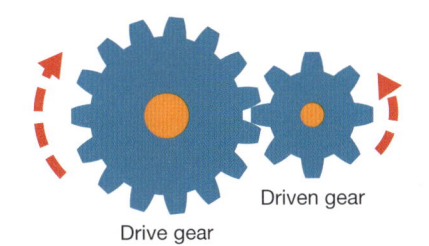

To calculate velocity ratio (VR), use the formula:

$$VR = \frac{\text{Number of teeth of driven gear}}{\text{Number of teeth of drive gear}}$$

To calculate the output speed, use the formula:

$$\text{Output speed} = \frac{\text{Input speed}}{\text{Gear ratio}}$$

In an example: Output speed = $\frac{\text{input speed}}{\text{Gear ratio}} = \frac{300}{1/2} = 300 \times 2 = 600$ rpm

Compound gears speed up or slow down the output.
Pairs of gears are positioned on the same axle.

To find the total VR of the compound gear train, work out each pair separately

The 1st pair (a-b) are: 20 teeth and 40 teeth

The 2nd pair (c-d) are: 10 teeth and 40 teeth

$\frac{40}{20} \times \frac{40}{10} = 8:1$ This means that the output speed is 8 times slower than the input speed.

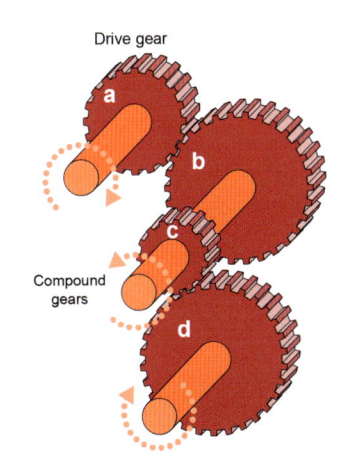

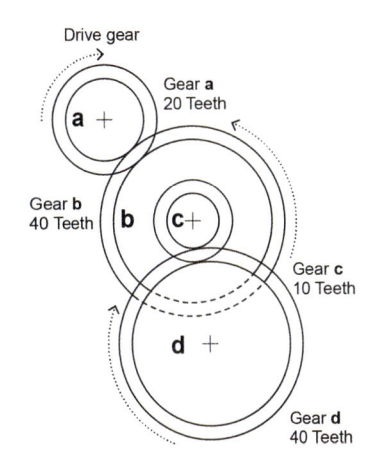

Idler gear

An idler gear is used to change the direction of rotation so that the driven gear goes in the same direction as the drive gear. The size of the idler gear does not matter as it just transfers the movement from the drive gear to the driven gear.

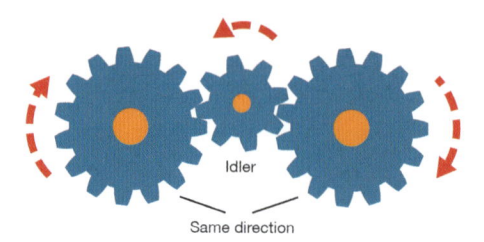

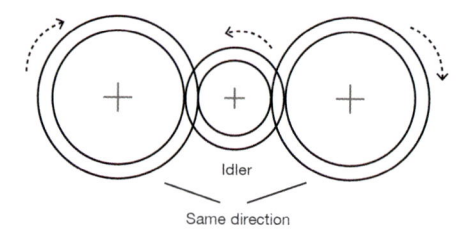

Bevel gears

These special gears change the direction of drive through 90 degrees. They are used on hand drills, some kitchen whisks and numerous power tools.

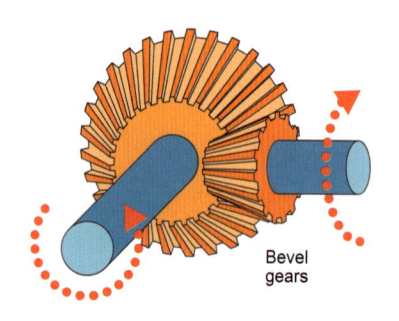

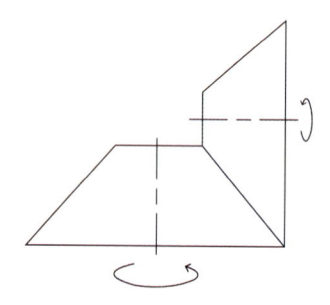

Rack and pinion

Rack and pinion gears convert rotational motion to linear motion and vice versa. They are commonly found on steering systems but can also be seen on pillar drills to raise and lower the table.

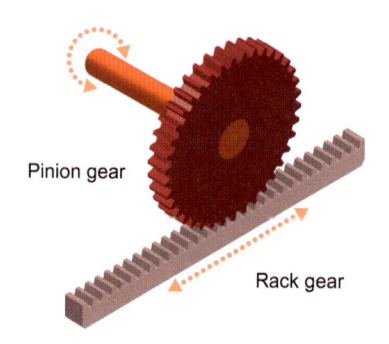

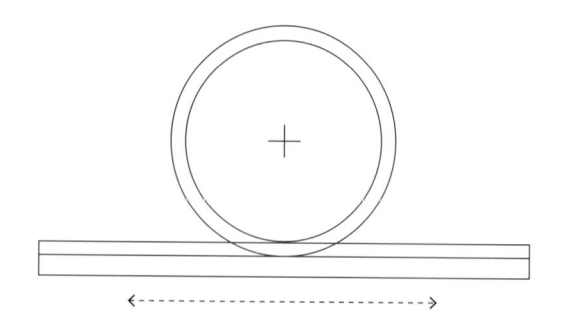

To calculate the distance a rack gear moves per revolution of a pinion gear we use the following calculation:

$$\frac{\text{Number of teeth on pinion gear}}{\text{Number of teeth on rack gear per metre}} \times 1 \text{ metre}$$

Therefore, if a pinion gear has 20 teeth and a rack gear has 160 teeth per metre then 20 ÷ 160 = 1/8 metre = 125mm

> **Q10** If a pinion gear has 30 teeth and rack gear has 120 teeth per metre, how far will the rack gear move in half a revolution?

Chapter 14 – Electronic systems

Objectives

- Understand how electronic systems provide functionality to products and processes
- Know the working characteristics, advantages and disadvantages for a range of sensors, control devices and outputs

Systems

A **system** comprises parts or components that work together to control a task or activity. A system consists of inputs, processes and outputs. All design and manufacturing tasks are made up of systems, from printing a simple image onto a piece of paper to manufacturing a sports car.

The role of switches in electronic systems

For a system to be controlled it either needs to be manually triggered or it needs to sense an environmental change such as heat, sound, movement or light. To do this it needs an input component or sensor.

Some electronic components have **polarity**. This means that they have a positive and negative side to them and therefore it matters which way around they go in a circuit. Most switches do not have polarity, but they do have a **pole** and a **throw**. Electricity in a circuit will only travel from the pole to the throw or vice-versa.

The simplest form of switch is a single pole single throw (SPST) which is perfect as an on-off power switch, as it can make (connect) or break (disconnect) a circuit. The single pole double throw (SPDT) has two options for the throw. This could be used to control two outputs such as a red bulb for stop or a green bulb for go. Toggle switches latch on or off when pressed where as momentary switches (push switches) only operate for as long as they are pressed. There are two types of momentary switches; push to make (PTM) and push to break (PTB). These are frequently used to trigger circuits such as that used for a door bell.

Other input devices include **thermistors** to detect heat and cold, **light dependent resistors** (**LDR**) to detect light or dark and pressure sensors to detect changes in force.

> **Q1** Which type of switch would be used for the following actions:
> (a) a light switch?
> (b) remote control buttons?
> (c) trigger switches at pedestrian crossings?

Common input components

Name and symbol	Appearance	Image	Characteristics	Uses
Toggle switch (latching)	Available in a variety of shapes, sizes and switching positions depending on the task		Off and on positions, once switched they stay on (latched) until switched again	Lighting, power switch, control panels
Push to make (PTM) switch normally open	A wide variety of shapes, colours and sizes		The legs of the switch are only connected when the switch is pressed (momentary); it is normally open, no polarity	Door bell, intercoms, keyboards
Push to break (PTB) switch normally closed	They are identical to PTM switches so you may need to check the connectivity		The legs are only disconnected when the switch is pressed (momentary); it is normally closed, no polarity	Alarm systems, control systems
Light dependent resistor (LDR)	Small light sensitive panel often in plastic shroud, two wires for mounting to circuit		Resistance increases in the dark and decreases in the light, no polarity	Street lights, solar garden lights, security and child night lights, low-light meter for sporting events
Thermistor	Small coloured disc, two wires for mounting to circuit		Resistance changes with a change in temperature, no polarity	Thermostats on central heating systems, fridges and freezers, digital thermometers

> **Q2** Explain how a sensor might work automatically in place of a switch being manually pressed.

Transistors

Transistors are small silicon semi-conductors and are used in systems to process or control information. Transistors have two common applications. Firstly, they can be used as electronic switches, where they can detect very small amounts of current which can trigger the flow of a much larger current. This application can be seen in use with touch sensitive devices. Secondly, they can be used as an amplifier, where a small input current can be increased to become a much larger output current. This can be explained well by using an amplifier to increase the signal from an MP3 player through a loudspeaker. Transistors are classified as **transducer drivers** which are components that boost or amplify weak signals.

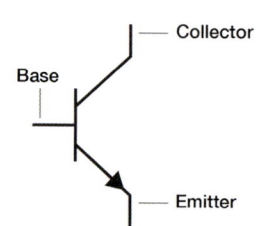

Circuit symbol for an NPN transistor

Resistors

Other components such as resistors, diodes and capacitors can vary in shape, size, voltage and power-handling, and need to be used appropriately for the specific task required.

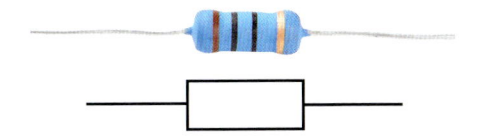

Resistors are passive components that restrict the flow of electricity in a circuit. They can be used for various applications including lowering the voltage within a circuit, protecting other components or stabilising digital switches. There are a number of different styles of resistor, but they will either be a fixed-value resistor, or a variable resistor, which can be used to control the level of resistance.

Resistance is measured in ohms (Ω). A resistor has a series of coloured bands painted onto its body. Each set of bands represents a specific value. To work out the value in ohms of the coloured bands we use the resistor colour code. See page 261.

> **Q3** Look up the resistor colour code to learn how the value of a resistor is worked out.

The role of outputs in electronic systems

Output components are used to give off a stimulus such as light, heat, movement or sound. Some output components such as light emitting diodes (LEDs) require very little power to drive them but others, such as heating elements, require a lot of energy. Output components sometimes need to be connected to devices called **transducer drivers**, such as transistors, which increase the power available and help a circuit perform correctly without overheating.

Most output components (excluding lamps) have polarity. Two common output devices are buzzers and light emitting diodes (LEDs).

Name and symbol	Appearance	Image	Characteristics	Uses
Light emitting diode (LED) — Anode / Cathode	Available in a variety of sizes, shapes and colours, most commonly 5mm round		Produces light, connected by an anode (+ve) and cathode (-ve), has polarity. Low voltage, low power consumption, long-lasting, can be hard to change if broken	Low power lighting, torches, TV screens, power indicators
Buzzer	Small compact units in plastic casing, available in a variety of sizes and sounds		Mid- to high-pitched buzz created by fast oscillating electromagnetic parts, has polarity	Alarm systems, door entry systems, children's toys, electronics and games

> **Q4** In which situations would LEDs be a more appropriate output than a buzzer for a door entry system?

Chapter 15 – Programmable components

Objectives

- Understand how programmable components provide embedded functionality to products
- Be aware of the performance and functional capabilities of programmable components
- Understand how flowcharts are used to simplify the programming of components
- Understand the difference between the processing of digital and analogue inputs

Processing using programmable components

Special **integrated circuits** (**IC**) known as microcontrollers can be used for multiple processes. Traditionally ICs were selected to perform a certain task or process. Although these ICs are still used, many modern products use **microcontrollers** as they can be programmed to take over the role of many ICs. This means fewer ICs need to be used and therefore circuit boards are smaller, often meaning that products become smaller too. This saves natural resources and can lead to cost savings. As most microcontrollers are reprogrammable, it also means that products can be updated with new firmware which can extend the life of some electronic products.

Programming microcontrollers

Microcontrollers come in many different forms and are also known as **peripheral interface controllers** (**PIC**s). There are many different varieties of PIC available. The brands that you are likely to find in schools include Picaxe, Genie and Arduino. Similar systems include the Raspberry Pi and the BBC Micro:bit.

PICs are programmed by sending code from a computer to the integrated circuit (IC) using a download cable, usually connected to the USB port. The code can be written directly on the computer in an appropriate programming language or the code can be generated using software that allows you to create a **flowchart** of the processes that you want the PIC to perform. The software then converts the flowchart into the appropriate code for the PIC. This saves having to learn a programming language, such as BASIC and can save time.

Digital and analogue signals

The most common processes performed by electronic circuits are timing, counting and decision-making. Inputs and outputs may receive or give out one of two different types of signal.

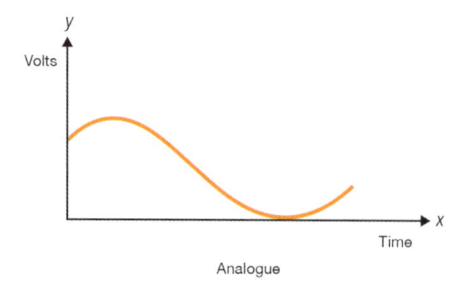

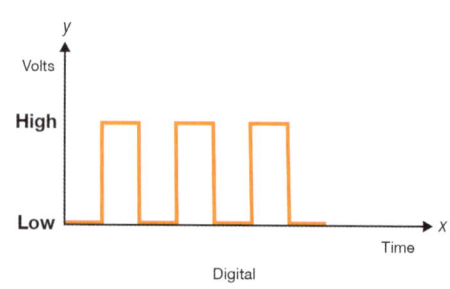

An **analogue signal** is continuous with an infinite range of values between minimum and maximum points. An analogue signal would be produced by a thermistor as it changes between hot and cold, or a light dependent resistor sensing change from dark to light.

70 Section 3 **Energy, materials, devices and systems**

A **digital signal** is either on or off and is the type of signal you would get from a switch. This is represented by 0 for off and 1 for on, creating the on/off symbol: O+|=⏻.

The voltage of an analogue signal can vary continuously, as opposed to the digital signal that can only be a series of highs and lows (or ones and zeros).

> **Q1** What type of signal would be sent from the following devices?
> (a) the thermostat on a central heating system
> (b) a microphone
> (c) a computer mouse

Flowcharts

Flowcharts are a graphical representation of a system or part of a system, known as a subsystem. The following symbols are used to create flowcharts.

Start / End	Arrows	Input / Output	Process	Decision
⬭	→	▱	▭	◇

The symbols are added together in a linear configuration with connecting arrows which indicate the direction of travel of information.

Switching outputs in relation to inputs and decisions

Using flowcharts, it is easy to control what happens to inputs, decisions and outputs in a system. In the following example a **passive infrared sensor** (**PIR**) is the input that detects movement as someone approaches some automatic doors. This triggers a time delay to be activated for a few seconds. During that time the output drives a motor which opens the doors while someone walks through.

The steps have been simplified for illustration purposes.

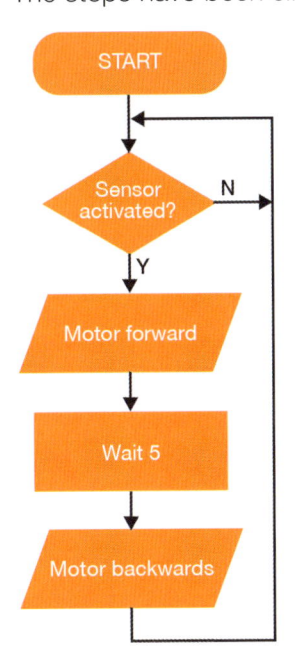

Start:

Decision: Has the motion sensor (PIR) connected to the input been activated?

If NO, continue to wait for the PIR to be triggered by movement.

If YES, continue with the program.

Output: The motor turns on and opens the doors.

Process: Delay for 5 seconds; the motor is on long enough to open the doors and let people through.

Output: The motor turns on again in reverse and the doors automatically close.

The circuit loops back to the top awaiting the next trigger of the PIR.

> **Q2** Explain how a time delay could be used to help encourage good oral hygiene.

The following is an example of a system that would turn on four LEDs in a running sequence like the type of program that would control a bike safety light. The **schematic** drawing below graphically explains the physical connections between the microcontroller, the input switch and the LEDs.

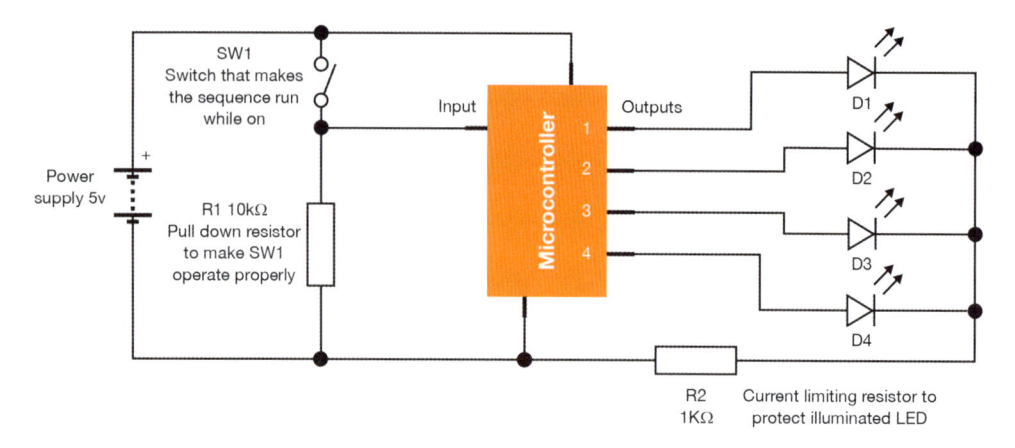

Below is the flowchart that would be converted into a program that would make the LEDs flash in sequence.

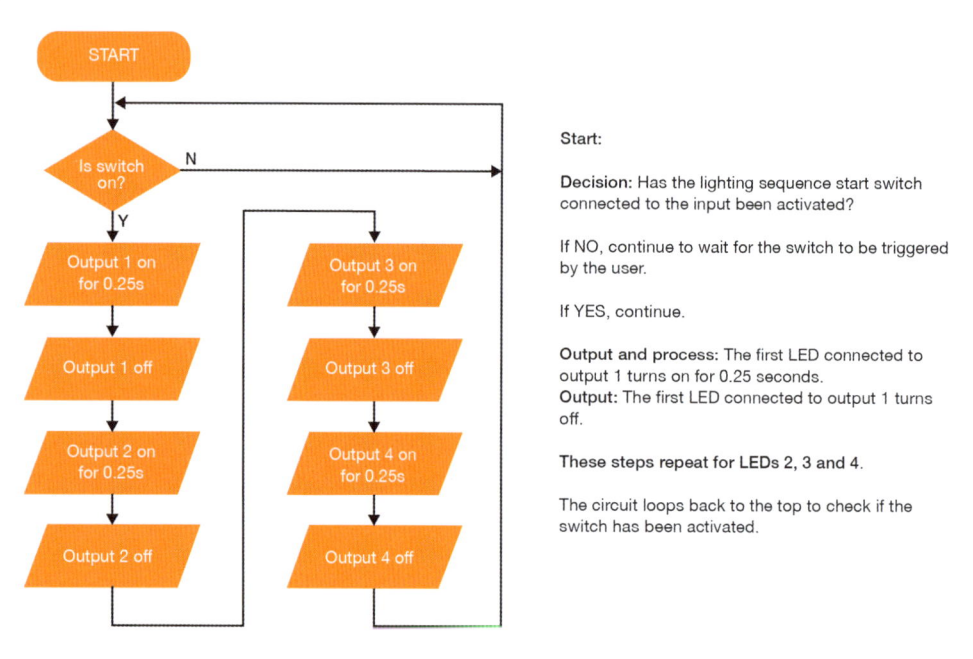

Start:

Decision: Has the lighting sequence start switch connected to the input been activated?

If NO, continue to wait for the switch to be triggered by the user.

If YES, continue.

Output and process: The first LED connected to output 1 turns on for 0.25 seconds.
Output: The first LED connected to output 1 turns off.

These steps repeat for LEDs 2, 3 and 4.

The circuit loops back to the top to check if the switch has been activated.

Processing and responding to analogue inputs

Sometimes a circuit needs to make a decision about a situation. As you will have seen from previous examples, detecting when a switch has been activated is very straightforward. However, if a street lamp is meant to turn on at a specific light level, then the decision is more complex.

The system needs to know exactly at which light level to turn the lamp on. To do this, the system detects exactly how much voltage it is receiving from the light dependent resistor and compares that to a pre-determined level that has been deemed 'dark enough' to turn the street lamp on.

The LDR is an analogue sensor and therefore, an analogue input is needed. This enables a variable number between 0 and 255 to be set as the trigger. LDRs have very low resistance in light and high resistance in the dark, therefore 0 could be set to bright sunshine and 255 to total darkness. Then you just need to decide at which point you want the street lamp to turn on. In the example following, 150 is used as the trigger level.

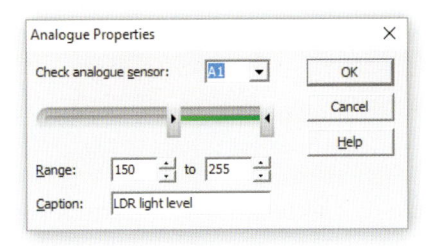

Analogue Properties dialog:
- Check analogue sensor: A1
- Range: 150 to 255
- Caption: LDR light level

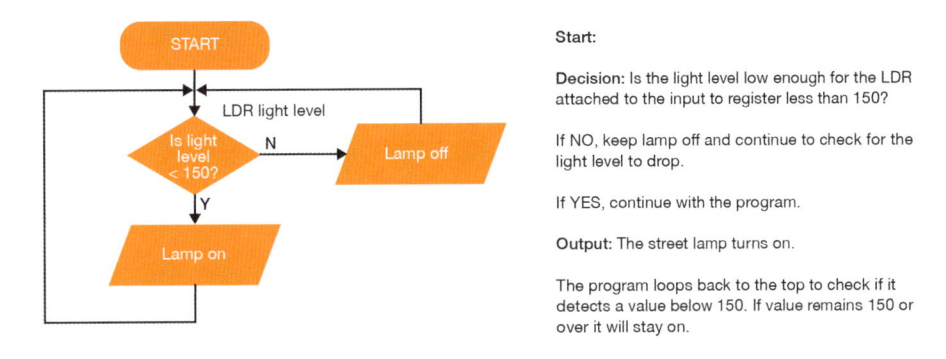

Flowchart: START → Is light level < 150? → Y: Lamp on (loops back) / N: Lamp off (loops back to LDR light level check)

Start:

Decision: Is the light level low enough for the LDR attached to the input to register less than 150?

If NO, keep lamp off and continue to check for the light level to drop.

If YES, continue with the program.

Output: The street lamp turns on.

The program loops back to the top to check if it detects a value below 150. If value remains 150 or over it will stay on.

> **Q3** Other than an LDR, name an input component that would require an analogue decision to work correctly.

Use of simple routines to control outputs

A large number of routines can be programmed into microcontrollers allowing them to control their inputs and outputs more effectively. The following selection of simple routines are among the most common.

Delays

We have seen time delays in action in both the automatic door system and the flashing LED examples. The two types of delay can be defined as follows:

Delay timers go on once for a set period of time and then turn off and wait to be retriggered. This type of timer can be best explained by an egg timer or a doorbell chime.

Repetitive timers constantly alternate between on and off states. This might be extremely fast or very slow and describes the type of delay used to control car indicators or the reversing beeps found on large trucks.

> **Q4** Which type of timer would be best for the flash facility on a camera?

Loops

The types of loops used with microcontrollers are **open loop**, and **closed loop** systems, which include **feedback loops**.

An **open loop system** has no feedback and is unable to make a decision. The input directly controls the output; however, the output is unable to influence the input. For example, a room heater remains on until it is manually switched off, regardless of the temperature being reached.

An **open loop system** is one that performs a routine once the program is run and then stops at the end of the program. In order to work again, the whole program will need to be re-run.

Chapter 15 **Programmable components** 73

Open loop system

A **closed-loop system** is able to make a decision using a **feedback loop**, usually from a sensor. For example, in a central heating system, the heating will be automatically switched on or off when the temperature reaches a certain value.

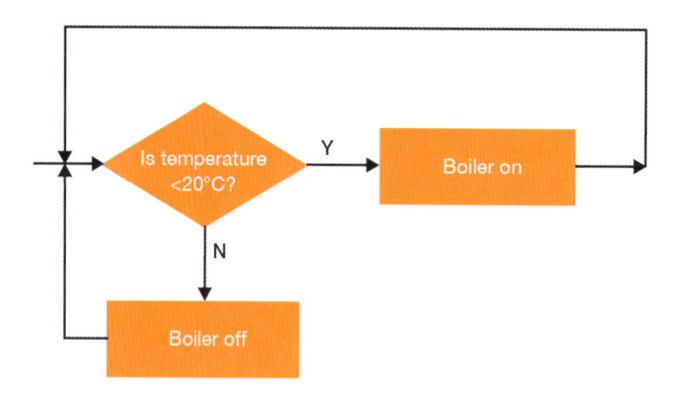

Closed loop system

A closed loop system is one that runs continuously until the system is turned off. It constantly makes decisions.

Q5 How could a feedback loop be used to trigger an alarm when a specific sound level is reached?

Counting

Counting devices are used in many applications. Microcontrollers can be programmed to count up or down which enables them to be used for numerous activities such as scoreboards, turnstiles and reaction timers. They can be triggered or 'clocked' with either a single manual input or an automatic series of input pulses. They can keep a tally of how many times an event occurs, and they can output information to a **7-segment display**.

A program could be set up to look for the press of a certain input before displaying a random number from 1 to 6, therefore replicating the roll of a die. It could perhaps be programmed to monitor cars entering and leaving a car park, therefore know the number of cars in the car park at any one time.

Q6 In snooker, a player can score between 0 and 7 points each time they strike the cue ball. Explain how the correct score could be displayed by pressing different buttons, each corresponding to the different numbers of points that can be awarded.

Exercises

1. Explain how electricity is generated from fossil fuels. [2]

2. (a) Name **three** different types of renewable energy. [3]

   (b) Describe the process of generating energy using **one** of the renewable energy sources you have named in your answer to part (a). [2]

3. This question is about batteries.

   (a) State the typical voltage provided by each cell in a 3 volt battery. [1]

   (b) A PP3 battery as shown below produces 9V.

   An electrical product requires an 18V supply.
   Calculate how many cells are used if **two** PP3 batteries are used. [3]

   (c) Explain **one** advantage of using rechargeable batteries. [2]

4. Describe how Nitinol, an SMA, could be used to control the fingers and thumb on a robotic hand. [2]

5. The picture below shows a baby feeding spoon.
   The polymer contains a thermochromic pigment.

   Explain **one** reason for using a thermochromic pigment in the polymer for the baby feeding spoon. [2]

6. Explain **two** advantages of making a hockey stick out of carbon fibre reinforced plastic rather than glass fibre reinforced plastic. [4]

7. Explain **one** reason why Kevlar is an appropriate choice of material for the firefighter protective gloves shown below. [2]

8. This question is about switches.
    (a) Draw the correct circuit symbols for a PTM and a PTB switch. [2]
    (b) Describe **one** operational difference between a PTM and a PTB switch. [2]

9. Use annotated sketches to show the difference between an analogue and digital electrical signal. [4]

10. (a) Name the type of motion shown below: [1]

    (b) Give **one** application or machine which exhibits the type of motion you have named in your answer to (a). [1]

11. Identify the class of lever shown below for the car foot pump. [1]

12. (a) Describe the action a follower goes through when following a drop/snail shaped cam. [2]
    (b) Name **two** types of cam follower. [2]

13. Explain **one** reason why an idler gear is used in a gear train. [2]

14. This question is about composite materials.
    (a) Explain what is meant by the term 'composite'. [2]
    (b) Give **two** composite materials. [2]

Section 4
Material types, properties and structure

In this section:

Design contexts and material properties		78
Chapter 16	Ferrous and non-ferrous metals	80
Chapter 17	Papers and boards	83
Chapter 18	Polymers	85
Chapter 19	Textiles	88
Chapter 20	Natural and manufactured timbers	93
Exercises		97

Design contexts and material properties

Material properties

Each of the specialist material areas cover material categories that have a range of different physical and working properties. The following terms and descriptions are given to help support the understanding and identification of the right material or material category for any given task throughout the core and specialist material areas.

When selecting materials for making into a product or prototype, it is essential to know how those materials will react and cope in different conditions. The following physical and working properties need to be considered so the correct selection is made.

The physical and working properties of materials can often be adapted and modified using different processes and techniques. Many of these techniques are covered throughout the specialist areas of Section 6. Not all terms apply to all material categories and the level at which they exhibit their properties will vary.

Physical properties

A physical property is an inherent property of a material. For example, metals are generally good conductors of electricity, and most natural textiles, and papers and boards will absorb moisture.

Absorbency – the tendency to attract or take on an element, usually a liquid such as water or moisture, but could include light or heat.

Density – the mass of material per unit of volume; how compact a material is.

Fusibility – the ability of a material to be converted through heat into a liquid state and combined with another material (usually the same) before cooling as one material.

Electrical conductivity – the ability to conduct electricity. An electrical insulator does not conduct electricity.

Thermal conductivity – the ability of a material to conduct heat. A thermal insulator does not conduct heat efficiently.

Working properties

Working properties describe how a material responds to use in a certain environment or in a certain way. For example, steel is malleable when heated as it can be shaped without cracking or tearing, and felt can be formed into a hat or similar when wet.

Strength – the ability of a material to withstand a force such as pressure, tension or shear. A material might possess one type of strength and not another, therefore it is better to justify the type of strength it possesses rather than simply to say it is 'strong'.

Hardness – the ability to resist abrasive wear and indentation through impact. Very hard materials can become brittle and can crack, snap or shatter.

Toughness – the ability to absorb energy through shock without fracturing.

Malleability – the ability to deform under compression without cracking, splitting or tearing.

Ductility – the ability to be stretched out or drawn into a thin strand without snapping.

Elasticity – the ability of a material to return to its original shape after being compressed or stretched.

Flexibility – the ability of a material to bend without breaking.

Printability – the ability of a material to be printed on to and absorb/retain ink or dye.

Biodegradability – the ability of a material to be broken down by microorganisms into organic matter.

Resilience – the ability for a material or fibres to spring back into shape following a deforming or compressive force. Often used in relation to textiles.

Durability – the ability to resist damage, pressure and the wear and tear of daily use.

Selection of materials and components

The pair of speakers annotated below is a typical product that uses many different materials in its manufacture. Every material for every component will have been selected based on a combination of its physical and working properties. The annotations explain a small number of the reasons for the specific material selection for some of the components.

As well as physical and working properties, a full materials analysis can include other factors such as:

Scale of production	Material processing	Availability - now and ongoing
Stock form	Sustainability factors	Environmental & ethical factors
Waste production	Cost	Assembly
Energy usage	Reuse/recyclability	Specialist tooling and machinery

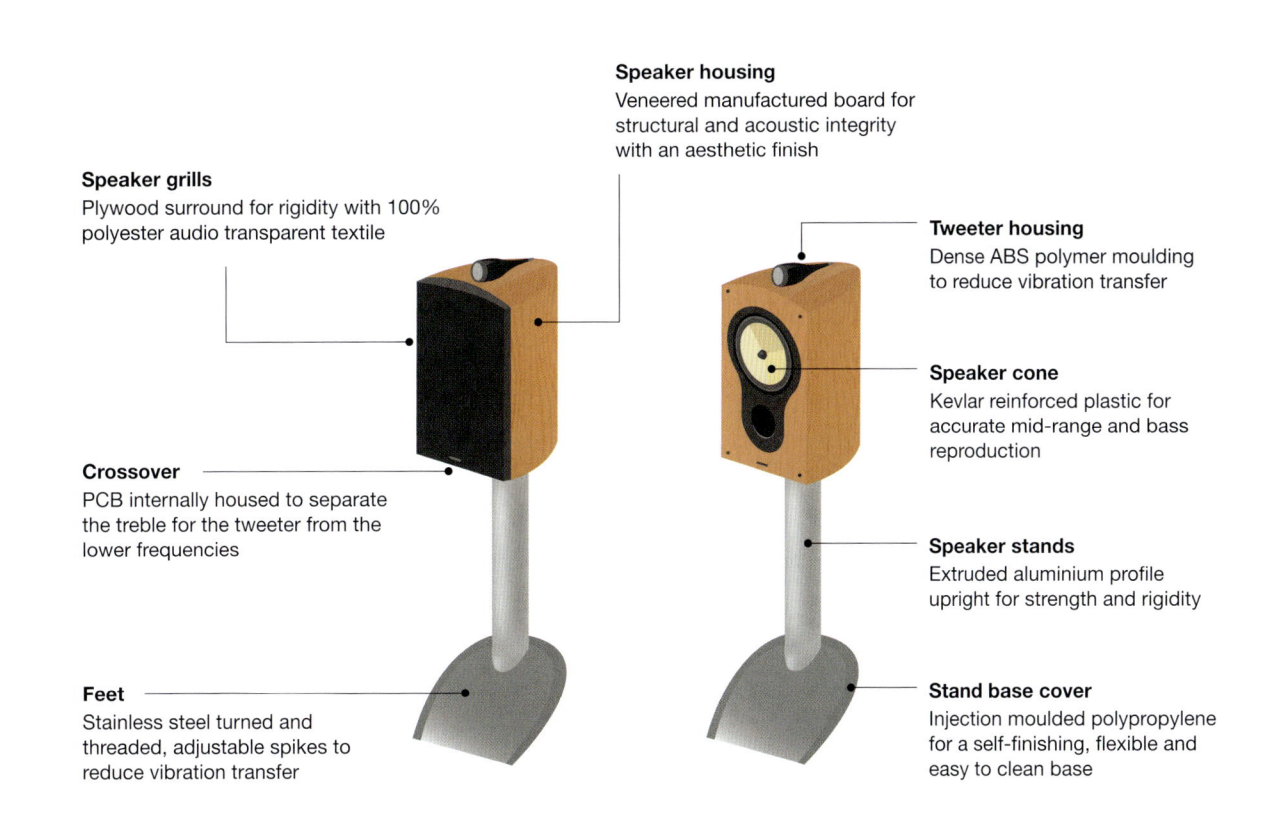

Speaker grills
Plywood surround for rigidity with 100% polyester audio transparent textile

Speaker housing
Veneered manufactured board for structural and acoustic integrity with an aesthetic finish

Tweeter housing
Dense ABS polymer moulding to reduce vibration transfer

Speaker cone
Kevlar reinforced plastic for accurate mid-range and bass reproduction

Crossover
PCB internally housed to separate the treble for the tweeter from the lower frequencies

Speaker stands
Extruded aluminium profile upright for strength and rigidity

Feet
Stainless steel turned and threaded, adjustable spikes to reduce vibration transfer

Stand base cover
Injection moulded polypropylene for a self-finishing, flexible and easy to clean base

Chapter 16 – Ferrous and non-ferrous metals

Objectives

- Know the primary sources of materials for producing metals and alloys
- Be able to recognise and characterise different types of metals and alloys
- Understand how the structure and working properties of a range of metals and alloys affect their performance

Ferrous and non-ferrous metals

Humans have used metals for many thousands of years. They generally have a high strength to weight ratio and have become an essential construction material in our modern society. Metals are categorised as either **ferrous** or **non-ferrous**, although a third group, known as **alloys**, is created when two or more elements are blended together, where at least one is a pure metal.

Metals are resistant materials and are found in the earth's crust. Some pure metals are mined as a whole metal but many are extracted from an **ore**. Ore is a type of rock that contains a pure metal in small quantities. The ore is obtained through mining, then the metal is often extracted from the ore using large furnaces. The extreme heat of the **furnace** separates the metal from the ore and it is drawn off as a molten liquid and processed into the metals that we commonly use. **Bauxite** is crushed and the aluminium is extracted via the process of electrolysis.

Ferrous metals contain iron and can rust

Non-ferrous metals do not rust, but can oxidise

Ferrous metals

This group of metals all contain iron (ferrite). Most ferrous metals are magnetic and will rust if exposed to moisture without a protective finish. Common examples include mild steel, carbon steel and cast iron. Very small amounts of other compounds or metals can be combined with non-ferrous metals to enhance their properties. Carbon is a common additive used to increase the hardness of the iron.

Q1 Explain the major difference between an alloy and a pure metal.

Q2 What factors make metal an expensive material to obtain?

Q3 Why is mild steel such a popular material for the construction of buildings and vehicles?

Common ferrous metals

Name	Appearance	Image	Characteristics	Example uses
Low carbon steel (Mild steel) Carbon content 0.05 – 0.3%	Bright grey with a smooth texture that quickly oxidises if not protected		Tough and ductile, easily machined, formed, brazed or welded	Construction girders, screws, nails, nuts and bolts. Many car bodies and bike frames
Cast iron Carbon content 2.4 – 4%	Dull, varying shades of grey depending on type, rough texture unless machined, less prone to rust		Hard but brittle in thin sections. Easily cast into complex shapes, but some types are hard to machine	Kitchen pots and pans, machine bases and bodies, vices, manhole covers, post boxes

Q4 Explain why rust can be an issue for structural products made from low carbon steel.

Q5 What is the chemical symbol for iron?

Non-ferrous metals

This group of pure metals is generally not magnetic and does not contain iron. Non-ferrous metals do not rust, but they can oxidise. Oxidisation causes the surface of the metal to change colour and dull with time. This rarely affects the working properties of the metal and is used by some designers as an aesthetic benefit. Copper, for example, turns a deep turquoise called verdigris and is used as a bespoke roofing material. The thin oxide layer is known as patina.

Non-ferrous metals come in many colours. They include precious metals such as gold, silver and platinum and others including lead and mercury, that are poisonous.

Q6 What factors can make precious metals more expensive to obtain?

Common non-ferrous metals

Name	Appearance	Image	Characteristics	Example uses
Aluminium	Light grey, can be polished to a mirror finish but often has brushed matt finish		Lightweight, high strength to weight ratio, ductile but can be difficult to weld	Pots and pans, sports car body panels, bike frames, drinks cans, foil or take-away trays
Copper	Light reddish brown, polishes well, oxidises to an attractive green- grey shade		Ductile, malleable and a good electrical conductor that is easily joined by soldering	Plumbing supplies, electrical cables, bespoke roofing and guttering

Alloys and ferrous alloys

Alloys are a mixture of at least one pure metal and another element. The alloying process combines the metals and other elements in such a way as to improve the physical and or working properties or even the aesthetics.

Alloy

Name	Appearance	Image	Characteristics	Example uses
Brass Copper 65% Zinc 35%	Yellowish gold, polishes well and oxidises to a dark antique brown		A heavy alloy of copper and zinc that is malleable, easy to cast and machine, and has naturally low friction	Musical instruments, bushes, plumbing fitments, ornate artefacts and hardware

Ferrous alloy

Name	Appearance	Image	Characteristics	Example uses
Stainless steel Low carbon 0.03–0.08% Chromium 10.5–26%	Silver hue that can be polished to mirror finish. Resists rust well		A ferrous alloy with chromium, nickel and manganese. Hard, very smooth but difficult to weld	Cutlery, kitchen and medical equipment

Chapter 17 – Papers and boards

Objectives

- Know the primary sources of materials for producing papers and boards
- Be able to recognise and characterise different types of papers and boards
- Understand how the working properties and structure of a range of paper and board products affect their performance

Papers and boards

Papers and boards are usually made from wood pulp and converted to their finished forms at a paper mill. Other cellulose sources can include textiles such as cotton, where the resulting paper, known as rag paper, can be of very high quality and can last many hundreds of years.

Wood pulp at a paper mill

Common papers

Paper is measured by weight in grams per square metre **(GSM)**. Weights and measurements of paper and board are covered in more detail in Section 6-3.

Name	Appearance	Image	Characteristics	Example uses
Copier paper	Usually brilliant white with a smooth texture		70 – 150gsm. Lightweight, low cost, good for laser printing toner	Photocopying, general use in home printers
Cartridge paper	Thick white paper with a slightly rough surface texture		120-150gsm, completely opaque and more expensive than photocopier paper	Pencil and ink drawings, sketching and watercolour
Tracing paper	Off white, low opacity sheet. Translucency decreases as gsm increases		40-120gsm, translucent, takes pencil and most colours well	Copying and tracing images. Used with a light box, overlays for design adaptations and working drawings

Chapter 17 **Papers and boards** 83

Common boards

Board thickness is usually quoted in **microns** (μm) or grams per square metre (GSM). 1000 microns is equal to 1mm of thickness. The lower the number, the thinner the paper or card. Weights and measurements of board are covered in more detail in Section 6-3.

Name	Appearance	Image	Characteristics	Example uses
Folding boxboard (FBB)	Either a natural brown or bleached white finish, however a dyed top coating can be added		275-560gsm. A layered board with a central layer of mechanical pulp sandwiched between two layers of chemical pulp which can be bleached. The top layer can have an optional coloured coating and has good printability	Packaging for foods - from cereals to biscuits, as well as many household goods such as tissues and toiletries
Corrugated board	Natural brown board finished on one or both sides with bonded paper		1000-5000 microns, strong, lightweight and rigid perpendicular to corrugations. Insulative and easily printed on	Packaging, boxes and impact protection
Solid white board	High quality card, brilliant white smooth finish on both sides		200-500gsm, stiff board, holds colour well, easily cut or creased	Many uses including greetings cards, packaging and advertising, base material for hot foil stamping and embossing

Q1 Why is it better for the environment to use softwood rather than hardwood for paper pulp?

Q2 Justify which papers or boards listed you would use for the following tasks:
(a) Creating a colourful piece of artwork to be framed
(b) Creating the net for a box to transport a cake
(c) Producing a high quality point-of-sale advertising stand to hold leaflets

Q3 What factors make corrugated cardboard such a popular material as packaging for transportation?

Chapter 18 – Polymers

Objectives

- Know the primary sources of materials for producing polymers
- Be able to recognise and characterise different types of polymers
- Understand the working properties and structure of a range of thermoforming and thermosetting polymers

Polymers

Plastics are mainly synthetic materials made from **polymers** traditionally derived from finite petrochemical resources such as oil, gas and coal, but they are increasingly produced from sustainable sources such as vegetable starches. There are also some naturally occurring polymers such as amber and rubber.

Categorisation

Plastics are categorised into two types; **thermoforming** and **thermosetting** plastics. They can be derived from three sources: synthetic compounds, naturally occurring compounds and plant-based starches. Synthetic polymers are by far the most common.

Thermoforming polymers

This group, known as **thermoplastics**, is generally more flexible, especially when heated. This is owing to their physical structure; polymer chains are quite loosely entangled with very few cross links. This allows the chains to easily slide past each other when heated. They can be formed into complex shapes and many can be reformed multiple times. Thermoplastics are commonly used in processes such as vacuum forming, injection moulding and blow moulding. They are also easier to recycle.

Thermosetting polymers

Thermosetting plastics or **thermosets** are more rigid and, as the name suggests, once they are formed or 'set' they cannot be reformed. The long polymer chains have many more cross links between them which stops the molecular chains in the plastic moving. As a result, they are generally harder and more brittle than thermoplastics. They make excellent electrical insulators and have good resistance to heat and chemicals. When thermosets are heated, they tend to burn rather than melt making most thermosetting plastics difficult to recycle. New types of recyclable thermosetting plastics are being developed. This technology has the potential to reduce waste.

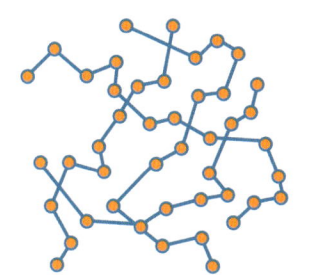

Thermoforming polymer

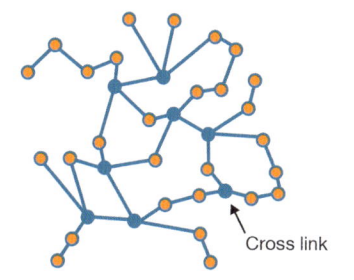

Thermosetting polymer (Cross link)

Q1 What molecular property allows thermoplastics to have more flexibility when heated?

Common thermoforming plastics

The following tables gives the properties for some of the most commonly used plastics. Most have similar properties, but they all have slight variations and some have specific applications.

Name	Appearance	Image	Characteristics	Example uses
High Impact Polystyrene (HIPS)	Flat, clear or coloured sheets for vacuum forming		Flexible, impact resistant, lightweight, can be food safe, sheet used for vacuum forming. Very toxic when burnt	Vacuum-formed products such as food containers or yoghurt pots
Acrylic (Poly-methyl Methacrylate – PMMA)	Thick to thin sheets, bars and tubes in huge colour ranges with a smooth finish. Can be spun into thread and woven. Very versatile		Tough but brittle when thin. Easily scratched, formed and bonded. Common in school workshops with laser cutting and line bending	Car lights, display stands, trophies, table tops, modern baths, jumpers, hats and gloves

Common thermosetting plastics

The properties of the most commonly used thermosetting plastics are similar to each other but most are quite easily distinguished from thermoplastics. They are rigid but brittle and they are all better at withstanding heat.

Name	Appearance	Image	Characteristics	Example uses
Urea formaldehyde (UF)	Very smooth finish, mainly white, limited colours available. Very versatile		Heat resistant, very good electrical insulator, hard, brittle, easily injection moulded	Electrical fittings, casings, buttons and handles. Also used as an adhesive or to treat fabrics to enhance easy-care properties
Polyester resin (PR)	Similar to epoxy resin, it is supplied as two liquids, a resin and a hardener (catalyst). Sets very clear, very smooth and can be coloured		Reasonably strong, heat resistant and a good electrical insulator. High VOCs when curing	Encapsulation of artefacts, waterproof coatings, flooring, used in the lamination of fibreglass

Biodegradable thermoforming plastic

This plastic is made from vegetable starches and is fully biodegradable but it is not recyclable.

Name	Appearance	Image	Characteristics	Example uses
Polyhydroxy-butyrate PHB Biopol™	Smooth or textured finish, easily coloured		Quite brittle with limited chemical resistance. Non-toxic, slow but fully biodegradable, easily processed and moulded	Bottles, pots, household items and disposable food containers

Q2 What are the basic common characteristics that nearly all plastics possess?

Q3 Justify which category of plastic would be best suited to making drinking straws.

Chapter 19 – Textiles

Objectives

- Categorise textiles based on their primary sources
- Recognise and characterise different types of textile
- Understand how the working properties and structure of a range of textiles affect their performance

Textiles

Textiles are highly adaptable and can be constructed to maximise different properties including a very high strength to weight ratio, which means less material can be used to make strong and robust products.

Availability of textiles

Textiles are available in many different forms including rolls, yarns and fibres. They can be made into a multitude of shapes and products using different processing methods. Some textiles can be very cheaply produced and some are extremely expensive, especially when using rare fibres and labour intensive techniques.

Categorisation of textiles

The categories of textile that are covered in this chapter include:

- natural fibres
- synthetic fibres
- woven fabric
- non-woven fabric and
- knitted textiles.

Some of the most commonly used textiles are included in the following tables, although many more varieties are available.

Plant-based natural fibre

Plant fibres can be spun together to create yarn. Fabrics made from plant-based materials are renewable but some can take a long time to grow.

Name	Appearance	Image	Characteristics	Example uses
Cotton	White fluffy 'boll' taken from the cotton plant; contains fibres that are combed and spun into yarn. Takes dye readily		Soft and strong, absorbent, cool to wear and easily washable. Cotton fabrics can be given a brushed finish to increase their thermal properties	Most clothing, especially shirts, underwear and denim can be made from cotton. Also used for towels and bedsheets

Animal-based natural fibre

Animal fibres can be spun in the same way as plants fibres to create yarn.

Name	Appearance	Image	Characteristics	Example uses
Wool	Animal fleece, most commonly from sheep, is spun into yarn. It is easy to dye and available in many colours and textures		From fine and soft to thick and coarse, it is warm, breathable and naturally crease resistant. Can shrink. Often blended to add functionality	Jumpers, coats, suits and accessories worn for warmth. Specialist wools are very soft and expensive. Felt products and carpets

> **Q1** What properties of wool make it suitable for making a quality suit?

Synthetic fibres

Name	Appearance	Image	Characteristics	Example uses
Polyester	Can be made into different fabrics including rip-stop, satin, tent and sail material, and brushed Polartec® fleece		Tough, strong, hard wearing, very versatile, holds colour well, non-absorbent so quick drying, machine washes well. Often blended with other fibres. Easily coloured	Clothing, fleece garments bedsheets, carpets, wadding, rope, threads, backpacks, umbrellas and sportswear
Acrylic	Soft, smooth, woven or knitted		Strong, soft, warm, easily machine washed and versatile. Poor absorbency so quick drying. Easily dyed	Clothing, faux fur products, soft toys, upholstery, carpets

> **Q2** Why are most synthetic fibres so water resistant and quick drying?

Woven textiles

Evidence of handwoven cloth dates back as far as 7000BC and the same basic techniques are still used today. Weaving is the most common way to produce cloth from yarn. The cloth is made up of two sets of yarns which are threaded at 90 degrees to each other. The **warp** threads are fixed in the loom and run the length of the fabric. The **weft** threads run across the width of the fabric from selvedge to **selvedge**.

There are many different types of weave, the most common of which is plain weave.

Plain weave is a very simple weave. The weft yarn goes alternately under and over the warp yarns. It is the most basic pattern and hence tends to be the cheapest to produce.

The finished fabric is identical on both sides. Common examples of plain weave fabrics include poplin, muslin, calico and rip-stop nylon.

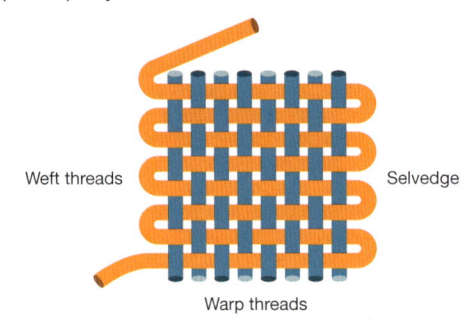

Weft threads   Selvedge

Warp threads

Name	Appearance	Image	Characteristics	Example uses
Plain weave Calico	Threads are interlaced at 90 degrees to each other, warp threads run the length. Same pattern on front and reverse		Simple and cheaper to produce than more complicated weave patterns	Used on textiles such as cotton calicos, cheesecloth and gingham, found on table cloths, upholstery and clothing

Q3 What equipment is needed to make a woven fabric?

Twill weave is a more complicated technique than plain weave as the weft goes over two or more warp yarns to create a diagonal striping on the fabric. It is used in the production of many popular fabrics including denim. Twill weave can create a number of interesting patterns such as houndstooth and herringbone.

A garment that has been cut on the bias uses fabric with the warp and weft threads at a 45° angle. This creates greater elasticity and movement.

Name	Appearance	Image	Characteristics	Example uses
Twill weave Denim	Threads give a distinctive diagonal line running across the fabric		Creates a tougher, stronger and thicker fabric than plain weave	Used on textiles such as denim but also found on curtains and hard-wearing soft furnishing covers, like sofas

Q4 Study items of clothing that you are wearing to see if you can identify any that have plain or twill weave.

Non-woven textiles

Non-woven fabrics are made directly from fibres without being spun into yarns. The most commonly available non-woven fabrics are bonded fabrics made from a web of fibres held together with heat or adhesive. Common uses of non-woven fabrics include disposable products such as garments worn by surgeons and crime scene investigators, dishcloths and interfacings. Non-woven fabrics can be given special treatments such as flame resistance to make head rest covers on trains and aircraft.

Felting is a mechanical process which has traditionally been done by hand but is now mainly machine produced. It involves matting together wool or synthetic fibres using a combination of heat, pressure, moisture and movement to mesh the fibres together in a random way. Felt can be formed into shapes when wet (see drape formed hats in Chapter 59), but it does not have any elasticity and will not drape well when dry. It is not strong and can pull apart under tension, but unlike woven fabric, will not fray when cut.

Name	Appearance	Image	Characteristics	Example uses
Bonded fabric	Random laid fibres are visible in the fabric, it can have small holes or a textured surface		Fabrics lack strength, they have no grain so can be cut in any direction and do not fray	Disposable products such as protective clothing worn for hygiene purposes, tea bags, dish cloths and dusters
Felted fabric	Matted fibres randomly interspersed, wide range of colours and thicknesses		Can be formed with moisture and heat; once dry it has no elasticity or drape, and can pull apart easily. Woollen varieties can be expensive	Hats, handicraft, pads under furniture to prevent scratching, soundproofing and insulation

> **Q5** What is meant by the term grain in relation to textiles?

Knitted textiles

Knitting is a traditional technique of interlocking yarn loops together to produce a fabric and has been used for well over 2000 years. There are two types of knitted fabric called weft knit and warp knit. With all knitted fabric, if a yarn breaks then it can come apart or ladder.

Weft knitting

Weft knit fabrics are made by hand or by machine using a single yarn that forms interlocking loops across the width of the fabric. They tend to be quite stretchy due to the method of interlocking and can therefore lose their shape quite easily. Weft knit fabrics are very warm owing to the amount of air trapped.

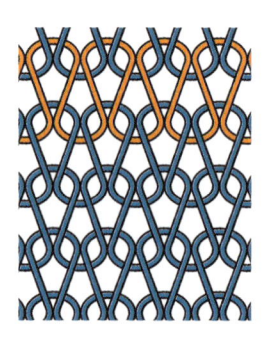

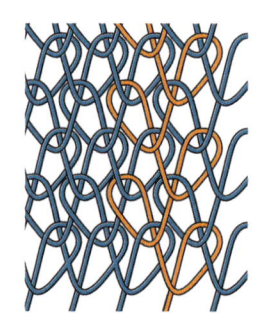

Weft knitting   *Warp knitting*

Warp knitting

The loops in warp knit fabrics interlock vertically and are less prone to unravelling and laddering, which makes them easier to cut into sections and sew together for the construction of complex garments. They are less stretchy than weft knits and tend to hold their shape more effectively.

Warp knit fabrics are complex structures, often using multiple yarns and are therefore made by machine rather than by hand.

Name	Appearance	Image	Characteristics	Example uses
Knitted fabric	Loops of yarn are interlocked with each other using needles or machines. Plain or very decorative patterns can be produced		Warm to wear, different knits have different properties such as stretch and shape retention. Weft knits ladder and unravel more easily than warp	Jumpers, cardigans, sportswear and underwear fabrics, socks, tights and leggings, craft items such as soft toys

> **Q6** Explain how a ladder is formed in a knitted garment.

Chapter 20 – Natural and manufactured timbers

Objectives

- Know the primary sources of materials for producing natural and manufactured timbers
- Be able to recognise and characterise different types of natural and manufactured timbers
- Understand how the working properties and structure of a range of natural and manufactured timbers affect their performance

Specialist tools equipment, techniques and processes

Natural wood is categorised as **hardwood** or **softwood**. These names reflect the cell structure of the tree and not the strength of the wood. Hardwood is from a **deciduous** tree, usually a broad-leafed variety that drops its leaves in the winter. Softwood is from a **coniferous** tree, one that usually bears needles and has cones. These are frequently called **evergreen** trees as most of them keep their needles all year round.

Wood is a resistant material and has always provided humans with essential heat and shelter. It is a versatile material and demand for it continues to increase, especially as it can be a very sustainable resource if harvested responsibly and ethically. Trees take a very long time to grow.

Some softwood trees can reach maturity in around 25 years, but hardwoods can take hundreds of years or more. A native British oak tree's growth rate slows down after 80 to 120 years. The slow growth of most hardwood trees is the main reason that hardwood tends to be more expensive than softwood.

Hardwood tree (deciduous) *Softwood tree (coniferous)*

Felling is the term used for cutting down a tree. Traditionally this was done by hand using an axe or a very long saw. Trees are now felled using chainsaws and modern chainsaw attachments are available for agricultural machines that can fell a tree, de-branch it and cut it into equal-length logs in one action.

> **Q1** A sustainably managed forest contains 1000 trees.
> (a) If these were softwood trees felled at 25 years of age and 1/25 of the trees are harvested each year to ensure consistent supply, how many trees are felled?
> (b) If the same forest was planted with hardwood trees that mature at 40 years of age and 1/40 were felled annually, how many trees would be felled each year?

Hardwood

Hardwoods generally have a less porous and denser cell structure than softwoods. This makes many varieties harder wearing and less prone to rotting. Note however that balsa wood, a very lightweight and fragile wood commonly used in modelling, is in fact a hardwood.

Hardwood comes in a variety of colours and has many sought-after aesthetic and physical properties. As the value of hardwood is so high there is much illegal felling of trees, especially in rainforest areas. Although the devastation from deforestation is slowly reducing, large areas have already been totally cleared, adversely affecting the natural environment and wildlife habitats. It is essential to source all wood from sustainably managed forests and reputable suppliers.

Common hardwoods

Name	Appearance	Image	Characteristics	Example uses
Beech	Dense/close grain with an attractive pink hue		Fine finish, tough and durable	Children's toys and models, furniture and veneers
Mahogany	Rich reddish brown		Easily worked, durable and finishes well	High end furniture and joinery, veneers
Oak	Light brown with an interesting and variable grain		Tough, hard and durable, high quality finish possible	Flooring, furniture, railway sleepers and veneers
Balsa	Pale cream/white. An open grained, large and unusually fast growing hardwood tree		Very soft and spongy, very lightweight, can snap in thin sections	Prototyping and modelling - especially model aircraft

Softwood

Softwood generally has a more porous cell structure than hardwood. If left unprotected from the elements, it can absorb moisture and begin to rot, although some softwoods, such as cedar, contain natural oils which protect them and make them suitable for exterior use. Cedar shingles are often used for roofing.

Softwood cedar shingles contain a natural oil making them suitable for exterior roofing

Softwood is not available in as many colours as hardwood – however, it is easy to add stain and it is frequently coloured to look like more expensive hardwoods. Softwood is commonly used in the construction industry; it is relatively cheap and readily available. It is the most sustainable wood owing to its faster growth rate and is widely planted, especially in Europe and Scandinavia.

Name	Appearance	Image	Characteristics	Example uses
Cedar	Reddish brown, with straight, fine, even grain. Very aromatic		Easy to work, can blunt tools, finishes well, naturally resistant to rot	Outdoor furniture, fences, cladding for buildings, roof shingles
Pine	Pale yellow to pale brown, attractive grain that darkens with age		Lightweight, easy to work, can split and be resinous near knots	Interior construction (and exterior if treated), cheaper furniture, decking

Manufactured boards

Manufactured boards are usually sheets of processed natural timber waste products or veneers combined with adhesives. They are often made from waste wood, low-grade timber and recycled timber. Manufactured boards have a pale brown natural finish but can be covered with thin slices of high quality wood to give the appearance of solid wood. This covering is called a veneer.

Veneers are produced by taking thin slices of a natural wood from the trunk of a tree. Synthetic polymer veneers are also available. They are then bonded to the surface of cheaper sheet materials, such as medium density fibreboard (MDF) or plywood. The veneering process is covered in Chapter 30.

Name	Appearance	Image	Characteristics	Example uses
Medium density fibreboard (MDF)	Smooth, dull, light brown finish available in many veneered options. Edges can be hard to finish well		Rigid and stable, good value with a smooth, easy to finish surface. Very absorbent so not good in high humidity or damp areas	Flat pack furniture, toys, kitchen units and internal construction
Plywood	Alternating layers of natural grain veneers with the outer material usually of a higher quality for aesthetics		Very stable in all directions due to alternate layering at 90°, with outside layers running in the same direction. Thin flexible versions available (flexiply)	Furniture, shelving, toys and construction. Interior, exterior and marine grades available for greater water resistance

Q2 Justify which softwood you would select to construct a garden shed.

Q3 From the manufactured boards listed above, justify which you would select to construct a shelf unit in a shower room.

Q4 State **two** ways in which softwoods or manufactured boards can be made to appear as more expensive hardwoods.

Exercises

1. Give the definition of the following properties.
   (a) Ductility [1]
   (b) Resilience [1]
   (c) Density [1]
   (d) Biodegradability [1]

2. Paper products are measured in grams per square metre (gsm).
   Calculate the weight of the following paper products to the nearest gram.
   (a) 10 x A3 sheets of 150gsm cartridge paper (A3 = 420mm x 297mm) [3]
   (b) 1 x A2 sheet of 40gsm tracing paper (A2 = 594mm x 420mm) [3]

3. For each of the applications below, select a suitable type or form of paper or board.
   (a) An artist drawing a portrait in charcoal. [1]
   (b) A picture framer wrapping a framed picture to transport to a customer. [1]
   (c) Copying a section of a drawing to create an overlay. [1]
   (d) Making a handmade greeting card. [1]
   (e) Making packaging boxes for a range of cereals. [1]

4. Give **two** differences between a hardwood and a softwood. [2]

5. Mahogany is a hardwood.
   (a) Describe the appearance of mahogany. [2]
   (b) Give **two** applications of mahogany. [2]

6. (a) Name the **two** elements alloyed to make low carbon (mild) steel. [2]
   (b) Give **two** properties of low carbon (mild) steel. [2]

7. Explain **two** properties of copper which make it an appropriate material for use as electrical cables. [4]

8. Explain **one** reason why HIPS (high impact polystyrene) is an ideal material from which to make yoghurt containers such as the one shown below. [2]

9. Give **two** properties of urea formaldehyde that make it an appropriate material for use as electrical sockets. [2]

10. This question is about textile fibres.
    (a) Give **two** animals that produce wool. [2]
    (b) Name **one** plant-base natural fibre. [1]

11. Explain the aesthetic difference between twill weave and plain weave. [2]

Section 5
Designing principles

In this section:

Chapter 21	Social and economic challenges	100
Chapter 22	The work of others	105
Chapter 23	Avoiding design fixation	109
Chapter 24	Developing design ideas	112
Exercises		119

Chapter 21 – Social and economic challenges

Objectives

- Explain the opportunities and constraints resulting from environmental, social and economic factors
- Appreciate the diverse needs and values of different social, ethnic and economic groups
- Discuss how products can be designed and analysed to reduce environmental impact
- Explain how products are developed according to the capabilities of humans and machines

Different social, ethnic and economic groups

Developing a detailed understanding of the market place in order to launch new technologies is one of the most difficult aspects for designers and manufacturers. Many aspects need to be taken into consideration when launching a product including social, ethnic and economic profiles of potential users. Many companies now employ specialist management consultants who analyse data to see which products would be successful in which areas.

People across the world can have very different needs and tastes, and products successfully launched in one country can be a complete failure in another.

Culture is an amalgamation of the ideas, beliefs, customs and social behaviours of a society or group of people. It often manifests itself through ritual, art and fashion. It is important for designers to be aware of the society around them and to try to understand the different cultures that exist within it.

Some parts of the world are still dominated by one type of culture, especially where a government or a particular religious belief has a very powerful hold over the population. Designing products for these countries may be considered easier, as there is less diversity and the majority of people have similar lifestyles. The downside of this, from a manufacturer's point of view, is that they may require a limited range of products. Above all, respect must be given to diversity and all social, ethnic and economic groups should be considered.

Products can fail for a number of reasons; some avoidable and some not so easy to predict. One of the easiest mistakes for a company to make is the use of a brand name that means something else in a different country.

Plopp chocolate has been a Swedish favourite since 1949

Ensuring that cultural influences and sensitivities are considered is essential. It would not be good for a company's image if a product was inappropriately placed – a roulette game being sold in a country where gambling was illegal could be disastrous.

A designer has to be responsible for considering the wider implications of a product launch within certain communities. Cosmopolitan and mixed communities are perhaps more difficult to prepare for because of the wide range of faiths and beliefs. There are many more potential pitfalls in mixed communities; however, they can be more understanding and tolerant of other views than some, where one faith or belief is followed by the majority.

Case study: £5 note

Hindu, Sikh and some other faith-based communities may choose to follow a vegetarian diet, and this is part of their culture. In addition to not eating meat, many followers of these faiths, as well as vegans and vegetarians, take every opportunity to avoid using animal products in their day-to-day lives.

The revelation in 2016 that the new polymer Bank of England £5 note contained tallow, an animal fat-based substance, upset a number of communities. There was a prompt call for the Bank of England to find an alternative way to produce the note and in the first two days of an official petition well over 100,000 signatures were received.

Shortly after the Bank of England admitted that the new polymer £5 note contained the animal by-product, some establishments refused to take the notes as a method of payment. One café owner was repulsed by the idea that the note contained tallow and believed that her customers supported her view. They received no complaints.

The Bank of England say they currently have no plans to change the manufacturing process.

Q1 What type of market testing should a company use to see if a product is ready for launch?

Appreciating environmental, social and economic issues

It is helpful to understand the influences that environmental, social, ethnic and economic factors can have on the designing and making of products. As designers and manufacturers, we are living in a world that is becoming increasingly aware of the effect human activity is having on the planet's natural resources and its contribution to global warming. Responsible designers and manufacturers automatically look for ways to reduce consumption of limited resources, along with finding innovative alternatives to meet customer demands.

Good design is about challenging oneself to come up with solutions to tricky problems. Some of the most successful and innovative designers turn environmental, social and economic challenges into opportunities for successful products and business ideas. The **Fairtrade** Foundation (covered in Section 2) is a lifeline to many farmers and small producers in developing countries, and is an example of how a challenge can be turned into a success.

Q2 Find out about an individual or company that has come up with an innovative way to produce a product or service that has tackled an environmental, social or economic problem. Explain how they have turned the problem into an opportunity.

Adidas and Parley manufactured the first pair of shoes to be made from waste ocean plastic

Designers and manufacturers inevitably have a negative effect on the planet however a number of actions can be taken to reduce and even negate this effect. Companies can invest in **carbon offsetting** activities which effectively cancels out the carbon produced by their businesses. The prime example is the planting of trees, which directly absorb CO_2 and emit oxygen. In addition, they add to ecosystems and provide sustainable building and heating materials.

Another way designers and manufacturers can help is by planning for **sustainable product disassembly and disposal**. This involves designing products with a limited number of materials that are easily recyclable. The key factor is that the different materials should be easy to separate at the end of their working life. Disposal is planned around the recyclability of the product components.

There is a growing desire among consumers to know the provenance of the products that they are buying. This means that designers and manufacturers need to know not only where all of the materials and components to make the products come from, but also where they were originally sourced, what the conditions were like for the workforce there and whether they were paid a fair wage. Only then can they be sold as ethically sourced and produced goods.

Green design

When products are made, natural resources are used, so designers and manufacturers have to make decisions which have a direct impact on the consumption of the earth's resources. By designing products efficiently and, where possible, reducing the burden on finite resources, products can be made more sustainable. The impact can be further reduced with clever thinking and planning around how the product will be distributed and what will happen to it once it is no longer needed.

Q3 Explain how designers and manufacturers can help to reduce the impact of raw materials being harvested.

Recycling and reuse

Reusing products multiple times for the same purpose is also known as **primary recycling**. Reusing a product in a different way from the one it was designed for is known as **secondary recycling**.

The classic glass milk bottle is reused many times before it reaches the end of its useful life, at which point it is recycled. A plastic milk bottle, however, is intended to be used only once, although it can have many different subsequent uses.

Donating to and buying from charity shops extends the life of products and in recent years there has been a resurgence in products having second lives. Websites and apps such as eBay, Gumtree, Freecycle and Shpock are designed to allow users to sell or give away used or unwanted items.

It is very popular for furniture and other household items to be **upcycled** with a coat of paint and some minor repairs or adaptations, extending their useful life by many years.

> **Q4** How does the secondhand market play an important role in reducing demand for new products?

Tertiary recycling, although a very important stage, is lower down the hierarchy of preferred options because most materials that are recycled this way tend to be of lower quality than the original material. It takes a lot of energy to recycle materials – although not as much as creating new ones.

This form of recycling requires the reprocessing of the material and in many cases involves chemicals and/or heat to recover the recycled materials. Metals are melted down and can be very high quality if separated correctly before processing. Plastics are separated into their different forms and reprocessed separately. The same applies to different colours of glass, although most recycled glass has a pale tint, usually green. Paper is graded and made into different paper products.

All councils in Britain operate recycling centres and will recycle nearly all household waste. More complex items are sent to specialist centres for processing. Batteries and electrical appliances are particularly difficult as they may contain toxic metals and chemicals that need careful processing, as these may leach into the environment if incorrectly disposed of. The WEEE directive is covered in Chapter 2. More detail on batteries is covered in Chapter 9.

In an ideal world, tertiary recycling would remove all recyclable materials from our household waste so that only biodegradable materials would be left. Only very few parts of the world are set up to cope with this level of processing. The percentage of waste materials being recycled continues to grow however, and as the supply of finite materials becomes more limited, the demand for recycled materials will increase further, forcing countries to become even better at dealing with their waste.

Human capability

Designers need to think about the physical and mental capabilities of the proposed user in order to make products accessible and safe to use. Making products too complicated or difficult to operate can exclude a group of potential customers, for example many elderly people find digital devices hard to use and many packaging materials almost impossible to open. Conversely, some products are specifically designed to be inaccessible to certain users, such as child-proof lids for medicine and chemical bottles.

Cost of materials

Creating a product with a fixed selling price is important, but not just as easy as adding the cost of raw materials and manufacturing costs together and working out an acceptable profit margin. The true cost of materials involves many factors including the fluctuations in raw materials costs over time, cost of any bought in components, cost of tariffs and taxes on some goods and cost of any waste produced and the disposal of it. Additionally, the environmental cost needs to be considered.

Manufacturing capability

When designing a product for manufacture, the limitations of any materials, equipment, tooling and processing needs to be known well in advance. That doesn't mean that new and ground-breaking developments are avoided but it does mean that working within known manufacturing capabilities will produce a product more quickly and to a known standard or quality.

Manufacturing considerations include using standard stock forms and components to reduce costs and ensure good availability. Designs are simplified to use fewer materials and parts using items repeatedly where possible, which also make disassembly and recyclability easier at end of life. Additionally, manufacturing procedures must be considered such as limiting the different processes required, utilising jigs, templates, dies or formers to speed up the manufacturing time and planning quality control procedures to enforce strict tolerances. A successful product is well designed, well planned and well manufactured, making it right first time and attaining higher customer satisfaction.

Environmental impact – life cycle analysis (LCA)

As part of planning for manufacture, the environmental impact of a product needs to be considered. As we saw in Chapter 7, a **life cycle analysis (LCA)** can be conducted to assess whether everything that goes into the making of a product has a negative or positive impact. Responsible manufacturers will look for a way to ensure the product has as little impact as possible. Revisit Chapter 7 to refresh the five stages of an LCA and the wider implications of conducting one.

Chapter 22 – The work of others

Objectives

- Know how to investigate, analyse and evaluate a given product and the work of others
- Understand how investigating the work of other designers and companies can inform design

Product analysis

"Standing on the shoulders of giants"
Bernard of Chartres, 12th century

This famous quote personifies the reasons for conducting a product analysis. It was further enhanced as a method of discovery when in 1675 Isaac Newton said "If I have seen further it is by standing on the shoulders of Giants" meaning that the knowledge and understanding of our forefathers is a good starting point. This does not mean that plagiarising the work of others is acceptable, and all **intellectual property** must be respected, however it does mean that we don't need to reinvent the wheel.

When conducting a product analysis, we need to consider a wide range of criteria including:

Form – the shape and aesthetic appearance of a product

Client and user requirements – are the users' needs met

Systems, materials and components – what a product is made from and how it operates

Sustainability – what is the environmental impact of the product from cradle to grave

Marketability – how feasible is the product and how might it sell

Function – what the product does

Performance requirements – how a product performs its task

Scale of production and cost – the number of units being produced will affect production methods and unit cost

Aesthetics – how visually appealing is the product

Consideration of innovation – does it use ground breaking ideas or **disruptive technology**

The Technics SL1200 came to market in 1972 and was followed by the iconic SL1210 which is still the preferred vinyl turntable of club DJs. Many have tried to copy and better this classic design, but none have succeeded.

> Conduct your own product analysis of this or another design classic of your choosing. Ask searching questions using the headings above to uncover how the product is made and what makes it work.

The work of past and present designers and companies

Alessi est. 1921

Founded by Giovanni Alessi in 1921, the company started by producing a range of metal tableware. Over the decades their portfolio increased to include many other household items. From 1955 onwards they began to collaborate with outside designers, forging very successful relationships with some of the world's greatest product and industrial designers including Aldo Rossi, Ettore Sottsass and Philippe Starck.

Many of Alessi's products are recognisable due to the use of stainless steel mixed with bright colour schemes and fun characterful designs.

Apple est. 1976

In 1976 Steve Jobs, Ronald Wayne and Steve Wozniak founded Apple, now ranked the largest Information Technology company in the world. Starting off by developing personal computers, Apple sometimes struggled to be competitive, however its innovative designs made sure it had a core of enthusiastic followers. In 1983 they introduced the first personal computer to have a graphical interface operated by a mouse.

Apple's current success has been helped by the introduction of the first commercially available finger-only operated smartphone; until then screens relied on buttons and a stylus. The launch of the iPhone in 2007, designed by Sir Jonathan Ive, was unlike anything that previously existed. Although frequently updated, the basic design is relatively unchanged to this day. The iPod and the iPad have also become incredibly popular items for people of all ages. Apple believe in using robust operating systems that are simple and intuitive to use, inside products that are finely crafted and desirable.

Joe Casely-Hayford 1956-2019

British fashion designer, Joseph Casely-Hayford OBE, started creating exceptionally tailored couture from 1983 but joined with his wife Maria in 1984 to create the Casely-Hayford brand. Having trained as a tailor, he went on to be the first designer commissioned by Topshop to create an exclusive range for them. His own brand was aimed at both women and men, and in 2005 he became creative director at Gieves and Hawkes of Savile Row. He has dressed many influential clients over the years, in particular musicians, including Lou Reed, Take That and U2.

Raymond Loewy 1893–1986: Example case study

Hailed as the Father of Industrial Design, Raymond Loewy's influence has touched everyone in the modern world and gave the American way of life a distinct identity which has travelled across the globe. He said of himself "… I have made the mundane side of the 20th century more beautiful".

Loewy was born in Paris to Austrian-French parents and distinguished himself at the age of 17 by designing the winning model aeroplane in the Gordon Bennett Cup, which then went on to commercial success in the following year.

After World War I, he moved to New York and worked as window designer for various large department stores as well as working as a fashion illustrator for Vogue and Harper's Bazaar. His first industrial design commission was in in 1929 to redesign the appearance of the Gestetner duplicating machine, a design that persisted for the next 40 years. This was the first instance of the streamlined look that characterised Loewy's work which went on to include the Greyhound bus, the Coca-Cola bottle, and the GG1 and S1 locomotives.

In the 1930's, his successful styling of the Hupp Aerodynamic motor car paved the way for automotive design to become a legitimate profession. Motor manufacturers began to use external stylists like Loewy, who then designed the classic 1953 Studebaker Starliner.

He was quick to realise that a product's appearance was a saleable commodity and his streamlined look became the emblem of western society. He also understood that appearance had a knock-on effect on production cost and performance, and enhanced the product's standing in the marketplace: stating that of two similarly specified products, the most aesthetically pleasing would be the most successful.

In addition to his automotive designs Loewy was also a prolific commercial artist and illustrator with simple but effective graphic designs. Of the many logos he created, he said, "We want anyone who has seen the logotype even fleetingly to never forget it."

Loewy's ideal of creating beauty through function and simplicity is still in tune with the requirements of industrial production today and his work still influences designer and consumer decisions.

Zaha Hadid RA DBE 1950-2016

Known as the 'Queen of the curve', Dame Zaha Hadid was an Iraqi-British architect who often pushed the boundaries between sculpture and architecture. In 2004 she became the first woman to receive the Pritzker Architecture Prize and went on to scoop the prestigious Stirling Prize in 2010 and 2011. In 2016 she was awarded the Royal Gold Medal from the Royal Institute of British Architects - the first and only woman to have received this accolade so far. Her architectural achievements are many and include the London Aquatics Centre built for the 2012 Olympics, the Guangzhou Opera House in China and Port House, Antwerp, Belgium.

Heatherwick Studio est. 1994

Set up by the British inventor and designer, Thomas Heatherwick CBE, in 1994, Heatherwick Studios have been responsible for a growing number of modern icons such as the spun chair and the new Routemaster bus. They also took centre stage at the 2012 London Olympics by creating the magnificent Olympic Cauldron composed of 204 copper petals, one for every nation taking part. Their influence is undeniably unconventional, as can be witnessed in many of their architectural projects, such as the Nanyang Technological University Learning Hub, Singapore, and the UK Pavilion built for the Shanghai World Expo in 2010 in which the acrylic rod structure held 250,000 seeds.

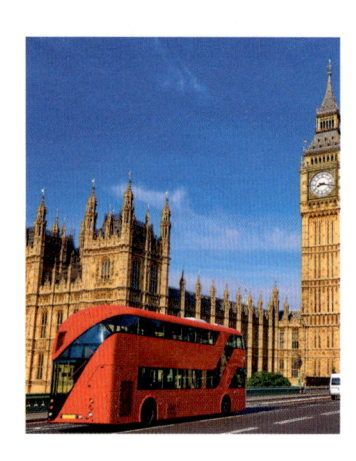

Pixar est. 1979

Having started life as Lucasfilms' Computer Division, Ed Catmull was tasked with developing a number of digital film editing systems. In 1982 they completed the first fully computer animated sequence in a feature film. In 1986 Steve Jobs bought the company from George Lucas and rebranded it Pixar. The famous Anglepoise lamp 'Luxo Jr' won them critical acclaim and an Oscar nomination for best animated short film. In 1991 Pixar started work on Toy Story for Disney which was released in 1995. Since then they have gone on to create some of the most watched animated films including Monsters INC, Up, Finding Dory, Inside out and Coco.

Tesla est. 2003

Tesla is an American company based in California, known for its world-leading all electric cars and solar charging systems. Built around an ethos of harnessing renewable energy to power not only transportation, but eventually the home as well, the company have invested heavily into research and development. They have created solar rooftiles and the Tesla Powerwall, which is a battery pack designed to power the home.

In early 2019, Elon Musk CEO stated that Tesla was releasing all of the electric car patents in order to 'accelerate the advent of sustainable travel' to help fight climate change. Both Tesla's flagship vehicle, the Model S and the more affordable Model 3 are in very high demand and can travel over 300 miles on one charge.

Chapter 23 – Avoiding design fixation

Objectives

- Be able to use a range of design strategies to help produce imaginative and creative design ideas
- Explain design fixation and how to avoid it

Strategies, techniques and approaches for generating design ideas

Before, during and even after designing and making prototypes and products, information needs to be gathered. This information is used to help ensure that the design fully meets the client's needs. Research comes in many forms and it is not always possible to gather all information before designing begins.

Iterative design involves making small steps with constant changes as feedback is gained. Stages in the process include formulating ideas, making prototypes, testing, analysing and evaluating the latest version (iteration). **Feedback** is used to refine and modify areas and some, or all of the process is then repeated. Additional investigation may be needed at any point in the process to help clarify an issue or problem.

Investigation may involve asking users' views or finding out about new materials and processes. It may include testing or measuring elements of a design proposal, or perhaps calculating costs to see if something is a viable option. Whatever information is needed should be collected as efficiently as possible and applied so that it has positive impact on the design.

Any information and data that are gathered should come form primary sources whenever possible as they are usually specific to the design challenge. Primary data sources include:

Primary data sources

- Interviews
- Questionnaires
- Focus groups
- Case studies
- Physical material testing
- Product analysis

Secondary data sources

Data obtained from secondary sources means that other people have gathered and presented it first. Secondary data sources include:

- written articles such as books, magazines, internet pages
- official data, such as government statistics and company information
- media such as news, radio and television broadcasts
- exemplar work of other designers and/or students

> **Q1** How can primary data help a designer understand a client's needs?

Design strategies

Designs come to life in many different ways and there are no right or wrong methods. This chapter looks at some well-established techniques that may be used to help you solve design challenges. The design strategies used can change as a project progresses and different areas of a project may demand a different approach.

Collaboration

Working with others to share the gathering of data, come up with design proposals or solve problems can be a really good way to get creativity flowing. A number of design companies ensure designers work in teams, as this has been shown to improve the range and quality of ideas produced. Designers can feed off the ideas of colleagues and inspire others around them.

> **Q2** Discuss the phrase *'a problem shared is a problem halved'* in relation to collaborative design.

User-centred design

User-centred design is based around understanding and fulfilling the wants, needs and limitations of the clients or users of products. The client or user group is the main focus throughout the whole design process and is consulted at every stage.

Types of information gathering include:

- ongoing interviews and questionnaires
- video and audio capture of the testing of existing products and new prototypes
- behaviour analysis of the observations captured

This questioning and testing is ongoing throughout the whole design process and for many companies, it continues even after a product is launched. This helps them understand any potential issues that arise as well as how the next iteration of the product may need to be modified to ensure sales volume is maximised.

> **Q3** How could anthropometric data be used to inform user-centred design?

Systems thinking

When designing certain products, such as an electronic device, a different technique may be required. Planning the layout for the correct sequence of inputs, processes and outputs or other interactions in an electronic or mechanical system needs a logical and ordered method. The systems approach is a method to show a sequence in a visual way using a systems diagram.

Systems diagrams are simple versions of flowcharts that clearly lay out the input, process and output stages of a system. One block may consist of a complex process but the separate operations involved in that process are not broken down at this stage. It is common to use only one style of box for all operations.

Here is a simplified example of a systems diagram which explains how an automatic door works.

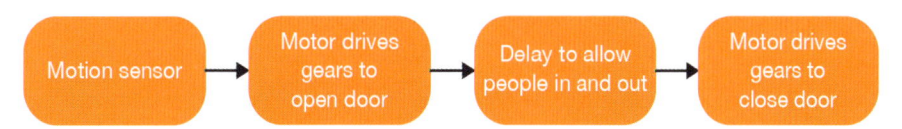

Motion sensor → Motor drives gears to open door → Delay to allow people in and out → Motor drives gears to close door

Design fixation

Some designers have the ability to come up with concise and complete designs with very little effort and in some cases they get it right first time. This is known as **intuitive design** and, although it is quite a rare gift, even the best intuitive designers need to change design strategies to avoid getting stuck on their first idea, especially if it gets rejected by a client.

Design fixation is a common condition for designers and design students alike. It simply means that they become stuck in a rut and can only produce a range of similar designs, blinkered or blind to alternative ideas available.

Factors that can make design fixation worse include the fear of making mistakes, playing safe and not taking risks. Don't assume your first idea is best and allow enough time to explore other routes. Avoid doing too much research if this leads you to look only at existing solutions. Budget and time constraints may restrict the ability to develop a wide range of proposals. Once these and other constraints have been recognised and acknowledged, the challenge is to attempt something different from what you have been doing.

The most common strategies used to avoid design fixation are as follows:

- Work with others – use collaborative design techniques, even just having a quick exchange of ideas with another student or a teacher can break the gridlock. You could ask a few friends to review your work and give you feedback.

- Accept and understand the design fixation and force yourself to use a new starting point. For example, you could start a design with a random shape and adapt it, rather than starting with a box, or change materials, change size, change the scale you are working in or even the medium you are using. For example, swap from pencils to marker pens, use A4 or A2 instead of A3 paper. Any change is good.

- Stop drawing and start making – model something in 3D from the medium of your choice or whatever is to hand, pipe-cleaners, clay, card, dowels, felt, papier-mâché and so on.

- Get some failures out of the way – do not be afraid to get it wrong a few times and move on quickly. It is widely believed that the more you fail the better you become.

> **Q4** Why is it important to avoid clichéd subject matter when beginning design ideas? Examples include starting with someone's initials, a cartoon character or a sports team.

Chapter 24 – Developing design ideas

Objectives

- Explain how to develop, communicate, record and justify design ideas
- Be aware of a range of techniques to support clear communication and presentation of design ideas

Communication techniques and media

Communicating ideas, recording important information and justifying designs are important skills to learn and develop so that designs can be clearly explained to others when needed. When done successfully, a range of techniques and different media may be used depending on the task, the product, the client and the stage in the design process.

Freehand sketching (2D and/or 3D)

Getting ideas down quickly is really important and sketching is the best way for most people. When an idea hatches, it can be easily lost if it is not acted upon promptly. Getting simple sketches on paper and not worrying about the quality of the drawing helps the idea to develop. There is always time later to tidy up the design and make it presentable if needed, as long as you can convey the concept of the idea to others working with you.

Deciding on the best method to visually explain an idea can be a challenge. Usually ideas are drawn in 2D or 3D. A combination of the two styles can provide the best detail needed to convey certain design ideas and concepts clearly.

Both 2D and 3D drawing techniques can be used for freehand sketching or they can be used more formally using drawing aids or used with CAD packages.

Two-dimensional design is better for plan views and for expressing size by adding dimensions. It can also help explain mechanical and electrical concepts clearly.

Three-dimensional design is better for conveying the overall shape of a design and for visually explaining aesthetic properties.

The 3D sketch of the bottles allows the viewer to imagine how they might feel in the hand, whereas the 2D version gives a technical profile that could be measured more accurately.

Annotated sketches

Adding notes to explain the detail that a drawing cannot convey is important to ensure others can understand your designs. Notes can add detail such as identifying the material being used, the manufacturing technique being considered or how the design meets a certain specification point or sustainability issue. It can also express the views of potential users or the client. Annotation should be clear, concise and specific to the design.

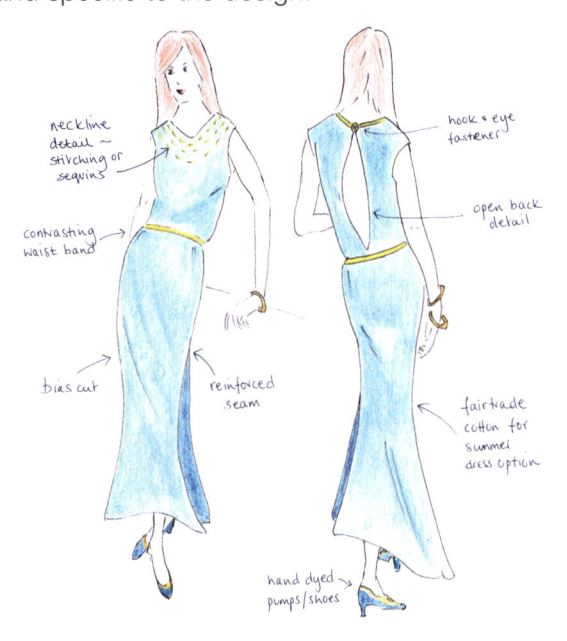

Q1 Why should any annotation be positioned close to the area of the design that it relates to?

Q2 How might colour coding different types of annotation help to visually explain a design idea or a development drawing?

Cut and paste techniques

Using mixed media to create a style, a story or mood board can be a very quick and inspirational way to get ideas down. It is good for expressing ideas, experimenting and can lead to quick design decisions and new ideas. This technique is often used by interior designers and those working with colour and texture pallets, such as fashion and set designers.

Digital media recordings – Photography, video and audio

Whether creating a digital portfolio or just collecting data to write up later, using audio and/or video recordings alongside plenty of photographs, is helpful. Recorded data can be used during research for client interviews, site studies and user group feedback. It can also help you gather ergonomic and anthropometric data. Video recordings of tests can be replayed to gather precise details.

Most modern smartphones have both audio and video recording facilities. Some devices also have slow-motion or time-lapse modes which can be very helpful in explaining some forms of testing.

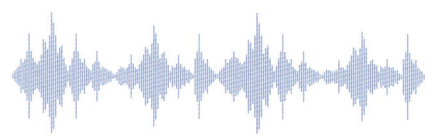

The use of photographs to record information throughout a portfolio is highly recommended. It is particularly helpful for gathering research, capturing developments, evidencing manufacturing and recording tests. Photographs of your prototype or product can be useful to help show how you analyse and evaluate issues and suggest modifications, for example, analysing how a dress hangs or is worn by a model.

3D models

Quick and simple modelling techniques are very good for testing ideas in 3D to see if they have any potential. By using cheap and easy-to-shape materials such as cardboard, masking tape, straws and other stationery products, 2D sketches can become 3D models in very little time. This technique can capture the initial energy of the idea and act as an important stepping stone to a potentially more successful version later in the process.

Models can be constructed to test different elements of a design to help work out how viable it is likely to be. Modelling can involve creating a whole scaled up or down product or it may just be needed to help work through an important element of a design.

The materials that are used for model making vary depending on the material area that you are working with, as well as what you hope to find out from the activity. If you are judging aesthetics then the modelling material may not be so important as long as it looks right, but if you are judging the weight of something and how it feels when held, then the material selection would be crucial. If the model is used to calculate loading or stress testing, then the materials used for the model need to be the same as the proposed product, otherwise the results could not be relied upon.

Modelling textile garments often requires making a **toile** garment, which is a full version made from a cheaper material. For electronic circuit modelling you may use a **breadboard** to connect the actual components so that it can be seen working.

3D drawing techniques

There are three main types of 3D drawing styles that you are likely to use within your portfolio. These vary in their level of complexity to produce and have different advantages and disadvantages.

Oblique projection

Oblique projection uses a 45-degree angle to draw lines that represent the depth of the side (end) and the top (plan) of the drawing. The front of the drawing is face on to the viewer which actually creates a visual lie. It is impossible to see the front of a cuboid straight on and also see the side and the top.

Oblique projection is a technique that can get an idea across quickly and simply. It can be very useful in the early stages of developing ideas

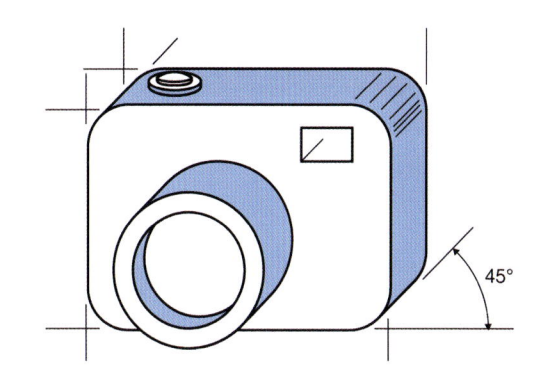

Isometric projection

Isometric projection uses a 30-degree angle and is much more realistic. For a basic cuboid, all of the height, width and depth lines follow the 30-degree isometric grid lines. Dimensioning can be done accurately and, by using simple techniques, complex shapes can be constructed or carved out of the main cuboid.

Isometric projection is very good for design ideas that have a geometric shape. With some practice, it is also good to convey ideas quickly and to show where components and parts fit in relation to others.

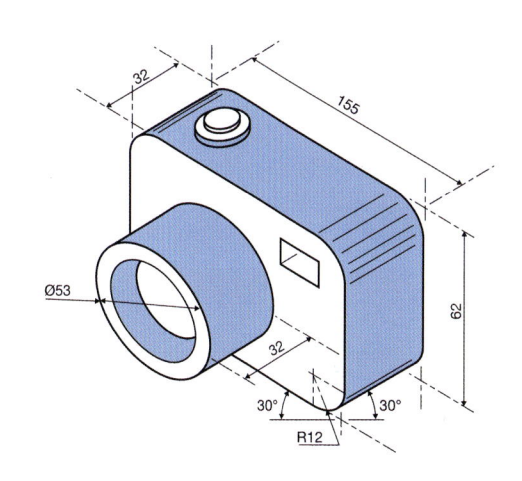

Perspective drawing

Two-point perspective uses two **vanishing points** that are set to the outer edges of the page. The main **construction lines** that create the width and depth are all projected back to the two vanishing points.

Two-point perspective gives the most realistic view as it emulates the way the viewer's eye sees perspective, meaning that things get smaller the further away they are. It is a great technique to give a realistic view of what a product or prototype might look like. It is not so easy to add dimensions, in comparison to isometric projection.

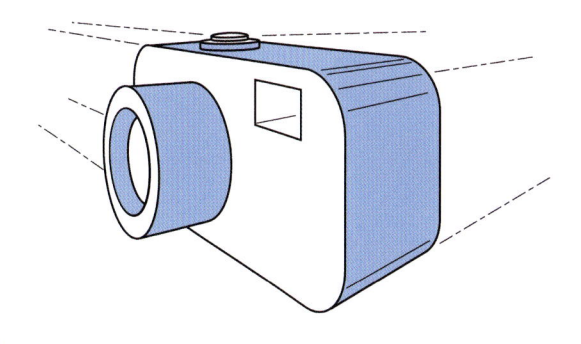

Q3 Which 3D drawing technique would you choose if you were intending to make an accurate prototype of a product from it?

Orthographic drawing

To enable enough detail for prototype or product manufacture to take place, a working drawing needs to be produced. This normally needs to include a front, end and plan view (elevation) of the design. A textiles pattern may simply include a front and back view. Drawings could also include other elevations if not all of the important detail has been shown. Some very detailed products require a **sectional view**, which enables you to see inside a design as if part of it had been removed or if it had been cut through.

Working drawings are best presented in **orthographic projection**. The two types used are first angle and third angle orthographic projection. Third angle projection places the plan elevation above the front elevation; the right end elevation is placed to the right and so on. First angle differs in that the plan elevation is projected below the front elevation and the left end elevation is positioned to the right.

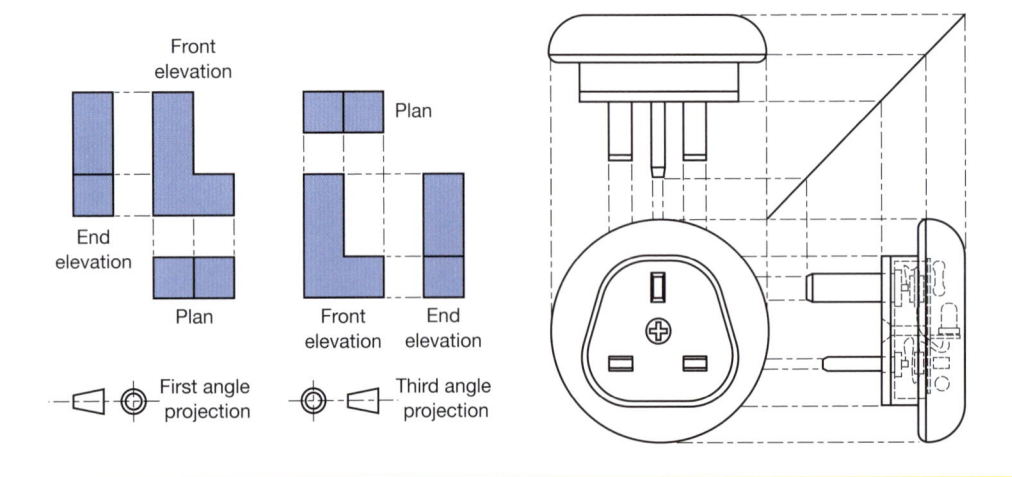

Q4 What factors make working drawings an appropriate format to enable manufacturing to take place?

Exploded views

An **exploded drawing** can be very helpful to show how the component parts of a product fit together. The parts are drawn as if they are separated from each other, but using paths that represent the way they are assembled. Exploded drawings are a good way to show separate components that would normally be hidden in a solid drawing.

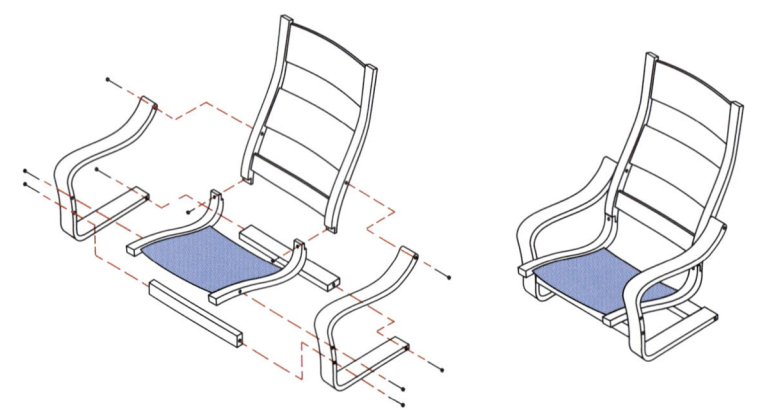

Q5 Why are exploded drawings helpful when constructing flat-packed furniture?

Assembly drawings

Assembly drawings are often a collection of different drawing formats and styles that explain how a product goes together. All parts are named and labelled to avoid confusion. For engineering projects, components may have both orthographic views with sectional information showing hidden details. They may be accompanied with 3D drawings to explain how they connect together and may also be exploded. Any electronic elements may include schematic diagrams (see below) or wiring diagrams.

Customer-facing assembly drawings are usually simpler and are best described by their use in flat-packed furniture or Lego instructions. Usually, a combination of 2D and 3D sketches with a number of exploded views show the customer how to assemble the product.

System and schematic diagrams

Flowcharts, system diagrams and schematic diagrams are used to describe procedures and concepts using logical layouts of words and/or symbols. Flowcharts (covered in detail in Chapter 15), use symbols to describe a series of events or a computer program. Systems diagrams (covered in detail in Chapter 23), use blocks of information to describe complex systems so logical planning can be structured.

Schematic diagrams are used in electronics to describe the connections and electronic relationship between the components. Schematic diagrams use international circuit symbols to represent each of the components, which in turn are given codes or numbers for identification, and values so the correct component is selected or used. Special software can be used to lay out a schematic diagram and can even test the design through simulating how it will respond in real life. Some software can route the design as a printed circuit board (PCB) layout ready for manufacture.

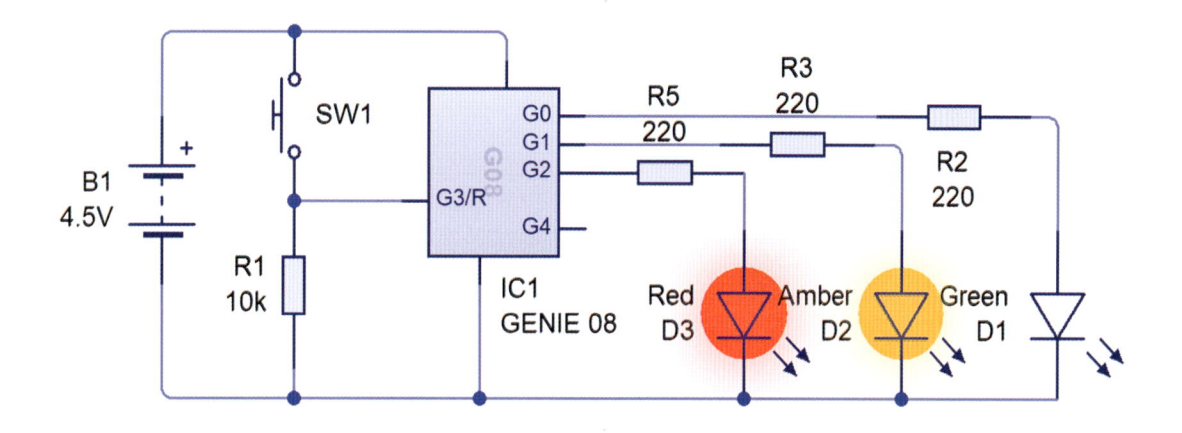

Schematic diagram of a microcontroller connected as a set of traffic lights

Computer aided design (CAD)

There are many different types of CAD software available and appropriate selection depends on the task. 2D and 3D packages are now commonplace in all design and manufacture situations. Most schools will have appropriate software to create 2D and 3D shapes for designing and also for outputting to various CNC manufacturing hardware such as 3D printers, CNC routers and laser cutters to make components from different materials.

As well as standard 2D and 3D packages, software allows designers to test and simulate designs. This means that designs can be given a set of parameters, such as material properties. For example, a virtual model of a building can be created with all of the material properties of the real building. It can then be placed under certain simulated conditions, such as stress loading, extreme weather conditions and even earthquakes. The data collected is used to find potential weaknesses and guide modifications. Other simulation software is used in the field of electronics, where circuits can be tested and analysed for performance. The software can also route the circuit on to a PCB layout finding the most efficient way to place components, saving space and materials.

Record and justify design ideas

Just as designers record as much information, and as many ideas, as possible, students should do the same. Keeping a rough notebook to hand for sketches and thoughts and taking as many photos as possible for inspiration and evidence is strongly advised. The data collected will help inform design ideas and will also act as a justification where required. The more evidence you can gather the easier it is to form and justify design ideas.

Exercises

1. Describe **two** different design strategies used by designers. [4]

2. Explain the term 'design fixation'. [2]

3. Describe what is meant by each of the following terms.
   (a) Ergonomics [2]
   (b) Anthropometrics [2]

4. The drawing below shows an orthographic drawing of a wooden toy building block.

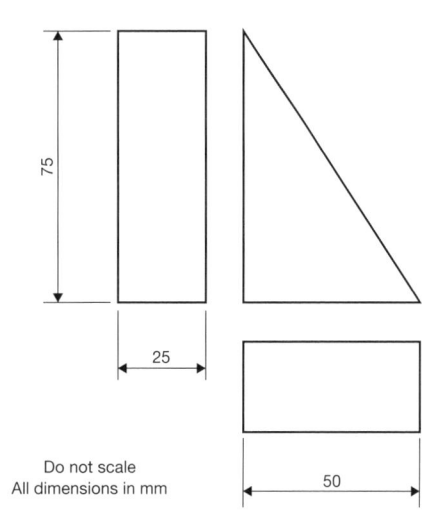

   Do not scale
   All dimensions in mm

   Use an annotated sketch to show an accurate isometric view of the toy wooden building block. [4]

5. Explain the difference between primary and secondary data sources giving **one** example for each in your answer. [4]

6. Give the most applicable presentation technique or drawing style to use for the following tasks:
   (a) Planning out an electrical circuit. [1]
   (b) Designs for a bride to choose a wedding dress. [1]
   (c) Flat pack furniture instructions. [1]
   (d) 3D view of a product with dimensions [1]
   (e) Accurate drawing of a product with dimensions ready for manufacture. [1]

7. Discuss the use of cheap materials such as corrugated card and masking tape, toile, breadboards and components for early prototypes of 3 dimensional products. [6]

8. Name **two** types of designers that may benefit from using cut and paste techniques for their early presentations to clients. [2]

9. Explain how digital media recordings can assist when gathering primary data. [2]

10. Discuss how using a 'green design' strategy improves the social and ecological footprint of a company. [2]

11. Study the picture of the two different types for milk bottles below.

    Evaluate the reuse of glass milk bottles compared to the recycling of polymer milk bottles. [9]

12. Choose **one** of the designers or design companies from the list below and evaluate their work considering their influence on modern society. [9]
    - Apple - Industrial/product design
    - Alessi - Industrial/product design
    - Joe Casely-Hayford - Fashion
    - Heatherwick Studio - Industrial/product design and architecture
    - Pixar - Animation/digital design
    - Raymond Loewy - Industrial/product design and architecture
    - Tesla - Industrial/product design
    - Zaha Hadid - Architecture

Section 6-1
Timbers

In this section:

Chapter 25	Sources, origins and sustainability	122
Chapter 26	Physical and working properties	126
Chapter 27	Selection of materials and stock forms	129
Chapter 28	Planning and production methods	136
Chapter 29	Material processing and joining	141
Chapter 30	Material treatments and finishes	148
Exercises		150

Chapter 25 – Sources, origins and sustainability

Objectives

- Explain the sources, origins and properties of a range of natural and manufactured timbers
- Be aware of the social and ecological footprint of timbers
- Understand the processes involved in growing, felling and processing timber

Sources of timber

The word 'wood' refers to the cellulose fibrous material that trees are made out of. The term is usually used before trees are felled and after the material has been used in manufacture for example, 'wooden furniture' or 'made from wood'. Timber is the term used to refer to wood after the tree is felled and processed.

From a fuel to create heat to a building material to create shelter, timber has been a vital part of day to day human existence for thousands of years.

Trees

Trees are divided into two classifications, hardwood and softwood. Hardwood trees are largely deciduous, broad leafed trees that lose their leaves in winter. They are slow growing and the timber tends to be close grained.

Softwood trees are coniferous with needles instead of leaves. Most are evergreen and will retain their needles all year round however some softwood trees, for example, larch, do drop their needles. Softwood trees are faster growing and therefore better for commercial crop growing.

Forests

4000 years ago, the United Kingdom and mainland Europe were heavily forested. By the early 1900s it was calculated that forest covered only 5% of the UK land mass. Indigenous trees like oak were plentiful and were felled and used for building ships and homes.

Forests are vital to our ecosystem both as habitats and as a filter for the air that we breathe. Since 1900, planting initiatives have seen a rise in forest plantations in the UK.

Forests of the world

Climate dictates the forests that grow in different geographical locations. In cooler climates, alpine forests are predominantly home to coniferous trees such as pine, cedar and larch, whilst in the more temperate European climates, a mixture of softwoods and hardwoods thrive including oak, ash, beech and birch. In Amazonian rainforests, tropical hardwood trees such as mahogany and teak flourish in the damp, warm environment.

Sustainable timber production

Wood is considered to be a sustainable product, as new trees can be grown to replace those used for timber and fuel. The main issue facing timber production is that in many parts of the world, it is being used at a far greater rate than it is being replanted. The result is an unsustainable supply of timber, which is frequently illegally obtained. This **deforestation** is causing many problems and areas are suffering from **desertification** as a result. This activity is also thought to be a contributing factor in **global warming**.

To ensure that timber comes from a reputable source, it is vital to know the **provenance** of the wood. This means that the supplier or retailer should be able to prove that it has been sustainably harvested. This can be very difficult to do, so there are organisations that make the process much easier. The Forest Stewardship Council® (FSC®) and the Programme for the Endorsement of Forest Certification (PEFC™) are both dedicated to ensuring that timber supply is regulated. If a product is labelled as approved, the company selling it will need to have proved that the timber came from a properly managed forest. FSC and PEFC timber is readily available in the UK, Europe and a growing number of countries worldwide.

Greenpeace actively promote the sustainable use of timber and a detailed report of woods to use and avoid can be found on their website www.greenpeace.org.uk.

Destroyed tropical Amazon rainforest in Brazil

> **Q1** If you had the choice between two identical tables made from mahogany, one sustainably sourced which costs £200 and one from an unmanaged supply at £100, which would you choose, and why?

Forestry management

Managed well, forestry as an industry has many advantages. New plantations create habitats and environments for leisure activities as well as creating employment opportunities.

To ensure future availability, felled trees are replaced with new seedlings and as the trees grow, smaller saplings are thinned to give the remaining trees the space and resources to thrive. The thinnings do not go to waste. They are cut or chipped for a variety of applications including fuel, mulch or manufactured boards.

Traditionally cut down with axes and long saws, tree felling is now done using chain saws or on a larger scale with specialist logging machinery which also removes branches and cuts logs to length ready for transportation. Logs are then taken by road, rail or sea to sawmills for further processing.

A lumberjack de-branching felled logs with a chainsaw

Timber conversion

After a tree is felled and cut into manageable lengths, it is then converted into planks at which point it is known as timber. Timber is supplied in two main types of finish: **rough sawn** or **planed**. Rough sawn timber has not been planed and is rough to the touch. It is often used for exterior tasks or where the finish is not important. Planed timber has a much smoother finish as it has been mechanically planed. It is used for furniture and internal features such as windows and doors. Finishes such as varnish or paint can be easily applied. Planed timber is also less absorbent than rough sawn timber.

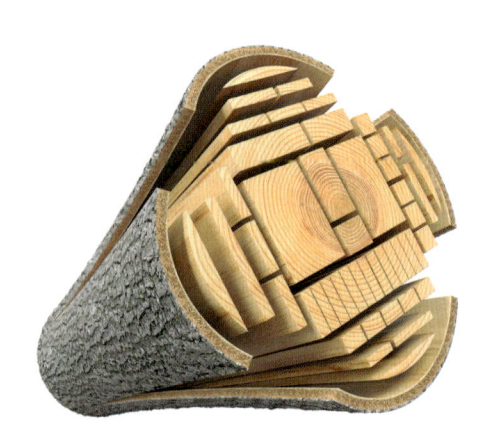

Timber is available in many different shapes and sizes, standardised to enable different varieties to be used together. This is covered in more detail in Chapter 28.

Q2 Which type of timber surface finish do you think is the most expensive to produce and why?

Seasoning

Once timber is converted into a workable form, it is **seasoned** in order to reduce the moisture content. Typically, a newly felled tree will have a moisture content of over 50% and is known as green timber. The moisture content needs to be reduced below 20% for most exterior applications, below 15% for interior work and below 10% for interior areas that are constantly heated. Uneven evaporation of the water content can cause some common faults to occur such as twisting, cupping and bowing which can render the timber useless for many tasks. If the end grain dries too quickly it can cause the plank to split.

There are two methods of seasoning; air-drying or kiln-drying. Air dried timber is stacked so that air can circulate around the planks and evaporation can take place naturally. It takes approximately one year per 25mm of plank thickness to season and in the UK the moisture content typically reduces to around 18%.

Kiln dried timber can have a much lower moisture content and it is a much faster process, meaning the timber can be sold much sooner. It costs more than air drying, as heat and pressure are used, but no additional land is required to store the timber while seasoning takes place. Kiln dried timber is less prone to faults and the heat also kills off bacteria and insects that may attack the timber.

Q3 Why does timber for interior use need a lower moisture content?

Q4 How long would it take a 100mm thick piece of timber to air dry?

Q5 The end grain of timber planks is often covered with a sealant. Why do you think this is done?

Chapter 26 – Physical and working properties

Objectives

- Describe the advantages and disadvantages of manufactured boards and natural woods
- Be aware of the physical characteristics and working properties of hardwoods, softwoods and manufactured boards
- Understand methods used in the disposal and reuse of natural timbers and manufactured boards

Natural timbers

When hardwood and softwood trees are converted to timber they display a range of physical characteristics that make them desirable for different applications. For example, **beech** is often used for making toys and kitchenware due to its fine close grain, toughness and durability. **Cedar** contains natural oils which provide water resistance making it ideal for roof shingles.

Physical characteristics

- **Knots** are natural blemishes found in most timbers. They are caused by the removal of branches at the point where they grow out of the trunk and so are more prolific in softwood timbers like **pine** that have lots of low branches. Knots can be seen as an attractive aesthetic feature, however, they can sometimes shrink and fall out as timber dries and are often hard and resinous which can damage cutting tools.

- **Colour** varies enormously and many timbers are sought after because of their natural tones. Colour will change as timber dries and ages. Softwoods are often quite pale when cut but may yellow as they age. Hardwoods differ enormously from the deep reddish brown of **mahogany** to the pale creamy white of **birch** with many colours and shades in between.

- **Grain structure** will depend on the type of tree, its age, the speed at which it grew and how it was sawn and converted. It is revealed by slicing through the natural fibres and pores that run the length of the tree trunk and the growth rings that radiate from the heart of the tree. Faster growing softwoods tend to have wider, more pronounced grain patterns whereas slower growing hardwoods have closer grain patterns. Some hardwood timbers display more open vessels, this is called open or coarse grain and these grains may need filling before finishes are applied.

- **Density** is affected by grain structure, growth rate and moisture content. **Balsa** is a hardwood and like other hardwoods, has a straight even grain pattern. It is fast growing and has a very high moisture content. When felled and kiln dried, much of the moisture is removed leaving a comparatively light low-density timber.

Working properties

The working properties of timbers affect their selection and application. **Hardness** is important where a timber surface may be subject to wear from repeated use, for example in the seat of a bench or chair. **Toughness** and **durability** would be valuable in a timber floor.

Some timbers such as ash have good **elasticity** which allows it to bend under load, and absorb and disperse shock before returning to its original position when the load has been removed.

Timbers used in construction, for example, **oak** need to have good **tensile** and **compressive strength**. Tensile strength is the ability to resist pulling forces whilst compressive strength is the ability to withstand pushing or crushing forces. In both cases, denser timbers used in the direction of the grain tend to be stronger. For property definitions, see Section 4.

> **Q1**
> (a) Which members of this chair are under tension and which are under compression?
> (b) What other working property would be required from the timber used here?

Additional natural timbers

In addition to the timbers in Section 4, you should know and understand the properties and uses of the following hardwoods and softwoods.

Additional hardwoods

Name	Appearance	Image	Characteristics	Example uses
Jelutong	Creamy yellow, close, fine grain		Low density, very easy to work/carve	Carvings, patterns for sand casting and model making
Birch	Pale cream, fine dense grain		Durable, easy to work, low resistance to rot	Furniture, veneers and facing plywood
Ash	Pale brown / grey and cream with distinctive grain		Tough, shock resistant, good elasticity, resistant to splitting	Tool handles, sports equipment, furniture

Additional softwoods

Name	Appearance	Image	Characteristics	Example uses
Larch	Yellow to reddish brown, with straight, distinct grain pattern, sometimes knotty		Tough, hard, good resistance to rot, easy to work but resinous and may blunt tools	Outdoor furniture, fences, cladding for buildings, boat building

Manufactured board

Natural timber is combined with adhesive to make manufactured boards. They can be made from waste, low-grade and recycled timber and are usually produced in a pale brown natural finish.

Each manufactured board is produced in a slightly different way; the two main processes used are **lamination** and **compression**. Plywood and blockboard use the lamination method where layers of wood are bonded together using an adhesive. Medium density fibreboard (MDF), chipboard, orientated strand board (OSB) and hardboard use the compression method where wood is shredded, chipped or pulped, then heated and compressed under high pressure, in most cases using adhesives to bond the particles together.

Advantages and disadvantages of manufactured board

Advantages	Disadvantages
• Available in large sheets, very stable which saves time and energy joining narrow planks together	• Adhesives used to bond the boards can contain hazardous particles or VOCs
• No defects such as warping, twisting, cupping and splitting which occur in natural wood, meaning less waste	• Machining and sanding some boards, especially MDF, causes very small particles of dust to be released which can be breathed in, even through a mask
• They do not have knots or resin pockets which can be hard to work around, avoiding waste	• Tools can blunt easily owing to the adhesives in the boards
• Smooth finish requiring little preparation	• Many traditional wood joints cannot be used effectively with manufactured boards
• Makes use of low grade, recycled and waste wood	• Edges can be hard to finish
• Available in many different finishes, veneers and laminates	• Most boards can absorb moisture if not treated

Additional common manufactured boards

In addition to the manufactured boards in Section 4, you should know about the properties and uses of **Chipboard**.

Name	Appearance	Image	Characteristics	Example uses
Chipboard	Grey brown, lightly textured, natural wood chips compressed and bonded		Rigid and even strength, poor resistance to moisture, may chip when cut	Construction, flooring, flat pack furniture

Q2 Chipboard is commonly used as a flooring in loft and attic spaces. Suggest **one** advantage and **one** disadvantage of this application.

Chapter 27 – Selection of materials and stock forms

Objectives

- Be aware of how environmental, cultural and ethical issues influence material choices
- Explain how environmental factors influence the disposal of timber based products
- Be aware of the forces and stresses that act on timbers and how they can be reinforced and stiffened
- Understand the availability of various stock forms and sizes of timbers and manufactured boards

Selecting suitable natural and manufactured timber

Which type of timber-based material to use for a product depends on a number of factors, including:

Aesthetics	Cost	Social influences
Size and weight	Size of material available	Desired properties
Where it will be used	Required finish	Workability
Stability	Availability of stock	How long it is to last

Aesthetic factors

Timbers and manufactured boards are available in a variety of different stock forms which will be explored in more detail later in this chapter. A designer or manufacturer will consider the **form** the timber takes and how easy it will be to shape. The **colour** and **texture** of timbers and manufactured boards also influence their selection. A cabinet maker may select a thin timber veneer with a rich colour and attractive grain pattern however they must also ensure it will take the form they wish without cracking or splitting.

Curved oak cabinet draw front-face using oak veneer

Environmental factors

The sustainability of forests is only possible through the responsible use of timber. Designers, manufacturers and consumers all have a responsibility to check that the timber they buy is sustainably sourced.

Historically, demand for valuable and exotic timbers like mahogany has resulted in devastating deforestation. Whilst the harvest and use of exotic hardwoods is now regulated, illegal logging still takes place and so it is vital that all timber selected displays the Forest Stewardship Council® (FSC®) or the Programme for the Endorsement of Forest Certification (PEFC™) marks to verify its provenance.

> **Q1** What factors drive illegal logging?

The quality of timber varies and manufacturers increasingly look for consistency. **Genetic engineering** is used in forestry to modify or change the DNA of trees to make them grow faster, straighter and with fewer low branches to maximise the speed and quality of their output. They can also be made more resistant to disease and rot.

Seasoning is another factor a producer needs to consider. Whilst air drying is the more environmentally friendly option, it takes a long time and there are several variables including weather and temperature. Kiln drying is controlled and much faster however fossil fuels are burned to heat and dry the timber using energy and producing harmful atmospheric emissions.

Manufacturers should also consider how their products will be dealt with at the end of their useful lives. Timber products can usually be broken down and the timber reclaimed and reused, pulped for paper or chipped for use as bio-mass fuel, in gardening or landscaping.

Used timber products may also be **upcycled** and given a new lease of life. This is either done by repurposing, making a new product out of an old one; or renovating, stripping, painting and changing features.

Old kitchen chairs painted and repurposed as a garden bench

Availability factors

A range of factors influence the availability of timber including the productivity of managed forests, the demand for timber and specialist timber products and trends in consumer demand.

In the UK, organisations like **Forestry England** use growth and yield data along with climate predictions to predict availability from managed forests over the next 50 years.

Trend forecasting is also used to predict future demand. Factors such as house building initiatives can increase the demand for certain timbers used in construction whilst fashions for different timbers and manufactured boards in interior and product design can also be influential.

The environmental impact of climate change is another consideration as long term drought would affect growth and, hence, the long term supply of timber. Extreme weather conditions can cause more immediate issues with hurricanes and storms able to decimate forests. Disease and pests can endanger whole species of trees.

> **Q2** What other effect of climate change might impact forestry?

Case study: Ash dieback

Ash dieback is a fungal disease that particularly affects younger trees, making them vulnerable to other pests and diseases, it is often fatal. The first infected trees in the UK were discovered in 2012. Spores can be spread by the wind or by the movement of infected plants and logs. The BBC reported in 2019 that the disease could cost the economy as much as £15bn.

A lesion on the bark of an infected Ash tree

Cost factors

Several factors influence the cost of timbers and manufactured boards. The quality and type of timber affect its price as does the distance it has to travel from forest to consumer.

Some timbers are graded depending on the numbers of knots, blemishes and faults. Lower grade timber will be less expensive. Constructional timbers are also given structural gradings depending on their strength. C16 is a common structural grade whilst C24 is stronger with fewer defects.

Pressure and chemical treatment, such as tanalising, is used to protect timber from rot and pests. Fire proofing treatment is used in construction timber and, like tanalising, will increase the cost of the material. Manufacturing set-up costs and scales of production have cost implications and whilst many manufacturers will use standard stock forms where possible, some applications call for specialist machines and cutters.

> **Q3** What specialist machines might be used in timber manufacture?

Social influences

Designers and manufacturers need to understand their target market and the social group it represents. This understanding affects their selection of materials, product cost and chosen aesthetics. An individual might commission a one-off or bespoke piece of furniture from a carpenter or cabinet maker. This piece would be predominantly hand made to a high quality and materials and labour would be expensive, but the piece would likely be seen as an investment. In this case, the product may not appeal to, or be accessible to other social or economic groups. Many products are batch or mass produced and are aimed at a broader market. In this case, less expensive materials and construction methods using manufactured boards and knock down fittings may be used.

Furniture maker hand finishing a bespoke product

Whilst it is important that a product is fit for purpose, consumer choice is often influenced by fashions in design, lifestyle trends and the popularity of particular materials. Fashions and trends can be influenced by the past, however they are often led by evolutions in material technology.

Case study: Charles and Ray Eames

In the 1940s, designers Charles and Ray Eames discovered a way of moulding wood, heated under pressure, that led them to create plywood splints and stretchers that were used in World War II.

After the war they refined that manufacturing technique and found that it lent itself to mass production. Through a process of prototyping, testing and refinement they developed a moulded plywood chair that fitted the human body comfortably.

In 2001 it was awarded 'Design of the Century' by Time magazine.

The Plywood Group LCW chair, is still in production today.

Ethical factors

To be viable, products must meet the needs of the target consumer without causing offence or endangering others. Colours, symbols and language have different meanings in different cultures and product designers must consider this, not only in designing the product itself but in the design of any packaging, instructions or advertising information material.

> **Q4** (a) Many international companies use pictorial instructions, why do you think this is?
> (b) What could be added to these instructions to make them accessible to visually impaired consumers?

There is an expectation of quality and longevity in the timber and manufactured boards used in the construction industry but the trend for 'fast' and 'disposable' fashion is influencing the design of furniture and smaller timber-based products. Many consumers will not buy a product expecting it to last a lifetime; in fact they may only want it to last a matter of years before changing their look.

In responding to fashion and changing trends, some manufacturers make products that are specifically built to last for a finite time; this is called planned or **built-in obsolescence**. As the product is not expected to last, cheaper, lower quality materials like chipboard and chipboard laminates are used. The resulting product may be cheap and appealing, however, a problem arises when the product fails and needs to be disposed of. Cheap furniture is often taken to landfill as its quality makes it difficult to repair or upcycle.

Natural forces and stresses

Before timber is used in construction and manufacture it is subject to forces and stresses. Trees are living organisms and as such they experience growth stresses. When a tree is felled and converted to timber, these stresses are released and can cause faults including splitting, cracking and warping. Removing these faults creates waste material which can be recycled.

Improving functionality

Timber for construction needs to withstand several forces including tension, compression and shear force.

Pre-stressing timber beams makes them stronger when stress loaded. In a timber roof truss, the cross beam may be pre-stressed through controlled pulling or stretching, making it more able to withstand tension when in use. This is usually done through a process of lamination.

Laminating

Laminating involves bonding strips of material together in layers. It can be done with thick materials in order to create very strong structures which can be used as roofing beams and bridge supports.

If thinner materials are used for laminating, the curves made can be quite complex and have reasonably tight radii. The process involves layering the material with adhesive and holding it in the chosen position using a **former** or **jig** with clamps or by using a **vacuum bag press**. Flexi-ply is often used for lamination as it is very workable and can make a robust product with a high quality finish.

> **Q5** What must you check for before releasing a shaped laminate from the former?

Lamination is also used to pre-stress timber beams. Curved members that would otherwise be forced into compression and tension under load are constructed by laminating thin layers of timber which are then glued in under pressure and heat over a former, creating a pre-stressed curved beam.

Glued, laminated (Glulam) beams used in a timber roof construction

Braces and ties can be used to reinforce timber structures. Usually made of steel, they triangulate structures to add strength and rigidity.

> **Q6** What are the benefits of triangulating a structure?

Timber products can be reinforced and their properties enhanced by adding other materials, forming a composite material. GRP (**glass reinforced plastic** or **fibreglass**) wood composites are used in used boat building, the production of doors and windows, flooring and decking, furniture and sports equipment including snowboards, skis, oars and paddles.

Standard material stock forms, types and sizes

Most wood-based material comes in a range of standard shapes and sizes. This enables materials to be more interchangeable, and the manufacturers of tools to be aware of the material they will need to cope with. When ordering material, you should ensure you have the correct measurements to hand. Standard practice is to use length x width x thickness for planks and boards, and length x diameter for rods and dowels.

Board and plank sizes

- Manufactured boards come in a series of standard sizes. Thicknesses tend to start at 3mm and 4mm. From 6mm thicknesses, they rise in 3mm steps to 9mm, 12mm and so on.
- Single veneer thicknesses vary from 0.4mm to 4.5mm but are commonly 1.5mm thick.
- A full size sheet of manufactured board is 2440mm long by 1220mm wide (based on the old imperial size of 8 feet by 4 feet). Boards are commonly available in half and quarter sheets and frequently smaller. Many DIY stores and timber suppliers offer a cutting service and will prepare the exact size needed.
- Planks are available in different levels of finish. Rough sawn, planed square edge (PSE) (where one reference side is planed straight for use as a datum edge) and planed all round (PAR).
- Plank widths are of standard sizes and generally increase in 25mm stages (again based on the imperial for 1 inch). A common size is 50mm x 25mm, used for frame and carcase construction. 50mm x 25mm would be the size of the rough sawn version; however, if you were to ask for it planed all round (PAR), it would measure approximately 45mm x 20mm as this would account for the material removed by the planing process. The PAR sizes will always be 2-3mm less per side in width and thickness than rough sawn, meaning around 5mm less width and 5mm less thickness will be available. This reduction needs to be considered when designing, as it could lead to inaccurate construction sizes.
- Planks are measured by cross-sectional area (width x thickness).
- Plank lengths vary and can often be bought by the metre. Common lengths are 1.2m, 1.5m, 1.8m, 2.4m, 3m and 3.6m, normally increasing to a maximum of 4.8m.

Q7 How many square metres of material are there in a standard full size board of 2440mm x 1220mm?

Q8 What would be the finished PAR width and thickness of a piece of timber that was machined from a sawn plank starting out at 150mm x 50mm?

Dowels and mouldings

Many specially shaped sections of wood are available and these are known as **mouldings**. The most common variety can be seen around door frames and is called **architrave**; you may also have noticed ornate **skirting boards** in older style houses which is another form of moulding. Some modern mouldings are made from manufactured board such as MDF and can come pre-painted – however, the majority are made from different types of timber.

Dowel rods are circular sections of timber that come in many different diameters. Some dowel is pre-cut and ridged for use in a dowelled wood joints. Dowels and mouldings are machined using industrial milling machines and routers. Dowel rods are usually sold in standard lengths of 350mm, 600mm, 900mm and 2400mm.

Chapter 28 – Planning and production methods

Objectives

- Be aware of the advantages and disadvantages of different manufacturing processes for various scales of production
- Understand how production aids and quality control procedures improve manufactured products

Marking out timber and manufactured boards

A sharp pencil and steel rule or straight edge are invaluable tools when marking out timber and manufactured boards however there are a range of other tools that enable accurate measuring and marking.

> **Q1** What is the disadvantage of marking out with a pencil? Name an alternative.

Name	Uses	Image	Name	Uses	Image
Vernier calipers	Used to accurately measure the thickness of timber, board and moulding		Mortice gauge	The adjustable stock and two spurs allow the accurate marking of two parallel lines for a mortice joint	
Tri square	Used to ensure components are at 90° to one another		Marking gauge	The adjustable stock and single spur allows a single parallel line to be marked along an edge	
Sliding bevel	Adjustment of the straight edge allows different angles to be marked including a 45° mitre		Combination gauge	A straight edge, tri square and sliding bevel. The combination gauge incorporates a scale and spirit level for accurate marking of angles	

When preparing any timber, a **reference** or **datum face** called the **face edge** is created, in PSE timber this has been done for you. From this accurate datum edge the 'face side' can be created by planing and checking it against the face edge using a tri square. Once you have created and marked an accurate face side and edge the remaining sides and edges can be planed by hand or the plank can be run through a planer thicknesser using the prepared faces as reference surfaces.

Quality control

When products are made, checking that they are being produced correctly is an essential stage. This is known as **quality control (QC)** and ensures dimensional accuracy is consistent as well as visual inspections of surface quality and constuction. This ensures the product is safe to use.

To save checking every vital measurement on every product with an accurate measuring device, special tools known as **go/no go** gauges are used. These tools are set to the specific minimum or maximum **tolerances** allowed for that particular component. It is then a simple task of placing the fixture onto the part of the workpiece being measured. The gauge will indicate whether the part is 'go' or 'no go' (too big or too small) and can be easily rejected if it is the incorrect size.

> **Q2** What are the benefits of using go/no go fixtures in product manufacture?

Scales of production

A range of techniques and processes are used to cut and shape timber and manufactured boards. The nature of the process and type of tools or machinery used will vary depending on the scale of production.

In **one-off** or **bespoke production**, highly skilled crafts people, in workshops similar to those in schools, work with hand tools, power tools and some machinery to produce predominantly hand made products. Processes are labour intensive, materials are high quality and the resulting products tend to be relatively expensive.

Small workshops may **batch produce** some products and will use tools and machines such as routers and mortices to enable them to repeat processes more accurately and consistently.

In most workshops timber preparation and dimensioning is done by **sawing**. Table saws, radial arm saws, panel saws and mitre saws use circular blades to rip saw (along the grain) and cross cut (across the grain) of the timber.

Bandsaws use toothed steel bands which are narrower than a circular saw blade. The band enables gentle curves and details to be cut. When using any type of mechanised saw, PPE must be worn and where applicable, guards, guides and fences should be used.

A **router** is a hand held power tool although it can also be mounted in a table. It is used with different shaped cutters (bits) for creating slots, rebates and mouldings. Cutters rotate at high speed and can be 'plunged' into the material to a set depth dictated by a depth stop. Correct PPE must be worn and precautions taken when using a router including using the correct sized cutters, checking cables are out of the path of cutter, traversing the router away from you and holding it in place until the cutter has stopped rotating.

Morticers are commonly used in joinery where large numbers of mortise and tenon joints are cut. The machine uses a hollow square chisel which contains a central drill bit. The chisel is moved laterally to elongate the cut and the depth can be adjusted. The drill removes the bulk of the material while the chisel ensures the sides of the mortise are square.

A **bag press** uses a constant vacuum to form intricate shapes using lamination. Instead of clamping the laminates between male and female formers whilst the glue cures, a bag press uses air pressure to keep the formers in place. Laminates are glued up and laid over a single former or mould. This is placed in the bag and a porous fabric placed on the lamination. The bag is then sealed so that it is air tight and a pump is attached to a valve in the bag. The pump sucks the remaining air from the bag and the resulting atmospheric pressure forces the lamination over the mould. The lamination remains in the bag until the glue has cured.

> **Q3** What is the function of the porous material that is placed over the lamination whilst in the bag press?

In batch production, **patterns**, **templates**, **jigs** and **fixtures** are used to enable repetition, improve accuracy and to save time. Patterns and templates are shapes or a collection of shapes cut out of cheap materials like cardboard or hardboard and used to allow makers to repeatedly mark out a part or parts of a product repeatedly. This might simply involve drawing around a shape but templates and patterns may also include details like the positioning of holes and slots. The term pattern is also used to describe the timber shape (often made from jelutong) used in the sand casting process.

Jigs are devices that help to hold a workpiece in place and guide the tool being used for example, a drilling jig may be used to ensure the accurate location of holes for fixings. Fixtures hold the workpiece in position on the machine bed whilst it is cut or shaped. They are usually larger and more permanent than jigs.

A drilling jig enables angled holes to be drilled accurately

Mass and **continuous production** methods utilise a higher level of mechanisation and automation to enable fast and accurate repetition of processing. These methods are usually used for smaller, more common parts such as cocktail sticks or dowels.

Commercial routing and turning

In industry, most machining and shaping of furniture, artefacts and components is now done using **CAM, (Computer-Aided Manufacturing)**. **CNC (Computer Numerical Control)** routers are used for flat materials and CNC lathes for cylindrical objects. Great repetitive accuracy, and a level of detail that would be very difficult to manage by hand, can be achieved. Routers are available in very large formats that are capable of producing flat-packed furniture but they can also create detailed ornate profiles if required.

Machine operator routing the detail into a wooden door

In mass production, **sub-assembly** is used to manufacture and assemble components of larger products. These sub-assembled parts are products in their own right and as such are quality controlled and tested by the manufacturer.

> **Q4** Which parts of the office chair above may have been sub-assembled?

Material selection

Commercial products are nearly always aimed at a specific price point which often determines the quality of the chosen construction material.

Traditional wooden toys are frequently made from beech as it has a fine dense grain which gives it resistance to splintering and chipping when dropped or thrown. It is also non-toxic and finishes well. It can be sanded to a very fine and smooth finish and is equally appealing either in its unfinished pinkish grain or painted.

If a manufacturer wanted to save on production costs, they could decide to use a softwood such as pine or spruce. The result would have slightly different aesthetics, being yellower with a more pronounced grain. The blocks would be prone to denting and splitting over time due to a more open grain structure which makes the wood softer and less durable than beech.

Toy building blocks in beech and pine

Flat-pack furniture

Manufactured boards are most often seen commercially in flat-pack products.

Advantages of flat-pack furniture	Disadvantages of flat-pack furniture
• Compact for ease of transportation	• Needs to be constructed yourself or by someone else at additional cost
• Low cost compared to traditional furniture	• Not as robust as traditional furniture
• A large choice of styles and finishes	• Can be complex to construct for some
• Easy to assemble with limited tools and experience	• Prone to damage by moisture
• Can be disassembled for storage/moving	• Can chip and break more easily

As manufactured board is so dimensionally stable it can be processed, transported, stored and assembled without the risk of developing the faults of natural timbers. It is, however, prone to absorbing moisture in damp and humid conditions which makes shipping and storage more complex.

Q5 What are the advantages to manufacturers of producing a range of flat-pack furniture?

Q6 What factors make flat-pack furniture cheaper than traditional pre-assembled furniture?

Chapter 29 – Material processing and joining

Objectives

- Understand the application of specialist techniques when manufacturing products
- Be aware of the advantages and disadvantages of specialist techniques
- Be able to select appropriate specialist techniques and joining methods

Shaping, processing and machining wood

A vast array of tools is available in workshops in order to help make the products we require. Tools enable us to mark out materials, cut to them size, waste them (remove material), shape them and apply a finish.

Drilling

Drilling a hole into a piece of wood seems a simple task but there are a number of factors to consider. Selecting the correct type of drill bit is important so that the right amount of material is removed. Additionally, the correct speed is needed; large drill bits require a slower speed than smaller diameter bits to avoid overheating and potential scorching of the wood. The depth of cut needs to be considered as you may not want to drill all the way through a piece of material, as does the feed rate which can put excessive strain on the drill and the drill bit if it is too fast.

A pillar drill is good for accuracy and it is powerful enough to drill larger holes in thicker materials. A cordless drill is very adaptable and usually has variable speeds and a clutch which can help avoid overtightening of fixtures and fittings.

Common drill bits used with wood-based materials

Name	Uses	Image	Name	Uses	Image
Wood drill bit	Designed to drill holes in wood, flutes carry waste wood away		Hole saw	Used to cut large holes, they can easily overheat due to high peripheral speed	
Twist drill bit	General purpose bit, also used on plastic and metal		Flat bit	Efficient way to make larger holes, removes waste efficiently, long shank for greater depth	
Countersink bit	Used to allow a countersunk screw head to be flush with the surface		Forstner bit	Accurate hole cutting bit, good for flat-bottomed partial-thickness holes	

Q1 What is the most essential piece of PPE to be worn when using a drill?

Cutting and sawing

Saws are used to cut materials and joints to size. The tenon saw, rip saw and cross-cut saw are common hand saws that are used for cutting straight lines in wood. The tenon saw is used for cutting wood joints and for small section material. Rip and cross-cut saws are used for cutting large panels. The coping saw enables curved lines to be followed. The bandsaw is powered and can be used for straight cuts and gentle curves through thick and thin material.

The bandsaw is a powered tool used to cut curved lines through thin material.

> **Q2** Do some research on saw blades and explain the following:
> a) Tooth pitch   b) Kerf

Tenon saw   *Coping saw*   *Rip saw / Cross-cut saw*

6-1 Wasting and abrading by hand

Using hand tools to accurately shape wood is a skill that is learned over many years. Accuracy is vital and mistakes are easy to make which can be costly. Practice is needed in order to achieve the quality that you need at GCSE level, therefore it is recommended that you use some scrap wood to become acquainted with the following tools first; especially chisels. Planes can take some delicate setting up before they work correctly but it is worth taking time to ensure an even cut is made.

Wasting tools			Abrading tools		
Name	**Characteristics**	**Image**	**Name**	**Characteristics**	**Image**
Smoothing plane	Smoothing plane removes very thin layers of wood, smooths and flattens along the grain		Rasp	Like a file with very rough teeth for fast removal of material, different profiles available	
Chisel	Different versions used with a mallet to remove wood to form rebates and recesses		Surform	For fast removal of material, a cheese grater-like blade is sharp but brittle, different profiles available	

Sanding

Sanding wood to give it a smooth finish can be performed with machines or by hand. A disc or belt sander is best used for easy-to-reach sections that can be held safely. There are also cylindrical sanding machines called bobbin sanders which are useful for internal curves.

Hand sanding using **glasspaper** is best for hard-to-reach areas and it also allows you to apply the force where it is needed most, perhaps to remove scratches or a glue stain. Glasspaper comes in different grades; the grit density (measured in grit per square inch) determines how rough or smooth it is. 40 to 60 grit is very coarse and will scratch most materials, 600 grit is very smooth and has almost a polishing effect. Electric hand sanders are useful and some come with accessories for working on hard-to-reach areas.

Bobbin sander

> **Q3** Which three pieces of PPE would be most appropriate to use when mechanically sanding?

> **Q4** When sanding a rough piece of timber to a smooth finish, would you start with a high number grit and work lower, or a low number and work higher?

Wood turning and carving

Wood lathes are used to turn bowls and spindles. The size of the material being turned is important; the speed needs to be reduced as the diameter of the object being turned gets larger.

A special set of chisels is used to shape the wood when turning. The most commonly used tools are the scraper, the gouge and the parting tool. Spindles are usually turned between centres whilst bowls are mounted on a face plate so that the inside of the bowl can be hollowed out. If the base of the piece needs to be rebated, they can be mounted in a chuck.

Carving

Wood carving is a traditional skill where chisels of different profiles are used to create decorative relief patterns. A special rounded mallet is used with the chisel to remove materials. Carving is usually done by hand although similar effect can be achieved using CNC routers or mills.

Wood joints

One of the most effective ways to join two or more pieces of wood is with a wood joint. Wood joints can be used to fabricate carcase constructions e.g. a drawer or bookshelf, and frame constructions e.g. tables, chairs and picture frames. Joints need to be made precisely and time should be taken to mark out accurately and ensure that any cuts are made on the waste side of the marked out lines. Joints are best pared down with a chisel if they do not fit first time. It is preferable to have wood joints that are a tight fit rather than ones which are too loose and require filling, as this can weaken them.

Name	Characteristics	Image
Butt joint	The most basic joint, not very strong due to little surface area for the adhesive and no mechanical advantage. Pins or nails often used	
Dowelled joint	Similar to the butt joint but with wooden dowels that add strength and assist rigidity. Dowels are glued in for extra strength	
Mitre joint	More attractive than the butt joint and used for picture frames and surrounds. Weak due to lack of surface area, metal splines can be used to help strengthen them	
Lap joint	Full or half lap joints. Stronger in crossed lap form. Used in furniture construction and shelving	
Housing joint	A stronger joint that has larger surface area for glueing and the physical advantage of the wood being supported by three sides	
Mortise and tenon joint	A strong joint used in table and chair construction. Very large surface area for glue and good physical advantage created by the tenon	Mortise / Tenon
Dovetail	A strong attractive interlocking joint commonly used to join drawer fronts and sides and in decorative box construction	

Q5 Which joint from this selection do you think would best suit the following tasks?

(a) A shelf

(b) Architrave around a door frame

Adhesives

In applications where temperature and humidity may change, some wood joints are left dry so they don't crack or break with movement however most of the joints created in the workshop will be glued. A good joint is most commonly achieved using wood glues such as **PVA (polyvinyl acetate)**. This glue is white in colour but dries clear. It also has a reasonable open working time allowing adjustments to be made before clamping and curing. PVA is not gap-filling and so the joint being glued must be tight.

Contact adhesives are sometimes used to glue other materials to timber or board such as veneers. Both surfaces need to be coated with a thin layer of the adhesive and, when it is tacky, they are pressed together. The adhesive 'grabs' and there is no opportunity for repositioning either piece. This is often used for larger surface areas.

Woodscrews

To fix two pieces of wood together, woodscrews are used. They are available in many different lengths and diameters. Screws come with different driving methods, the most common being slotted, Phillips and Pozidriv®. Allen key and Torx® drive are becoming more widely available and offer a more reliable connection when using powered screwdrivers, as they are less prone to slipping and result in fewer stripped heads.

Slotted   *Phillips*   *Pozidriv®*   *Allen*   *Torx®*

When connecting two pieces of timber together it is best to select a screw that has a shank so that it does not grip the first piece of timber and create a gap between the two separate pieces.

First, a pilot hole of about the core diameter of the screw is drilled through both pieces of wood. Then a clearance hole is drilled through the top piece only, to at least the diameter of the shank.

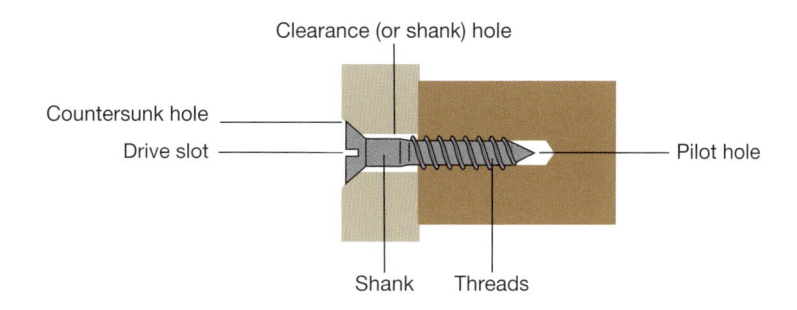

Finally, if using a countersunk screw, a countersunk hole should be drilled to the depth of the head of the screw, so the screw lies flush with the surface of the material. A countersink bit is used for this purpose.

> **Q6** Why is it good practice to drill a pilot hole?

> **Q7** Why are Allen key and Torx® screws less prone to slipping when being driven in?

Nails and pins

Nails and pins are threadless versions of screws and are either hammered into position or a powered nail gun can be used along with special cartridges of nails. They are generally used for permanently fixing wood together. Pins tend to be thinner than nails, have less of a pronounced head and are used to attach materials that have finer detail as the head is easily hidden below the surface.

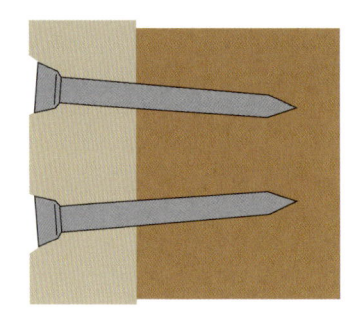

To attach two pieces of wood together, a method of skewing the nails or pins at an angle (known as 'dovetail' nailing) is ideally used, as it gains some mechanical advantage and reduces the chance of the joint working itself loose through vibration and pressure.

Common types of nails and pins

Name	Characteristics	Image	Name	Characteristics	Image
Round wire nail	All-purpose nail with a wide flat head, can be galvanised for exterior use		Oval wire nail	Shaped nail with small head, prevents wood splitting, best for interior use	
Panel pin	Thin diameter with a discrete small head, pin punch used to set below surface		Tack	Sharp, short, wide head, used to attach material such as upholstery or carpets to wood	
Clout nail	Very wide head, often galvanised, used to attach roofing felt and plaster board		Lost head nail	A thicker version of a panel pin, used where the head should not be visible. A pin punch is used to set down	

Knock-down fittings

Flat-packed furniture relies almost entirely on different types of **knock-down fittings (KDF)**. These are a form of temporary fixing that joins two or occasionally three pieces of material together, normally via a screwing method. They provide a secure and tight joint (although not as rigid as a permanent joint), and they are easily dismantled for transportation or storage. You may have used these before or have identified them on furniture you have seen.

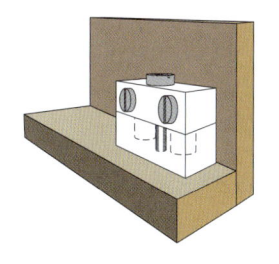

Connecting or block fitting 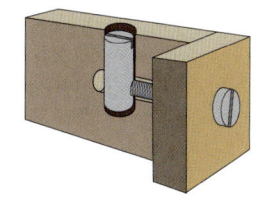 *Cross dowel fitting* 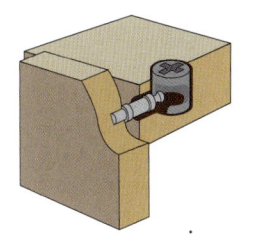 *Cam lock fitting*

Hinges and ironmongery

Hinges are used to attach doors, windows and other openings to frames and carcases. They can be made from many different materials but most commonly are metal. Many varieties are made from polished brass or steel and are often sold in pairs.

Hinges need to be carefully aligned to ensure accurate operation. The process of **rebating** or recessing the hinge is used to ensure a flush fit between the frame and the door or window.

Common **ironmongery** includes handles, door knockers, bolts, catches and brackets. Drawer sliders may also be commonly required in furniture.

> **Q8** How can steel hinges be modified to protect them from rust?

Common types of hinge

Name	Characteristics	Image	Name	Characteristics	Image
Butt hinge	Standard hinge for doors and windows, needs rebating to fit flush	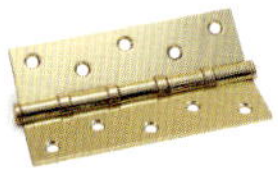	Piano hinge	Long butt style hinge, cut to required length, fine and close join possible	
Flush hinge	Not as robust as a butt hinge, does not require rebating		Concealed hinge	Used in flat-packed furniture and kitchens, specialist jig needed to fit	
Butterfly hinge	Decorative version of the butt hinge, used in cabinet making		Tee hinge	Often galvanised, painted or black japanned for outside use on sheds and gates	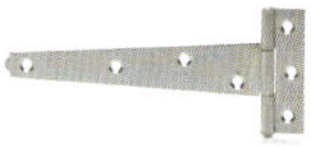

Chapter 29 **Material processing and joining**

Chapter 30 – Material treatments and finishes

Objectives

- Be able to select appropriate treatments and finishes and understand their application
- Be aware of the advantages and disadvantages of finishing techniques and preservation methods

Surface treatments and finishes

Most woods, whether natural or manufactured, perform better if they have a finish applied to them. The reasons for applying a finish fall into two main areas: aesthetics and protection.

Aesthetics can mean colouring or staining to:

- match or contrast with existing materials
- enhance the natural grain of the timber
- give it a sheen or shine or even a matt surface finish

Protection can mean making it:

- waterproof
- less prone to fungal or insect attack
- tougher so it resists knocks and bumps
- easy to wipe clean and disinfect

When purchasing rough-sawn timber, particularly for outside use, there is the option of having it pressure-treated or **tanalised**. This is a process of forcing wood preservative into the cell structure of the timber under pressure in a vacuum. The wood preservative does not go right through the timber but the process is more effective than painting it on the surface alone.

Tanalising protects timber from fungal and insect attack and will delay the onset of rot but it does not make the wood waterproof.

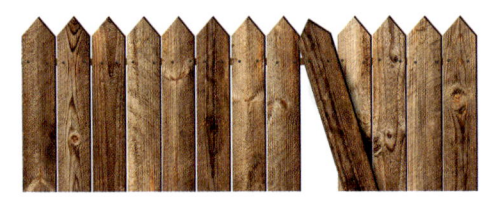

What treatments might be applied to a spruce garden fence?

Common protections and finishes for timber-based products

Most finishes for woods are available with a range of different base liquids. The three categories are oil-based, solvent-based and water-based. Traditionally oil and solvent-based products were used, and these are still considered the longest lasting. However, they are not very environmentally friendly as they can contain high levels of **volatile organic compounds (VOCs)**. This means that they give off fumes that are considered hazardous to health and should be used according to the manufacturer's instructions, normally wearing a mask in a well ventilated area. Water-based products are becoming much more popular and are kinder to the environment. These are non-toxic and are safe to use around children and animals.

Name	Characteristics	Image	Name	Characteristics	Image
Shellac	Shellac is a natural resin and is used in French polishing. It primes and seals, giving a high-gloss finish		Paint	Painted with brush or roller, usually needs primer and undercoat on bare wood, wide range of colours available	
Varnish	Protects from moisture, can be coloured with stain, enhances grain, gloss, satin or matt finish, yellows with age		Stain	Permanently colours wood, does not protect it, results vary depending on base wood and colour	
Oil	Similar effect to varnish but soaks into the timber rather than sitting on the surface, needs reapplying frequently		Wax	Rubbed into the wood with cloth or wire wool, enhances natural grain, needs regular reapplication	

Q1 Why should you reapply surface treatments and finishes in accordance with the manufacturer's instructions, or when signs of wear occur?

6-1

Veneer

Veneering is a surface finish that is usually used to enhance manufactured boards. This can be both decorative and functional. Natural wood slices are taken from the trunk of a tree and are bonded to the surface of cheaper sheet materials. Veneers are commonly seen on medium density fibreboard (MDF) and plywood.

There are two methods of veneer production; rotary and knife cut. Rotational veneer production produces the longest sheets and involves rotating a whole tree trunk on an industrial machine similar to a wood turning lathe. It is a bit like a huge pencil sharpener creating one long ribbon of veneer.

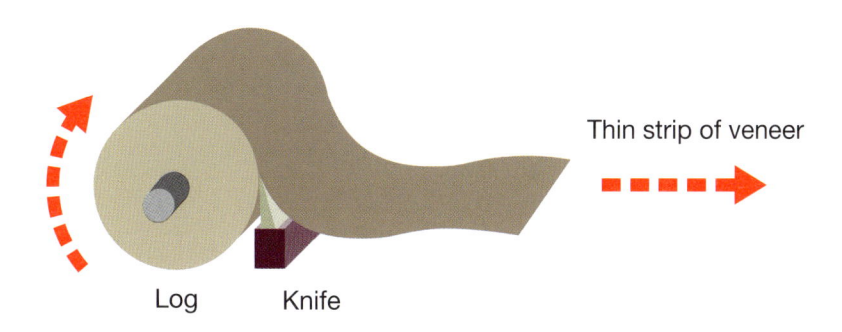

Rotational veneer method

Exercises

1. Use notes and sketches to show the process of laminating a curved form from oak veneers [4]

2. Oak is a hardwood.
   (a) State **one** geographical region oak would be sourced from. [1]
   (b) Name **one** stock form in that oak would be available in. [1]
   (c) Explain how an oak frame structure can be stiffened to withstand forces and stresses. [2]
   (d) Explain the difference between PAR and PSE timber. [2]

3. Describe **one** method that is used during the production of products in quantity to ensure that dimensional accuracy is maintained. [2]

4. When selecting natural timber for the manufacture of a product, designers should consider the sustainability and recyclability of any materials used.
   Discuss the sustainability of natural timbers in manufacture, in use and end of life. [6]

5. Study the desk pictured below. It is sold flat-packed.

   (a) Name the type of assembly fittings that would be used in the assembly of the flat-packed desk. [1]
   (b) Give **two** advantages of the desk being sold flat-packed. [2]
   (c) Name a specific type of manufactured board that would be used to manufacture the flat-packed desk. [1]
   (d) Use notes and sketches to show how the desk top would be attached to the upright sides of the desk. [4]
   (e) Explain **one** advantage of using a concealed hinge to attach the door to the upright sides of the desk. [2]

6. Timber can be treated for functional and aesthetic reasons.
   (a) Name **one** surface finish or treatment that can be applied to timber to enhance the functional or aesthetic qualities of the timber. [2]
   (b) Use notes and sketches to show how the surface finish or treatment named in 6(a) would be applied. [4]

7. Study the wooden bowl shown below.

   (a) Give the name of the machine that would have been used to manufacture the wooden bowl. [1]

   (b) Use notes and sketches to show the process of manufacturing the wooden bowl. [4]

8. Which **one** of the following processes would have been used to produce the ornamental relief pattern in the timber shown below? [1]

   ☐ Planing
   ☐ Laminating
   ☐ Carving
   ☐ Veneering

9. Wood joints are used to construction and the manufacture of furniture.

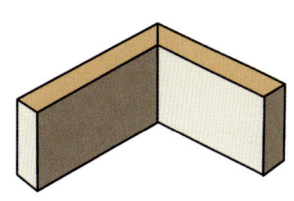

   (a) Name the type of joint shown above. [1]
   (b) Give **one** application for the joint shown above [1]
   (c) Give **one** advantage of using a dovetail joint to join the sides of a drawer to the front. [1]
   (d) Draw an annotated 3D sketch of a dovetail joint labelling the parts as appropriate. [4]
   (e) Explain **one** reason why a mortice and tenon joint is ideal for furniture construction. [2]

Section 6-1 **Exercises** 151

Section 6-2
Metals

In this section:

Chapter 31	Sources, origins and sustainability	153
Chapter 32	Physical and working properties	157
Chapter 33	Selection of materials and stock forms	160
Chapter 34	Planning and production methods	166
Chapter 35	Material processing	170
Chapter 36	Finishing	180
Exercises		183

Chapter 31 – Sources, origins and sustainability

Objectives

- Explain the sources, origins and properties of a range of ferrous and non-ferrous metals
- Understand the processes involved in mining, extraction and refining to produce metal
- Be aware of the sustainability of metals and their ecological footprint

The origin of metals

The discovery of metal ores dates back to around 9000BC and humankind have been mining, refining and working with metals ever since. It is estimated that 65% or more of the copper ever mined is still in circulation today.

Mining for metals

Metals are a finite resource found in the earth's crust and are obtained through mining. Two main types of mining for metal and ore are **surface mining** and **underground mining**. Both methods cause some destruction to the natural environment but surface mining creates much more of a visible scar. Vast amounts of energy are required to mine and transport the raw materials for processing.

An open cast iron ore mine

Iron ore and steel production

Iron ore is mined in many countries however the largest producers today include the USA, Russia and Sweden.

When an iron ore deposit is located it must first be extracted from the surrounding rock. This is usually done by drilling or by blasting with explosives. Once mined, the broken ore is loaded onto dump trucks and taken away for processing. On arrival at the processing plant, the ore is crushed, washed and impurities are removed before it is sent on to a refinery. The process is energy intensive and relies on the use of heavy machinery for transportation.

Iron is the most commonly used metal worldwide, largely due to the fact that it is the key ingredient in steel. Historically Britain, USA and Europe all produced steel, however, due to the size of the workforce and rapid economic growth, China is now the largest producer, contributing over 50% of the world's steel.

Bauxite

The largest producers of aluminium are the USA, France and particularly Australia where it is extracted from bauxite; the most abundant ore on the planet. Once the bauxite has been mined it is washed to remove clay minerals and other impurities. The resulting aluminium oxide is then extracted using electrolysis; an expensive process which consumes a lot of electricity. The aluminium, in its liquid form, is separated from any unwanted elements and cast into the required forms for further manufacturing. It takes approximately 4kg of bauxite to produce 1kg of aluminium metal.

Copper and tin

Copper is thought to be the first ore discovered and extracted many thousands of years ago. Nowadays both surface and underground mines are used with Chile, the USA, Russia and Zambia being some of the key producers. Copper is sometimes found in pure form but can also be extracted from a mineral called chalcopyrite. The mined material is crushed and ground up to release the mineral. To seperate the mineral from the waste material a process called flotation is used, the mineral (which is hydrophobic) will float to the top.

Like copper, tin ore (also known as cassiterite) is mined both over and underground, however underwater dredging is also used as deposits may be found in the sea bed. Tin mining today is focused in Indonesia and China where the ore is also processed.

Extracting metals

Once the raw material has been mined, the metal is separated from any waste material. This is usually done in a furnace although different metals are processed in different ways.

The process of extracting iron from iron ore is called **smelting**. This involves a blast furnace that can reach temperatures of around 1,700°C. Iron melts at 1,538°C and therefore starts to become liquid as it descends through the furnace, eventually running free from the rest of the ore, which becomes a waste product known as **slag**.

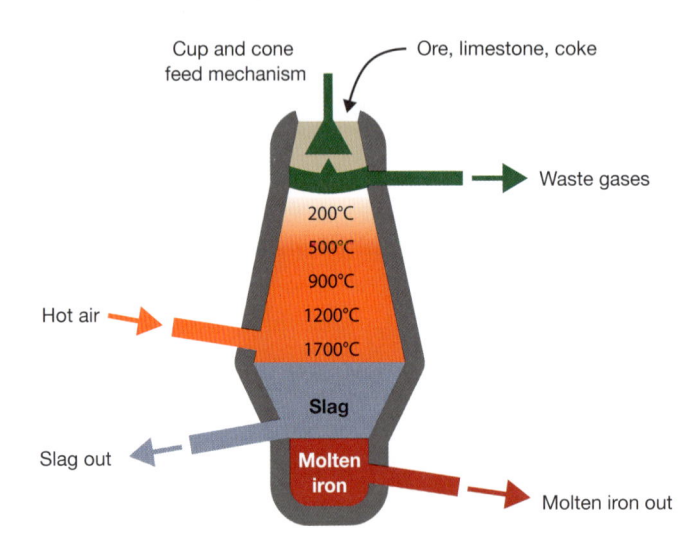

The molten iron is heavier than the slag and therefore sinks below it to be collected at the bottom of the furnace where it is drained off and cooled into rectangular blocks. At this stage it is known as pig iron.

This unrefined iron has a very high carbon content and is very brittle. It usually undergoes further processing to remove the carbon and other impurities to make steel.

Refining metals

The process of refining metals simply means purifying them to improve their quality and functionality. It involves removing impurities and waste materials that must be treated or disposed of. Different processes are used to refine different metals and the level of purity obtained also varies.

Q1 Explain the factors that make metal such an energy hungry material to produce.

Q2 Which physical properties can be gained by reducing the carbon content of pig iron?

The environmental impacts of mining and extraction

The mining, extraction and transportation of metals are resource intensive and their impact can be far reaching. Heavy machinery is used to displace, break up and transport rock or sediment which can cause air and water pollution as well as noise pollution.

The impact on the landscape and wildlife can be considerable as the disturbance of natural habitats and deforestation, coupled with soil erosion and the contamination of ground water can result in a loss of biodiversity. This, in turn, can cause significant changes to the way the ecosystems function.

The effects of mining on communities are both positive and negative. Mines and processing plants may bring investment and job opportunities, however a sudden influx of workers can put pressure on infrastructure and services, and can change the social dynamics of a community.

Fine dust from the mining process causes air pollution

Q3 How might the building of transport links to enable raw materials to be sent for processing affect a community?

Sustainability of metals

Almost all metals are recyclable. When a metal is recycled and melted down the resulting recycled metal is of the same quality as the original. By contrast, when other materials such as paper and plastic are recycled, the resulting recycled materials tend to be of a lower quality.

Ferrous metals are picked up by a giant magnet at a scrap yard

Metals are considered a **finite resource**. Designers must therefore consider the amount of metal needed in a product and how easy it will be to recycle when the product reaches the end of its life. Metals must be separated into their pure form when being recycled, as small amounts of other metals in the recycling process can degrade the quality of the recycled metal. Any contamination will affect the properties of the recycled metal and limit its use.

Almost all metals can be recycled as long as they are separated. The process involves shredding, melting and purifying the used metal and this can be done repeatedly without the metal losing its properties. Whilst the recycling process still requires energy and resources they are significantly less than those required to mine and process new metal.

Metals require vast amounts of energy to produce and to recycle, but metal products tend to last a long time, thus reducing the need to replace parts or products so frequently. When metals are not recycled, they are often dumped in landfill sites, from where some poisonous metals, such as lead and cadmium, can leach into the soil and the water table. This can cause pollution in nearby rivers and farmland, causing harm to animals and the environment.

Q4 What are the implications of metal being considered a finite resource?

Q5 What are the positive impacts of recycling metals?

Chapter 32 – Physical and working properties

Objectives

- Be able to discriminate between and select from a range of ferrous and non-ferrous metals
- Understand the advantages, disadvantages and applications of ferrous and non-ferrous metals
- Be aware of the physical characteristics and working properties of ferrous and non-ferrous metals
- Be aware of the forces and stresses that act on metals

Physical characteristics and working properties

Metals have a range of different physical characteristics which make them suitable for different applications.

- **Conductivity** denotes how well a metal conducts heat or electricity.
- **Magnetism** causes metals that contain iron to produce fields that attract or repel other magnetic objects.
- **Density** dictates the weight of a metal.

When selecting metals, the working properties will be considered. **Ductility** and **malleability** are important if a metal is going to be shaped, formed and drawn whilst **hardness** and **durability** are vital to a product that may be subject to wear or damage. Properties are covered in detail in Section 4.

A metal that has good **toughness** is more able to withstand impact and absorb energy without breaking or fracturing. **Elasticity** is important if a metal part or product is required to bend and stretch but still return to its original shape.

> **Q1** What is the difference between a physical characteristic and a working property?

Forces and stresses

Like other materials, metals used in products and construction are subjected to different forces and stresses. Forces may be still - **static** or they may be moving - **dynamic**.

Tensile and **compressive** strength should be considered where metal components are subject to pulling and pushing forces for example in the construction of towers and bridges.

The metal used for the blades of a pair of scissors apply a **shear force**, where two surfaces move against one another in a 'shearing' action. This can also be seen in the moving blades of electrical hair clippers or garden shears.

Electrical garden shears create a shearing action

SECTION 6-2 METALS

Electrical cables and contacts like those found in plugs, switches and light fittings need to have good conductivity to allow the flow of electrons creating electric current. High-powered devices can get warm in use.

Magnetic forces mainly attract metals that contain iron. In Japan, Maglev trains use an electrodynamic suspension system (EDS), which is based on the repelling force of magnets to propel the trains along the track. The Shanghai Maglev train has a top speed of 430 kmph (267 mph).

The Shanghai Transrapid SMT Maglev train

> **Q2** Discuss which forces are at play on your chair as you sit down.

6-2 Additional metals and alloys

In addition to the metals covered in Chapter 29, it is worth knowing about the properties and uses of ferrous metals: high carbon steel and tungsten steel, and the non-ferrous metals, tin, titanium and 7000 series aluminium.

Additional ferrous metals

Name	Appearance	Image	Characteristics	Example uses
High carbon steel (Tool steel) Carbon content 0.6 – 1.5%	Similar to mild steel but does not rust as easily, smooth texture		Less ductile and harder than mild steel due to higher carbon content. Very hard wearing and holds edge well	Garden or workshop tools, blades, scissors, masonry nails, wood and metal cutting tools
Tungsten steel (HSS) Alloys can also include: Chromium Molybdenum Vanadium Cobalt Carbon	Smooth, silver grey colour, some drill bits have a gold ferrous oxide coating		Hard, tough, greater ability to retain cutting edge, heat resistant	Drill bits, milling bits, saws, tools, taps and dies

Additional non-ferrous metals

Name	Appearance	Image	Characteristics	Example uses
Tin	Silvery white, often used as a plating on steel giving a shiny finish		Soft, malleable, ductile, good electrical conductor	Coatings on cans to protect contents, soft solder, toys, alloyed with copper to form bronze
Titanium	Bright silver in color, lustrous		Low density, good strength to weight ratio, corrosion resistant, ductile, poor conductor	Medical implants, golf clubs, watches, aircraft parts, armour plating
7000 series aluminium. Aluminium alloyed with: zinc, magnesium and copper	Bright silver grey, often used with a matte finish		Good strength to weight ratio, relatively corrosion resistant (due to copper content)	Laptop, phone & watch casings, bicycles, aircraft, sports equipment

Metals for commercial products

Metals are used in commercial products for many reasons. Most metals have particular properties that are hard to find in other materials. It is often its high strength to weight ratio that means metal is frequently selected over other materials.

Although some metals can be very expensive, many offer good value for money. Cooking utensils, for example, must meet quite a demanding set of criteria in order to perform their function well. They need to be tough and durable, flame and heat resistant to a very high temperature, waterproof, corrosion resistant, dishwasher safe and hygienic with a scratch resistant surface. It helps sales if they look good too. There are very few materials that will perform these tasks as well as stainless steel.

Q4 Why is stainless steel used for kitchen utensils and not mild steel?

Q5 What are the advantages and disadvantages of using aluminium over stainless steel for kitchen utensils?

Chapter 33 – Selection of materials and stock forms

Objectives

- Be aware of how environmental, cultural and ethical issues influence material choices
- Explain how environmental factors influence the disposal of metal products
- Understand how metals can be reinforced and stiffened
- Understand the availability of various stock forms and sizes of materials

Selecting suitable metals

Choosing an appropriate type of metal-based material to use for a product depends on a number of factors, including:

Aesthetics	Cost	Weight
Size of product	Size of material available	Desired properties
Where it will be used	Required finish	Workability
Stability	Availability	How long it is to last
Environmental issues	Sustainability	Social influences

Suitability

Function and performance are key factors in selection. A metal must be both **fit for purpose** and safe when used for its chosen application. For example, it would be inappropriate to select a metal that corrodes easily for use in an application where it will be exposed to air and water.

Aesthetics

The aesthetic qualities of metals including **form**, **colour** and **texture** influence their selection. Metals are available in a variety of different stock forms which will be explored in more detail later in this chapter. The colour of some metals like brass, copper and aluminium are distinct and present the designer with aesthetic opportunities. Certain metals colours may have associations, for example brass is often used in products that are perceived as high end or valuable. Historically, this was because it was aesthetically very similar to gold and could be polished to a high shine.

Ornate antique brass door handles

Metals also vary in texture and whilst many can be polished, brushed or blasted, they are often used unfinished where natural oxidisation or a more industrial aesthetic is desired.

Environmental factors

When selecting metals, a designer or manufacturer needs to consider the sustainability of the material. If the product is to be produced continuously or on a large scale, then they need to know that the material will be readily available for as long as it is in production.

> **Q1** How does using recycled metals benefit a manufacturer of metal products or parts?

> **Q2** What factors could cause degradation of recycled metal?

Metal can in the early stages of corrosion and degradation

Availability

The sustainability and long-term availability of a metal is also linked to its market price. Metals are listed as commodities on the stock exchange and their price may be influenced by various factors that affect supply and demand, including the increase or decrease of producers, productivity levels, transport availability, legislation and political factors.

Greater availability is not always good for the market. Whilst it creates competition which may result in lower prices for the consumer, it can also drive producers to cut costs in the production stage and, where there is not sufficient scrutiny, the quality of resulting products may suffer.

Costs

Manufacturers must also factor in other costs when selecting metal for use in production. Different metals require different tools and machinery so that they can be formed, fabricated, joined and finished. This will affect manufacturing costs including premises, fuel and energy, and also labour.

Trend forecasting

Like any other material, metals are affected by design trends and fashions. The growth of personal, portable digital technology, for example, watches, phones, tablets and laptops illustrates the fluctuating trends in size, weight, form and finish.

Advancements in production capability and material science have also influenced these changes. A predominantly metal phone casing may have been unthinkable 20 years ago as the weight it would have added to the product would have been unacceptable, whereas now, new machining methods and advanced alloys allow strong, lightweight casings to be produced.

Ultra-thin smartphone in 7000 series aluminium casing

As a potentially highly sustainable material, metals are now experiencing a resurgence in popularity and are replacing other materials like plastics.

Social influences, cultural and ethical considerations

Changing fashions influence **consumer demand**. There is a growing ethical pressure against the 'throw-away' society. As a consequence, longevity (or how long a product will last), is reemerging as a growing consideration. Changing fashions, however, present manufacturers with the opportunity to constantly reinvent new or modified products and designs in order to meet the collective consumer need to be 'on trend'.

Meeting **market pull**, especially the demand for affordability and choice, inevitably drives some manufactures to look for areas where they can cut costs. Unfortunately, these can include outsourcing production to countries where conditions and pay for workers are not regulated or where materials do not meet required standards of quality.

Single use PET bottles and a reusable aluminium drinks bottle

Q3 What are the arguments for changing to a refillable metal bottle instead of repeatedly purchasing water in plastic bottles?

Q4 What other trends have influenced the use of metals in product design?

Q5 What duty of care do British companies have to the workers who manufacture their products in factories around the world?

Improving functionality

Metal products and components may be subject to forces, stresses, weather and the wear of regular use. When a manufacturer considers their choice of metal, they will also take into account how its properties may be enhanced or changed to improve functionality.

The performance of a metal can be improved in various ways. Metals used in construction can be formed into **shaped beams** that reduce weight and improve strength, often allowing loads to be spread more evenly. These rolled steel joints (RSJs) are commonly formed with I, U, T or C shaped cross sections.

Steel 'I' Beams used in the construction of a warehouse

Metals can be **work hardened** by repeatedly hammering, bending or rolling the metal whilst cold. This changes the crystalline structure of the metal. Whilst it improves hardness, it also makes the metal more brittle. **Annealing** can reduce the effect of work hardening. This is done by heating the metal to a specific temperature and then cooling it slowly.

Hardening medium- and high-carbon steel is done by heating it to a pre-determined temperature and quenching it in water or oil. This makes the steel harder but it also makes it more brittle and prone to splintering or shattering.

Some tools need very hard parts but if the whole tool is too hard it may break or snap. A file needs to have a hard blade capable of cutting through steel and other metals. The pointed tang which goes into the handle is much thinner and needs to be tougher and less brittle to cope with the force being applied without snapping.

The process to make the steel for the tang tougher and less brittle is called **tempering**. It involves heating the required area of the steel back up to a specific temperature between 230°C and 300°C and quenching it again. The exact temperature will depend on how tough or hard it needs to be.

Steel parts are hardened by heating in a temperature controlled kiln before being quenched in a tank of oil

Raising the carbon content of a metal makes it easier to harden using heat however the additional carbon also makes the metal more brittle.

> **Q6** Explain why the blade of a chisel needs to be hardened and tempered.

Standard material stock forms, types and sizes

Metal-based materials come in a range of standard sizes and shapes including sheets, rods, bars, tubes and wire. Standardisation enables materials to be interchangeable and for manufacturers of tools to be aware of the material they will need to deal with.

Standard dimensions for metal-based materials are given as *length x width x thickness* for sheet and flat bar. For box sections and many other shaped profiles, you will need the *profile shape*, and the *diameter x length*. Threaded rod – known as studding – needs *diameter x length*. The *pitch* of the thread will need to be considered if fine or coarse threads are required.

Metal stock lengths vary and are usually bought by the metre. Some sections can be bought in very long lengths if required.

Sheet, bar, tube, rod and wire sizes

Metric is the standard measuring system for metal material forms. Sheet material normally starts around 1mm thick up to 6mm thick; lengths and widths are usually measured in 500mm sections but smaller sheets are available. Flat bar sections can be between 3mm to 20mm thick and round bar can be from 3mm to well over 100mm **diameter**. Wire thickness is measured in mm or gauge.

> **Q7** Explain the difference between bars, tubes and rods.

Tube and box sections are a little more complicated to order as you need to decide on the **wall thickness** that you require. Too thin a wall section could mean a product lacks strength and too thick could add unnecessary weight and cost to a product.

Wall thickness is often measured in millimetres; however, traditionally thickness is known as **gauge** and many metals are still sold by gauge. From the chart you will see that as the gauge number increases the wall thickness actually decreases, making gauge 10 around 3mm thick.

Imperial gauge	Imperial conversion	Metric sheet equivalent
10	3.25mm	3.0mm
12	2.64mm	2.5mm
14	2.03mm	2.0mm

The cross-sectional area of a stock form is the area of the shape revealed when you cut through a part, just like the slice created when cutting through a loaf of bread.

The cross-sectional area of a round metal bar or any cylindrical solid can be calculated by finding the area of the circle, $A=\pi r^2$.

The cross-sectional area of a square or rectangular bar is simply the area of the square or rectangle $L \times W$.

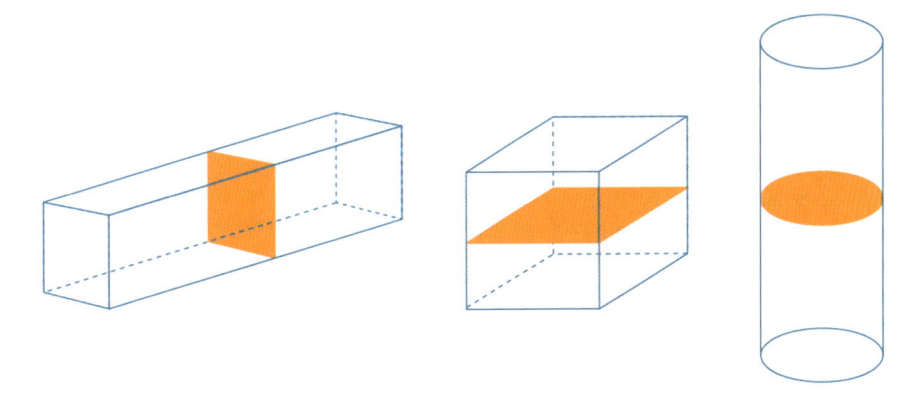

Cross-sectional area of shapes

Q8 Why is it important to calculate the correct wall thickness of a tube for a given task?

Production of stock forms

How stock forms are produced depends on the metal used, dimensions, and profile of the form. Most commonly this is done by **casting**, where molten metal is poured into a die or mould; **extrusion**, where the metal is forced through a shaped die resulting in long, consistent profiles and **powder metallurgy**, where powdered metal is compressed into a mould and then bonded or 'cured' using heat, a process called **sintering**.

Extruded aluminium profiles used in windows and doors

Q9 What properties of metals would make them more suitable for extrusion?

Chapter 33 **Selection of materials and stock forms**

Chapter 34 – Planning and production methods

Objectives

- Be aware of the advantages and disadvantages of different manufacturing processes for various scales of production
- Understand how production aids and quality control procedures improve manufactured products

Marking out metals

When giving the dimensions of a metal part, **tolerances** are often indicated to ensure accuracy and fit. A tolerance is the acceptable margin of error. For example if a steel pin is to be made to fit a hole and it is made too big it will jam in the hole and if it made too small it will fall out. The margin of error may be as little as +/-0.01 mm so the tool used to measure and mark it out must be very accurate.

Reference surfaces or datum points are used to take all other measurements from. Tools should have accurately machined surfaces and calibrated readings.

- Digital callipers are used to measure thickness or gauge and need to be set to zero before use.

- Odd-leg callipers do not have integrated measuring. They are hinged with one straight leg with a sharp end and one bent leg. Odd-leg callipers are used to mark parallel lines by hooking the odd leg over the edge of a metal piece and running the sharp point along its length.

- Scribers are hard, sharp steel tools used to mark a line on a metal surface and are often used with a steel rule or an engineer's square which enable the accurate marking of a 90° angle.

- Micrometres and gauges are used to measure thickness and gauge. Fine pitched threads allow accurate measuring.

- A dial test indictor or DTI uses a probe to test accuracy from a specific reference point.

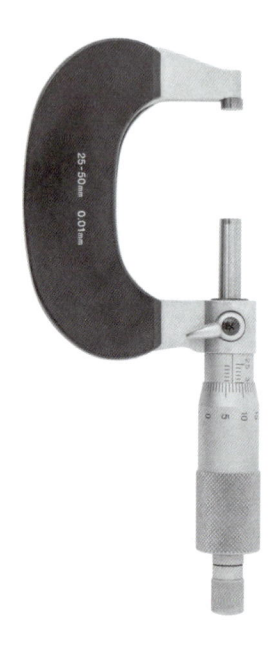

Micrometre

Q1 How might the properties of a scriber be altered to improve its performance?

Accurate measuring, marking and use of tolerances assist efficient cutting which minimises waste and ultimately reduces material costs. Quality control checks are used to ensure the dimensional accuracy of products.

Production aids may also be used to ensure the accurate shaping and machining of metal parts. **Jigs**, **templates**, **patterns**, **fixtures** and **moulds** help manufacturers produce consistent results. These are covered in more detail later in this chapter.

Quality control

Quality control (QC) checks ensure dimensional accuracy is consistent.

A **depth stop** can be found on most pillar drills and can also be fitted to the drill bit itself. The depth of the hole required is set on the gauge, tested once to check that the correct depth has been set, and then all subsequent holes will be the correct depth.

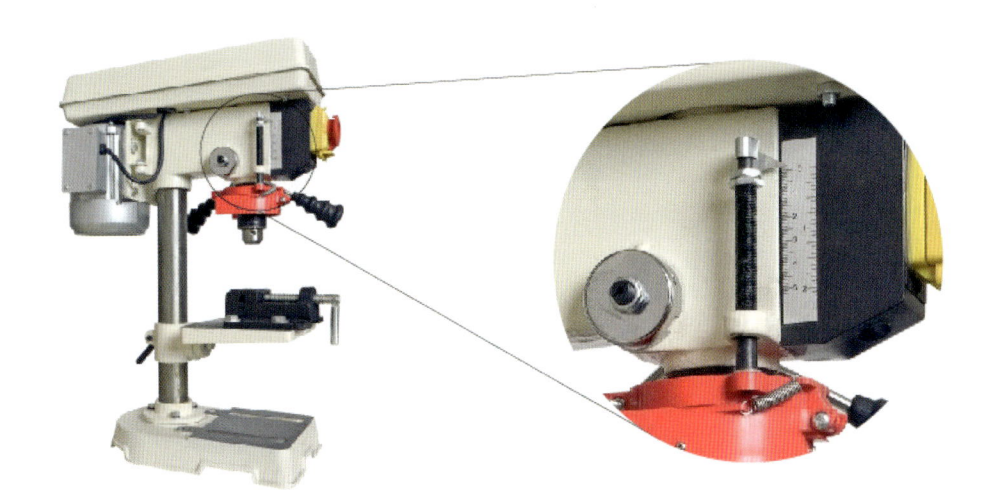

Other quality control tools known as **go/no go fixtures** are available to ensure accuracy and consistency. These tools are set to the specific **tolerance** allowed for a particular component.

Scales of production

Metals are used in every scale of production. **One-off** or **bespoke** production is labour intensive, time consuming and usually results in a more expensive product, however, there is a value to having a product created specifically to your own specifications. Blacksmiths and sculptors use their skills and specialist hand tools to form unique creations.

Forging

Forging is a method of one off production that uses heat to increase the metal's malleability. The metal is then beaten into shape, often over an anvil. Farriers still use this method to shape and fit horse shoes.

Batch production utilises production aides to ensure that the run of products produced are accurate and consistent. A manufacture may use a **jig** to ensure the accurate welding of a right angled joint or a fixture bolted to the bed of a pillar drill to allow repeated drilling of holes.

Templates help ensure consistent shapes and forms are produced. They are usually stored and reused for the next run of similar items.

Commercial casting

Foundries form metal into a multitude of different shapes, sizes, components and parts. Highly skilled workers are able to cast items ranging from small artefacts to huge parts weighing many tonnes. They use the same labour-intensive process as sand casting in the workshop, although on a much larger scale.

Each casting initially needs to have a **pattern** made to precise measurements. Although much of this is now automated using CNC machines, pattern-makers have traditionally hand-made them.

Industrial casting at a foundry

Drop forging

Drop forging is often used in batch production. Instead of beating hot metal by hand, mechanical hammers are repeatedly dropped onto the hot metal billet which is consequently pressed into a die. Whilst this process is automated, skilled workers are often still required to finish the process.

Commercial welding

In batch production, jigs and fixtures are used to ensure that joints are accurate and welds can be repeated consistently. In mass and continuous production, robotic welding arms are used. Integrated, non-destructive testing scans each weld to ensure their integrity.

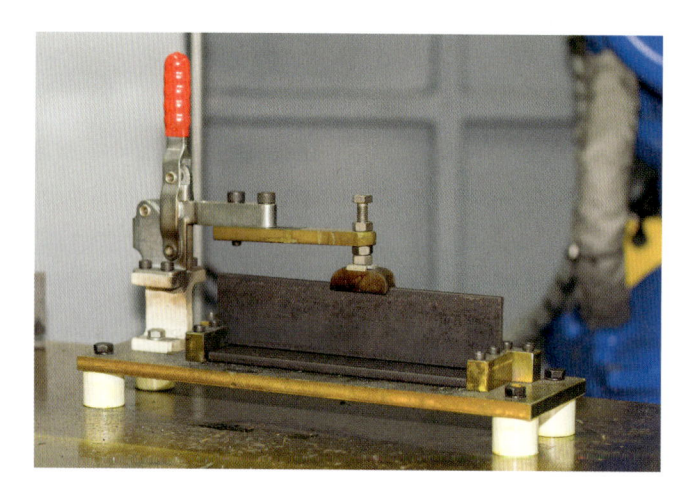

A welding fixture for use in batch production

Computer-aided manufacture CAM

Computer-aided manufacture or **CAM** lends itself to batch, mass and continuous production methods as it enables processes to be repeated accurately and often, and reduces human error.

Machinery including laser cutters, CNC routers, lathes and milling machines read code generated by **CAD** software which then plot an optimum path for the laser or cutting tool to follow. This means that layouts can be maximised and cutting paths can be optimised for speed, cutting lead times and costs.

> **Q2** What are the benefits to the manufacturer of optimising layouts for components needing to be cut?

Mass production methods utilise production lines to maximise efficiency and increase output. The manufacturing and assembly processes are highly automated. However, some operatives are still needed to carry out checks and perform assembly tasks.

In a car production plant some components such as pressed panels are manufactured on site. Other parts and components may be produced in separate cells or off site by other specialist manufacturers and then introduced into the assembly line at the point of need, this is called **sub-assembly**.

Cars held in cradles on an overhead assembly line

Continuous production, also known as **flow production** is used where there is a higher demand, often for products that are seen as single use or disposable, for example, packaging. Like mass production, processes are highly automated, but, in this case, machinery runs 24 hours a day managed by shift-workers. To ensure maximum productivity, lines only stop for annual maintenance.

> **Q3** What manufacturing methods lend themselves to mass and continuous production?

Production aids

Production aids are especially common in batch production and are used to save time and increase accuracy. Production aids include **jigs**, **templates**, **patterns**, **fixtures** and **moulds** – some of these terms are interchangeable and have different meanings in different material areas and industries.

- **Pattern** – a wooden shape used for creating a mould when casting metal - often made as two parts known as a split pattern
- **Mould** – a negative shape which liquid metal is poured into when casting or cold metal can be forced on to under pressure
- **Templates** – used for marking out a shape or profile repeatedly and accurately

Jigs and fixtures safely hold a workpiece in place while being processed.

- **Jigs** – used when repetitive tasks such as cutting, drilling or machining need doing accurately
- **Fixtures** – tend to be larger devices secured in a position to which other devices such as jigs can be fitted

Chapter 35 – Material processing and joining

Objectives

- Understand the application of specialist techniques when manufacturing products
- Be aware of the advantages and disadvantages of specialist techniques
- Be able to select appropriate specialist techniques and joining methods

Manufacturing methods

A range of tools is available to mark out materials, cut them to size, waste them (remove material), shape them and apply a finish.

Before undertaking any activity in a workshop, you need to be aware of the health and safety rules that apply to each of the machines, tools, equipment and materials that you use. Your teacher will guide you in this area, but you must ensure that the correct **personal protective equipment (PPE)** is worn when operating machinery and using tools and equipment.

Cutting and shearing metal

The hacksaw and junior hacksaw are common metal-cutting hand saws that are used for cutting straight lines. The **Abrafile** is a thin, abrasive steel rod that uses the same frame as a **coping saw** or **junior hacksaw**. It enables cuts in any direction to follow curved lines in sheet metal. The hacksaw has a robust blade and can be used for thicker material than the junior hacksaw.

Hacksaw   *Junior hacksaw*   *Abrafile*

Some jobs require a different method of cutting, for example where metal sheet is particularly large and difficult to access or to clamp, or if it is too thin and may become damaged. In this case **metal shears** can be used. Sometimes referred to as 'tin snips', they exert a **shearing force** on the metal sheet and produce a clean cut. Metal shears are available for left and right handed users.

A metal-cutting bandsaw is powered and can be used for straight cuts through thicker section material. **Cutting fluid** will need to be used for most cuts to lubricate and cool the blade which protects it from overheating and becoming blunt prematurely.

Metal-cutting bandsaw

Appropriate PPE needs to be considered when using saws. The metal-cutting band saw can have age restrictions applied to its use; your teacher will advise you on its use in your school.

> **Q1** Research metal cutting saw blades and explain the following terms:
> (a) Tooth pitch (b) Kerf

Drilling

Selecting the correct drill speed helps to avoid overheating the metal workpiece and the drill bit, which could cause it to become blunt quickly. Large drill bits require a slower speed than ones with a smaller diameter. The depth of hole also needs to be considered as you may not want to drill all the way through a piece of metal, therefore you will need to set a depth stop on a pillar drill. The **feed rate** is critical when drilling metal, as applying too much force can put excessive strain on the drill and the drill bit, again causing overheating. To avoid overheating you should use cutting fluid, allowing for a smoother cut to take place. This is especially the case when using large diameter drill bits and when drilling deep holes.

A pillar drill is great for accuracy and it is powerful enough to drill larger holes in thicker metals. A cordless drill may struggle to get through metals other than a fairly thin sheet or bar.

Drill bits used with metal-based materials

Name	Image	Characteristics	Name	Image	Characteristics
Twist drill bit		General purpose bit, can also be used on plastic and wood	Countersink bit		Used to allow countersunk screw or rivet head to be flush with the surface

Twist drills are usually made from high-speed steel (HSS). This is a type of tool steel that is more resistant to overheating than high-carbon steel due to the alloying of other metals such as tungsten and vanadium.

Turning

A centre lathe is used to turn metal, and there are a number of techniques and different cutting tools used for different tasks. The piece of metal to be turned is known as a **billet** and is held in the chuck which is attached to the headstock.

A three-jaw chuck is used for round or hexagonal bar and tube as it is self-centring, and a four-jaw version is used for square and rectangular sections. Special faceplates can be used for other odd shaped billets.

The tailstock can be used to centre longer pieces of bar. This technique stops the billet having excess movement known at chatter. Chatter reduces accuracy and the quality of the cut and finish. The tailstock, fitted with a chuck, can be used for drilling into a billet.

As with drilling and milling, the diameter of the billet needs to be taken into account when working out the correct speed. Larger workpieces generally mean a slower speed – however, it also depends on the type of metal, the cutting technique being used, the depth of cut and the feed rate. Coolant should be applied when necessary to avoid a build-up of friction and heat.

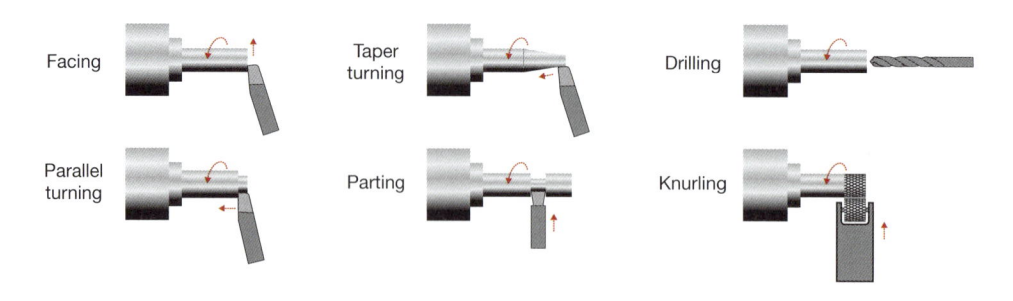

Lathe turning techniques and tools

> **Q2** Which type of turning technique would be used to create a grip on the end of a bar?

Milling

There are two types of mill; a vertical mill and a horizontal mill. The vertical mill is the most common in schools and colleges. The mill is similar to a large pillar drill, with cutters which can cut slots as well as drilling holes. These machines are used for fine and accurate wasting of metal. The workpiece is attached to a moving bed which is driven past the cutter.

Milling cutters

Wasting and abrading by hand

Using hand tools to accurately shape metal takes practice in order to achieve the quality that you need at GCSE level.

Abrading metal to give it a smooth finish can be performed with machines or by hand. Hand abrading using files, emery cloth or wet and dry paper is best for hard-to-reach areas and it also allows you to apply force where it is needed most. (Perhaps to remove cut marks left by a hacksaw or surface scratches.)

Emery cloth and wet and dry paper come in different grades; the grit density (measured in grit per square inch) determines how rough or smooth it is. Coarse emery cloth is 40 to 60 grit and will visibly scratch most metals; 320 grit is very fine. Wet and dry paper starts at 150 grit and is available up to 2000 grit which has a polishing effect as it is so fine.

Wasting and abrading tools and materials

Name	Image	Characteristics	Name	Image	Characteristics
Files		Steel file with serrations on the blade that smooths the surface. Different shaped profiles and grades of cut available	Angle grinder / abrasive wheels		Abrasive wheels cut through and smooth metals. Age restriction on use
Emery cloth		Cloth-backed abrasive material for cleaning up and preparing surface finish, very coarse to fine grades available	Wet and dry paper		Paper-backed abrasive material used to clean up and apply a smooth surface. Used wet or dry, medium to very fine grades, used for 'brushed effect'

Casting

Casting is the process of heating metal into its liquid form and pouring it into a **mould**. The sand-casting process offers the most flexibility and enables complex shapes such as engine parts, vice bodies and traditional British post-boxes to be made.

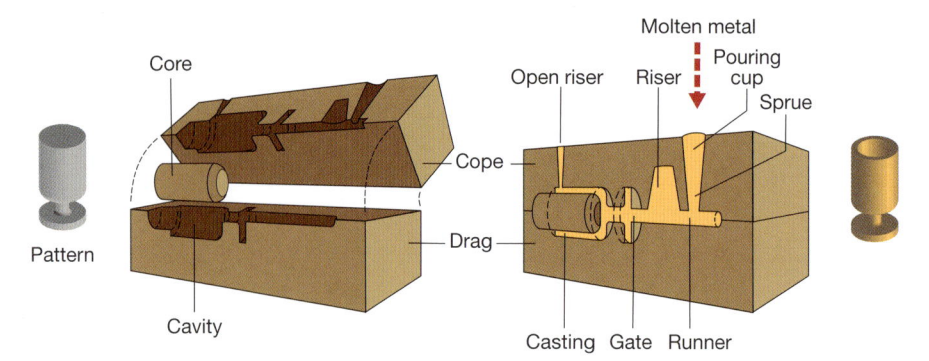

A **pattern** of the finished casting needs to be accurately made first and then placed in the lower part of the flask called the drag. A release agent called parting powder is sprinkled onto the mould and then special sand known as 'green sand' is compacted into the drag and then levelled. The drag is then turned over and the cope is fitted on top.

The second part of the pattern (if required) is located on top of the first and again powdered and packed with green sand. Special channels called runners, risers and sprues are created to allow the molten metal to flow freely around the casting and trapped air to escape. The two parts are separated and the pattern is carefully removed before being put back together.

When casting, the molten metal must be poured in one consistent pour to avoid inconsistencies in the finished casting. Once the casting has cooled it can be removed from the sand. The runners, risers and sprues are be removed before it is cleaned up. Any removed metal can be recycled and the sand can also be used again.

Casting can be very hazardous and great care must be taken throughout the process. The correct PPE must be worn including leather apron and leather gauntlets, appropriate footwear and a face visor. The process gives off harmful gases so should be done in a well ventilated area with good extraction.

> **Q3** Which tools and materials would be best to use to remove the runners and risers and clean up a casting?

Forming and de-forming metals

Pressing, also known as stamping, is the process of using pressure to force a cutting or forming die onto sheet metal in order to cut out a **blank**, **punch** a hole or create a shaped form. A machine called a press, often powered by hydraulics, forces the die to perform its specific task.

A variety of procedures can be performed by this method including:

Blanking – cutting out flat sheets to make 'blanks' ready to be formed into another shape

Punching – cutting out a hole or shape in a blank or sheet

Bending – deforming the sheet or blank along a straight line

Drawing – the sheet or blank is stretched or 'drawn' into a different shape

Embossing – a die with a shallow impression is pressed into the sheet or blank and leaves a decorative raised profile

With punching, the ejected material is scrap. With blanking, the punched sheet metal is scrap and the ejected material becomes the work for the next stage of the manufacturing process.

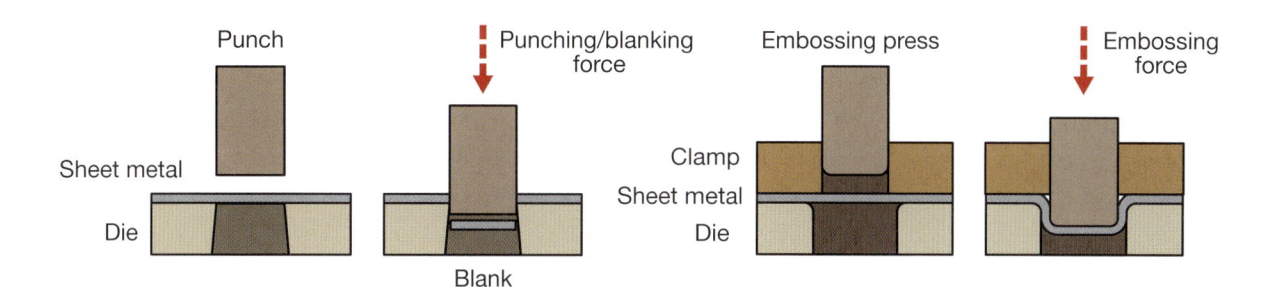

Q4 Which pressing procedures are used to produce the curved fork pictured from a flat sheet? Justify your answer.

Joining metals

Rivets

Rivets are used to join two or more pieces of metal together and are often used on sheet metals to create a very strong **semi-permanent fixing**. They are heavily used in the aircraft, shipbuilding and automobile industries as they avoid the need for welding, which can warp and twist delicate sheet metal due to the heat.

Rivets are available in steel, aluminium, copper and brass and come in different lengths and diameters. There are also a number of different head types depending on the task and the finish required.

There are two main types; cold-formed rivets and pop rivets.

Riveted aluminium aircraft panels

The **pop rivet** is the simplest type to use and requires a tool called a pop rivet gun. As pressure is applied to the handles of the tool, the pop rivet domes over and the shaft 'pops' off leaving the deformed rivet holding the materials together. Pop riveting only needs access from one side making it easier to use where access is limited or awkward.

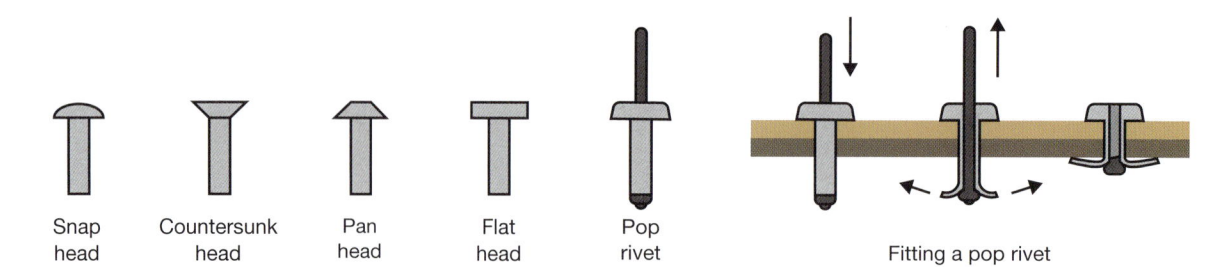

Snap head   Countersunk head   Pan head   Flat head   Pop rivet   Fitting a pop rivet

Cold-formed rivets use a tool called a snap which helps to set the rivet in place while the other end is domed over to form the joint. This can also be formed as a countersunk finish to create a smooth surface.

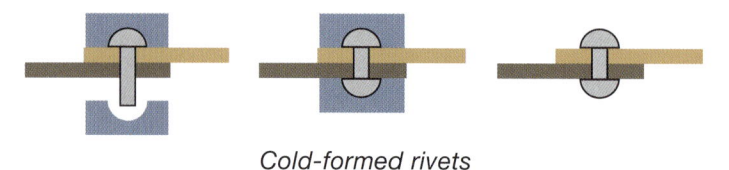

Cold-formed rivets

Welding

There are a few different types of welding but they all involve fusing together two metals of the same type using a filler. This means that both adjoining surfaces partially melt together becoming one piece. The joint is as strong as the parent material.

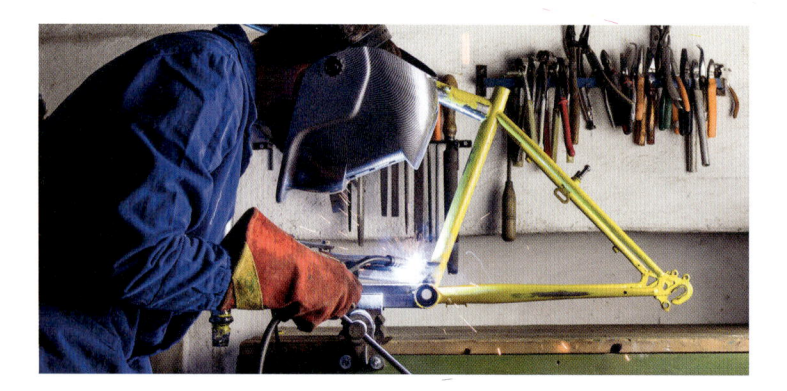

Common welding methods are **oxyacetylene** which is a very hot gas flame, MIG (metal inert gas) and TIG (tungsten inert gas). **MIG** and **TIG** are both electric arc welding methods, where a very powerful electric current is used to create the heat.

Brazing

Brazing is a process of permanently joining two pieces of metal together through heating by adding a filler material called **spelter**. The joint is first cleaned with emery cloth to degrease and remove any rust or oxide. Then **flux** is added all around the joint to stop oxidation during the heating process and to improve the flow of the spelter around the joint. The joint is evenly heated with a gas torch to melt the spelter as it is applied to the joint. If the joint has an even and close fit, then **capillary action** will assist the spelter to flow along the joint. The joint can then be quenched and cleaned.

Brazing differs from welding in that the two base metals are not melted enough to fuse, but are bonded together by the filler material, similar to glueing two materials together. Welding also uses a filler material but it is the same as the material being welded, known as the 'parent material'.

Q5 What could potentially happen if no flux was added to a joint before brazing?

Q6 Which is the strongest permanent joining method: brazing or welding? Justify your answer.

Soldering

Like welding and brazing, soldering is another permanent joining method. There are two types of soldering, **soft soldering**, which is most commonly used in plumbing and circuit boards, and **hard soldering** or silver soldering used in jewellery making and silversmithing.

Solder melts at a lower temperature than the brazing filler rod, spelter, and so soldered joints are not as mechanically strong.

An electrician uses soft soldering to repair a motherboard

Silver solder can be alloyed with other metals to produce solders with different melting points. This enables a jewellery maker to solder a number of joints in close proximity to one and other without the first ones melting and springing apart.

Tapping and threading

Taps and **dies** are used to create temporary joints. Tapping is the process of creating an internal thread and requires the metal part to be pre-drilled. A set of three sequential taps are used to cut the thread, a taper, plug and bottoming tap. Each one is held in a **tap wrench** which enables the user to exert rotational pressure.

Tapping a hole in a stainless-steel block

Cutting an external thread using a die in a die stock

External threads are cut using a die in a **die stock** which enables the die to be rotated down the workpiece. When both tapping and threading, it is good practice to use a **cutting compound** to lubricate the tools and to make one turn forward and then half a turn back. This clears the swarf created in cutting the thread. When threading, the die stock must be held perpendicular to the workpiece otherwise the thread will not be straight, which is known as a **drunken thread**.

> **Q7** What are the roles of the tap wrench and die stock?

Machine screws

Machine screws differ from wood screws by having a finer thread and a parallel shank with no point on the end. They are available in many different lengths, diameters and thread pitches.

Machine screws are available in different driving methods. The most common are slotted, Phillips and Pozidriv® although Allen key and Torx® drive are becoming more widely available.

Nuts and bolts

Like machine screws, nuts and bolts are available in many different lengths, diameters and thread pitches. Bolts come fully threaded or partially threaded; the unthreaded part is called the shank.

The shank has two uses; firstly, it may support a moving or rotating part, for example a child's swing. The shank would create less friction and reduce the shearing force applied to it. Secondly, the length of the shank reduces the elasticity of the bolt and certain engineering tasks may require greater or lesser levels of elasticity to perform efficiently.

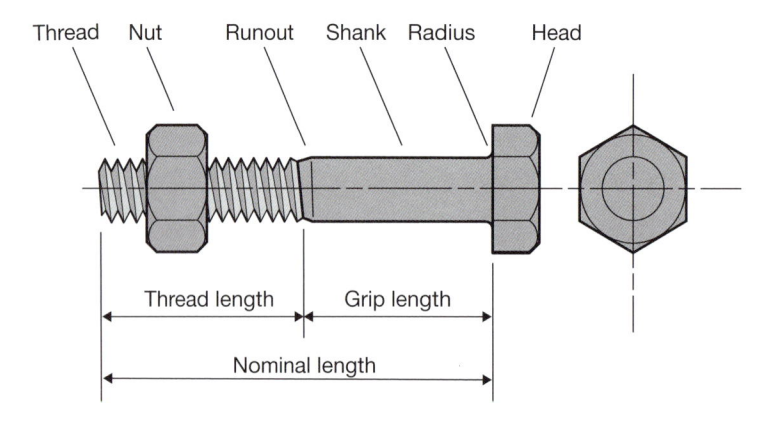

Most nuts and bolts come with hexagonal heads although there are many varieties depending on the task. Some are decorative and some are functional.

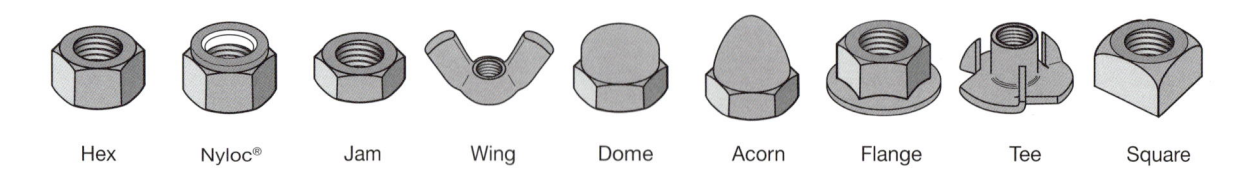

Hex, Nyloc®, Jam, Wing, Dome, Acorn, Flange, Tee, Square

> **Q8** Justify which type of nut would be best used for:
> (a) Children's garden play equipment such as a climbing frame
> (b) Quickly adjusting the height of a music stand

Common types of metal fixings

Name	Image	Characteristics	Name	Image	Characteristics
Nut		Usually a hexagonal profile used on bolts and machine screws to apply pressure	Nyloc		Single use vibration resistant nut that stays in position, nylon insert tightens up on thread
Bolt		Usually a hexagonal profile used with a nut to apply pressure	Grub screw		Headless screw with sharp point used to secure items such as a door handle to a shaft
Machine screw		Many different driving methods and profiles, very versatile	Snap rivet, cold-formed		Semi-permanent joining of two or more metal parts, access to both sides needed
Pop rivet		Semi-permanent joining of two or more pieces of metal, only one-sided access needed	Washer		Used with machine screws, nuts and bolts to spread the load, some prevent loosening

Adhesives

Whilst not normally associated with joining metals, there are applications where adhesives are the only option, for example where proximity to electrics or flammable materials makes joining using heat impossible.

Epoxy resin is a two-part adhesive; when the resin and the hardener are mixed in equal parts, the hardener acts as a catalyst and within minutes the mix cures hard. Because it does not set instantaneously, the pieces being joined usually need to be clamped whilst the resin cures.

Contact adhesives do not form as strong a join and therefore are usually used where larger surfaces are to be joined, e.g. sheet materials. Contact adhesives, which are also known as grab and impact adhesives, should always be applied to both surfaces and left to go tacky before joining. Positioning is key as once the two surfaces make contact the bond is instant.

> **Q9** How should metal surfaces be prepared before applying epoxy resin to ensure a strong joint?

Chapter 36 – Finishing

Objectives

- Be able to select appropriate treatments and finishes and understand their application
- Be aware of the advantages and disadvantages of finishing techniques and preservation methods

Metal surface treatments and finishes

The reasons for applying a finish to metals fall into two main areas; protection and aesthetics. Most ferrous metals last longer if they have a finish applied to them as this helps to prevent corrosion.

Aesthetics can mean colouring by **painting**, **powder coating**, **anodising** or **electroplating** with a desired finish such as chrome, nickel, bronze, silver or gold. Metal can be enhanced to give it a sheen, shine or even a matt surface finish by lacquering or blasting. It can even be coated in plastic.

Protection can mean making it waterproof, less prone to rust and other forms of corrosion and oxidation. It can also be made tougher so it resists knocks and bumps.

Preparation

Metals need to be prepared before they can take a finish or treatment. If the metal substrate isn't clean and free from rust, dirt and grease then the finish will not adhere and so will not function properly to protect the metal underneath.

Various methods can be used to prepare metals for finishing. New bare metal may simply be wiped down with a solvent or detergent based degreaser.

If there is an existing finish, this is usually removed using solvents and then the piece can be shot or sand blasted to remove any residual paint, rust or loose material. In the workshop this can be done using emery cloth.

Often a metal surface needs to be made slightly rough before coating. The rough surface is known as a **key** and ensures that the finish is able to grip.

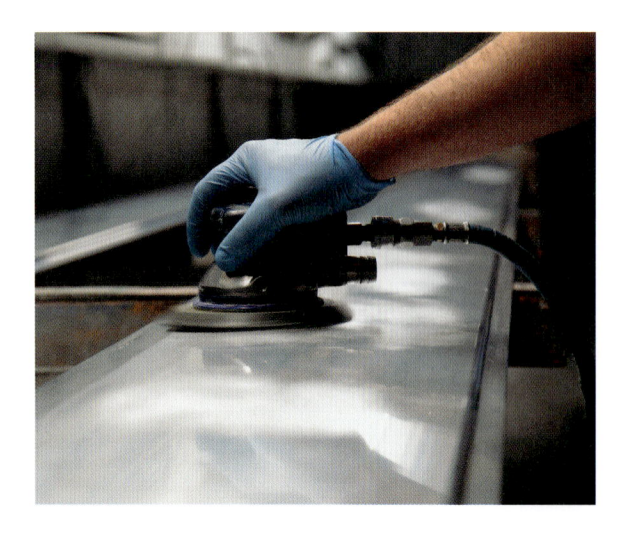

Using an orbital sander to prepare a metal panel

Shot blasting industrial beams before painting

Finishes will give best results if the work area is sufficiently prepared. This means ensuring that there is adequate ventilation or extraction, that the temperature is appropriate and that if working outside, there is protection from wind, rain and direct sunlight. Some paints and varnishes only perform within strict temperature parameters. The area must also be clean and free of dust particles.

You should ensure that the area is either screened off or that any surrounding objects are covered to protect from over spray or splash.

It is a good idea to use a check list as thorough preparation will give the best results.

- ✓ Check that the workpiece is clean and free of debris
- ✓ Check that you have the correct personal protective equipment readily available
- ✓ Check that the work area is clean, ventilated, well lit and protected
- ✓ Check that you have a sufficient supply of the correct finishing products
- ✓ Check there is appropriate storage for the finishing product after use

> **Q1** Why should most professional paint finishes not be applied in extremely cold conditions?

Common protections and finishes for metal-based products

Metal finishes vary dramatically in finish and method of application. A number of specialist techniques are on offer depending on the desired finish and level of protection required. Many paint-on and spray-on products are oil or solvent-based and are not very environmentally friendly. They can contain high levels of **volatile organic compounds (VOCs)**. This means that they give off fumes that are considered hazardous to health and should be used according to the manufacturer's instructions – normally wearing a mask in a well-ventilated area.

Respirator with detatchable filters

> **Q2** Why is a dust mask insufficient protection when using products containing VOCs?

Name	Image	Characteristics	Name	Image	Characteristics
Plastic dip coating		Metal is heated and dipped in powdered plastic that bonds, protects, insulates and adds grip and aesthetics	Powder coating		Electrostatically applied dry powder paint that is cured by heat and bonds to metal, tough, even finish
Metal laquer		A clear varnish-like finish, applied to metal (often sprayed) to protect and create a sheen, gloss to matt finish available	Metal primer and paint		Special primer and paint used to protect metal from the elements
Hot blackening		A black oxide finish is obtained by dipping into heated tanks of chemicals and oil	Electro-plating and anodising		Both use an electric current. Plating adds a layer of another metal to the surface. Anodising changes the surface structure
Polishing and brushing		A natural finish for aesthetics, the surface is buffed to a mirror finish or uniformly scratched	Galvanizing		Zinc is coated over steel products to protect from corrosion. Hot-dipped or electroplated
Rust stabiliser		A liquid painted on to rusty steel to harden any corrosion and prevent further occurrence	Shot / sand blasting		Particles of sand or lead shot are fired under pressure to remove layers of paint or to create an aesthetic effect

Aluminium anodising process

The aluminium is first prepared by cleaning. It is then chemically etched for a matt finish, or chemically brightened for a smooth finish before being anodised to form the aluminium oxide layer. It is dyed to the required colour and finally sealed to stop the oxide layer from being porous and to prevent colour fade.

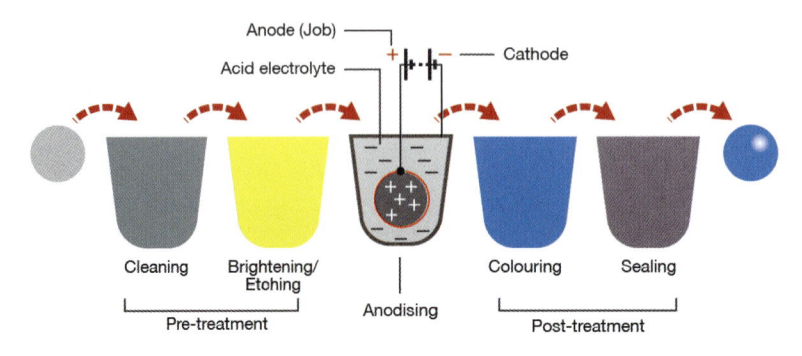

Exercises

1. The materials that products are made from are chosen because of their characteristics. Figure 1 shows a table of products.

   For each of the products shown, give **one** property of the material it is made from that makes it suitable for the product. The first one has been done for you.

Product	Description of product	Property
	Stainless steel juice extractor	*Corrosion resistant*
	7000 series aluminium laptop casing	[1]
	Titanium dental implants	[1]
	Tungsten tipped circular saw blade	[1]

2. Choose **one** of the products in the table below.

Products		
Low carbon steel bucket	Aluminium travel mug	Handles of a pair of high carbon steel garden shears

   (a) Name **one** surface finish or treatment that can be applied to the material to enhance the functional or mechanical properties. [1]

   (b) Use notes and sketches to show how the surface finish or treatment can be changed. [4]

3. Give **two** different processes that are used to manufacture metal products. [2]

4. Iron is a ferrous metal.

   (a) State **one** geographical region iron would be sourced from. [1]

   (b) Name **one** stock form in that iron would be available in. [1]

   (c) Explain **one** difference between ferrous and non-ferrous metals. [2]

   (d) Explain **one** way in which in which iron can be modified to improve its properties. [2]

5. When selecting metals for the manufacture of a product, designers should consider the sustainability and recyclability of any metals used.

   Study the aluminum foil pie tin above.

   Discuss the sustainability of aluminium for use as a takeaway food container, in use and end of life. [6]

6. Describe **one** method that is used during the production of products in quantity to ensure that dimensional accuracy is maintained. [2]

7. The metal name plate below has been mounted with screws.

   (a) Name an appropriate semi-permanent fixing method for joining the metal name plate to a metal cabinet assuming you can only access one side of the metals to be joined. [1]

   (b) Use notes and sketches to show how the process named in part (a) above is carried out. [4]

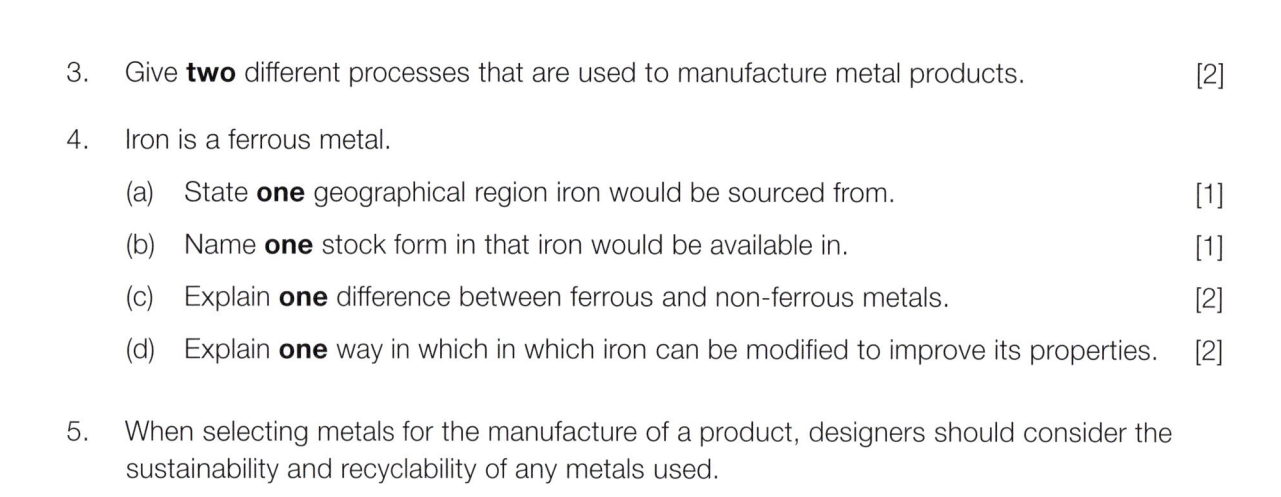

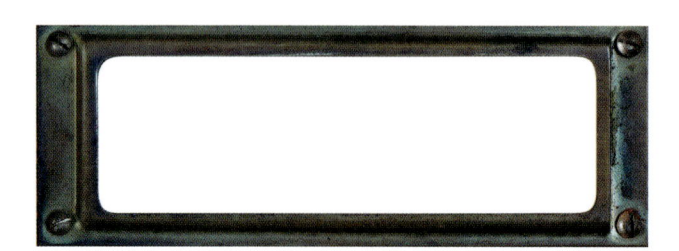

Section 6-3
Papers and boards

In this section:

Chapter 37	Sources, origins and sustainability	186
Chapter 38	Physical and working properties	190
Chapter 39	Selection of materials and stock forms	192
Chapter 40	Stock forms, planning and production methods	200
Chapter 41	Material processing	208
Chapter 42	Finishing	213
Exercises		216

Chapter 37 – Sources, origins and sustainability

Objectives

- Understand the sources and origins of papers and boards
- Know about different types of papers and boards and their applications
- Explain social, cultural and ethical factors in the production and use of papers and boards

Sources of papers and boards

Paper and board are made from a pulp which is a mixture of cellulose fibres and up to 99% water. The cellulose fibres are usually derived from finely shredded wood, but other types of fibres such as hemp, flax, bamboo, sugarcane and straw can also be used. Wood generally gives the best results and both deciduous and coniferous trees can be used, with fast growing softwoods such as spruce and fir being the most common.

Much of the world's pulp, paper and board production comes from China, the United States and Japan. Germany is the largest paper producer in Europe, and Finland and Sweden are the largest producers of paper pulp. Some specialist papers are produced elsewhere; rice paper for example is mainly produced in China and Vietnam.

Pulp – A mechanical process converts debarked logs into fine chips which are then added to a chemical solution and cooked in large tanks under pressure to make the paper pulp. Depending on the desired colour of the finished product, the resulting fibrous liquid is then bleached or dyed accordingly.

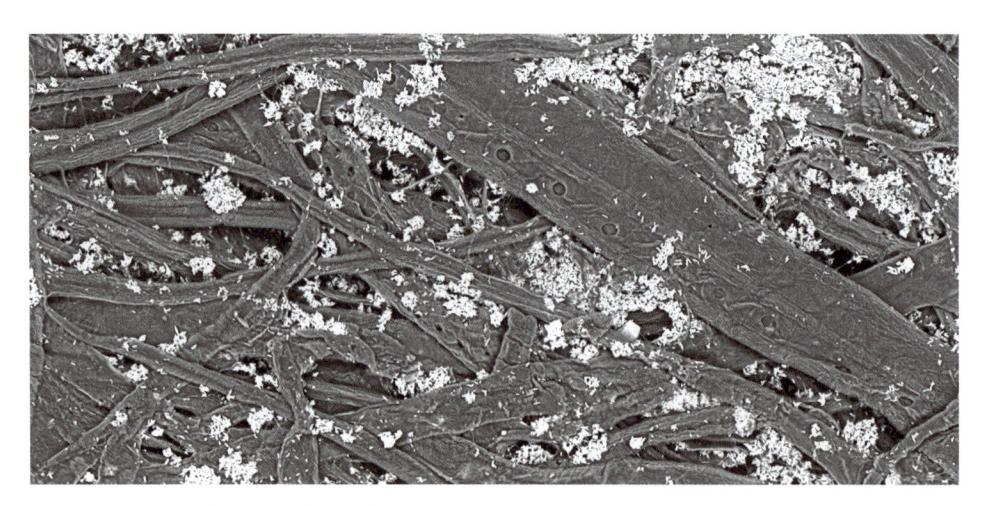

Paper fibres shown under an electron microscope

Sizing – The pulp is then beaten with other chemicals or additives according to the required finish. This process is called sizing. Sizing stops the paper from being so absorbent, thereby allowing it to be printed, photocopied or painted on. Paper with little sizing is very absorbent, such as toilet tissue or kitchen paper.

Converting pulp to paper – The pulp is fed onto a mesh conveyor belt which allows much of the water to drain away. It then passes onto a series of rollers which squeeze out any excess water. Next, it goes through a series of drying rollers and onto a final set of rollers called calender rollers. These give the paper the desired finish, for example, satin or matt. Sometimes a final coating or sizing is added before the paper is cut to size.

Draining a handmade paper sheet through a fine mesh frame mould

Mechanical paper production

> **Q1** What level of sizing would paper intended for the cover of a glossy magazine be likely to receive?

Sustainable paper production

The UK uses over 12 million tonnes of paper every year. It takes roughly 25 trees to produce one tonne of paper. On average, each person in the UK uses around 200kg of paper products per annum, equivalent to about five trees. As trees grow, they take in carbon dioxide (CO_2) and give out oxygen, but a lot of energy is required to chop them down and make paper. Trees are a renewable resource and if forests are sustainably managed, producers can meet the high demand for the raw materials for paper pulp.

Paper production is both water and energy intensive and creates waste that must be treated to prevent water and soil contamination. Many paper producers now recycle waste water, clean it and reuse it in the pulping process. If waste paper is sent to a landfill site it decomposes, giving off a greenhouse gas called methane. It is therefore better to recycle it.

Recycling paper and board is easy, and the amount being recycled continues to rise. When paper is recycled it is graded. High quality glossy magazines produce higher quality recycled paper products than newspapers or cardboard. Twice as much is paid for recycled white office paper waste than for cardboard. Recycled paper uses between 40-70% less energy to produce than paper made from virgin pulp.

> **Q2** What are the benefits of recycling paper and board?

Q3 What are the negative effects of sending paper and board to landfill sites?

Q4 To help picture what 200kg of photocopy paper would look like, calculate how tall a stack A4 paper would be if you placed one ream on top of another. One ream (500 sheets) of 80 gsm A4 photocopy paper weighs 2.5kg and is 55mm tall.

Ecological footprint

Paper is so widely used day to day that we may not always consider the environmental impact of this omnipresent material. The advent of mechanisation meant that harvesting, processing, production and printing were made faster, more efficient and resulted in a material that was cheap and abundant.

All these industries have left their **carbon footprint** however in recent years the paper industry has sought to take a more sustainable approach.

Harvesting

The vast majority of the paper we use is made from wood fibre. This means the paper industry is reliant on forestry to maintain the supply chain. Unfortunately, where there is demand there is often a rush to meet that demand and this can lead to practices such as illegal logging. This has resulted in deforestation and the loss of vast swathes of valuable forest habitat as well as widespread devastation of communities and a loss of biodiversity.

To ensure the industry has a sustainable resource to draw on, some managed forests are grown solely to supply the paper and board industry. Other sources include thinnings from managed forests grown for timber or processed recycled timber.

Processing, wastage and pollution

Processing the wood to obtain the fibrous pulp is an energy and water intensive process. Harmful chemicals are used to break down the lignin in wood and during the bleaching process; these chemicals can find their way into water courses if not carefully filtered from the waste water. Waste water from the paper processing industry can also contain chemicals like chlorine and organic matter and it is hard to make it safe for disposal. Processing plants that clean and treat their water to a level where it can be recycled within the plant and used again in the paper making process may take advantage of cost savings.

Fibrous raw material being processed at a paper mill that reuses waste water

Transportation

Any transportation of materials or products, whether by truck or, if sourced abroad, by container ship, requires the use of fossil fuels and increases product miles. This causes CO_2 emissions which are a significant contributing factor in global warming.

Social footprint

A **social footprint** is a measure of the impact that a company's social policies have on its employees, partners or subcontractors and on society as a whole. Companies have an obligation to protect the environment by reducing their ecological footprint wherever possible, but they also have a duty to consider the effect that company policies have on all those affected.

Most developed societies have a set of rules that govern working conditions for employees, but many countries do not protect their workers to the same extent. Much of the planet's workforce has little or no protection against their employers; they can be paid very low wages and have to work excessively long hours in poor conditions. One of the biggest problems workers face is the lack of health and safety provision to protect them from danger whilst at work. This may include unsafe levels of light or dust, inadequate PPE, poorly maintained machinery and the structural integrity of buildings.

Brand identity

As manufactures rethink their packaging options they also must consider how they maintain brand identity. For decades, companies have used packaging to increase consumer awareness of their brands using recognisable logos, marketing messages and colour schemes. As consumers we are susceptible to this, and if a campaign is successful, it will encourage consumerism and consequently, can increase waste.

Many companies use **market research** and **trend forecasting** to predict future trends in consumer demand. If there is a trend towards using less packaging, companies can maintain a positive brand identity by being seen to respond to this.

Examples include the trend to move from plastic drinking straws towards paper alternatives, or coffee chains moving from single use cups to reusable ones. Single use cups are usually made from laminates which are very difficult to separate and recycle. They generally end up in landfill. Increasingly consumers have called for something to be done about this and in response, Bio PLA paper cups made from corn starch have been developed. Coffee shops are also offering incentives to encourage the use of reusable cups.

> **Q5** What type of incentives do you think coffee retailers might offer customers to encourage the use of reusable cups?

Chapter 38 – Physical and working properties

Objectives

- Be able to discriminate between, and select from, a range of different papers and boards
- Understand the advantages, disadvantages and applications of papers and boards
- Be aware of the physical characteristics and working properties of papers and boards

Physical characteristics and working properties

How papers and boards look and feel depends on the physical characteristics they display.

- **Transparency** and **opacity** – these describe how see-through the paper or board is.
- **Density** – this is reflected in the weight of the paper and its absorbency, the denser the paper is, the less absorbent it will be.
- **Texture** – papers and boards may be smooth, rough or embossed depending on the fibres and manufacturing processes used.

The working properties of a paper or board affect the way it behaves when used. Depending on the application certain working properties will be more important than others.

A paper used for photo-quality printing needs a smooth **surface finish** so that the photo is crisp and clear. Copier or bond paper used for printed text must also be **flexible** to allow it to be fed through the printer and have relatively low **absorbency** so that the ink does not bleed; papers used for printing are said to have good **printability**.

A watercolour artist may require a slightly textured paper that is a heavier **weight**, commonly 300–600 gsm to prevent buckling when wet, and for it to be fairly absorbent, providing a good key for their paint. Boards used in single use packaging products need to offer a range of working properties including a good surface finish and printability. Additionally they need the flexibility to allow for folding or creasing, low absorbency to prevent leakage, and increasingly, **biodegradability**, to ensure that when they are disposed of, they can degrade naturally.

> **Q1** What common DIY application requires a paper that can be smooth or textured and is fairly absorbent on one face?

> **Q2** What type of paper, commonly used in schools, needs to have good transparency?

Uses of common papers and boards

In addition to the detailed list of papers and boards in Chapter 17, you need to know about the other common types listed below. The weights and measurements of paper and board are also covered in Chapter 17.

Additional papers

Name	Appearance	Image	Characteristics	Example uses
Bond paper	Often brilliant white but also available in a range of colours, smooth, sometimes features a watermark		80–160 gsm. Fairly dense, high quality, made from bleached rag pulp, originally used for bonds and deeds	Printing, handwritten letters, important documents
Heat transfer paper / Sublimation paper	A white paper coated on one side only with a film layer, very smooth		45–140 gsm. High quality, low absorbency, holds ink on the surface which is transferred by using a heated press	Printing onto a number of substrates including fabric, ceramics, plastic and glass

Additional boards

Name	Appearance	Image	Characteristics	Example uses
Foil-lined board	Smooth and white on one face, metallic and shiny on the other		From 240 gsm. Foil creates a moisture barrier, board adds rigidity	Takeaway food packaging, cake boards, party plates
Tetra Pak® Packaging laminate	A patented six-layer laminate that has a smooth outer surface. It's fairly thick and the layers can be seen when cut or torn		An outer polyethylene layer protects a second printable paperboard layer. Inner layers act as a barrier to heat, light, air and contaminates	Used in cartons for food and drink, mostly liquids

Packaging laminates are created by adding layers of different material that improve both the physical and the working properties of the finished materials. **Paperboard** is a lamination of paper and board used to create a strong material, thicker and more rigid than paper alone. It is used as an art material, in book covers and packaging, and is smooth and printable. **Polyethylene** is often added to paper and board used to create an impermeable layer, this is used in food and drink packaging as a barrier to moisture, preventing leakage. When **aluminium foil** is laminated with paper, it creates an opaque material that also acts as a thermal insulator and as an oxygen and biological barrier. It is often used in bags and containers for hot food.

Owing to their varied properties, from lengthening shelf life to helping to maintain nutrients and taste, packaging laminates are wildly used; however, because they consist of layers of different materials they can pose a problem to recyclers. Not all local authorities will recycle these laminates. Some kerbside schemes and recycling centres will take them and increasingly manufacturers, including Tetra Pak®, provide guidelines for recycling on their websites.

Chapter 39 – Selection of materials and stock forms

Objectives

- Know and understand the way in which the selection of papers and boards is influenced
- Understand the impact of forces and stresses and how they can be reinforced and stiffened
- Know the commercial stock forms, types and sizes of materials in order to calculate quantities

Selecting suitable papers and boards

Which type of paper or board to use for a product depends on a number of factors, including:

Aesthetics	Cost	Weight
Size of product	Size of material available	Desired properties
Where it will be used	Required finish	Printability
Stability	Availability of stock	How long it is to last

Suitability

When deciding which paper or board to use, a manufacturer will consider its suitability for each specific application. There are several key factors to consider including longevity – how long that product is expected to last and the circumstances in which the product will be used. Board or packaging laminate used for a takeaway cartons will likely be '**single use**'; it therefore needs to effectively hold the food, keep it warm and prevent it leaking for as long as it is in transit and before it is served. In contrast, a **Tetra Pak**® carton containing milk or juice needs to keep the contents fresh and sealed in until at least the use by date, which could be several years.

Aesthetics and surface graphics

Aesthetics play a significant part in creating our first impression of a product. Papers and boards can vary in colour, texture and form and each of these factors will affect the way a product is perceived. A book with a coloured, embossed paperboard cover, and pages made from 120 gsm silk white paper, may initially give the impression of being a more valuable product than a paperback with 80 gsm ivory matt paper, regardless of what is printed inside.

Form

Papers and boards are available in a range of weights, thicknesses and stock forms. The form of the paper or board selected for an application will depend on the intended construction methods and the required shape of the finished product. For example, a packing box constructed from a flat net will be made from corrugated cardboard sheet which needs to crease and fold cleanly. The material must be rigid enough to give the box structural integrity whilst being pliable enough to construct without cracking.

Texture

Texture may depend either on the fibres used in the manufacture of the paper or on a treatment it has undergone. Papers made from bleached wood pulp may be very smooth in contrast to papers made from flax or hemp. A textured finish can add a home-crafted touch and handmade papers are becoming very popular for cards and gifts.

Colour

Colour is added to paper pulp during the manufacturing process. Papers and boards are available in a wide spectrum of colours, however, the paper we consume most of is simply white. Colour, or lack of it, can make type more impactful and different colours can convey different impressions depending on the products application or target audience. Packaging made from brown paper and board for example may seem to indicate recyclability, modesty and social consience whereas packaging made from a gold foil laminated board might be seen as decadent and expensive even if both packages have the same contents.

> **Q1** What paper stock would you choose to package some new jewellery or hand-baked bread?

Surface graphics

Any paper or board intended to display surface graphics must do so effectively and should be able to be printed on by whatever means is appropriate. Test runs ensure that both text and images are sharp and clear with no bleeding or smudging.

> **Q2** What properties does photographic paper have that ensures the surface graphics are sharp and bleed free?

Environmental factors and genetic engineering

Understanding the lifecycle of a product helps manufacturers respond to environmental factors that may contribute to its sustainability. Ideally raw materials should be ethically sourced and their processing and production methods evaluated, so their negative environmental impact is reduced. The resulting materials and products should also be able to biodegrade or be recycled easily.

Much of the paper we use is made from wood pulp. The Forestry Stewardship Council (**FSC**) and the Programme for the Endorsement of Forest Certification (**PEFC**) enable manufacturers to check the source of their wood comes from sustainably managed forests. The FSC also encourages the employment of local workers, the provision of training, correct safety equipment and a fair salary.

As part of the processes of turning wood chip into paper pulp, **lignin** has to be removed from the fibres. Lignin forms an integral part of the organic structure of the tree, however, it increases the acidity within paper and as the paper ages it becomes brittle and yellow. Paper which is low in, or free of, lignin is less prone to yellowing and lasts much longer. The removal of lignin is a costly, energy intensive process which involves using hazardous chemicals and produces waste.

Increasingly, genetic engineering is used in trees grown for the paper industry to reduce their lignin which in turn reduces the need for chemical processing and ultimately saves money. Genetic engineering is also used to create faster and straighter growing trees capable of withstanding different climates and disease.

Q3 What disadvantages might there be in reducing the lignin in trees?

Availability and costs

Before a manufacturer commits to a production run, they will need to ensure that all materials are readily available and that they are available in the stock forms required. Continuity of supply is vital, especially where products will be mass produced.

Rolls of paper in a print company warehouse

Decisions regarding costs are also made prior to production and include the purchase of raw materials and finishes, manufacturing processes and scale of production. Purchase planning involves an evaluation of materials needed including the quality, appropriate stock sizes (that enable efficient cutting and minimise waste) and the availability and cost of any specialist materials. There may be pros and cons that need to be weighed up, for example using recycled paper pulp from over virgin pulp can reduce costs, but quality will suffer as a result since paper products degrade as they are recycled. These costs will be calculated, and economy of scale considered prior to order.

Like other materials, the commodity price of the raw material used to make papers and board fluctuates, therefore, if the price is low it may be economically wise to procure more stock with a view to continued production. There is a risk that if an order is cancelled you will be left with excess stock that takes up warehouse space.

Other considerations include the set-up and running costs of plant and machinery, especially where specialist decorative techniques are used. Dies used for cutting or embossing are made to a client's specification, are costly to produce and may not then be re-used once the order is fulfilled so these must be incorporated into costings.

Social influences and ethical considerations

Products made from papers and boards are often used to display imagery and marketing information. Whether retail packaging, magazines or advertising hoardings, manufacturers should ensure that the imagery and wording used does not cause offence, incite hatred or exploit any religious, ethnic or social groups. Manufacturers need to consider the cultural and social expectations of their target audience.

All products are subject to trends and fashion and those made from papers and boards are no exception. Nowadays there are many more ways for companies to carry out market research so they can more easily design for specific target markets, age and social groups. Imagery, colour and text are all used in this way but, whilst it is legitimate to design to appeal to one section of society, that does not mean it is acceptable to alienate or offend another section. Designers and manufactures must therefore take care; if producing a set of instructions for a product that will be sold internationally they could ensure they were translated into many languages. This, however, is not always practical owing to the number of possible languages so instead they may consider using predominantly pictorial directions to ensure the document is accessible to all.

Colours can also cause confusion. In many eastern and western cultures colours have different meanings and connotations for example in many western cultures, the colour purple represents wealth and royalty, however in some Asian and Latin American cultures it represents death and mourning.

A Japanese decorative envelope for wrapping money given at a funeral

The demand for choice and variety, especially in products often seen as disposable or single use, has been driven by the consumer society and the effects of mass production. When manufactured in greater numbers, a product becomes cheaper and thus more accessible to the mass market; this can devalue the product in the eyes of the consumer. Some manufactures have reacted to this trend by attempting to add value to their products. Making the consumer aware of the sustainability issues relating to a product can help achieve this and many companies will display regulatory information like the FSC mark and even information about the source. They may also print advice on sustainable disposal and recycling drawing the consumers attention to the real value of the material.

Reinforcing and stiffening

Papers and boards are subject to forces and stresses in everyday use. Simply being stored on a roll, paper is in **tension** and **compression**. A wet paper towel is subject to **torsional** forces when we wring it out and a **shear** force when we tear the next sheet off the roll. Whilst heavier weight papers and boards may be relatively strong, for many applications they may need further stiffening or reinforcement.

Bending

A material is subject to bending forces when it is rolled, folded or creased. Some paper and boards need to maintain rigidity and **stiffness** to fulfil their application and therefore need to resit bending forces. The stiffer the material, the greater the force it will require to bend it. The material may crack when this force is applied whereas a thinner, more flexible paper like copier paper or folding boxboard can bend and fold more easily.

Torsion

Torsional or **twisting forces** affect a number of paper-based products in use and in production. Paper bags and boxes are subject to twisting forces when lifted and moved however some paper ropes and strings are twisted or woven in production to create a stronger material.

A parcel tied with twisted paper string

Shear

Shear force is exerted when two planes move against each other in opposite directions. An obvious example of shear force at play in paper products is tearing. The **tear strength** of some papers is more important than others, indeed some papers require a low tear strength so that they can be torn easily. A greater tear strength can be achieved by using different or bulkier fibres in the paper pulp that are more resistant to tearing. Tearing can be assisted with the addition of perforations.

Compression

Most papers and boards will be subject to compressive or pushing forces during manufacture and printing, even when stacked in storage. As a paper is fed through the rollers of a printer or photocopier, pressure is exerted. In a letterpress or during screen printing, pressure is applied through plates and screens. The material must be **resilient** enough to withstand this force without permanent deformation.

Laminating / encapsulation (school-based)

Laminating is the process of encapsulating paper or thin board inside a plastic pouch that is bonded to the surface through heat. It improves functionality by protecting the contents, making it water-resistant, more rigid, easy to clean and keeps it hygienic. It can also enhance aesthetics by giving the contents a gloss, satin or matt finish. The pouches come in a huge range of sizes and thicknesses as well as a choice of surface finishes. The thickness of the film is measured in microns. Thin pouches are around 50-75 microns and heavy-duty versions can be as thick as 350 microns.

> **Q4** Why is a laminating pouch slightly larger than the ISO sheet size it is designed to be used with?

Lamination (commercial)

Lamination in printing is the application of a polymer film (usually polyethylene) to the surface of a product. This protects the printed document to ensure it lasts longer and is less prone to damage from grease and moisture. It can be applied single or double sided, however it does not seal around the edges like encapsulation lamination (laminating pouches). This leaves the edges vulnerable to absorption.

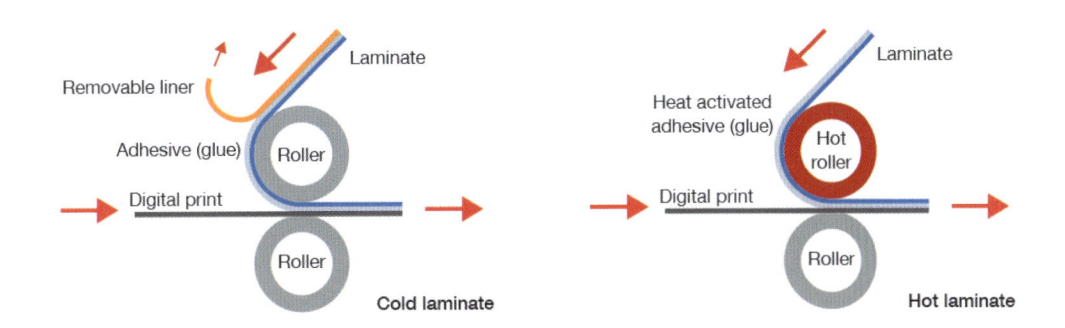

Polymer laminate can be applied as a film, either cold or with heat. New processing techniques also allow it to be applied as a liquid. Laminate is often applied to the covers of paperback books and can be identified by the outer cover which is smooth and usually shiny, whereas the inside cover is left unprotected.

> **Q5** Look at the paper covers of a few textbooks and detect whether they have been laminated or not. Note any damage occurring to the unsealed edges.

Corrugation

Corrugation is the term used to describe the adding of fluted paper layers to flat faces to add rigidity without adding excess weight. Flat outer faces are alternated with corrugated layers forming walls, this is a form of **sandwich construction**. The number of walls increases the impact resistance.

> **Q6** (a) Suggest an application for single face corrugated card.
> (b) Suggest an application for triple wall corrugated card.

Layers and plies

Increasing the number of flat layers or **plies** adds strength to fine papers and increases their ability to withstand tearing and to absorb moisture without disintegrating. They also enable carbon copies to be produced on a second and even third ply. **Ply form** contains layered sheets of paper in either sheet or roll form. It is used for packaging, till rolls and invoicing paper as well as kitchen and toilet roll. The layers are held together using **embossing** techniques and/or glue.

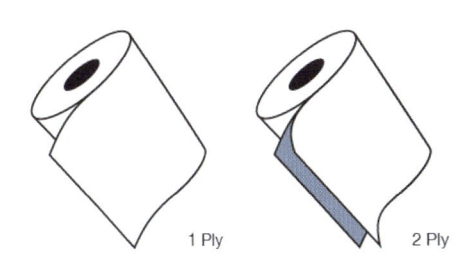

Adding ribs

Another way of adding strength, rigidity, shape and tear resistance to a lighter weight paper is by adding **ribs**. Some papers may have desireable physical characteristics for an application however their working properties may mean they are not mechanically suited. Tissue papers are often used for lanterns and lamp shades, they are suitable as they are available in a huge range of colours and patterns and are semi-transparent allowing light to suffuse in an attractive way. On their own however, they are not strong or rigid enough to hold a form and so metal or wooden ribs are used to create a skeleton over which the paper is laid.

Wooden ribs used to reinforce a tissue paper fan

Q7 Suggest other paper products featuring mechanical ribs made from wood, metal or plastic.

Standard material stock forms, types and sizes

Papers and boards are available in three main formats; rolls, sheets and ply. **Rolls** are commonly used in the printing industry for large and continuous runs. **Sheet** form is used in printing, art supplies and consumer-based goods.

Paper sizes

Paper is cut into a series of standard sizes set by the International Standards Organisation (ISO). There are three different series;

- A series includes the main sizes used in schools, at home and at work
- B series which is used more in industry, especially for the printing of posters and in publishing
- C series which is usually used for envelopes

The most commonly sold paper size is A4 (210mm x 297mm) which is used for most non-commercial printing. A3 is a popular format for school art or design and technology projects. The dimensions of **A series** paper halves each time the size goes up a number. Therefore, A0 is twice the size of A1, A3 is twice the size of A4 and so on.

Foolscap (216mm x 343mm) was a traditional imperial size of paper that is no longer used but may still be found in historical and archive documents. **Letter** (216mm x 279mm) is a size more commonly used in the United States however you will find it in the options menu of most printers.

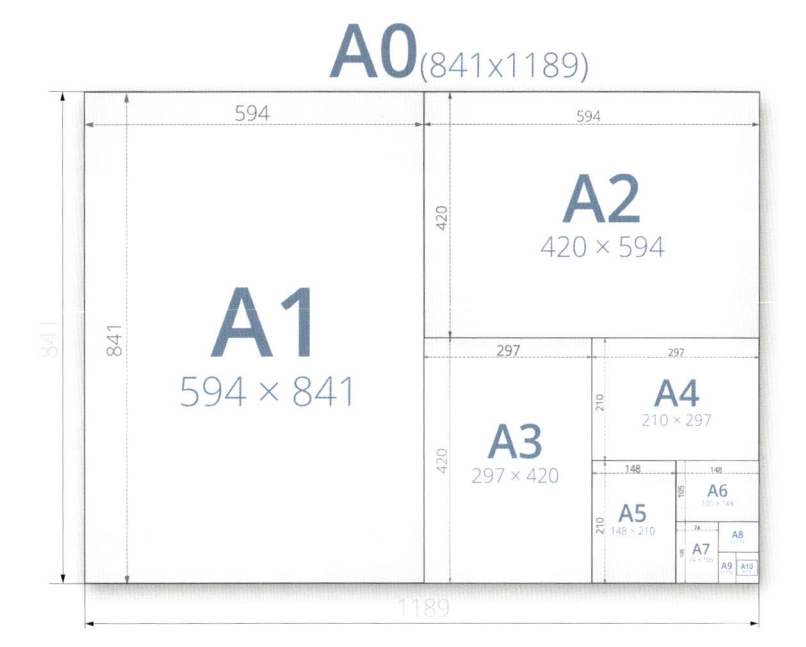

Q8 Calculate the area in cm² of:
(a) an A4 sheet
(b) a foolscap sheet

Q9 Find out which size of C series envelope holds a sheet of A4 paper without being folded.

Paper weight and thickness

The stiffness of paper or board is probably the most important factor in determining if it will perform a specific task successfully. Paper is measured in **grams per square metre (gsm)**. The lightest is tissue paper ranging from 10–35 gsm, and most A4 and A3 photocopying paper is around 80 gsm. Material up to and including 200 gsm is called paper and over 200 gsm is known as board. You will find that many products are sold as card and these range from roughly 120 gsm to 250 gsm.

Board is measured by its thickness rather than its weight. It is measured in **microns**; 1 micron (1μm) is 1/1000th of a millimetre. Board that is 300 microns thick will be about 0.3mm which is the thickness of a good quality greetings card.

Q10 How thick in microns is 1.5mm board?

Cardboard postal tubes are used to store and send larger A and B series paper sizes. Not only do they give protection, but rolling the paper means the package is more compact and easier to send. Tubes come in different lengths, diameters and wall thicknesses to accommodate the different size papers.

Q11 A heavy duty postal tube for A1 paper has an external radius of 40.6mm and a wall thickness of 2.5mm.
Calculate the **internal** diameter.

Chapter 40 – Planning and production methods

Objectives

- Be able to discriminate between different methods of processing including printing, cutting and modelling
- Be aware of the advantages and disadvantages of different techniques for quantity production
- Understand why registration marks are used to enhance quality control

Printing methods

Images and text can be transferred to a substrate using several different methods. Thousands of years ago ancient civilisations discovered they could use tools to imprint characters in clay. Since then, **stamps** and **blocks** have enabled man to record events and tell their stories.

Letterpress

In Germany in 1436, Johann Gutenberg created a printing press which used movable metal type. Each block of type was cast with the character in relief. Metal type made a cleaner print than the earlier carved wooden blocks. The characters could be assembled in a frame with spacers to create a legible page of text, a process called **type setting**. Ink was applied to the type with leather pads and the paper mounted in a frame, moved under the press and pressure was exerted using a lever to turn the screw which lowered the platen and pressed the paper against the inked type. Once printed, the blocks would be reused.

In 1476 William Caxton established the first printing press in London and it remained the primary method of printing for the next 500 years. In the early 1900s, offset printing took over, however letterpress printing remains popular with traditionalists and has seen several revivals, especially in the production of posters, shop signs and artwork.

A tray of metal letterpress type blocks

> **Q1** Typesetting was a time-consuming process. Suggest some other disadvantages of letterpress printing.

Screen printing

Screen printing is a process which can be used on a wide range of substrates. It is time consuming and therefore suited to one off and batch production. The screen consists of a very fine mesh fabric stretched across a frame and fixed in place. The mesh is first coated with photo emulsion and once that has dried, a silhouette of the artwork to be printed is laid onto the screen as a mask. This is often done using a printed transparency. Light is shone onto the screen; this fixes the photo emulsion that is left exposed and after this, the mask is removed, and the unexposed photo emulsion is washed away.

A different screen has to be made for each different colour and **jigs** are often used to help align the screens for printing. To make a print, the screen is laid on top of the substrate, ink is applied at the top of the screen and pulled across the screen using a squeegee. Screens can be washed and reused.

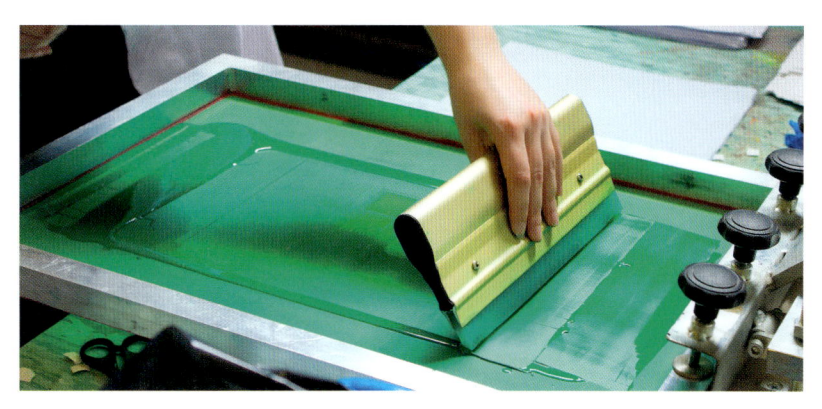

Drawing the ink across whilst making a screen print

Colour printing

Commercial colours are based on blending specific amounts of base colours to form the required shade or tone. The full-colour printing process uses **CMYK** (cyan, magenta, yellow and key [meaning black]) to form colours.

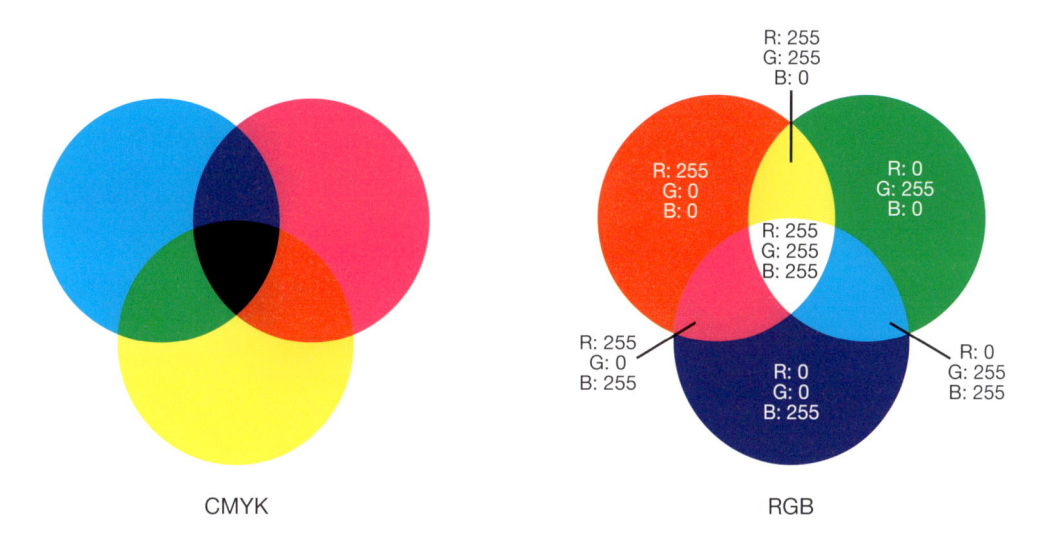

CMYK

RGB

Home printers often have a combined colour ink cartridge containing three colour wells and a black ink cartridge. Larger printers and commercial printers have separate inks (usually CMYK).

Companies such as Pantone® produce a huge range of colours that are given a specific combination of values for either RGB or CMYK. Digital colours on computers tend to use **RGB** with values for each colour between 0 and 255. Therefore 255, 0, 0 will be process red.

Q2 How many different combinations of colour are there in the digital RGB system?

Offset lithography

Mass produced printing and very long print runs tend to use **offset lithography**, also known as offset printing. An aluminium sheet (plate) is exposed to a laser image to create a page master. The sheet is then attached to the plate cylinder.

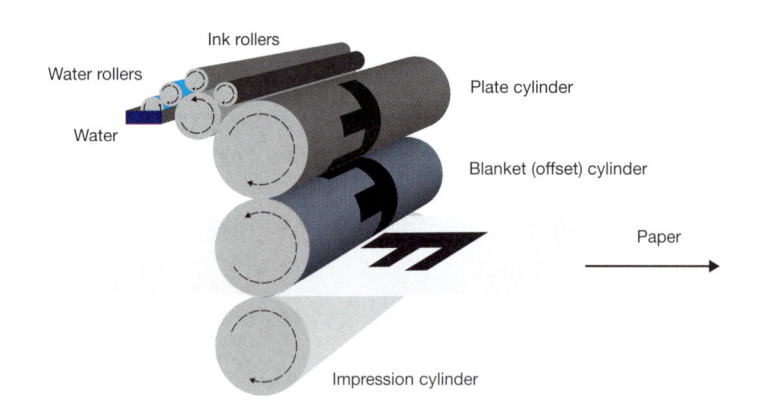

Ink and water are applied via rollers to the plate cylinder. Parts of the plate cylinder are kept wet by the water rollers so the ink does not stick to these areas. This creates the image area. The inked plate cylinder transfers the image to the rubber blanket cylinder (offset cylinder). At this point the image is mirrored. Finally, it is transferred to the material. This process is repeated for each of the colours required.

> **Q3** Why is the image mirrored on the offset cylinder?

Registration marks and crop marks – Quality control (QC)

As part of **quality control** procedures, commercially printed products need to be checked to ensure that all the different coloured inks are correctly aligned. It can be difficult, looking at an image, to detect whether all the colours are correct, so to make the process easier, **registration marks** are used.

One set of registration marks is correctly aligned and another poorly aligned

Crop marks are used to show the printers where to trim or guillotine the sheet. Registration marks are placed outside the crop marks so that they can be checked without interfering with the image.

Colour bars are also used to help the printers see whether the colours are true and of the correct intensity and whether any adjustment is needed.

> **Q4** Look for examples of registration marks, crop marks and colour bars. Cereal boxes are usually good to try; open up a finished one and have a look.
> See if you can detect any poor registration.

Digital printing

Used in industry and in the home, digital printing has relatively low set up costs, however the inks used can be costly. A wide range of digital printers are available for different applications and quality can vary.

Digital files can be edited prior to printing and then sent straight to the printer, removing the need for typesetting, printing plates or screens. Despite its speed and ease, digital printing tends to be used for single or shorter print runs as it is not as accurate or as cost effective as other methods.

Ink jet and laser printing

Both popular in the home, **ink jet** and **laser printers** may appear similar, however there are fundamental differences. The ink jet uses cartridges which feed the printhead. This passes across the substrate moving from left to right and depositing ink straight onto the surface.

The laser printer uses a laser to negatively charge areas of the printer drums and a positively charged toner powder which adheres to those negatively charged areas. A transfer belt then picks up the toner from the drums and transfers it to the substrate.

Photocopying

Much like laser printing, **photocopying** uses positive and negative electrostatic charges to transfer toner powder to the substrate. The toner is fixed to the paper using heat; this is why fresh laser prints and photocopies feel warm.

Cutting

Most papers and boards will require cutting at some stage of production. On a small scale when modelling or in **one off** or **small batch production**, cutting may be done by hand using scissors, scalpels or craft knives in conjunction with steel rules and cutting mats. Manual guillotines enable accurate dimensioning and right-angle cuts with their integrated measuring scales and fences, and a lever arm adds mechanical advantage allowing thicker board or layers of paper to be cut cleanly.

Printed papers need to be trimmed to the **crop lines**, a process usually done using large pneumatic CNC (computer numerically controlled) **guillotines** with integrated fixtures that ensure paper stacks are flat and sides are at 90°.

Die cutting

Commercial products like the food cartons pictured are commercially **die cut**. The die consists of special steel rules that either cut, crease or perforate the material they are being pressed into.

One of the most common die cut features that you will recognise is the euroslot. It consists of an industry standard set of dimensions for the hole which slides onto euroslot display stands in retail stores.

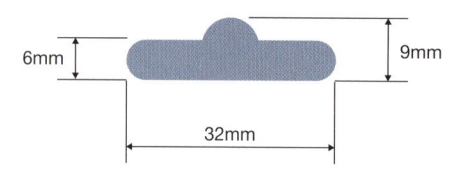

The industrial die cutting process starts with the manufacture of the die. It needs to be accurate and hardwearing as some machines are capable of producing over 400 presses per hour. Dies are usually constructed from laser cut plywood with steel rules inserted to the correct depth.

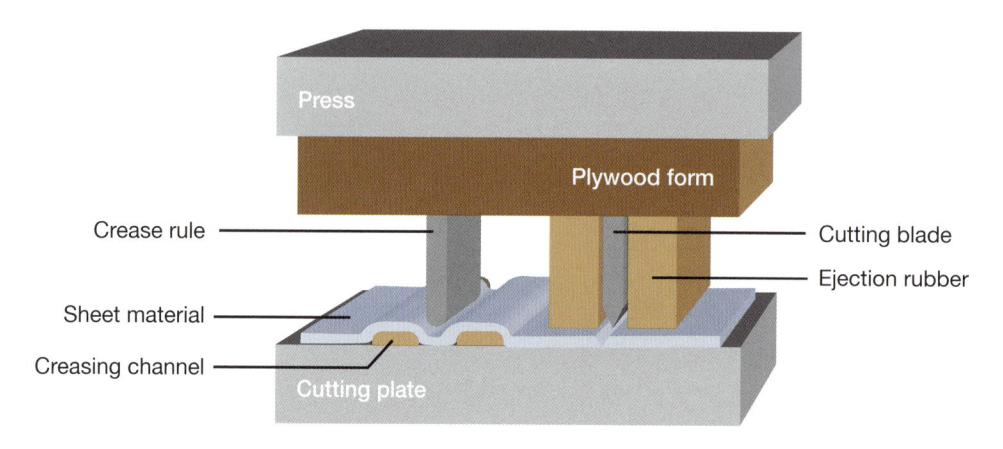

Q5 Why is laser cutting a suitable technique for making a plywood base for the die?

Laser cutting

Used in industry for some time, **laser cutters** are now more commonplace in schools. They can be used to cut a variety of materials including papers and boards. As long as the settings are adjusted to prevent scorching, laser cutters can produce clean accurate cuts and are useful in achieving very fine detail. CAD software enables designers to plan layouts, tessellating nets or shapes to increase efficiency and limit waste.

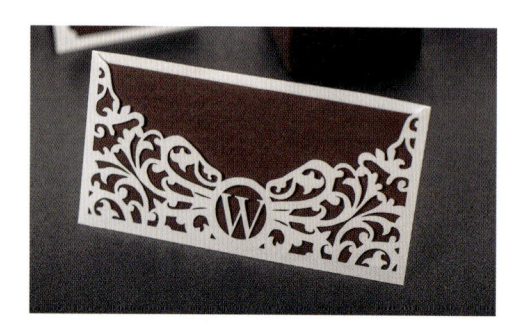

Laser cutting enables intricate shapes and fine detail

Cutting plotters

Advancements in **CAD** and **CAM** mean that highly accurate **cutting plotters**, smaller versions of those used in industry, are now available to schools and hobbyists. Plotters enable design and layout to be done on the computer before the file is sent to the machine. A very fine knife is used to cut the material and the pressure can be adjusted enabling it also to crease, score and perforate. As long as the knife size is right and the pressure is appropriate for the material used, a plotter can provide a very clean cut. Plotters are often used for cardmaking, prototyping, packaging and shop and exhibition displays.

> **Q6** Suggest **one** advantage of using a CAM cutting plotter over a die cutter.

Modelling

All of the cutting methods mention can be used to create shapes, nets and components for modelling.

Intermediate modelling

Papers and boards are often used to create **intermediate models** and prototypes to mock up and help visualise design ideas and concepts. They are readily available, easy to work with, available in range of thicknesses and relatively inexpensive. Paperboard and foamboards lend themselves to architectural modelling where as corrugated card, a more robust material, may be used in product and furniture design. Models may be constructed using adhesives or tape or they can be slotted together; cardboard can also be cut and layered to create a stronger laminated material.

An intermediate architectural model made from papers and boards

Test modelling

Board may be used to **test model** a product enabling designers to check for flaws in their design before it is put into production. A cardboard prototype allows the form, size and ergonomics of a product to be evaluated and test models may even be used as templates for the final product.

Frame modelling

The **frame modelling** method is used by some architects and engineers to create models of structures. It involves rolling up paper or board to create tubes which can imitate joists or beams. Schools sometimes use paper straws in this way when constructing bridges and towers.

Production aids

Jigs, **fixtures**, **templates** and **patterns** are used at all scales of production to help ensure accuracy and enable repeat production.

Fixtures

As the name implies, fixtures are usually fixed to the machine bed like those used on manual and automated guillotines. Sometimes these are adjustable like fences and clamps however they are integral to the machine or tool. Fixtures reduce the need for measuring and marking and can speed up the cutting and trimming process.

An operative using an automated pneumatic guillotine with fixtures that position and clamp the paper

Jigs

Jigs also aid manufacture but are more temporary than fixtures. A jig might be used to help in folding a net and make sure that creases run perpendicular to the edges of the box or carton. Jigs vary in complexity depending on the level of use.

Templates and patterns

Templates are more commonly used in small batch production runs to help lay out shapes for cutting or in work or school to assist with measuring, drawing or lettering. They are usually pre-cut from boards or more rigid materials like manufactured boards, metals or plastics.

Stencils

Stencils are templates. Usually used to enable paint to be applied to a substrate accurately within a predetermined shape. Often made from papers and boards, they can be hand cut or produced using machines such as laser cutters or cutting plotters. They are commonly used for lettering and increasingly for stencil art such as the works of Banksy.

Scales of production

Whilst we might immediately associate paper products with mass and continuous production methods, papers and boards are used at all scales of production.

One-off production

Crafts people and artists create a wide spectrum of hand made one off or bespoke products from artwork and handmade cards to origami and paper cuts. These are usually time consuming, require a high level of skill and practice and will usually be expensive to produce and purchase. Architectural model makers are also highly trained and use paper and board to create accurate scale models of structures and buildings that are considered art works in their own right.

Young people learning the traditional art of papercutting

Batch production

Batch production is a broad term for production runs of anything from ten to tens of thousands of products. The key common factors are repetition and the need for consistency to which end jigs, templates and patterns are used to aid replication. Processes are more highly mechanised than in one-off production and workers have to be trained to use specialist machinery. There is usually a certain amount of down time between batches, whilst tooling and setups are changed so that a new product can be produced.

Newspapers and many books as well as some packaging products are batch produced. Batch production is ideally suited to seasonal products as runs are finite and will likely change in response to trends year on year.

Mass and continuous production

More highly automated than batch production and requiring less skilled labour, mass production uses a production line to produce high numbers of identical products quickly. These are often common day to day products which are used briefly, disposed of and then repeat purchased such as food packaging, paper bags and serviettes. Materials for mass production are usually purchased in bulk and whilst set-up costs may be high, the need for less skilled labour and the high level of output help to lower costs. Continuous production is similar, however as the name suggests, there is no downtime and so it is ideal for products like toilet roll and copier paper for which there is continuous demand. These production lines run 24/7 and are run using shift workers. The set-up of the production line rarely needs to change.

Chapter 41 – Material processing

Objectives

- Understand the application of specialist techniques when manufacturing paper and board prototypes
- Be aware of the advantages and disadvantages of specialist techniques
- Be able to select appropriate specialist techniques and joining methods

Paper and board shaping, cutting and fabricating

A vast selection of tools is available in workshops in order to help us make the products we require. Tools enable us to mark out materials, cut to size, waste (remove material), add material, deform, reform and apply a finish.

Marking out and cutting tools

Name	Image	Use	Name	Image	Use
Steel rule		Measuring and assisting with the drawing of straight lines	Paper shears		Used to cut paper and card, very long blade for even cut
Maun safety rule		Helping to score or cut a straight line safely as it prevents a knife from slipping	Rotary cutting wheel		Cuts a line through paper and card, good for curved cuts
Craft knife		General cutting and scoring of various materials	Drawing aids		Drawing and measuring various angles
Scalpel		Fine cutting and scoring, selection of replaceable blades for different tasks	Cutting mat		Safe anti-slip, self-healing matt to protect work surfaces
Perforating tools		Creates perforations to allow easy folding or tearing off of sections	Rotary paper trimmer		To cut paper and light card to size
Creasing tools		Used like a knife to create a crease, often made from bone	Creasing machine		Creates crease line to enable folding

Cutting, scoring and perforating

Cutting and scoring lines on paper and board involve the same process but differ in the amount of pressure used. Score lines are partially cut through the material, but not all the way and allow for accurate folding or articulation of an edge, joint or feature. Cutting goes through the whole thickness of the material. Many products require a combination of both in order for them to function correctly.

A Maun safety rule is the best tool to use to help create a safe score or cut. It allows for even pressure to be applied to the material to stop it moving and its high sides prevent the blade from riding over the rule edge. This prevents potential cuts to fingers.

Perforations are a series of punched holes or short cut lines that allow for a section of paper or board material to be removed with ease by allowing the tear to follow the perforated path. The perforations create a weakness in the material, so the force when tearing is directed to the weakness allowing the perforated section to be removed. Perforations tear more efficiently when folded first.

Paper engineering

Paper engineering is the manipulation of papers and boards by folding, creasing and cutting to produce a relief or three-dimensional form. Pop-up story books are a good example of paper engineering, using tabs and flaps to enable intricate paper shapes to 'stand up' as the pages of the book are turned.

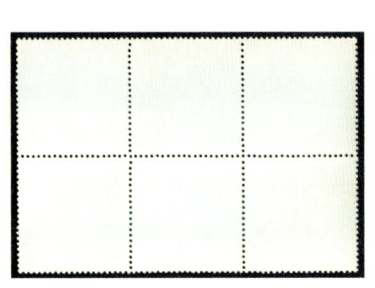

Block of six blank postage stamps with perforations

> **Q1** Why should you use a cutting mat when cutting and scoring with a blade?

Creasing and folding

A crease is the line or mark that remains present when a material has been folded. Creasing and folding involves crushing the fibres of the paper or board in order for it to remember a shape. Once folded and creased, the fibres are slightly weakened and the line of weakness remains. This can be used to our advantage as it allows us to make complex three-dimensional shapes from two-dimensional materials. Scoring can also be used to create a sharp fold line.

The ancient art of origami is based on paper folding. Kirigami is a similar art that applies cutting techniques as well as folding. Both methods allow the creation of imaginative three-dimensional structures.

Many of the complex net designs used in modern packaging have been developed using ancient paper folding and cutting techniques. It is a good idea to practice a few basic nets to get used to cutting, scoring, folding and creasing. There are many imaginative nets available to download and print from the Internet.

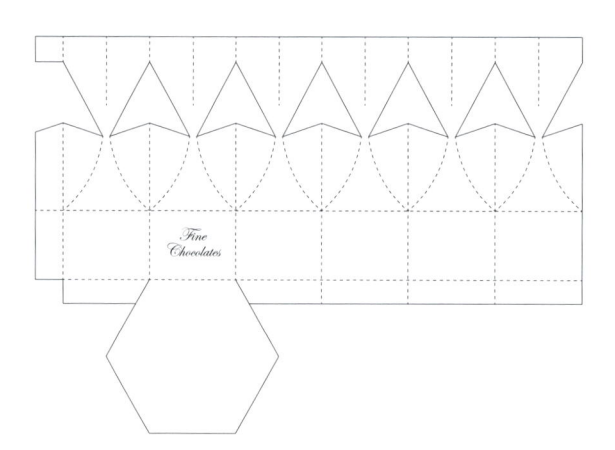

> **Q2** Draw the net for a cube that has a side length of 50mm. Add tabs in the appropriate places so that it can be joined.

> **Q3** Draw a net for a pentagonal prism with all lengths at 30mm, add tabs then score and cut the appropriate lines before folding into shape.

Notching

Cutting small **notches** in a paper nets removes excess paper making them easier to fold and allowing tabs to fit neatly. Notches are also used in modelling to allow curved strips of thicker card or board to be manipulated so that they can be joined to flat surfaces.

At school this would be done by hand using a scalpel or scissors however in industry, notches are either incorporated into dies or CAD layouts or cut after production from stacks of sheet using pneumatic machines with shaped die cast cutters. Notches are used in paper dressmaking patterns to denote where two pieces of the pattern should join together.

Manipulation

Rolling, folding and cutting are common methods of manipulation and sometimes it is necessary to laminate layers of material to strengthen the prototype. To fabricate your prototype, you will also need to consider which joining methods are appropriate.

Machinery and digital design

Machines for use in the manufacture of papers and boards can be very expensive and whilst they can improve accuracy and speed up processing, they are not always cost effective for small scale production. Some tools and machines used for processing other materials may be used with papers and boards, for example scroll saws and drills. Some CAM cutting plotters are also used in schools and small die cutting machines are also popular.

Digital design and prototyping

In addition to hand tools and equipment, digital CAD software enables us to design and create prototypes using CAM machinery like laser cutters and cutting plotters. (See Chapter 40.) These machines are an expensive investment; however, they can be used to create multiple, accurate prototypes quickly. The advantage of modelling using CAD is that we can change, adapt and develop ideas easily without having to produce a physical model each time, saving time and money.

Standard components

A huge range of useful products are available to facilitate the paper and board industry. Many everyday items have been designed to make managing paper-based products easier.

Common fasteners and joining methods

Fasteners attach paper-based products or other materials together. Most are temporary and can be removed or undone easily. A few are permanent or more difficult to remove.

Name	Image	Characteristics	Name	Image	Characteristics
Paper fastener - split pin		Joins paper and card through a punched hole, good for joints and linkages	Map pins		A temporary fixing. Pins can act as pivot points for movable parts
Adhesive tape		Provides an instant but visible bond, can damage substrates if removed	Masking tape		Can usually be removed without damaging the substrate, used to mask areas when painting or using spray adhesive
Hot-melt glue		Often used in packaging and modelling, dries quickly and can bond dissimilar materials	PVA		A water-based adhesive, can be used as a sealant as well as glue, must be applied thinly with a roller or brush
Spray adhesive		Used for mounting, creates a permanent or repositionable bond depending on type, can be difficult to control.	Staple		Semi-permanent, way to hold sheets together, different depths and thicknesses available, special tool helps removal

Q4 The paper fastener/split pin is the best fastener to use for making mechanisms with moving part or joints.

(a) Explain why it is the best fastener for this purpose.

(b) (i) Which other fastener from the selection shown would also work?

(ii) Why is it not as adaptable?

Addition of materials

Various other materials and components can be added to paper products to enhance their function. A wide variety of seals are available for different applications.

Name	Image	Characteristics	Name	Image	Characteristics
Self-adhesive foam pad		Semi-permanent method of attaching materials, good for wall mounting, can be hard to remove	Tamper-proof stickers		Paper sticker that tears when removal is attempted
Rivets		Permanent method of holding material together, different lengths and diameters available	Windows		Clear plastic windows enable addresses to be seen, can cause issues with recycling
String and button		Reusable envelope closing method	Eyelets		Eyelets can be inserted to reinforce holes for string, metal rings or ribbon for gift bag handles

Common binding methods

When creating a pamphlet or brochure, or presenting an essay or larger publication, there are a number of different methods of binding the pages together. Most of the following techniques are designed to be permanent; however, some can be taken off and replaced if necessary.

Name	Image	Characteristics	Name	Image	Characteristics
Perfect binding		Method used by most magazines, and paperback books, smooth flat spine	Coil or spiral binding		Coil is twisted onto the pages through punched holes
Wire binding		Wire loops attached to the spine are threaded through punched holes and closed	Comb binding		Very popular low cost binding, plastic comb is inserted through punched holes
Hard-cover binding		Traditional method for hardback books, long lasting and robust method	Saddle stitch		Normally stapled top and bottom and sometimes in the centre, inexpensive method reliable up to 40 sheets thick

Q5 Find examples of as many different types of binding as possible and try to identify them. Use the library and have a look at home. List your findings to see if particular types of publications fall into the same binding categories.

Chapter 42 – Finishing

Objectives

- Be able to select appropriate treatments and finishes and understand their application
- Understand how the application of surface treatments and finishes can modify the functional and aesthetic properties of paper and board products

Finishes for commercial products

We come into contact with industrially produced paper and board products on a daily basis and many of these will have surface finishes and treatments. From the cover of the book you are reading, to the wrapper of a sandwich; all contribute to the estimated 200kg of paper and board we use per person each year in the UK. This chapter looks at some of the different surface finishes and treatments that are applied to papers and boards.

Varnishing

A protective coating or laminate helps paper and boards to look professional. **Varnish coatings** are available in gloss, satin and matt finishes and whilst they offer a relatively low degree of protection compared to other surface finishes, they do offer a low-cost flexible finish which is easy to apply.

Varnishes can be applied like an ink, 'in line' as part of the printing process. It can be used to cover the whole surface or just used to highlight certain areas. Varnishes are safe and odourless when dry, however many liquid varnishes contain **VOCs** (volatile organic compounds) and should always be handled and applied with care.

UV varnishing (spot varnishing)

UV varnishing or **spot varnishing** is a technique that enables all, but more usually, part, of the surface of card or paper to be printed with a shiny transparent varnish. This decorative technique gives a high-quality finish to brochures, cards and documents, adds protection and prevents yellowing. The varnish is applied through a stencil and is then exposed to ultraviolet light which cures (sets) the varnish instantly.

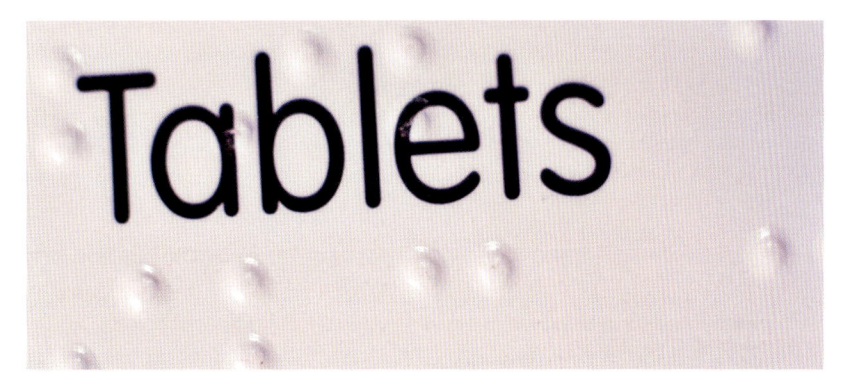

Braille is often spot varnished onto food and medical products

Packaging laminates and films

As discussed in Chapter 39, layers or films made from different materials can be laminated with board to enhance function and aesthetics. Plastic films made from polypropylene (PP), Polyethylene terephthalate (PET) and low-density polyethylene (LDPE) add strength and offer a greater degree of protection than varnishes especially against moisture. Other materials including starch, gelatine and wax can also be effective.

Carton board and waxed paper products are very popular with fast food outlets and are specially coated to prevent absorbency when coming in contact with the food or liquid.

Case study: Tetra Pak®

One of the most popular card-based food packaging methods is Tetra Pak®. The company produce a layered card that can hold liquid and food products safely. Until quite recently Tetra Pak® products have been very difficult to recycle as the many different layers that they consist of were difficult to separate. Since 2011 the company has been using bio-based materials to allow the used cartons to be recycled more easily, reducing the amount going to landfill sites.

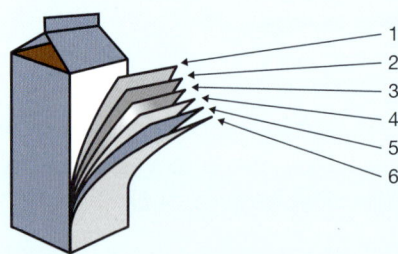

1. Metallocene polyethylene - Seals and protects the contents
2. Adhesive polymer
3. Aluminium foil - Prevents entry of light and oxygen
4. Polyethylene lamination
5. Paper board - For strength and durability
6. Polyethylene - Protects package from moisture and seals corners

Q1 Why is carton board an ideal material for the construction of fast food boxes?

Most takeaway food and drinks packaging are either plastic- or card-based. Plastics take a very long time to biodegrade whereas most paper and board products are fully biodegradable and recyclable. The main problem with card is that it is very absorbent if left untreated. Card can be treated and processed to improve functionality and enable it to be waterproof and greaseproof. However, some of these coatings can make the card harder to recycle and slower to biodegrade.

Q2 What are the advantages of using a waxed layer instead of a polyethylene layer on paperboard used for takeaway packaging?

Edge staining

Edge staining is a traditional practice most commonly seen in book binding and in high-end stationery.

Coloured dies or foils are applied to the edges of the pages or cards. To do this, papers or boards are stacked tightly and clamped, and the ink is applied using a roller. Sometime patterns are applied. The effect is attractive, eye catching and adds a sense of quality.

Hot foil blocking

A way of adding metallic foil to a material, **hot foil blocking** is a process where a pre-glued foil is pressed into a substrate using a heated die forming a permanent bond. It can be used for purely decorative reasons or as a security measure. **Holographic foils** are used on passports, bank notes and event tickets.

Holographic foil on a £10 note

Embossing

The paper embossing process (known as **blind embossing**) creates a raised profile or pattern on the surface of the paper. The process involves two plates being created known as the relief die (female) and the counter die (male). Just as in folding or creasing paper and card, the fibres are permanently compressed and stay in position.

The paper or card is placed between the two dies then pressure, and sometimes heat, is applied to the two parts of the die. The material is then removed and the raised pattern remains. Debossing is when the profile is recessed below the surface of the substrate.

One of the most significant uses of the embossing process is in the production of **braille** writing that can be found on many products, specifically medicine packages and labels.

> **Q3** Suggest **two** other places where you might find embossed paper or boards.

Exercises

1. Hot foil blocking is an example of a surface finish that can be applied to solid white board.
   (a) Name **one** other surface finish or treatment that can be applied to solid white board. [1]
   (b) Use notes and sketches to show the process of hot foil blocking. [4]

2. Give **two** different ways in which papers and boards can be shaped. [2]

3. This question has four parts.
   (a) State **one** geographical origin of wood pulp that is used to make papers and boards. [1]
   (b) Name **one** stock size that photocopying paper is supplied in. [1]
   (c) Explain how papers and boards can be stiffened to withstand forces and stresses. [2]
   (d) Explain what is meant by the term 'gsm'. [2]

4. Explain **two** ways in which brass split pins can be used in products. [4]

5. Explain **one** reason why corrugated board is an appropriate material to make a takeaway pizza box. [2]

6. Describe **one** method that is used during the production of products in quantity to ensure that dimensional accuracy is maintained. [2]

7. TetraPak® is a packaging laminate.
   (a) Give **one** other example of a packaging laminate. [1]
   (b) Explain **one** way in which lamination enhances the functional properties of Tetrapak®. [2]

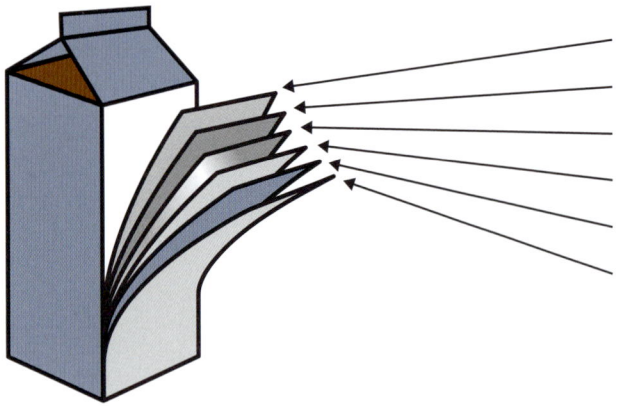

1. Metallocene polyethylene
2. Adhesive polymer
3. Aluminium foil
4. Polyethylene lamination
5. Paper board
6. Polyethylene

8. The booklets below have been bound by comb binding.
   (a) Give **one** other form of binding. [1]
   (b) Use notes and sketches to show the process of comb binding. [4]

9. When selecting papers and boards for the manufacture of products, designers should consider the sustainability and recyclability of any materials used.

   Discuss the sustainability of papers and boards in manufacture, in use and at the end of their life. [6]

Section 6-4
Polymers

In this section:

Chapter 43	Sources, origins and sustainability	219
Chapter 44	Physical and working properties	223
Chapter 45	Selection of materials and stock forms	227
Chapter 46	Planning and production methods	235
Chapter 47	Material processing	242
Chapter 48	Finishing	249
Exercises		250

Chapter 43 – Sources, origins and sustainability

Objectives

- Explain the sources, origins and properties of a range of polymers
- Understand the processes involved in mining, extraction and refining the raw materials to make polymers
- Be aware of the sustainability of polymers and their ecological footprint

The origin of polymers

Plastics can be created from three different sources. Most are made from petrochemical resources such as oil, gas and coal. Some are made from natural materials, such as amber and rubber. **Biopolymers** are natural polymers which can be made from starchy vegetables such as corn, or plants containing lots of fibre, fat or carbohydrate.

Crude oil, the source of many of the synthetic polymers we are familiar with, is a finite natural resource found deep underground and under the sea bed. To locate reserves at sea, seismic survey ships patrol the oceans using shock waves to identify areas of bedrock that might be feasible drill locations. Once assessed as viable, oil rigs are set up to enable drilling and extraction. On land, oil is sometimes located as a result of surface indications or seepage, however, geological surveys usually look for tell-tale shapes in rock layers to determine whether oil may be present. The only way to confirm the presence of oil is by test drilling and once tests confirm an oil reserve, drilling rigs and pumps are set up to extract it. Some rigs may reach up to 3km deep.

Oil is extracted all over the world, however the top crude oil producing nations are Russia, Saudi Arabia and the United Arab Emirates. **Crude oil** is transported to oil refineries by ship or overland using vast pipelines.

An offshore oil rig platform

Plastics are produced by polymerisation. This occurs when molecules of simple compounds known as monomers join to other monomers to form polymers. These atoms are joined end-to-end to form long chains. These chains are the building blocks of the plastics that we use.

The Trans-Alaskan oil pipeline in northern Alaska, USA

> **Q1** Describe how polymerisation is used to make plastics.

> **Q2** Which plant-based materials can be used to make sustainable plastics?

Refining crude oil with fractional distillation

Refining is the process of converting black sticky crude oil into other more usable products such as transportation fuel, including petrol and diesel, or oils for machinery. The waste product, bitumen, is used ias a binder n road surfacing.

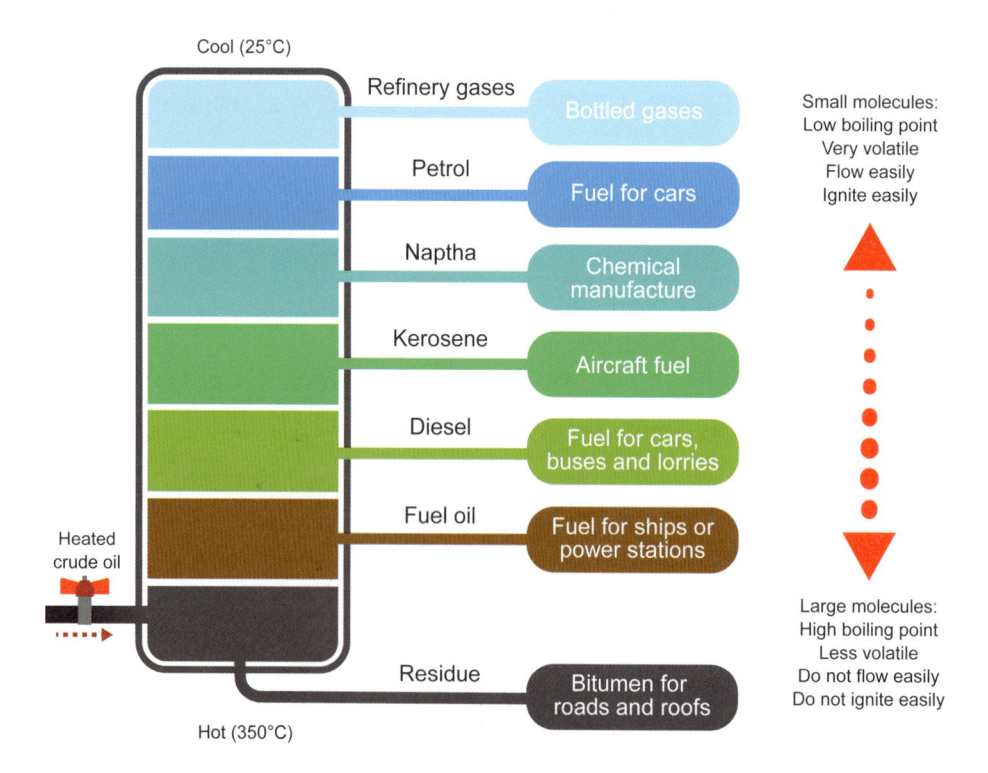

Cool (25°C)
- Refinery gases → Bottled gases
- Petrol → Fuel for cars
- Naptha → Chemical manufacture
- Kerosene → Aircraft fuel
- Diesel → Fuel for cars, buses and lorries
- Fuel oil → Fuel for ships or power stations
- Residue → Bitumen for roads and roofs

Heated crude oil
Hot (350°C)

Small molecules: Low boiling point, Very volatile, Flow easily, Ignite easily

Large molecules: High boiling point, Less volatile, Do not flow easily, Do not ignite easily

Fractional distillation occurs when crude oil is heated in the crude oil distillation unit (CDU). This process separates the heated crude oil into many different compounds or fluids using condensers. Each product has a different boiling point and condenses at a different temperature, thus allowing the multiple condensers to draw the product off separately at different stages.

Cracking

The separated fuel products from the fractional distillation process contain large hydrocarbon molecules which do not flow well and are not suitable to be converted into plastics. **Cracking** is the process of converting large hydrocarbons into smaller more useful versions.

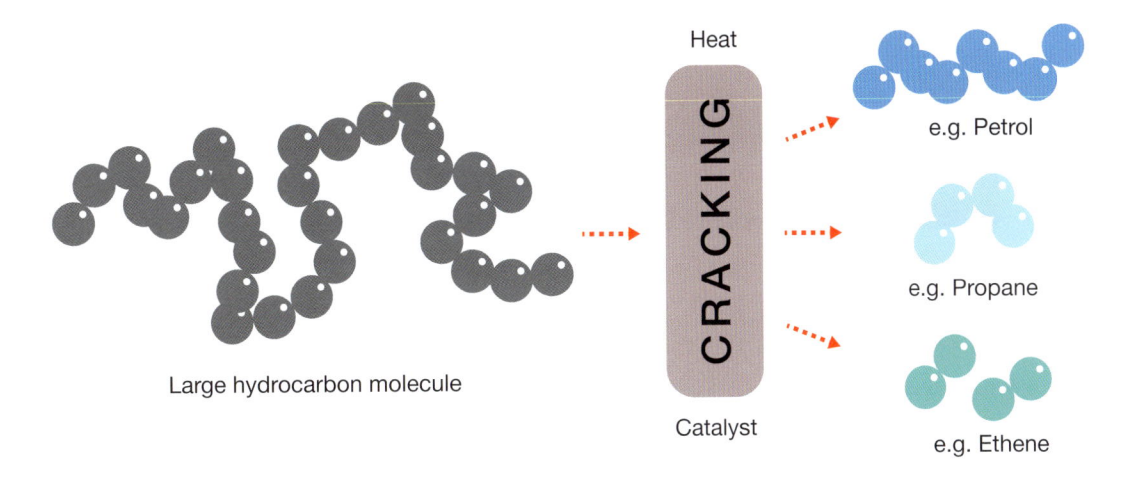

High levels of heat and pressure are used in the process, although this can be done at a lower temperature if a **catalyst** is used. The most significant products gathered from the cracking process for the making of plastics are ethene and propane.

The environmental impact of oil exploration and extraction

The drilling, extraction and transportation of crude oil is resource intensive and the impacts can be far reaching. The repercussions from setting up rigs are considerable as the disturbance of natural habitats and deforestation coupled with a loss of biodiversity can cause significant changes to the way the ecosystem functions.

Transporting crude oil to refineries by ship causes significant air pollution and vast pipelines can be subject to leaks, polluting the soil or water. In most oil producing countries, there is strict legislation dictating how waste materials are disposed of. Sadly, this is not the case everywhere. Waste disposed of irresponsibly contains harmful chemicals and metals like lead and mercury which leach through soil and can contaminate rivers and ground water.

The effects of oil extraction and refining on communities are mixed. Rigs and refineries may bring investment and job opportunities, however these are very specialist and life on an offshore rig is dangerous and isolated. Oil and drilling rigs are not particularly visually attractive, and their presence may affect tourism. Undoubtedly, oil brings money to a country and the local area, but it may not reach the pockets of the communities adversely affected.

Impact on wildlife

Whilst building rigs and refineries can cause deforestation and loss of biodiversity, damage to pipelines or spills from ships or underwater pipes can have an immediate catastrophic effect on sea and birdlife. When oil sinks below the surface of the water it has a very damaging effect on the fragile underwater ecosystem and fish and other organisms may be killed or contaminated.

Birds' feathers are naturally waterproof and oil can cause this to break down; it also hinders, or at worst prevents, flight and many birds caught in oil spills will die if not rescued. The environmental impact caused by spills also has long term implications, damaging plants and habitats.

Cleaning up a beach in Thailand after an oil spill

Trend forecasting

Crude oil and the resulting polymers are **commodities** and their prices are influenced by several key factors including their availability, demand and world economics and politics.

Trend forecasting is a method by which companies look at patterns of consumption in historical data to predict supply and demand. For example, the recent growth in the awareness of the long-term environmental damage caused by waste polymer products coupled with an increase in global oil prices has driven an increase in demand for bioplastics.

Whilst there is still a rising global demand for plastics used in packaging, new regulations imposed on the use of polymers are making many companies more cautious about using them.

6-4 Sustainability of plastics

End-of-life considerations are important for all products, but as most plastics take so long to biodegrade, extra care should be taken to decide how it should be managed. Many responsible companies producing plastic products conduct a **Life Cycle Analysis (LCA)** which informs them of the environmental impact of manufacturing their products. The information gathered helps them decide how to deal with their products when they have reached the end of their working life. (LCA is covered in detail in Chapter 2.)

Almost all plastics are recyclable or biodegradable in some form – however, the difference in the quality of the recycled product varies dramatically.

Thermosetting plastics are generally considered non-recyclable although they are frequently ground down and used as a filler material or they are used for **energy recovery** through incineration. **Thermoplastics** are more easily recycled for use as a recycled polymer product. If the polymers are carefully separated into the different types, the resulting material remains high quality and commands a higher price than mixed polymers. It is important to recycle as much as possible, as poorly discarded plastics are becoming a major environmental concern, especially in our countryside, rivers and oceans.

> **Q3** How can thermoforming plastics be recycled?

> **Q4** Why is it important to separate the different types of plastics when they are recycled?

Chapter 44 – Physical and working properties

Objectives

- Be able to discriminate between and select from a range of thermoforming polymers and thermosetting polymers
- Understand the advantages, disadvantages and applications of thermoforming polymers and thermosetting polymers
- Be aware of the physical characteristics and working properties of thermoforming polymers and thermosetting polymers
- Be aware of the correct procedures for the disposal and recycling of different polymers

Physical characteristics and working properties

Polymers have different physical characteristics which make them suitable for different applications.

- **Durability** denotes how well the material will resist wear and damage in use.
- **Density** dictates the mass of a material per unit of size. Density is equal to mass divided by volume.

When selecting polymers, the working properties will be considered. **Hardness** is vital in resisting indentation and abrasion whilst **plasticity** is important if a polymer is to be moulded or formed and then retain its shape. Some phone cases made from **ABS** are rigid forms that create a **tough**, hard, durable shell to absorb and protect the phone.

See Section 4 for detailed definitions of physical and working properties as well as to revisit the core polymers that you need to know about.

Q1 Why is plasticity an important working property of the ABS used in phone cases?

Forces and Stresses

Like other materials, polymers used in different products are subjected to different forces and stresses. Forces may be still - **static** or they may be moving - **dynamic**.

Tensile and **compressive** strength should be considered where plastic parts or products are subject to pulling and pushing forces. For example, a three-strand polyethylene rope used in a yacht's rigging will be in tension whilst in use, whereas expanded polystyrene packaging needs to be able absorb compressive forces to protect its contents.

The PVC seats in a sports stadium must be tough and strong in compression

Q2 Name some polymer-based products that need to have good tensile strength.

Thermoforming and thermosetting plastics

Plastics are categorised into two varieties; **thermoforming polymers** and **thermosetting polymers**. They have many properties in common but there are fundamental differences which are covered in greater depth in Chapter 8.

Thermoforming polymers are generally the most flexible, especially when heated. They can be formed into complex shapes and many can be reformed multiple times and are usually easy to recycle.

Thermosetting polymers are much more rigid and once they are formed and cooled, they set and cannot be reformed. They are excellent electrical insulators and have good resistance to heat and chemicals but they tend to be harder and more brittle. Thermosetting plastics cannot be easily recycled.

Thermoforming polymers can be reshaped when heated

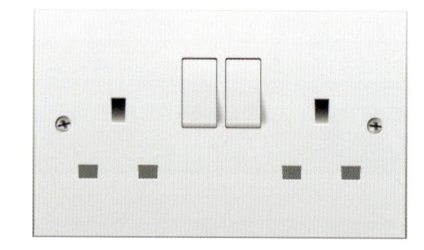

Thermosetting polymers are rigid

Additional polymers

In addition to the list of polymers in Section 4, you need to know about the following:

Additional thermoforming plastics

Name	Appearance	Image	Characteristics	Example uses
PET Polyethylene terephthalate (1 PETE)	Clear, easily coloured with a smooth finish		Dimensionally stable, easily blow moulded, chemically resistant and fully recyclable	Bottles, food packaging, sheeting and some food wraps
ABS Acrylonitrile butadiene styrene (7 OTHER)	Very smooth finish, can be textured, easily coloured		Tough, hard, good chemical resistance, good impact resistance, can be 3D-printed, easily injection moulded and extruded	Electronic casings, 3D printed products, hard-hats, Lego™
PVC Polyvinyl chloride (3 PVC)	Good range of colours with a high gloss finish. Available in sheets or shaped as rigid PVC		Flexible, high plasticity, chemically resistant, tough and easily extruded	Raincoats, pipes, electrical tape, air mattresses and self-adhesive vinyl
Rigid polystyrene (High density polystyrene) (6 PS)	Naturally clear but also available in a range of opaque and transparent colours, high gloss finish		Hard and brittle, low melting point, easily injection moulded and vacuum formed	Reusable drinks cups, CD cases, 'disposable' plastic cutlery, model making material
Urethane / Polyurethane (7 OTHER)	Available in liquid form, also as granules, sheet and foam		Hard and resistant to wear, flexible, good compressive strength	Carrier bags, bushes and bearings, upholstery and insulation foams, varnishes
Fluoroelastomer (7 OTHER)	A rubber like appearance, matt, available as sheet, tube, cable and strip		High temperature resistance, chemical resistance, flexible, good compressive strength	Seals and gaskets, fuel hoses and watch straps

Expanded and extruded thermoforming plastics

Name	Appearance	Image	Characteristics	Example uses
Expanded polystyrene	White, available in beads, sheets and blocks		Very lightweight, good ability to absorb impact, good buoyancy, difficult to recycle	Packaging, coffee cups, insulation, sound proofing, floats and life jackets, bean bag filler beads
Styrofoam™ (closed cell extruded polystyrene)	Available in sheet form, often blue in colour		Lightweight, good buoyancy, good insulator, difficult to recycle	Food and fast food packaging, insulation, craft and model making

Polymers for commercial products

Polymers are widely used in commercial products. They have particular properties, such as electrical and thermal insulation, that are hard to find in other materials and most of them are waterproof and hygienic. Many polymers, such as polyethylene used for plastic bags, possess a good strength-to-weight ratio. Polymers offer value for money as a manufacturing material.

Thermoforming polymers are a very popular material for seating products, as they are easy to mould and have a good level of flexibility. They are also lightweight, tough, durable, waterproof, corrosion-resistant and chemical-resistant making them easy to clean. Many polymers have a scratch-resistant surface which helps to keep them looking good for longer. They are easily coloured and can be given a textured surface if required.

Thermosetting polymers are generally harder but more brittle than thermoforming varieties; they do not melt if they get hot. This is the key property that makes them so useful for electrical fittings. Urea formaldehyde is the main thermoforming plastic used for electrical fittings and is an excellent electrical insulator with good tensile strength. It can reach a very high temperature before heat distortion occurs, making the fitting stable even if there is an electrical fault.

Q3 Why are polymers, such as polypropylene, an ideal material for large outdoor children's toys such as slides or climbing frames?

Q4 What are the advantages and disadvantages of using thermoforming polymers for kitchen utensils?

Chapter 45 – Selection of materials and stock forms

Objectives

- Be aware of how environmental, cultural and ethical issues influence material choices
- Explain how environmental factors influence the disposal of plastic products
- Be aware of the forces and stresses that act on polymers and how they can be reinforced and stiffened
- Be aware of the availability of various polymer stock forms and the sizes of materials

Selecting appropriate plastics

By applying the information regarding the different types of plastics covered, you will be able to work out which varieties would be best used for a given task. Considerations will include:

Aesthetics	Cost	Weight
Size of product	Social / environmental factors	Desired properties
Where it will be used	Required finish	Workability
Stability	Availability	How long it is to last

Suitability

Function and performance are key factors in selection. A polymer must be both **fit for purpose** and safe when used for its chosen application. For example, it would be inappropriate to select a polymer that has a low melting point for use in an application where it will be exposed to high temperatures.

Aesthetics

The aesthetic qualities of polymers including **form**, **colour** and **texture** influence their selection. Polymers are available in a variety of different stock forms which will be explored in more detail later in this chapter. Many polymers are available in a wide range of colours which presents the designer with aesthetic opportunities. Certain polymers have a very smooth high shine finish making them pleasant to handle and since most polymers are easy to mould, surface patterns and textures can be made to imitate the textures of different materials such as leather.

Leather-look ABS car door panel

Environmental factors

When selecting polymers, a designer or manufacturer needs to consider the sustainability of the material. If the product is to be produced indefinitely or on a large scale, then a manufacturer needs to know that the material will be readily available for as long as it is in production.

Many polymers are recyclable and, as long as they are not cross-contaminated, they can be recycled around 7-9 times. After this point, they can be turned into a product with a lesser value such as fleece for clothing or other fillings. This means that, whilst crude oil is a finite resource, recycled polymers can contribute to a reduction in the use of crude oil.

Recycling polymers as opposed to extracting and refining more crude oil reduces CO_2 emissions, ensures that there is ongoing availability and reduces processing and manufacturing costs. If they are not recycled, it is likely they will end up in landfill where they will only degrade very slowly, potentially taking hundreds of years to decompose.

Biodegradable plastics

Some newer plastics, including Biopol® are made from vegetable starches, and are fully biodegradable if composted. The natural bacteria in the soil break down the plastic very quickly, largely owing to being exposed to moisture and higher temperatures.

Modern biopolymer pellets are made from vegetable or corn starches

Bioplastics are non-toxic and are already being widely used in a range of products. Since biopolymers readily decompose, they cannot be recycled. Small amounts mixed in with other recyclable thermoplastics can produce low grade recycled plastic or render a batch unusable.

Name	Appearance	Image	Characteristics	Example uses
Polyhydroxy-butyrate PHB Biopol®	Smooth or textured finish, easily coloured		Quite brittle with limited chemical resistance. Non-toxic, slow but fully biodegradable, easily processed	Bottles, pots, household items and disposable food containers

Q1 Why does biodegradable plastic break down so readily when in contact with soil?

Q2 Why should biodegradable plastics not be recycled?

Availability of polymers

Plastics are abundant in our modern society and are available in many forms. They help us to solve complex design problems because they can be manufactured to have a very high strength-to-weight ratio and have many versatile properties. This means that we can use less material to make a stronger product. Plastics are generally cheap and last for a very long time which makes them good value-for-money.

Polymers are available in many different forms including sheet, rod, powder, granular, foam and film (covered later in the chapter). They are incredibly versatile and are made into a multitude of shapes and products through different types of processing.

> **Q3** Why are plastics so good at helping designers solve technical problems?

> **Q4** What factors make plastic a value for money material?

Cost factors

Manufacturers must factor in all costs when selecting polymers for use in production. Some polymers and other **specialist materials** require different dies and machinery so that they can be formed and may cost considerably more. The factors affecting manufacturing costs include premises, machinery, tooling, fuel, energy and labour. Oil and polymers are **commodities** and subject to price fluctuations on the world markets, this is covered in greater detail in Chapter 43.

Trends, fashions and popularity

Like any other material, polymers are affected by design trends and fashions. However ubiquitous, the popularity of a material cannot be taken for granted. Plastic is universally valued for its ease of manufacture, versatility and for its properties, like good strength to weight ratio and water resistance, and so demand for the material is unlikely to disappear, but it may change.

As previously mentioned, bioplastics have seen a surge in popularity in recent years and chemical engineers and materials technologists continue to develop new polymers in response to this demand. New materials initially carry the cost of the research and development process, however, as they gain popularity and manufacture becomes more viable, the cost will come down and they become accessible to all.

> **Case study: Development responding to demand**
>
> At the University of Tel Aviv, Earth scientists and chemists have been developing a bioplastic polymer called polyhydroxyalkanoate (PHA) that can be manufactured without the use of fresh water, an increasingly scarce resource. This polymer comes from micro-organisms that feed on seaweed. Neither the manufacturing process or the end product produce any toxic waste and, at the end of life it is biodegradable or can be recycled back into organic matter.
>
> The university is now expanding its research into bacteria and algae in the hope of developing further polymers with different properties.

> **Q5** What other trends have influenced the use of plastics in product design?

Social, cultural and ethical considerations

Many products are subject to trends and fashion and those made from polymers are no exception. There are many ways for companies to carry out market research, so they know how to design for specific target markets, age and social groups.

All products convey messages, whether it be obvious, through imagery and colour, or less so through cultural values or ethos. Whilst it is legitimate to create a design to appeal to one section of society, it does not mean it is acceptable to alienate or offend others. **Use of language and colour** in particular can cause confusion. In many eastern and western cultures, colours and words have different meanings and connotations, for example in many western cultures, the colour purple represents wealth and royalty, however in some Asian and Latin American cultures it represents death and mourning.

Incorrect use of **language** and different cultural values can sometimes get companies into trouble. Some words in one language can have very different meaning in another. Some cultures and countries do not allow gambling, therefore a polymer roulette wheel and set of poker chips would be considered offensive and would obviously not be very successful. This type of product would not be considered **suitable for the intended market**.

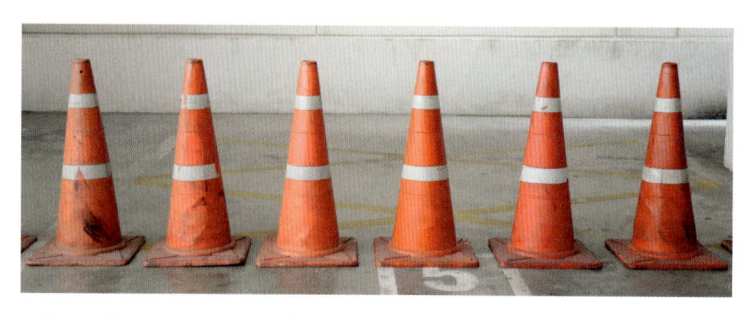

In the UK the colour red is a warning, meaning stop or danger, in China it is associated with joy and prosperity

> **Q6** Discuss what meaning different colours, gestures or words have in different cultures that could easily be misunderstood and cause offence.

The demand for choice and variety, especially in products seen as disposable or single use has been driven by the **consumer society** and the effects of **mass production**. When manufactured in greater numbers, a product becomes cheaper and thus more accessible to the mass market, which can devalue the product in the eyes of some consumers. Some manufactures have reacted to this trend by attempting to add value to their products by making the consumer aware of the sustainability issues relating to a product. Some companies display advice on the sustainable production of their product and what the correct disposal and recycling procedures are, drawing the consumers' attention to the value of the material.

Manufacturers must also consider the needs of different **social groups**. Plastics present an inexpensive and highly functional alternative to many other costlier materials making them accessible to a broader socio-economic market. They also offer weight and hygiene advantages and are much easier to keep clean than other materials, which is vital in countries where waterborne disease is commonplace. For some, plastics may be considered indispensable if not life-saving.

A community collects water in Tanzania re-using High Density Polyethylene (HDPE) containers

Our **consumer society** has given rise to **built-in obsolescence**. This is when products are designed to have a limited life span due to their quality, the materials used or indeed their aesthetics. With polymers, built-in obsolescence is linked to wear and tear as well as trends and fashions. New manufacturing technologies help develop and invent new products as well as driving sales. Low-cost, **mass produced** products make it easy for consumers to use and dispose of products quickly as trends and formats change. Built-in obsolescence is considered unethical by many, as it encourages consumerism and puts unnecessary pressure on our natural resources.

> **Q7** What duty of care do British companies have towards the workers who manufacture their products in factories on the other side of the world?

Reinforcing and stiffening

Polymers are subject to forces and stresses in everyday use. Simply being stored on a roll, polymer film is in **tension** and **compression**. A plastic bottle lid is subject to **torsional forces** when we twist it off and a shear force is exerted on a plastic coat hook. Whilst some polymers may be relatively strong, for many applications they need further stiffening or reinforcement.

Polymers are subject to forces and stresses in everyday use

Flexibility

Many polymers are flexible if produced in thin sheet or film form, however others are naturally rigid and brittle. Flexibility is an essential requirement for many applications where a selected polymer has to resist different forces and stresses. Stiffer, thicker materials need a greater force to bend them and may crack or buckle under too much pressure, whereas thinner, more flexible polymers like PVC can bend and roll without cracking. Thermoforming plastics become more flexible when heated which assists in manipulation and forming.

Tension

Tension or pulling forces affect many polymer products. Plastic bags and boxes are in tension when lifted, and polymers like polyethylene are used for ropes and string because of their excellent tensile strength.

Shear

Shear force is exerted when two planes move against each other in opposite directions. An obvious example of shear force at play in polymer products is tearing, for example in films used to wrap food or packaging which requires a low tear strength so that they can be torn open more easily.

Compression

Most polymers will be subject to compressive or pushing forces during manufacture and use, for example, when products such as plastic chairs are stacked in storage. As a polymer is injected, blown or pressed into a mould pressure is exerted. The keys on a keyboard are constantly being compressed with every letter typed as is the nib and body of a plastic pen in use.

Improving functionality

Frame structures

Polymer products are often used to create frame structures to support other materials. Rigid or flexible poles can simply be joined with injection moulded joints and sockets. Putting components in tension and compression creates a lightweight form or substructure that, depending on the shape, can resist different directional forces. **Triangulating** a form can further strengthen it. Triangles have a natural rigidity to them and are used in many strengthening techniques. Braces, ribs and struts are all used to improve strength through triangulation. Note the moulded ribs in the image below.

Polymers are shaped to improve their physical properties and to help resist forces and stresses

Plastic additives

Many different chemicals and compounds can be added to enhance the functional and aesthetic properties of plastics. **Pigments** are added to change the colour, **plasticisers** are added to increase flexibility and even **fragrances** can be added, as seen in some children's toys and air-freshening products.

Stabilisers can be added to make plastic resistant to heat and light. One of the main issues with plastic degradation is the effect that ultraviolet (UV) light has on it. Over time, plastic becomes brittle and can lose its colour, starting to yellow or fade. By adding UV stabilisers, this process can be slowed down, enabling a product to last longer and perform its task more efficiently.

UV light can make polymers become brittle and faded

Flame retardant additives

Whilst most plastics are not flame resistant they can be treated to improve flame retardant properties. Flame retardants are either incorporated into the polymer mix or added as a coating after polymerisation. Commonly used flame retardants contain either phosphorus or bromine.

Fire retardants make polymers more resistant to ignition, slow down the speed that the flame will spread, slow down the release of heat and slow down the generation of smoke and fumes. Polymers with fire retardant additives are used in roofing and cladding, films, tarpaulin and some electrical products. These additives are important as they help prevent the material from becoming a fuel which may increase the outbreak of fire.

Standard material stock forms, types and sizes

Most plastics come in a very wide range of standard shapes and sizes. This enables materials to be more interchangeable and for the manufacturers of specialist tools and equipment to be aware of the material they will need to cope with. Standard dimensions use length x width x thickness for sheet materials, length x diameter for rods, and length x diameter x wall (material) thickness for tubes.

Sheet, bar, rod and tube sizes

Metric is the standard measuring system for plastic forms. Sheet material normally starts at around 1mm thick and increases to over 20mm thick; lengths and widths vary depending on the type of plastic and the thickness required. Rod is available from 2mm to well over 100mm diameter and tubing is available from 5mm to around 1 metre in diameter.

Pipes or tubes are a little more complicated to measure, as you need to decide on the wall thickness you require. Too thin a wall section could mean the product lacks strength and too thick could add unnecessary weight and cost to a product.

Wall thickness is usually measured in millimetres; however, traditionally it is known as the **gauge** and some tubular plastics may still be sold by gauge. As the gauge number increases, the wall thickness decreases.

> **Q8** If a sheet of 3mm acrylic weighs 1.2kg, how much will the same size sheet weigh if it is 5mm?

The cross-sectional area of a solid square or rectangular bar is simply the area of the square or rectangle A = L x W and of a round bar A = πr^2

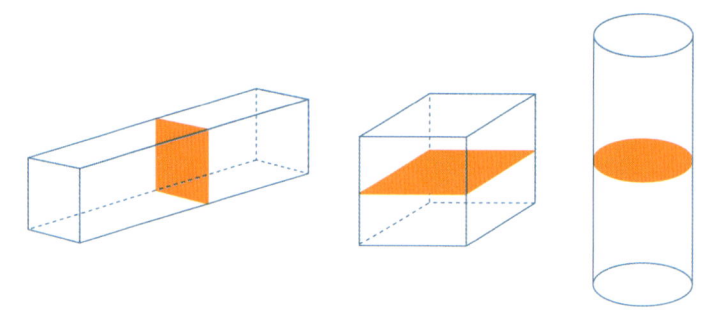

Cross-sectional area of shapes

Plastics as powder, granules, foam, films and resins

The majority of the polymers used in Design and Technology workshops tend to be sheet, rod or tube, but they are also available in a variety of other forms.

Powders and granules are mainly used in plastic processing such as plastic dip coating, injection moulding and extrusion (covered in Chapter 46). The granules are heated until they become soft and can then be shaped as required. Powders tend to be bonded to the surface of hot materials such as metals. Both are available in a wide range of colours.

Rolls of plastic film are widely used for packaging, especially in the food industry. Films can easily be heat-sealed to make them airtight and tamper proof.

Expanded plastics and foams are also used by the packaging industry, and one of the most common forms is expanded polystyrene. It is incredibly lightweight and protects the contents of a packet from impact damage. Expanded plastics are also used in cars to soften areas such as dashboards and bumpers, which are prone to impact. Plastic foams are used by the furniture industry to soften seating and beds and can even be used as floor coverings that are soft underfoot.

> **Q9** What are the physical characteristics of expanded polystyrene that make it able to resist impact?

Thermosetting polymer resins can be used to produce a variety of products by casting them into a mould where they set and permanently take on the shape of the mould. These polymers used in casting are made up of two parts; the resin itself and a hardener known as a catalyst.

Chapter 46 – Planning and production methods

Objectives

- Be aware of the advantages and disadvantages of different manufacturing processes for various scales of production
- Understand how production aids and quality control procedures improve manufactured products

Marking out polymers

When giving the dimensions of a plastic component, **tolerances** are often indicated to ensure an accurate fit. A tolerance is the acceptable margin of error, for example if a polyurethane bearing is made to fit a metal axle and it is made too big it will not run smoothly and if it is made too small it will jam. The margin of error may be as little as ±0.01 mm, so the tool used to measure and mark it out polymers must be accurate.

Reference surfaces and **datum points** are used to measure from. Measuring tools should have accurately machined surfaces and calibrated readings.

- Digital callipers are used to measure thickness or gauge
- Scribers are hard, sharp steel tools used to mark a line on a plastic surface and are often used with a steel rule or tri-square which enables the accurate marking of a 90° angle
- Micrometres and gauges are used to measure thickness and gauge
- Chinagraph pencils (pictured below) are used to create temporary markings on a variety of plastic surfaces. Different colours show up on different shades of substrate.

> **Q1** Other than those listed above, which tools are used to mark out sheet acrylic in a workshop?

Quality control

When products are made, checking that they are being produced correctly is an essential stage. This is known as **quality control** (QC) and is crucial to ensure dimensional accuracy is consistent and that the product is reliable and safe to use. Visual inspections are used to check the quality and consistency of the finish as well as the integrity of any joins and connections between components.

Production aids (see below) may be used in all scales of production to ensure the accurate shaping and machining of polymer parts. **Jigs**, **templates**, **patterns**, **fixtures** and **moulds** help manufacturers produce consistent results.

A number of quality control devices are either attached to machines or can be used to check for consistency. A **depth stop**, for example, can be found on most pillar drills. The depth of the hole required is set on the gauge, tested once to check that the correct depth has been set, and then all subsequent holes will be the correct depth. Other quality control tools known as **go/no go fixtures** are available to ensure accuracy and consistency. These tools are set to the specific **tolerance** allowed for that particular component.

Production aids

Jigs

Jigs aid manufacture and speed up repeat processes. A jig might be used to help fold a polymer sheet and to make sure that folds run perpendicular to the edges of the sheet. Jigs vary in complexity depending on the level of use and help with positioning and dimensioning for example when drilling a hole; they also reduce the time spent marking out. Jigs can help make accurate angles when line bending.

Templates

Templates are more commonly used in small batch production runs to help lay out and nest shapes for efficient cutting and drilling. They are usually pre-cut from boards or more rigid materials like manufactured boards or metals.

Patterns and moulds

Patterns are the positive forms used in resin casting to produce negative moulds which enable copies to be made. Patterns can be made from a range of materials including wood and silicone rubber and are usually sprayed with release agent before being cast to create the mould. The mould itself may be made from a range of materials depending on what is being cast or moulded and how many times it will be used, these include Plaster of Paris, silicon rubber, latex or GRP. Moulds used for vacuum forming in school may be made from wood, MDF and Styrofoam™. In industry, moulds are frequently made from tool steel to ensure a high-quality finish over thousands, if not millions of identical products.

Scales of production

Whilst we might immediately associate plastic products with mass and continuous production methods, polymers are used at all scales of production.

One-off production

Crafts people and artists create a wide spectrum of hand made, one-off or bespoke products from sculptures to handmade furniture. These are usually time consuming, require a high level of skill and practice and will usually be expensive to produce. Resins are commonly used for their decorative qualities and polyurethane varnishes are commonly used as a finish for wooden furniture. GRP is also commonly used to make individual pieces for specific tasks.

A bespoke table with polyester resin detail

Batch production

Batch production is a broad term for production runs of anything from ten, to tens of thousands of products. The key common factors are repetition and the need for consistency to which end jigs, templates and patterns are used to aid replication. Processes are more highly mechanised than in one-off production and workers have to be trained to use specialist machinery. There is usually a certain amount of downtime between batches, whilst tooling and set-ups are changed so that a new product can be produced.

Toys, moulded furniture and some packaging products are batch produced. Batch production is ideally suited to some drug packaging as runs will likely change in response to need. If you look closely at the blister packaging of health products and tablets you will usually find a batch number and date.

Mass and continuous production

More highly automated than batch production and requiring less skilled labour, mass production uses a production line to produce high numbers of identical products quickly. These are often common day to day products which are used briefly, disposed of and then repeat purchased such as food packaging, plastic bags and cups. Materials for mass production are usually purchased in bulk and whilst set-up costs may be high, the need for less skilled labour and the high level of output helps to lower unit costs.

Continuous production

Continuous production is similar to mass production, however as the name suggests, there is no downtime as only one product is made with very few, if any alterations. This is ideal for products such as HDPE milk bottles, PET drinks bottles and film used for refuse sacks and other plastic bags for which there is continuous demand.

Production techniques

There are many different plastic processing methods used in industry and in schools. The rest of this chapter looks at a selection that you need to know about.

Blow moulding

Blow moulding is used to make hollow shapes such as those used for bottles. An extruded plastic tube known as a parison is fed into a hollow mould. The parison is pinched at the bottom as the mould closes and is filled with heated compressed air until the parison inflates to fill the mould. The plastic cools and takes on the shape of the mould. The moulding is then released and trimmed. High production moulds are often water cooled to speed up the production process.

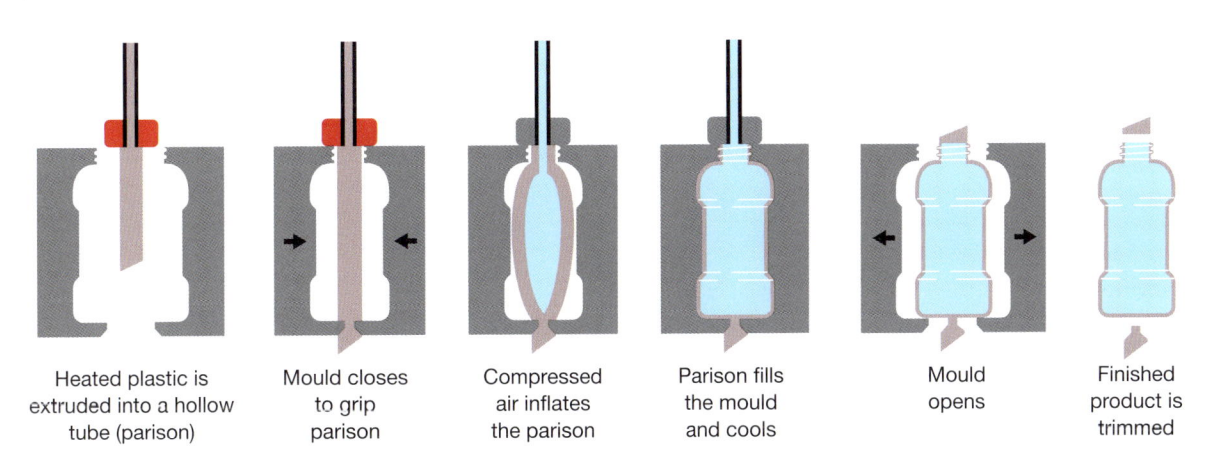

Heated plastic is extruded into a hollow tube (parison) | Mould closes to grip parison | Compressed air inflates the parison | Parison fills the mould and cools | Mould opens | Finished product is trimmed

Injection moulding

This process is ideal for complex shapes. Firstly, a mould needs to be made; these are generally constructed from steel in two parts. They must be very accurate as any blemishes will be transferred to every moulding produced. A number of different polymers are suitable for injection moulding and include ABS, acrylic and PVC.

Injection moulding process:

1. Granules of the chosen plastic are fed into the hopper
2. The hopper feeds the Archimedes screw that drags the granules past a heater, where they are softened and become plasticised as they travel forward
3. The plastic is in a soft, pliable form as it reaches the end of the screw, where it collects until there is enough to fill the mould
4. Next a hydraulic piston forces the softened plastic into the mould under pressure, filling it up
5. The plastic sets quickly, the mould is separated and **ejector pins** release the moulding
6. The process is repeated.

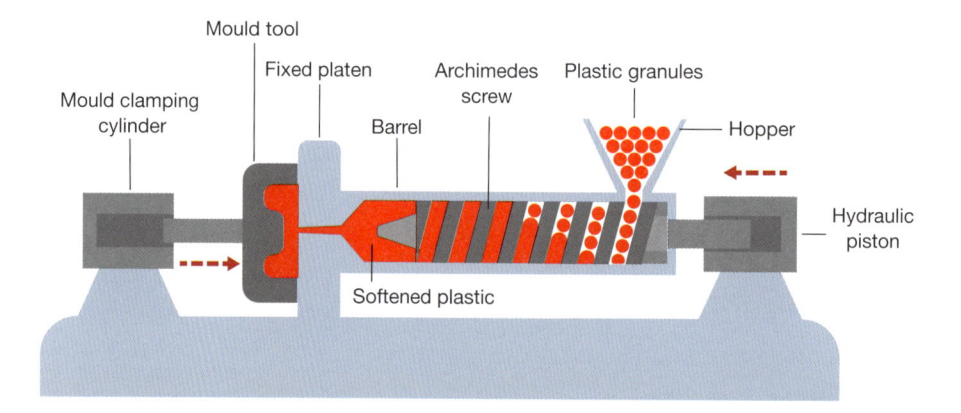

> **Q2** Suggest **three** objects other than bottle lids that are commonly injection moulded.

Polymer welding

Heat welding plastic involves using a special hot air gun which accurately heats the areas being welded together as well as a plastic filler rod that is applied to the weld joint. Filler rods are available in HDPE, rigid PVC, LDPE, PP and ABS making it a versatile way to join many plastics.

Hot gas welding a leak in a PVC pipe

There are several different methods of polymer welding including hot gas welding, hot plate welding, ultrasonic welding and laser welding. Hot gas welding uses a specialist heat gun or welder which fires a jet of hot air, softening both parts to be joined, and a filler rod which is run down the seam. The plastics joined must be similar and the resulting join will show. In laser welding, the finish is subtler as no filler rod is used. The two edges are cleaned and pressed together tightly, and a laser runs down the join, softening the polymers and creating a join.

Line bending

Bending most plastics involves heat unless they are very thin. Strip heaters are used for line-bending which is a good way to create a permanent fold in a piece of thermoplastic such as acrylic.

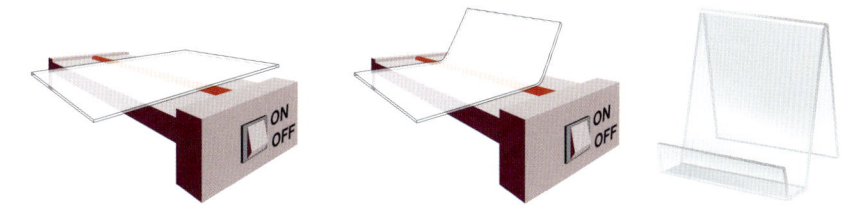

Line bending process:

1. Use a marker pen or chinagraph pencil to mark out where the bend lines will be
2. Turn on the stripheater so that it comes up to a working temperature
3. Put on heat-proof gloves and have a tray of water ready to cool the workpiece
4. Place the marked line of the workpiece across the heating strip
5. Allow the plastic to heat through (the time needed will depend on the thickness of the material, thicker materials may need to be turned over to heat from both sides)
6. Test for flexibility as the workpiece approaches the right temperature (too cool can lead to it cracking, too hot can lead to scorching and blistering). Bend the workpiece to the required angle (a jig or former may be used to ensure accuracy)
7. Once the workpiece has set it can be cooled in a water tray.

Press moulding

Press moulding, also known as compression moulding, is a process that requires two moulds, a male and a female which when pressed together, create a void. The moulds are first heated and then a charge or preform of polymer is placed between the moulds. The amount of polymer in the preform is usually slightly greater than that needed to fill the void which ensures no gaps are left. Pressure is exerted on the moulds which come together, heating the charge and forcing it into the void to create the part. It is then left to cool before removal using an ejector pin. This process is often used with thermosetting polymers and is used for fairly simple profiles such as electrical fittings.

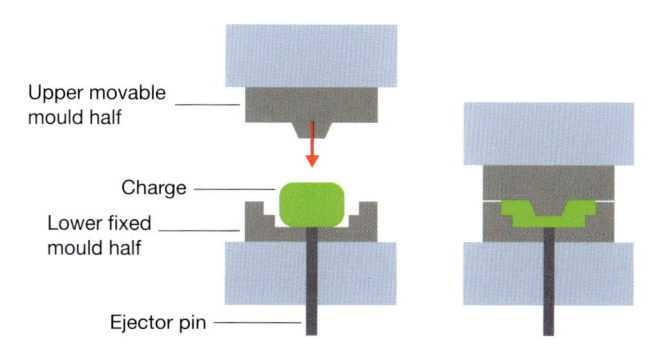

Extrusion

Extrusion is used to create a continuous flow of plastic that is pushed through a die to create a specific profile. Extrusion is used for cables, pipes, mouldings and even plastic film used for bags and packaging.

The extrusion process starts off in a similar way to injection moulding, using a die instead of a mould. The die sets the profile of the extruded plastic and must be made to a very precise tolerance. A continuous flow of the softened plastic passes through the die at just the right temperature and flow rate to hold the shape.

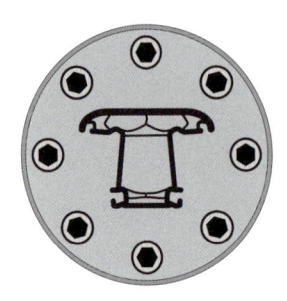

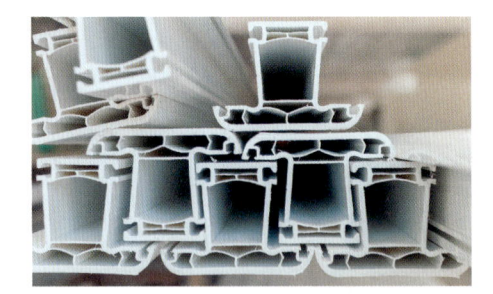

The extruded plastic then passes onto a cooling table or cooling trough where it fully solidifies and is either wound onto a spool or drum if thin and flexible, or cut into lengths if rigid.

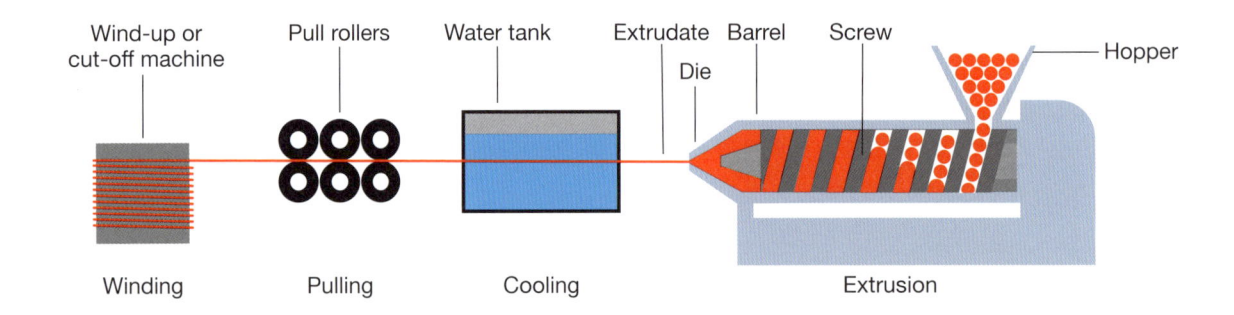

Q3 Why must the die be made to such a precise tolerance?

Computer aided manufacture (CAM)

Computer-aided manufacture or CAM lends itself to batch, mass and continuous production methods as it enables processes to be repeated accurately and often reduces human error.

Machinery including laser cutters, CNC routers, milling machines and 3D printers read code generated by CAD software which then plot an optimum path for the laser or cutting tool to follow. This means that layouts can be maximised and cutting paths can be optimised for speed, cutting lead times, wastage and associated costs.

3D printing

3D printing is an **additive manufacturing** process that enables physical objects to be formed from reels of thermoplastics. 3D printers use special CAD files, usually in STL or VRML format, and converts them into a series of coordinates that the printer will follow, building up the image in layers.

There are different types of 3D printers available, including the following:

- **Stereolithography** (SL) involves using lasers to part cure the printed shape from a bath of liquid resin. This is an expensive but very accurate method.
- **Digital light processing** (DLP) is similar to stereolithography but uses a powerful light source rather than a laser.
- **Laser sintering** uses a powdered material instead of a resin bath. The solid shape is created as the heat from the laser fuses and solidifies the powder.
- An extrusion method also known as **Fused Deposition Modelling** (FDM) is the most popular in schools and involves melting a plastic filament with a heated extrusion head.

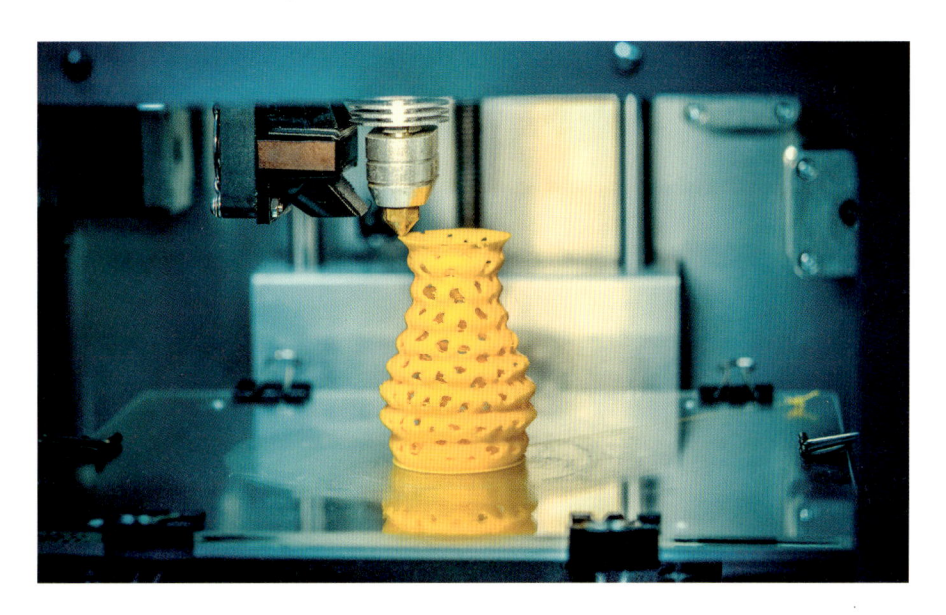

Fused deposition modelling 3D printer

The most common in schools are single-head printers that use reels of printable plastic filament. ABS and PLA are usually used in FDM style printers and come in pre-coloured cartridges. New and interesting materials are frequently being developed which allow for printing in wood, steel and brass effect. Soft rubbery materials are also becoming available, making prototype products even more realistic.

Very complex shapes can be 3D printed and some filament printers can print in more than one colour. Dry powder printers can even print in full colour.

> **Q4** Why are 3D printers so useful for creating prototypes and scale models?

3D printers can print other materials besides plastics, including metals, paper, ceramics and even food. 3D bio-printing is also being developed, meaning that in the future we may be able to successfully print replacement body parts.

Chapter 47 – Material processing

Objectives

- Understand the application of specialist techniques when manufacturing products
- Be aware of the advantages and disadvantages of specialist techniques
- Be able to select appropriate specialist techniques and joining methods

Shaping, processing and machining polymers

A vast array of tools is available in workshops in order to help us make the products we require. Tools enable us to mark out materials and cut them to size. They enable us to perform **wasting** (removal of material), **addition** (adding material), **deforming** and **reforming** techniques as well as applying a finish.

Before undertaking any activity in a workshop, you need to be aware of the health and safety rules that apply to each of the machines, tools, pieces of equipment and materials that you use. Your teacher will guide you in this area, but you must ensure that the correct personal protective equipment (PPE) is worn when operating machinery and using tools and equipment.

Drilling

Drilling a hole into plastic requires careful speed control. Large diameter drill bits require a slower speed than narrow ones to avoid overheating and the potential for the plastic to melt. The feed rate is another factor to consider – too much pressure can cause the plastic to crack.

A pillar drill is good for accuracy and is powerful enough to drill larger holes in thicker materials. A cordless drill is very adaptable and usually has variable speeds.

Common drill bits used with plastics

Name	Image	Characteristics	Name	Image	Characteristics
Twist drill bit		General purpose drill bit, also used on plastic, metal and wood	Hole saw		Used to cut large holes. They can easily overheat due to fast peripheral speed
Countersink bit		Used to ensure countersunk screw heads are flush with the surface	PCB drill bits		Very small drill bits for drilling copper-clad plastic board, fitted to a shank for ease of mounting

Bending polymers

There are many ways to bend polymers including **line bending** (covered in Chapter 46), oven forming, (also known as drape forming) or they can be flexed into shape and held under tension using mechanical fixings such as rivets, extruded channels or nuts and bolts. Heat guns can be used to bend rod and tube to an angle and **laminating** can create bends and curves in thin sections of polymer.

Cutting and sawing polymers

Saws are used to cut materials to size. The hacksaw and junior hacksaw are common plastic-cutting hand saws that are used to cut straight lines. The coping saw and Abrafile enable curved lines to be followed in thin material. The hacksaw has a robust blade and can be used for thicker material than the junior hacksaw, which is for light work.

The scroll saw and bandsaw are powered and can be used for curves or straight cuts through different thicknesses of material. With powered saws, you need to be aware that the plastic can easily overheat and melt. This can clog the blade and you may find the plastic bonds itself back together after being cut. If the blade is too course it can chip some polymers, therefore finer blades are recommended.

Extraction and appropriate PPE needs to be considered when using powered equipment.

Hacksaw *Junior hacksaw* *Abrafile*

Q1 What is the most essential piece of PPE to be worn when using a drill?

Q2 Research metal cutting saw blades and explain the following terms:
(a) Tooth pitch
(b) Kerf

Wasting by hand and abrading

Using hand tools and power tools to accurately shape polymers takes practice in order to achieve a high quality finish.

Abrading polymers can be performed by machines but is best finished and polished by hand. Hand abrading using files and wet and dry paper is best for hard to reach areas and it also allows you to apply force where it is needed most. Wet and dry paper comes in different grades; the grit density determines how rough or smooth it is. Similar to glasspaper, it is measured in grit per square inch – the lower the grit number, the rougher it is. Wet and dry paper starts at 150 grit and is available up to 2000 grit, which is so fine that it has a polishing effect.

A disc or belt sander is best used for easy-to-reach sections that can be held safely. Bobbin sanders can be useful for internal curves.

Wasting and abrading tools and materials

Name	Image	Characteristics	Name	Image	Characteristics
Files		Steel file with serrations on the blade that smooth the surface. Different shaped profiles and grades of cut available	Abrasive pads		Similar to abrasive paper, removes small surface scratches ready to be polished
Wet and dry paper		Paper backed abrasive material used to clean up and apply a smooth surface, used wet or dry, medium to very fine grades	Brasso®		Although designed for metal this polish gives polymers a very smooth and high shine finish, applied with a cloth

Q3 Which **three** pieces of PPE would be most appropriate to use when mechanically sanding?

Q4 When sanding a rough piece of plastic to a smooth finish, would you start with a high number grit and work lower or low number and work higher?

Addition, deforming and reforming

Laminating polymers

Laminating involves bonding strips or sheets of material together in layers. It can be done with thick materials in order to create very strong structures or very thin materials to create tough and flexible products. Polymers are frequently laminated with other materials such as glass or wood to improve aesthetics or functionality.

Laminated safety glass is now used in all car windscreens. It contains a thin film of plastic, usually polyvinyl butyral (PVB) or ethylene-vinyl acetate (EVA) which holds the inner and outer glass layers together when it is cracked or shattered. Without the laminated plastic layer, the glass would fly out, potentially causing serious injuries.

Laminated car windshield prevents shards of glass flying off

Plastic laminated boards are very popular for flooring products, kitchen worktops and some flat pack furniture. With these products, the plastic laminate is bonded to the surface of a manufactured board with adhesive – usually a **contact adhesive** that creates a strong and instant bond.

Plastic laminate comes in many colours and different effects. It can even be printed on with photographic images, commonly used to resemble marble or granite for kitchen worktops or woodgrain effects for flooring and furniture products. The quality can be so good that it is sometimes hard to tell if it is real or not.

The laminating process involves layering the materials with an adhesive and holding it in the chosen position using a former or jig. Pressure is applied through a press, a set of clamps or by using a vacuum. In industry, melamine formaldehyde is often used for lamination as it provides a very robust and hard-wearing surface and has a high-quality finish.

Vacuum forming

Vacuum-formed products include items such as plastic egg-boxes and bath tubs. A thermoplastic sheet is heated and pressed onto the former (mould) by atmospheric pressure, as the vacuum reduces the pressure below the softened thermoplastic. The plastic takes on the shape of the mould, then cools and sets in position before the mould is removed.

High density polystyrene is the most commonly used plastic to vacuum form within schools. In industry polyester PETG, ABS and acrylic are also used.

To ensure a good product is made, the mould must:

- have a positive draft angle > 3° to ensure easy removal of the material from the mould
- avoid undercuts that would make removal of the mould impossible
- not have too deep a profile so that the plastic is drawn too thin and could easily burst
- have vent holes drilled to avoid air pockets where there are dips in the profile
- have corners and edges rounded with a small radius to aid removal
- have a smooth finish so as not to adhere to the hot plastic – a release agent can be applied to the mould to assist removal

Internal radius   External radius
Draft angle

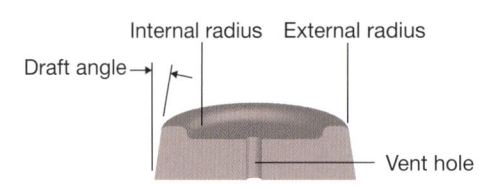

Vent hole

A suitable mould/former is carefully manufactured

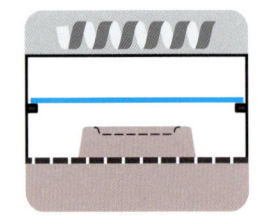

Plastic sheet is placed above the mould and clamped securely

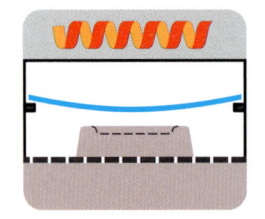

The electric heater is turned on to warm the plastic sheet which becomes flexible

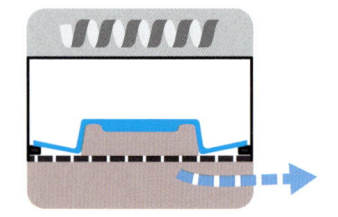

The air is pumped out below the plastic and mould

> **Q5** On the sketched former (pictured right), what features would you add or change to make it perform its job more efficiently?

Laser cutting and engraving

Laser cutters are one of the most accurate ways to cut many different plastics. The laser itself can follow a design to a very fine tolerance, but it must be set-up correctly. (Note that use of some plastics, for example PVC, should be avoided as they will give off poisonous fumes when heated.)

Lasers cut using a combination of speed and power to control the cut. The deepest cut would be on the slowest speed at the highest power and the lightest engraving would require the fastest speed and the least power. It is important to select the correct settings for the type and thickness of material and the type of cut or engraving required.

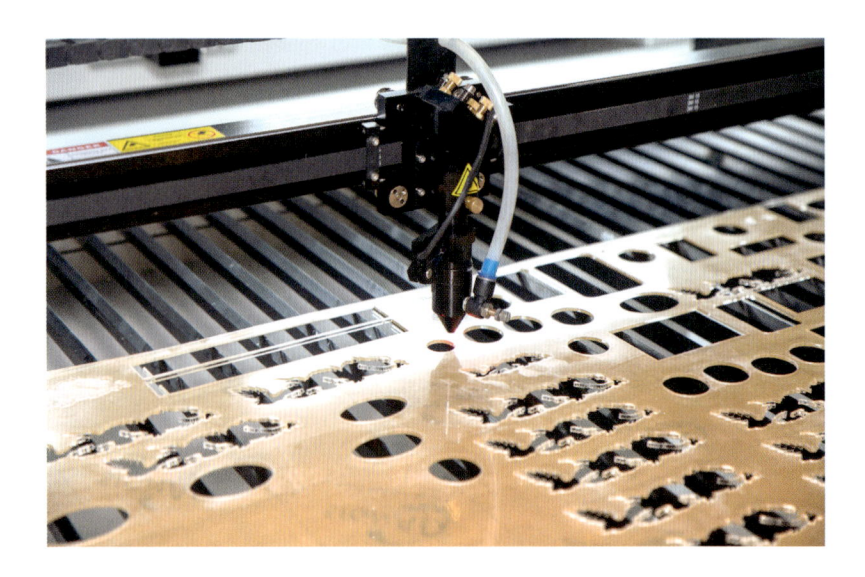

> **Q6** A material is being engraved using a laser cutter. The settings read 100% power and 100% speed. Which setting would you change in order to make a deeper engraving?

Joining polymers

Adhesives

Epoxy resin is a two-part adhesive; when the resin and the hardener are mixed in equal parts, the hardener acts as a catalyst and within minutes the mix cures hard. Because it does not set instantaneously, the pieces being joined usually need to be clamped whilst the resin cures.

Contact adhesives do not form as strong a join and therefore are usually used where larger surfaces are to be joined. Contact adhesives, which are also known as grab and impact adhesives, should always be applied to both surfaces and left to go tacky before joining. Positioning is key as once the two surfaces make contact the bond is instant.

Chemical welding is used in schools and involves using a solvent-based liquid that dissolves the surfaces of the pieces of plastic being joined. The two styles of chemical welds are liquid solvent cement and a thicker variety called dichloromethane methyl methacrylate, known as Tensol® 12. Both products are methane-based and need to be treated with appropriate care and PPE. Tensol® must be used in a ventilated room as it has high VOC levels.

Liquid solvent cement has a water-like consistency and is applied with either a fine-tipped paintbrush or a syringe. The surfaces being joined need to be flush as the cement will not fill any gaps. The cement is drawn along the joint by capillary action. Liquid solvent cement will join styrene, ABS, acrylic and butyrate in any combination. The join sets very quickly but is not particularly strong in thin sections. The solvent cement can damage the surface of the polymer if it is not applied carefully. **Tensol® 12** is best used on acrylic but will work with HIPS, PETG and polycarbonate. It is a much thicker solvent and is able to fill small gaps, but a flush accurate joint will always be much stronger. Tensol 12® is applied to the surface of the joint and can take around three hours to dry.

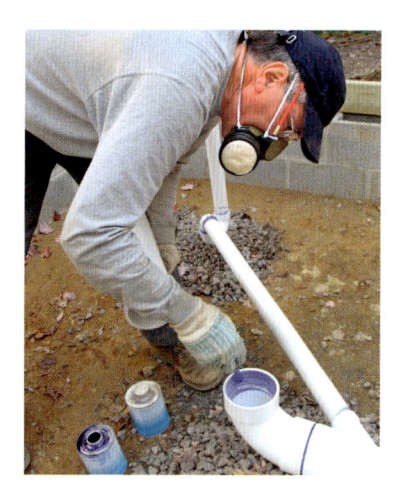

Standard components

To temporarily attach plastic to itself or to other materials many different methods can be used. **Machine screws** have a finer thread than self-tapping screws and they have no point on the end. **Self-tapping screws** can be used without the need for a screw thread to be cut first. This special screw cuts its own thread. The correct size pilot hole must be drilled first, otherwise plastics can crack or shatter as pressure is applied when it is screwed into position.

Like machine screws, **nuts and bolts** are available in many different lengths, diameters and thread pitches. Bolts come fully threaded or partially threaded; the unthreaded part is called the shank. **Washers** are used with machine screws and nuts and bolts to spread the load and prevent loosening.

Tapping and threading

Polymers can be internally **tapped** with a screw thread, allowing machine screws to be inserted, but the internal thread can easily strip if too much **torque** is applied. External threads can also be cut but can be easily damaged if too fine a pitch is used. Plastic nuts and bolts can be bought in and are frequently made from nylon as it is a self-lubricating material which stops threads becoming too difficult to operate.

Taps and **dies** are used to create the threads. Tapping an internal thread requires a pre-drilled hole. A set of three sequential taps are used to cut the thread, a taper, plug and bottoming tap. Each one is held in a **tap wrench** which enables the user to exert rotational pressure.

External threads are cut using a die in a **die stock** which enables the die to be rotated down the workpiece. When both tapping and threading, it is good practice to use make one turn forwards and then half a turn back. This clears the polymer **swarf** created in cutting the thread. When threading, the die stock must be held perpendicular to the workpiece otherwise the thread will not be straight; this is known as a **drunken thread**.

> **Q7** What are the roles of the tap wrench and die stock?

Name	Image	Characteristics	Name	Image	Characteristics
Nut		Usually a hexagonal profile used on bolts and machine screws to apply pressure	Nyloc		Single use vibration resistant nut that stays in position, nylon insert tightens up on thread
Bolt		Usually a hexagonal profile used with a nut to apply pressure	Grub screw		Headless screw with sharp point used to secure items such as a door handle or gears to a shaft
Machine screw		Many different driving methods and profiles, very versatile	Plastic nuts and bolts		Temporary fixing used for light applications, often made from nylon
Pop rivet		Semi-permanent joining of two or more pieces of material, only one-sided access needed	Washer		Used with machine screws, nuts and bolts to spread the load, some prevent loosening

> **Q8** Where it is physically possible, why is it better to use a metal nut to secure a machine screw as opposed to tapping a screw thread into plastic?

Chapter 48 – Finishing

Objectives

- Be able to select appropriate treatments and finishes and understand their application
- Be aware of the advantages and disadvantages of finishing techniques and preservation methods

Plastic surface treatments and finishes

The reasons for applying finishes to polymers falls into two main categories; protection and aesthetics. Most polymers are self-finishing, but a number of interesting finishes can be applied.

Adding aesthetic appeal may mean colouring polymers by adding pigment or applying graphics. Polymers can be enhanced to give it a texture of fine-grained surface finish, by using textured moulds in the manufacturing process or given a pattern (covered in Chapter 46) or lettering using laser engraving (covered in Chapter 47).

Common polymer-based finishing techniques

Polymer finishes vary dramatically in their method of application. A number of specialist techniques are available, depending on the desired finish.

Name	Image	Characteristics	Name	Image	Characteristics
Vinyl stickers		Printed and cut self-adhesive vinyl can be attached to most surfaces, specialist printer-plotter cutters are used	Textured moulds		Used to create subtle textures in the surface of the polymer. Can be used to imitate other materials such as leather
Laser engraving		Laser-engraved surface that can reflect light effectively, patterns and lettering can give a decorative finish	GRP pigments		Pigments are added to the polyester resins and gelcoats and mixed carefully to provide a deep uniform colour

Polishing

Polymers can become rough or scratched when they are processed and can also become weathered and faded if left outside. Polishing techniques can be used to restore a high-quality finish.

Brasso® is often used to give a lustrous shine to certain polymers such as acrylic. Many other specialist plastic polishes are available as are a number of products that restore faded and weathered plastics. Polishing can be done by hand or using a buffing machine. These are usually fitted with rotating cloth attachments called mops to which a polishing compound is added.

> **Q1** Find out about other polymer finishes including electroplating, flocking and rubberising spray.

Exercises

1. Acrylic edges can be polished on a buffing wheel.
   (a) Name **one** other surface finish or treatment that can be applied to acrylic. [1]
   (b) Use notes and sketches to show the process of how the edges of acrylic would be polished on a buffing wheel. [4]

2. Give **two** different moulding process that are used to manufacture polymer products. [2]

3. Biopol® is a thermoforming polymer
   (a) Explain **one** advantage of Biopol® over oil based polymers. [2]
   (b) Describe how Biopol® is manufactured. [2]
   (c) Explain **one** difference between thermoforming polymers and thermosetting polymers. [2]

4. Describe **one** method that is used during the production of products in quantity to ensure that dimensional accuracy is maintained. [4]

5. Give **two** properties of polyester resin that makes it an appropriate material for a shower tray. [2]

6. Study the PVC rainwater guttering pictured below.

   Give **two** features that makes the PVC rainwater guttering appropriate for manufacture using the process of extrusion. [2]

7. When polymers are selected for the manufacture of products, designers should consider the sustainability and recyclability of any materials used.

   Discuss the sustainability of polymers in manufacture, in use and at the end of their life. [6]

8. Use notes and sketches to show the process of bending acrylic using a strip heater. [4]

Section 6-5
Systems

In this section:

Chapter 49	Sources, origins and sustainability	252
Chapter 50	Physical and working properties	257
Chapter 51	Selection of materials and stock forms	263
Chapter 52	Planning and production methods	268
Chapter 53	Material processing and joining	277
Chapter 54	Finishing	283
Exercises		286

Chapter 49 – Sources, origins and sustainability

Objectives

- Explain where electronic products and the components within them come from and the raw materials they are made from
- Be aware of the social and ecological footprint of electronic products and components

Sources and origins

Electronic products and the systems used to control them are produced using a multitude of different materials sourced from all over the world. The following countries are amongst the most prolific producers of particular elements needed to create the electronic products that we rely on in our modern, connected society.

Russia, Saudi Arabia, and the USA are the main contributors to the wide variety of polymers that are refined from crude oil. These include **acrylic**, **high impact polystyrene** (HIPS) and **acrylonitrile butadiene styrene** (ABS). Each of these are used in the manufacturing of the cases that house many of our electronic products. China, Russia and the USA supply silicon, which is used to make the **semi-conductor** and **integrated circuit** which act as the decision making and processing parts of any electronic system.

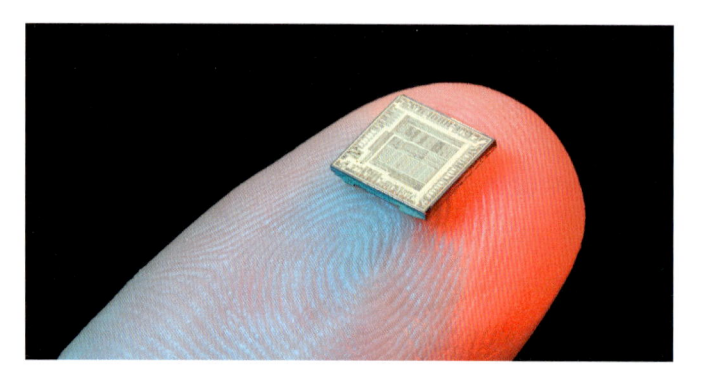

Silicone microchip etched on to a wafer of silicone

Gold is a valuable resource used in nearly all electronics as a plated covering of electrical connectors. A thin layer applied to a cheaper base metal gives superior connectivity and results in a higher quality and more reliable connection. China, Australia and Russia are three of the main suppliers of gold to world markets. Like gold, copper is another a metal with superior electrical conductivity, which is why it so commonly used for electrical cables. Chile, China and Peru are the world leaders in copper supply. China, Russia and Canada are the giants in the production of aluminium which is not only used for cheaper cabling and is an integral part of many electronic components, but is also a preferred casing material for high-end digital devices such as mobile phones, tablets and laptops.

To create batteries and other technical elements in screens and other components in digital devices, a number of **Rare Earth Elements** (REEs) are utilised. Increasingly harder to mine and expensive to buy, many of these elements can only be found in specific sites around the world including China, Australia and the USA. Lithium, a major ingredient in LiPo rechargeable batteries found in most modern digital devices, is frequently sourced from Australia, Chile and Argentina. Another common metal used in battery production as well as electroplating other base metals is nickel, which can be sourced from the Philippines, Indonesia, Russia, Canada and Australia.

Social footprint

A social footprint is a measure of the impact that a company's social policies have on its employees, partners or subcontractors and on society as a whole. Companies have an obligation to protect the environment by reducing their ecological footprint wherever possible, but they also have a duty to consider the effect that company policies have on all those affected. For example:

- Is there a flexible hours policy for parents who need to pick up children from school?
- Is the company understanding when a parent has to stay at home because a child is sick?
- Is the health and safety of all employees a primary concern?
- Are employees being paid a fair wage?
- Are there appropriate training schemes for employees?
- Are promising employees sponsored through university?
- Does the company contribute anything to the local community?

> **Q1** Discuss **two** other factors that you consider may contribute to:
> (a) a manufacturing company's social footprint
> (b) a school's social footprint

Communication technologies in society

Electronic systems play an important part in the lives of most people living in developed societies. Modern communications devices are now embedded in most cultures as they enable citizens to be 'connected' to their chosen networks, be it family, work or other social networks. Mobile- and smart-phones are perhaps the most common devices used, however computers and games consoles play increasingly significant important roles in many people's digital lives.

The average daily screen time for young children is recommended to be no more that two hours, however it is averaging to well over six hours a day in many countries. Additionally, it is hard for parents to monitor what their children are accessing or who they are able to contact or be contacted by. Cybersecurity is a big issue as is cybercrime and appropriate precautions need to be taken by all users.

The age of digital connectivity and instant communication has many positive factors and is transforming lives in many positive ways including access to medical advice and services, crowdfunding for innovative projects and awareness of important issues and human rights.

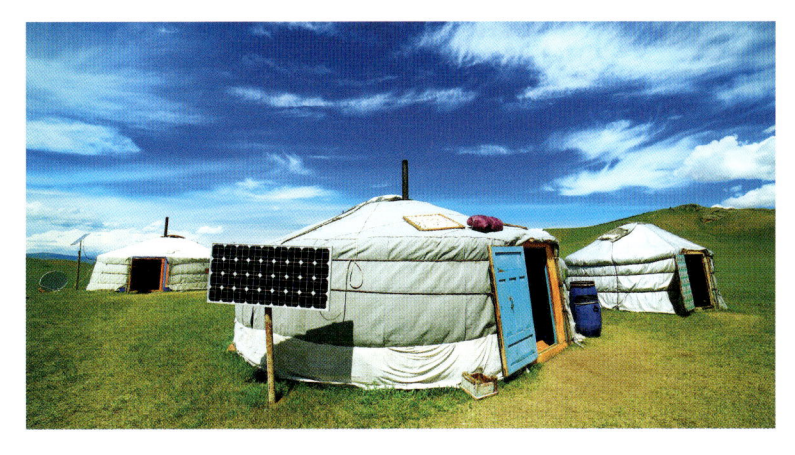

Mongolian ger with solar power and satellite television

Ecological footprint

When products are made, natural resources are used, so designers and manufacturers have to make decisions which have a direct impact on the consumption of the earth's resources. By designing products efficiently and, where possible, reducing the burden on finite resources, products can be made more sustainable. The impact can be further reduced with clever thinking and planning around how the product will be distributed and what will happen to it once it is no longer needed.

Material extraction and processing

When raw materials are harvested from the earth, it is inevitable that some disruption will occur. This is often done through mining which is a dangerous and disruptive process and in many countries is poorly regulated. The amount of environmental damage caused very much depends on the mineral being extracted. Once the raw material has been obtained, it normally needs to be processed into a usable form. This process of refining can also be very detrimental to the environment if it is not done responsibly.

Electronics manufactures rely heavily on scarce and/or hazardous elements that are used to make many electronic components and systems. Three of the main elements used are cobalt, tantalum and lithium. Manufacturers believe that supply is not keeping up with demand and there is a strong chance that shortages will lead to higher prices and reduction in the amount of products able to be produced.

Cobalt is used in the production of batteries and some specialist alloys but has a number of other uses including the colouring of pigments and dyes and as a catalyst for a number of chemical products. **Tantalum** is used in some types of capacitors and has very few alternatives in the electronics industry, meaning that it is in constant demand. Additionally, it is almost impossible to recover from products at end-of-life. **Lithium** is another metal used in batteries: rechargeable varieties in particular. With the global race for sustainable transport systems and our increasing reliance on mobile devices, rechargeable batteries have become one of the biggest growth industries and hence lithium is in extremely high demand.

Processing coltan ore, to extract tantalum, is poorly regulated in some parts of Congo

Built-in obsolescence

Many products are made to last and will have been engineered to a very high standard, however a growing number of products are made to last for a finite length of time and may well be designed and manufactured to meet a minimum set of requirements. There are a number of reasons for products having **built-in obsolescence** but one driving factor is repeat sales. Manufacturers want to sell the latest version, and this is particularly common with electronic products. Newer, faster, better upgrades are always available and compatibility with older models starts to become an issue very quickly, forcing products to be recycled or often just thrown away.

Effects of use

Most electronic products contain a combination of metals and polymers that are not good for the environment if disposed of incorrectly. Specialist recycling needs to be undertaken to reclaim and make safe any toxic elements and to recycle as much of the casing and other elements as possible.

Recycling batteries and PCBs

Non-rechargeable batteries and electrical appliances are particularly difficult to recycle as they frequently contain toxic chemicals and heavy metals. These need careful processing to ensure they do not leach into the environment if dumped into landfill sites. There are major concerns that soil and water contamination occur when poisonous heavy metals and chemicals find their way into the water table. This causes a real threat to wildlife and the environment.

In 2006 the **EU Battery Directive** set targets for the recycling of batteries and their separation from domestic waste in an attempt to reduce potential contamination.

PCBs are very difficult to recycle. A typical PCB will contain solder frequently made of lead and tin, copper track and many components with aluminium parts. Some electronic components contain mercury, lead, iron and cadmium; many electrical connectors are also gold plated. All of these metals can be recycled, but need to be separated from the PCB, which is usually made from fibreglass; another difficult material to recycle.

There are two ways that PCBs are recycled.

1. They can be dismantled by hand, which allows more parts to be recycled intact, but it is very labour intensive and costly.

2. They can be ground down and the separate elements collected from the powder.

Metals are separated from used electrical goods at a waste dump in Accra, Ghana

As many of the metals used in electronic products become more scarce and increasingly expensive, the profit in PCB recycling is improving, but many used boards are still shipped or dumped overseas.

> **Q2** What factors make the recycling of PCBs so difficult?

> **Q3** What are the ethical and environmental concerns facing overseas shipment of used electrical goods?

Environmental factors

A number of regulations are in place to make electronic products and components better for the environment and to protect workers and consumers from potential harm.

Restriction of Hazardous Substances (RoHS)

The **RoHS** directive was introduced in 2002 and implemented by all EU states from 2006 (updated 2018). Its aim is to restrict hazardous substances in manufacturing. The directive has had a major effect on the electronics industry as the reduction in the use of lead, mercury and cadmium are amongst its main priorities. Lead, at the time, was a major component in solder used for all PCB construction. Lead free solders have now been developed to replace toxic versions. Both manufacturers and importers are responsible for ensuring that products are RoHS compliant.

Waste Electrical and Electronic Equipment (WEEE)

The **WEEE** directive (Waste Electrical and Electronics Equipment) for recycling became UK law in 2014 and was updated in February 2019. It governs the recycling of the estimated two million tonnes of WEEE items that UK companies and households dispose of each year. These items cover almost everything that either has a plug or runs on batteries. The directive sets recycling and recovery targets for manufacturers.

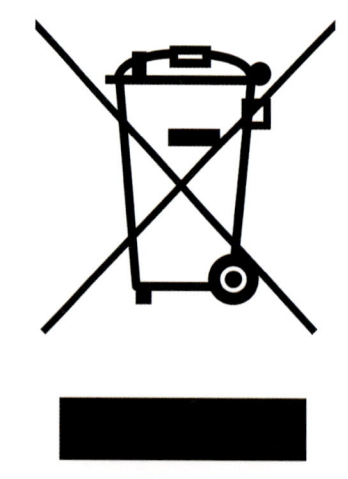

> **Q4** Find out the other substances that are monitored under the RoHS directive and which industries are exempt.

Chapter 50 – Physical and working properties

Objectives

- Describe the physical characteristics and working properties of electronic components and systems hardware
- Demonstrate an awareness of the influence of forces and stresses on electronic components and devices
- Describe a range of reinforcement and stiffening techniques in PCB and electronic product production

Physical and working properties

This chapter looks more deeply into the variety of components that are used when designing electronic products and electronic systems. It is essential to recap the information covered in Chapter 14 alongside the new components and processes listed here.

Inputs

Name and symbol	Appearance	Image	Characteristics	Uses
Moisture sensor	Available in different shapes and sizes. Usually two tracks close together on a PCB or two conductive probes		Detects levels of moisture in a substrate such as soil or responds to liquid levels in a system. Water conducts electricity; more moisture equals a greater reading	Automated watering systems, overflow devices, damp detectors
Piezoelectric sensor	Comes in many different shapes, sizes and colours of housings.		Detects physical pressure, can perform on/off tasks or detect gradual pressure being applied	Burglar alarm systems, video game floor mats, sensing fluid pressure in pipes

Control devices and components

The following group of components are used to control systems. Be aware of the different switches (toggle, rocker, push switches) and resistors covered in Chapter 14. In addition to those, the following components are used to develop and control electronic systems.

Name and symbol	Appearance	Image	Characteristics	Uses
Micro switch	Available in a variety of shapes, sizes and switching positions depending on the task		Momentary switches, usually SPDT, can be connected as normally open (NO) or normally closed (NC)	Triggering systems, safety shut off for tool guards, computer mouse, security systems, automated production lines

Chapter 50 **Physical and working properties**   257

Component	Description		Function	Applications
Reed switch	Glass tube with two spring steel contacts which overlap but do not touch with out a magnetic field present		The internal contacts are bought together when a magnet is nearby allowing electricity to flow	Security systems such as door and window sensors, proximity sensors
Variable resistors	Rotary and linear versions available, usually attached to a casing with a control knob		The resistor is connected so that one end of the rotation is at its minimum resistance and maximum at the other	Variable heating, volume and lighting controls, setting sensitivity levels
Transistor (bipolar)	A small semi-conductor in plastic or metal housing with three legs		Used as an electronic switch or as an amplifier to boost signals	Touch sensitive switches, sensing circuits
Microprocessor	Numerous pins connected to the semi-conductor processor, shapes and sizes vary depending on model / power		Transistors are etched on to a silicone processor, capable of processing information to operate computers	Processing information in smartphones, tablets, laptops and PCs
Microcontroller / PIC	Usually a dual in line (DIL) package, 8 to 40+ pins commonly available		Programmable flash memory makes these versatile ICs very adaptable for controlling electronic products	Controlling inputs and outputs in small to medium sized electronic devices, replacing numerous discrete ICs and other components
Relay	Electromagnetic coil used to connect and release spring switches in a housing		Uses a small voltage to switch on a potentially more powerful separate circuit. Also used as a latching device	Lighting circuits, controlling of high power devices such a motors, heating elements and solenoids

Q1 Name different types of switches available other than those listed here.

Outputs

As we discovered in Chapter 14, output components are used to give off a stimulus such as light, heat, movement or sound. Note that LEDs and buzzers are covered in Chapter 14 and need to be studied as well as those listed here.

Name and symbol	Appearance	Image	Characteristics	Uses
Motor (M)	Compact metal housing with protruding drive shaft, often with gear attached. Usually two or more wires for connecting to a power supply or drive unit.		Electromagnetic device that rotates the drive shaft in either direction depending on the polarity of the power supply	Mechanical toys, drones, electric transportation, washing machines, pumping systems, mobile phones
Loud speaker	Speaker cone shaped into magnetic coil at base, available in a wide variety of sizes		Full range of sound available, variety of power ratings (wattage), variety of frequency responses (treble to bass)	Headphones, music systems, intercoms, radios

Aesthetic factors

Electronic products are designed to appeal to consumers beyond their functionality. Designers spend time considering the aesthetic elements such as **form**, **colour** and **texture**.

A product's form and size will largely be dictated by the dimensions of any internal components, such as the PCB, a battery and the position of any input and output components. With the developments in PCB production and the miniaturisation of components, the form of many electronic products reduces in size over the years.

Note how the colour and texture of devices change with fashions and trends. Lots of sleek glass and aluminium, some anodised in subtle colours, is used in many modern devices. Some products are given colourful casings to attract certain users. Textured and rubberised ergonomic grips are frequently added to products to make them more accessible and user friendly to operate.

Q2 What factors have led to the changes in the form and appearance of mobile phones?

Forces and stresses

All materials, structures and products have to withstand stress as certain forces are applied to them when they are in use. The ability to withstand the stress is what allows them to perform their functions successfully. An electronic product will undergo a variety of different forces during regular operation, especially if dropped or misused. Manufacturers need to consider and test for all potential forces and stresses that their product may undergo prior to their product's release.

The different types of forces that you need to know about include:

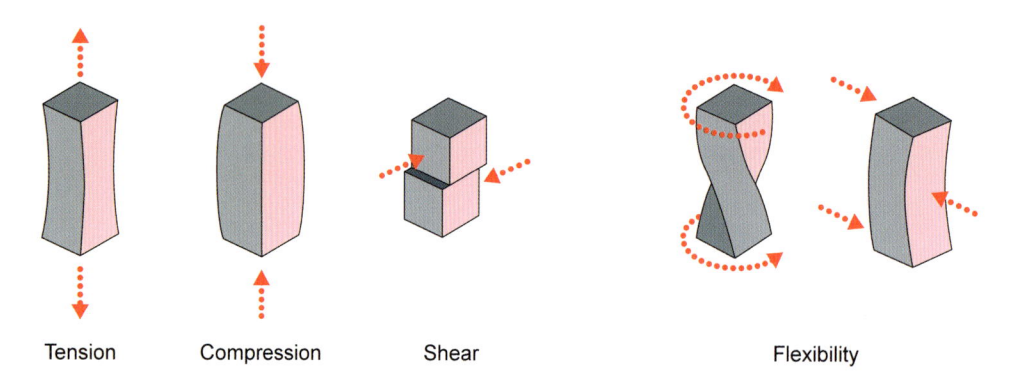

Tension   Compression   Shear   Flexibility

- **Tension** – Materials with high tensile strength resist pulling forces
- **Compression** – Materials with high compressive strength are resilient and resist crushing forces
- **Shear** – Materials that can resist two forces working against each other along an axis
- **Flexibility** – Flexible materials recover their shape after a bending or twisting force (torsion)

Reinforcement and stiffening techniques

Some forms of reinforcement involve stiffening a material through manipulation. Materials can be **laminated** to improve strength. **Folding** and **bending** techniques can be used to improve the mechanical and physical properties of a material and are often used in casings for electronic products.

Composite materials

PCBs are a composite material, being made from a combination of fibreglass and resin made into a rigid board with a layer of copper bonded to the surface. See Chapter 11 for more information on composite materials.

Printed circuit boards are a laminated composite material

Ribbing to strengthen case structures

Materials cost money and add weight to any product. Designers use a number of techniques to strengthen cases and reduce weight, saving valuable and expensive resources.

One way is to use **ribs** which come in many different forms, but generally involve thickening the chosen material in the specific areas that are subject to excessive strain or in areas of known weakness. Ribs save making the whole component extra thick making it lighter and more economic.

Physical and working properties, and characteristics

Materials and components are chosen for any number of specific physical characteristics that they may possess. Some materials used in electronics and systems have novel properties such as the piezoelectric effect, where movement becomes electrical energy and vice versa.

Resistor colour code

Resistance is measured in ohms (Ω). A resistor has a series of coloured bands painted onto its body. Each set of bands represents a specific value. To work out the value in ohms of the coloured bands, use the resistor colour code.

To identify the value of a resistor, read the colours from left to right. Firstly, hold the gold or silver band on the right-hand side. This is the fourth band and represents the **tolerance**, which is the permitted margin of error allowed in a resistor (see Chapter 51 for details). Then read the first band on the left; this is the first number. Next read the second band; this is the second number. Then read the third band; this is the multiplier, or the amount of zeros to add to the first two numbers. For example, red (2), red (2), yellow (4 zeros), gold, would be 220,000 Ω. It is actually written as 220k as the Ω symbol is not usually used and because 1,000 Ω is written as 1k, or 1 kilohm.

The resistor colour chart is used as a reference to work out the colour values for the four bands.

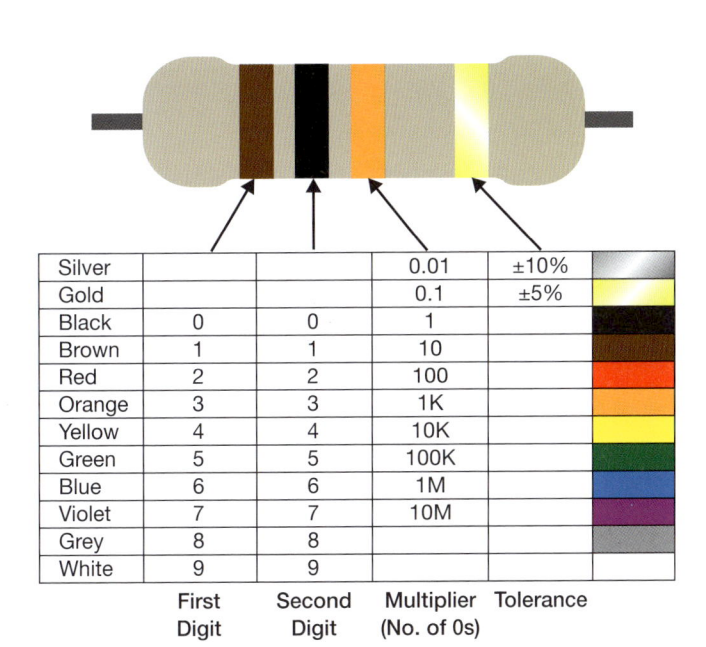

Colour	First Digit	Second Digit	Multiplier (No. of 0s)	Tolerance
Silver			0.01	±10%
Gold			0.1	±5%
Black	0	0	1	
Brown	1	1	10	
Red	2	2	100	
Orange	3	3	1K	
Yellow	4	4	10K	
Green	5	5	100K	
Blue	6	6	1M	
Violet	7	7	10M	
Grey	8	8		
White	9	9		

> **Q3** What is the value of the resistor shown in the diagram above?

Insulators and conductors

Most materials are either an electrical **insulator** or a **conductor**, meaning they either allow electrical energy to pass through them or not. As stated in Chapter 49, gold is a particularly good conductor, as are copper and silver. Polymers are particularly good insulators which makes them ideal for electrical shielding for cables and for making sockets, plugs and casings for electronic products.

As well as conducting or insulating electrical energy, materials can do the same for heat energy. **Thermal conductivity** is the measure of how well heat energy passes through a material. As you will know, most metals conduct heat well, whereas most polymers tend to be thermal insulators.

> **Q4** Discuss the insulative and conductive properties of glass.

Materials used for casings

Designers and manufacturers select materials on a number of criteria but usually the most important is the price. As products are made to a price point, the materials chosen must reflect those limitations. This is why polymers are such popular materials for case construction as they are robust, self-finishing, lightweight and natural **insulators**. The other most common material for casings is metal. Although it is heaver and a **conductor**, it is robust and lasts a long time.

There is a fashion for high-end electronics to have a metal finish to give the feel of luxury and longevity. Using metals over plastics does make a product more sustainable even though metals are a finite resource. This is because most metals are fully recyclable and if correctly processed they can be recycled without any loss of quality. Plastics, however, do not last as long, they are less likely to be recycled and even if correctly recycled, the quality does degrade.

Polymers take less energy to make into cases for products than metal and work out considerably cheaper. They are easily moulded into complex shapes, come in a broad range of colours and can be given a smooth or textured finish depending on the mould used. Polymers can be selected to be hard, durable and tough yet retain enough elasticity to resist being brittle.

The most common thermoplastics used in the making of cases for electronic products are ABS, acrylic and PVC and the thermosetting polymer urea formaldehyde is used for sockets and other electrical fittings. See the introduction to Section 4 for further information on the physical and working properties of materials.

Digital multimeter with combined polymer casing

Chapter 51 – Selection of materials and stock forms

Objectives

- Explain the different factors that influence the selection of electronic products and components
- Be able to calculate and determine the size and value of materials and components
- Identify a range of different stock forms

Selection of materials and stock forms

Most electronic components come in a range of standard shapes and sizes. Many are still based on an imperial system (favoured in the USA) using tenths of an inch as the standard distance between components.

Although commercial electronic circuits are becoming increasingly miniaturised and are using finer and even bespoke measurement systems, the through-hole technology that you are likely to be using in Design and Technology lessons will be based on a 0.1 inch grid.

The **integrated circuit** (**IC**), pictured right, is a **dual in-line layout** (**DIL**) which simply means that it has two rows of pins or legs. This particular IC is a 14 pin DIL (sometimes called a **DIP** or **dual in-line package**) as it has 2 rows of 7 legs. Other electronic components vary in shape and size but **through-hole** components usually have 0.1 inch, or multiples of, between legs.

A selection of different semi-conductors and an integrated circuit (IC)

As well as the physical size, the **voltage** and **current** rating of components needs to be considered when designing and making a circuit. Modern electronic products may well plug into the wall where, in the UK, the mains supply voltage is 230 volts (V). However, this is nearly always reduced or 'stepped down' internally with a transformer or **voltage regulator**.

> **Q1** What length on a PCB will a 40 pin DIL take up?

> **Q2** Many small electronic products are now designed to run from a USB port or USB charger. Find out what the supply voltage of a USB port is.

Availability factors

When planning the design and manufacture of a product, you should know the types, shapes, sizes and weights of standard **stock materials**. The majority of products can be made from stock materials but some products require **specialist materials** that are created for a specific product.

Stock materials for the electronics industry are generally mass-produced and include components, cables and circuit boards as well as a vast selection of different materials available for constructing and fabricating casings and housings.

Using stock forms offers several advantages to the manufacturer:

- Materials can be purchased repeatedly
- Repeat purchases will be consistent in terms of colour, quality and size
- Identical/similar products will be available from a range of different suppliers
- Cost of stock materials is lower than that of specialist materials due to economies of scale

Specialist materials are those which are commissioned or developed for a particular purpose or product. Specialist electronic components may be required by big electronics companies, where special software and even specific processors and other ICs are designed for a particular product or product range. Some companies develop new and bespoke components for their product ranges, for example Dyson have developed their own range of digital motors. The latest V10 model runs at 125,000 rpm.

The production run for specialist components may well be shorter than that for stock forms and hence will be reflected in the cost of the final materials. The exclusivity of specialist materials as well as the research and development necessary to bring them to market tends to make them more expensive.

Cost factors

There are numerous elements that make up the final selling price of a product. Fluctuations in the price of raw material and commodities have a knock-on effect on the price of stock materials. The quality of the materials and how widely available they are also play a role. The less the availability, the higher the price that can be charged, especially if demand is high. Additionally, more complex **manufacturing processes** and the greater the number of processes required will have an impact on the overall cost of production.

In industry generally, the narrower the level of **tolerance** required, the more an item will cost to produce. It is simply more time-consuming and therefore more expensive to make components and products very accurately. However, well-made products tend to work more effectively and last longer, so may in the end be better value for money.

Surface-mount technology (SMT) and through-hole components

Printed circuit boards are found in all modern cars and most domestic appliances. The single-sided, through-hole method used for prototyping in schools is not often used in industry. Instead, double-sided and multi-layered boards are used to save space and utilise component miniaturisation.

Surface mount technology (SMT) is often used instead of, and as well as, through-hole technology allowing components to be positioned on both sides of a board. Connections are easily made from one side or layer of a board to the connecting pins. SMT components are very small and take up far less space than through-hole components.

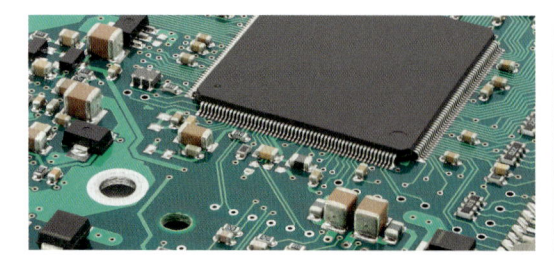

Surface mount components (SMT)

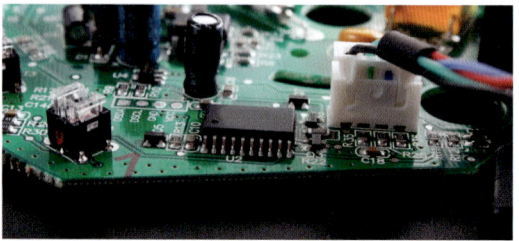

Combination of through-hole components and SMT

Stock forms and types

Preferred resistor and capacitor values

It would be impossible to have every value of resistor or capacitor available, therefore the 'E Series' of preferred values is used. The specific numbers are set component values.

The E12 and E24 series (pictured) are used for resistors. Capacitors come in a much smaller range of values. The values represent the first two numbers only and can be in any multiple or divisor of 10. For example, 12, 120, 1,200 and 12,000.

If an exact value is required, then a variable resistor should be used.

Component tolerance

When the value of a component is measured, it is not normally the exact stated value. The possible deviation from the indicated value is known as the **tolerance**, which could be between 1% and 10% with resistors, and as much as 20% with capacitors.

Resistors have a 4th colour band which represents the tolerance, or percentage accuracy. A 1K resistor is 1,000 Ω and if it had a gold 4th band, its tolerance is ±5%, meaning it could be between a lower value of 950 Ω and an upper value of 1,050 Ω.

E12	E24
10	10
	11
12	12
	13
15	15
	16
18	18
	20
22	22
	24
27	27
	30
33	33
	36
39	39
	43
47	47
	51
56	56
	62
68	68
	75
82	82
	91

Q3 What are the four colour bands of a 47k resistor with a 10% tolerance?

Q4 What value is a red, violet, green, gold resistor and what are the upper and lower limits?

Q5 If a student needed to protect an LED with a resistor and had worked out that it needed at least 330 Ω of protection, which E12 gold band resistor would you recommend and why?

Component ratings

Most electronic components carry maximum load ratings. This might be the maximum volts and/or amps that the component can handle before it overheats and potentially stops working.

It is really important to ensure that components are correctly rated for the task they are performing as some components can overheat and catch fire.

UK plugs carry protection fuses, rated in amps

Sizes and electrical units

Many units of measurement carry a prefix which is linked to a multiplier, meaning that it replaces a specific number of zeros. The table below shows the common prefix multipliers that you will come across whilst using electronic components and systems.

Prefix	Symbol	Multiplier	Factor
Tera-	T	1,000,000,000,000	10^{12}
Giga-	G	1,000,000,000	10^{9}
Mega-	M	1,000,000	10^{6}
Kilo-	k	1,000	10^{3}
Deci-	d	0.1	10^{-1}
Centi-	c	0.01	10^{-2}
Milli-	m	0.001	10^{-3}
Micro-	µ	0.000001	10^{-6}
Nano-	n	0.000000001	10^{-9}
Pico-	p	0.000000000001	10^{-12}

For example, a 2 kW (kilowatt) kettle uses 2000 Watts, and a 1 microfarad capacitor is equivalent to 0.000001 of a farad.

Unit of current (amp)

Ampere (amp) is the unit of measurement for electric current and uses the unit symbol A, however the symbol I is used in equations. Amps measure the flow of electricity past a point on a circuit or through a component.

Cables have ratings stating how many amps they can carry safely, as do many electrical and electronic components. Common household items are rated in the number of amps they draw in use. The mains electricity sockets in a domestic house are rated up to 13 amps maximum for each socket, and the ring main that they are connected to is normally rated between 30 to 45 amps.

Unit of resistance (ohm)

Ohms are the unit of resistance recognised by the Greek omega symbol Ω, however r is the symbol used in equations. R represents a specific resistor in question, rather than the value. Resistance is the measurement of the restriction in a conductor. Resistors are rated in ohms – the greater the number, the higher the resistance.

Unit of potential difference (volt)

Potential difference is stated in volts and uses the letter V as the symbol. Voltage is known as the **electromotive force** that relates to the flow of electricity in a circuit.

Applications of Ohm's Law

Ohms law describes the relationship between current, voltage and resistance in a circuit.

When resistance is increased, current is decreased. This is because a restriction slows the flow of electricity in a circuit. Additionally, when voltage increases, current increases as there is a greater electromotive force in the circuit increasing the flow.

Ohm's law states that voltage is equal to current multiplied by resistance or $V = I \times R$ or just $V = IR$.

This can be rearranged to $I = \dfrac{V}{R}$ or $R = \dfrac{V}{I}$

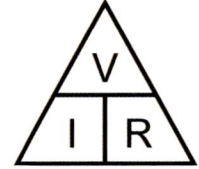

The Ohms law triangle can help to remember the different equations.

Resistors in series

To work out the total resistance value of resistors in series, simply add the resistor values together.

$R_{total} = R_1 + R_2 + R_3$ and so on.

Therefore, adding 1k, a 2k2 and a 47k resistor would be:

$1,000 + 2,200 = 3,200r$

Resistors in parallel

To work out the total resistance value of resistors in **parallel** use the formula:

$$\dfrac{1}{R\ total} = \dfrac{1}{R_1} + \dfrac{1}{R_2}$$

This formula can also be rearranged to give:

$$\dfrac{1}{R\ total} = \dfrac{R1 + R2}{R1 \times R2} \quad \text{or} \quad R\ total = \dfrac{R1 \times R2}{R1 + R2}$$

For example, if $R_1 = 1,000r$ and $R_2 = 2,200r$; R total = $\dfrac{1,000 \times 2,200}{1,000 + 2,200} = 687.5r$

Note that the total resistance is always less than the smallest resistor. This is because there are two routes for the electricity to go, meaning less overall restriction.

> **Q6** Calculate the total resistance of the following pairs of resistors, first in series and then in parallel.
> a) 10r and 20r   b) 330r + 470r

Rectangular area calculations

To work out area, multiply the length by the width: $A = L \times W$

To work out the area of a piece of printed circuit board that was 355mm long and 205mm wide, it would be: $355 \times 205 = 72,775mm^2$ which in cm^2 would be $727.75cm^2$.

Circle diameter and area calculations

The diameter of a circle is simply 2 × the radius.

To work out the area of a circle, such as the end of a round bar use the formula $A = \pi r^2$.

The area of a circle with a radius of 25mm = $\pi \times 25 \times 25 = 1963.495...$ rounded to $1,963mm^2$

> **Q7** What is the area of a 25mm radius circle to the nearest whole cm^2?

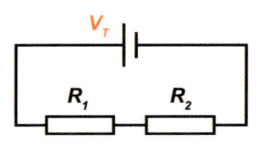

Chapter 51 **Selection of materials and stock forms**   267

Chapter 52 – Planning and production methods

Objectives

- Identify a range of different stock forms of circuit board
- Describe the characteristics of the different scales of production

Planning and production

Everything made needs to be designed, planned and manufactured. Bringing electronic products and systems to market takes meticulous planning and detailed production methods to ensure a successful product is achieved. At the heart of most systems is a circuit board.

Circuit boards

Electronic components are used to make circuits which perform certain tasks. Correct connections between components are vital for a circuit to work properly and a **printed circuit board** (PCB) is the best way to keep all the components in the correct place. Different types of circuit board are available, consisting of a non-conductive substrate (normally glass reinforced plastic or GRP) which holds everything in place, covered by a conductive layer (usually copper) which enables an electrical connection between selected components.

There are a number of different ways to make circuit boards. Most circuits start off on a prototyping board called **breadboard** which is a solderless way to plan and test a circuit. These are used for prototyping and form the basis for the planning of most GCSE projects. Most one-off and bespoke production will start off on a breadboard.

Breadboards are used to make physical prototypes for one-off production

The simplest form of circuit board is **stripboard**, also known by the trade name Veroboard. It is not a printed circuit, as you need to use the pre-laid tracks to route your circuit. Tracks can be broken with a track breaking tool to prevent a connection, and links are used to jump across tracks where new connections are required.

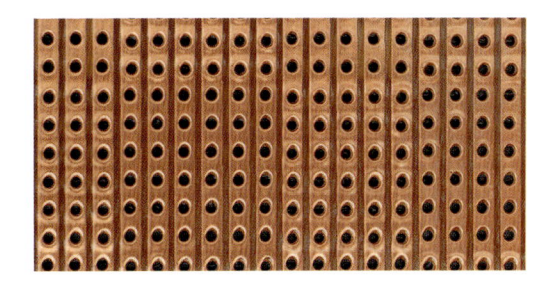

Printed circuit boards

There are two main types of PCB available; **copper clad PCB** and **photosensitive PCB** used in **photo etching**. Copper clad board consists of a layer of copper bonded to the substrate. This type of board is ideal for use with CNC routers and milling machines that are set up to create circuit boards.

Photo etching

Photo-resist PCB offers the ability to create an accurate image of a computer-aided designed circuit on the surface of the copper. This means that the circuit can be drawn, tested and printed from a piece of software, allowing for high levels of quality control.

The image is printed on the board using a mask in a UV light box. The board is then exposed to UV light which softens the photo-resist layer not covered by the mask. Developing solution is then used to dissolve the softened areas leaving just the masked tracks. The full photo-etch process is covered next.

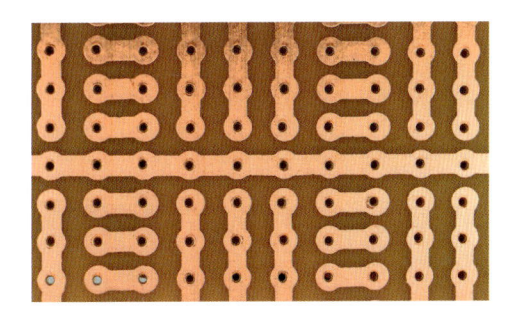

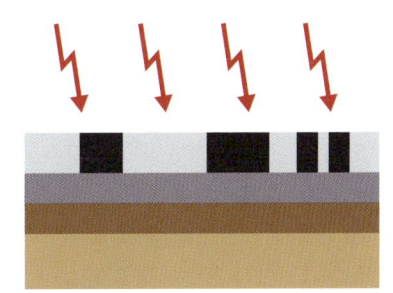

UV rays

Transparency (artwork)
Photo sensitive layer
Copper layer
Board (substrate)

The technique for making PCBs in school differs a little from commercial processes. Listed are the stages for using single-sided, photoresist board with through-hole components. The appropriate quality control (QC) steps are added along with specific health and safety (H&S) precautions.

1: Design and print mask:		2: Prepare board:	
Using a PCB specific CAD package is the best way to create a mask (circuit track layout). Print onto acetate and cut out. **QC:** Check quality of print. Hold up to a light source, tracks should be solid and dark. Poor quality mask leads to poorly developed tracks.	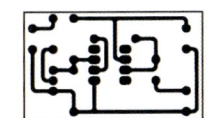	Using a PCB guillotine, cut the board to size using the most economical layout. **QC:** Use the cut-out mask to mark out the board before cutting to ensure the correct size is cut and waste is avoided.	

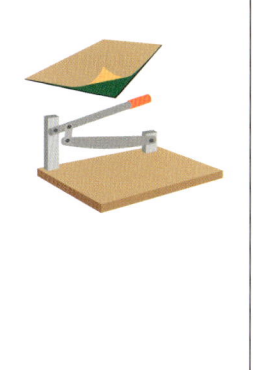

Chapter 52 **Planning and production methods**

3: UV light box:

Peel the protective plastic layer off the board. Place the mask on the board. Place mask side towards the UV light and close. Set correct exposure time (usually 6 mins).

QC: *Ensure mask is correct orientation (text reads normally). Check exposure time for selected photo-board. Once removed, check faint tracks are visible.*

4: Develop:

Quickly place the exposed board into premixed developing solution according to manufacturer's instructions. Agitate board for 15-30 seconds until tracks are visible.

QC: *Check for over- or under-developed board. Tracks should be solid and clear.*

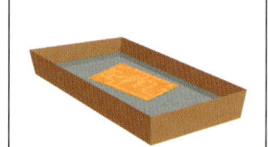

H&S: *Use gloves, tongs, apron and goggles as developer is an irritant.*

5: Rinse developer:

Promptly and thoroughly rinse off the developing solution in running water to halt the developing process.

QC: *Inspect tracks for quality. If underdeveloped, you may develop further. If over-developed a new board will be required as poor etching will result.*

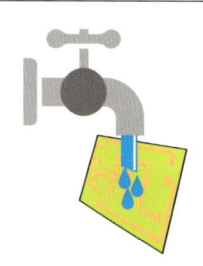

H&S: *Use gloves, tongs, apron and goggles as developer is an irritant.*

6: Etch:

Place board into developing tank. Times vary depending on type of tank, the age of the chemicals and the saturation of the solution. Bubble etch tank 15-45 minutes; rota etch around 90 seconds to 3 minutes.

QC: *Check board does not get over-etched resulting in thin or broken tracks.*

H&S: *Use gloves, tongs, apron and goggles as etchant is an irritant. Use in well-ventilated area as harmful fumes are given off.*

7: Rinse etchant:

Promptly and thoroughly rinse etchant off board to stop the copper tracks being etched away.

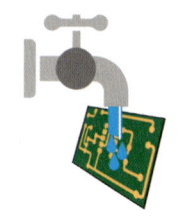

H&S: *Use gloves, tongs, apron and goggles as etchant is an irritant.*

8: Inspect:

Inspect copper tracks for quality.

QC: *If under-etched they may still be joined by undissolved copper and can be etched further. If over-etched they may not conduct, and they should be checked with a multi-meter for continuity.*

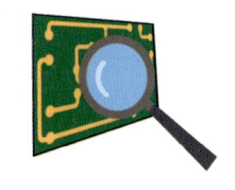

9: Clean board and drill holes:

Use PCB cleaning block or wire wool to remove etch resist. Drill holes in appropriate places.

QC: *Ensure the correct size drill bit is used for the correct holes as they can vary. Check all holes are drilled completely through. Visually inspect.*

H&S: *Wear goggles and ensure workpiece is held securely.*

10: Solder:

Solder in components. Follow detailed information on the next page.

QC: *Check solder joints are being formed correctly and that solder is not crossing tracks where it should not. Check component polarity is correct.*

H&S: *Correct PPE, use heat mat and fume extraction. Ensure workpiece is held correctly to avoid burns.*

PCB population – PCB drilling and soldering

The following tips should help you master the art of soldering – however, it is a skill that can take quite a while to perfect!

1: Set up the workstation:
Heat mat, soldering iron, solder, tools, fume extractor if required. Adhere to school PPE policies. Make sure tip of iron is clean (shiny).

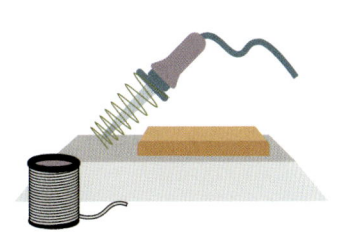

2: Check and clean PCB:
Sometimes the PCB tracks form an oxide layer on them, or the photoresist layer has not dissolved and needs to be removed.

Special cleaning blocks can be used but wet and dry paper will also work.

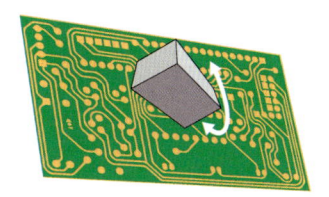

3: Hold workpiece steady:
Place components into the board or use helping hands or masking tape to hold components and wires still on your heat mat. Masking tape is great for holding things in place.

4: Tin items ready for soldering if required:
Tinning is a vital stage; it means applying a thin layer of solder to components and wires which helps them join together. Components going directly into the PCB do not need tinning but wires do.

To tin, apply a little solder to the iron tip and slide it along the wire or component, adding more solder if required. Tinning should be a very thin coating!

5A: Soldering components:
You are aiming to make a volcano-shaped joint and avoid a ball or onion shape forming. Only fresh, smoking solder will let this happen. The smoke is the flux burning.

Flux aids solder flow.

5B: To get a good joint you must:
- Wipe the tip clean then tin it with a small amount of solder
- While it is still smoking, heat the base of the joint (i.e. the track or pad) first for two seconds
- Then apply the solder to the track and not the tip of the iron
- Keep applying until you see the solder flow all round the joint
- Lift the soldering iron away in an upwards direction, this produces the volcano shape
- Put the soldering iron back in the stand to avoid burns

6: Tidy up wires as you go:
Cut back any protruding wires or component legs with side cutters. Be sure to snip them down towards the table as they can shoot off and be a potential hazard.

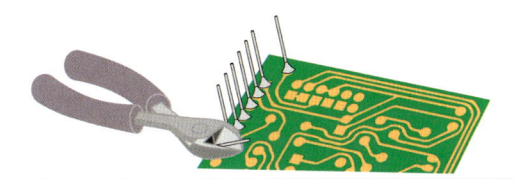

Other tips:
- Solder the flattest, smallest components to the board first and work up to the larger ones; it makes it easier to solder
- Leave flying leads until the end as they tend to get in the way
- Watch out for solder crossing tracks, clean up any splashes as you go
- Don't overheat the board as it can lift the tracks off the PCB

Chapter 52 **Planning and production methods** 271

Scales of production:

Products are manufactured in different volumes to meet consumer demand. The number of products being made determines the level of production required. There are no definitive quantities that make an item suitable for one type of production rather than another, but there are a few principles that make selecting the appropriate production method easier to understand.

The scales of production you need to know about are:

- **One-off production** – One unit is hand-made to suit the needs of a specific client
- **Batch production** – Products made in small batches to meet seasonal or sporadic demand
- **Mass production** – High-volume production required to meet demands of the mass-market
- **Continuous production** – Non-stop production required to meet constant demand

One-off production and prototypes

Electronic systems-based items suitable for **one-off** or bespoke production are limited but can include large projects such as security and surveillance systems, a scoreboard for a new stadium or a permanent sound system for a specific venue. Production requires highly skilled engineers and technicians to work out what installation best suits the systems requirements. This is usually a labour intensive and time-consuming process and usually results in a more expensive product. Higher value is associated with one-off products as they are designed exactly to a client's specification. System designers and manufacturers often work closely with their clients to deliver the desired outcome.

When products are being developed, designers will make a **prototype**. These are one-off versions of a product and are used to test out ideas and to receive feedback from user groups and potential clients. Many products made for theatre and television, such as a game show, are one-off products. A GCSE project will be a prototype and hence a one-off product.

A bespoke operation ratio display board in an industrial production line

Q1 One-off products are usually much more expensive than mass-produced goods. Using an example of a particular item, suggest reasons why a customer might ask a manufacturer to create a one-off product for them.

Batch production

Batch production is used when a certain number of identical products are required. This is known as a **batch**, as they will all have been produced together. One batch could contain a large or small number of products.

Batch production methods tend to use higher levels of automation than one-off production, but also have a high level of flexibility to meet changing demands. Machines may be specifically set up to perform certain tasks and **templates**, **jigs**, **patterns**, **moulds** and **formers** are used to save time and ensure parts are identical. Usually, once a batch has been produced some or all of the processes will be altered to produce the next batch. This may be as simple as changing the colour or size of a product for the next batch, or it may involve making a totally different product.

Batch production still uses some highly skilled labour. However, as some of the tasks are more repetitive, small production lines and semi-skilled workers may be employed. Expensive specialist tools and equipment are frequently needed to produce batches of products and initial set-up costs can be high. The more products being made, the cheaper the overall unit cost of each item. Products associated with batch production include seasonal, limited edition or novelty products.

The **lead times** on batch produced products are fairly short allowing manufacturers to respond to market demand quickly.

> **Q2** Explain what is meant by lead time.

Mass production

Mass-produced products tend to be items that are in constant use and where the design does not change significantly. Due to the large number of units produced and sold, high set-up costs can be justified, and the products can still be sold at an affordable price for the mass market.

When large numbers of products are required, the best way to produce them is to set up a dedicated production line that does not need to change. This way their manufacture can be highly automated and use as little skilled labour as possible. Where manual workers are needed, the tasks tend to be simple and repetitive. Production lines need to have some highly skilled technicians to keep them running efficiently, as any downtime could be very costly.

Continuous production

Continuous production is very similar to mass production although the products tend to be made to create stock or standard material forms (primary processing) before final processing or assembling elsewhere. The factory will operate up to 24 hours a day 7 days a week. Staff are mainly low-skilled and operate the factory in shifts. The products made rely on the highest levels of automation and this type of factory normally makes a very limited range of products. This saves any potential changes to the production line, avoiding any downtime. This scale of production is the least labour intensive and produces products with the lowest unit costs. Continuous production is suitable for products that are in constant demand such as batteries, cables and light bulbs.

With the introduction of digital techniques (such as laser cutting and engraving, and digital printing) a number of products that are **customised** and **personalised** for consumers blur the lines between one-off and other levels of production. Having your name engraved on something does not make the product a one-off. One-off products are not available for anyone other than the original client or purchaser.

> **Q3** Suggest a suitable scale of production for each of the following:
> a) led lightbulbs
> b) a light-up hat for a circus entertainer
> c) a light meter for a cricket match
> d) a walkie talkie.

Techniques for quantity production

Pick and place assembly

Once a circuit board has been manufactured, a solder paste is applied to the pads where components are to be placed. This paste is a tacky mix of flux and small solder particles. The flux stops oxidation and helps the solder to flow where it is required. Surface mount components (SMT) (covered in Chapter 51) are usually used with this form of manufacture.

Pick and place machines then select the appropriate components and place them in the correct position on the board. This is called populating the board. The CNC (Computer Numerical Control) machine uses components that are loaded into it via cartridges or reels. There can be hundreds of components on each reel which can be changed quickly and easily to avoid prolonged downtime.

Once assembled, the board can be soldered. With this type of assembly an industrial process for soldering is used called **flow soldering** (often called reflow soldering). The PCB is placed in a reflow oven where it is heated to the correct temperature to melt the solder paste without damaging the components.

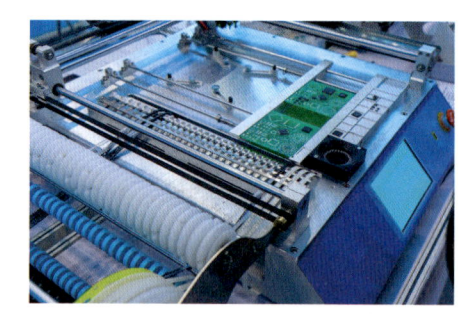

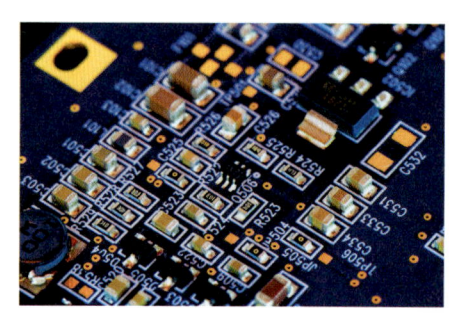

Quality control

When products are made, checking that they are being produced correctly is an essential stage, known as **quality control** (QC). This is vitally important to ensure dimensional accuracy is consistent and that any manufacturing imperfections are detected, so that the product will work correctly and is safe to use. Visual inspections are used to check the quality and consistency of the finish as well as the integrity of any joins and connections between components.

Production aids may be used in all scales of production to ensure the accurate shaping and machining of polymer parts. **Jigs**, **templates**, **patterns**, **fixtures** and **moulds** help manufacturers produce consistent results.

A number of quality control devices are either attached to machines or can be used to check for consistency. A **depth stop**, for example, can be found on most pillar drills. The depth of the hole required is set on the gauge, tested once to check that the correct depth has been set, and then all subsequent holes will be the correct depth. Other quality control tools known as **go/no go fixtures** are available to ensure accuracy and consistency. These tools are set to the specific **tolerance** allowed for that particular component.

Reference surfaces and **datum** points are used to measure from. Measuring tools should have accurately machined surfaces and calibrated readings. These points of reference are important to ensure prototypes and products work and fit correctly. If reference surfaces are poorly prepared then all other points taken from it will be incorrect and the resulting products could be unsafe.

Templates

Templates for casing manufacture are more commonly used in small batch production runs to help lay out and nest shapes for efficient cutting and drilling. They are usually pre-cut from more rigid materials like manufactured boards or metals.

Other forms of templates for electronic products include the CAD packages used for laying out a PCB. The templates for all component sizes and shapes are pre-loaded in the CAD software and are ready for you to use by simply dragging and dropping into position.

Patterns and moulds

Patterns are the positive forms used in vacuum forming. Patterns can be made from a range of materials including wood, MDF and Styrofoam™. They are usually sprayed with release agent before starting the process. industry moulds are frequently made from tool steel to ensure a high quality finish over thousands, if not millions of identical products.

Sub-assembly

Frequently products are constructed using components or parts that may have been made and assembled elsewhere, even by a different manufacturer. For example, the batteries used in an electric vehicle may well have come from a specialist manufacturer who will have designed them specifically. It is commonly more efficient to use the expertise of the battery manufacturer to sub-assemble the batteries and ship them to the electric car plant ready to be fitted to the vehicles.

Many parts within a computer are sub-assembled. The hard drive, the keyboard and even the motherboard may all come from different manufacturers and will be assembled before shipping to the customer.

Working within tolerance

The tolerance of components was covered in Chapter 51 but this section looks at accuracy of making. When giving the dimensions of a material component, **tolerances** are often indicated to ensure an accurate fit. A tolerance is the acceptable margin of error, for example, a laser cut front panel for a lighting circuit may require 10mm holes cutting to ensure the LED bezels fit flush to the surface. If the holes were too large the lights may fall out, if they were too small the lights would not fit into position. The margin of error may be as little as ±0.01mm, so any tools used to measure and mark materials must be accurate.

Efficient cutting to minimise waste

Whichever material is being used, efficient cutting involves forward thinking and planning. Regardless of the shape being cut, time should be taken to ensure that the most efficient cutting pattern is considered. This can utilise **nesting** and, if the shape allows it, **tessellation**. These techniques ensure that all waste materials are gathered together in to useful larger sections which may be used for other projects. All waste adds to the cost of a product and increases its **carbon footprint**.

Social, cultural and ethical factors

Our traditions, social and cultural beliefs and values all influence our selection of the products we buy. Many products are subject to trends and fashion, and electronic products are no exception. There are many ways that companies carry out market research so they know how to design for specific target markets, ages and socio-economic groups.

All products convey messages, whether they be obvious, through imagery and colour, or less so through cultural values or ethos. Whilst it is legitimate to create a design to appeal to one section of society, it is not acceptable to alienate or offend others. **Use of language and colour** in particular can cause confusion. In many eastern and western cultures colours and words have different meanings and connotations, for example in some western cultures, the colour purple represents wealth and royalty, however in some Asian and Latin American cultures it represents death and mourning.

Gambling machines are considered offensive in some cultures

Incorrect use of **language** and different cultural values can sometimes get companies into trouble. Some words in one language can have very different meaning in another. Some cultures and countries do not allow gambling, therefore betting machines would be considered offensive and would obviously not be very successful. This type of product would not be considered **suitable for the intended market**.

Our **consumer society** has given rise to **built-in obsolescence**. This describes products that are designed to have a limited life span due to their quality, the components used or indeed their aesthetic. In electronics, built-in obsolescence is linked to processing power and software capabilities as well as the normal trends and fashions. New technologies help develop and invent new products as well as driving sales. Low-cost, **mass produced** products make it easy for consumers to use and dispose of products quickly as trends and formats change. Built-in obsolescence is considered unethical by many, as it encourages consumerism and puts unnecessary pressure on our natural resources.

Q4 Name some music playing and recording formats that have become obsolete.

Chapter 53 – Material processing and joining

Objectives

- Describe and evaluate a variety of tools and techniques used to manufacture electronic products and prototypes

Material processing and joining

As with all specialist material areas, a specific set of tools and equipment are used in the development of systems-based products and prototypes. The following chapter looks at methods used in the school workshop as well as those used in industry.

Tools and equipment

Different sets of tools and equipment are used for making printed circuit boards than those for making their casings. You will learn about shaping and forming processes, deforming processes, additive manufacturing and wasting techniques.

> **Q1** What type of manufacturing process is 3D printing?

Hand tools used for PCB construction

Name	Image	Uses	Name	Image	Uses
Soldering iron, stand, sponge and heat mat		Electrically heated tip used to melt solder onto joint or PCB, damp sponge used to clean the tip	Solder		Solder is traditionally a mix of lead and tin, but lead free versions are best used for soldering in school. Solder contains flux
Side cutters		Used to cut components or wire. Can be used very close to PCB for a neat cut	Wire strippers		Many different versions available that are used to remove the outer plastic layer
PCB track cleaner		Used to remove oxide deposits from PCB tracks to make soldering easier	Fume extractor		Removes fumes when soldering, replaceable pads absorb the fumes
Helping hands tool		Handy tool to hold wire, components or boards while soldering	De-solder pump or tape		Used to remove molten solder incorrectly placed or to remove / replace components; de-solder tape is also available which acts like a wick

Manufacturing products and prototypes

Fabricating, constructing and assembling products and prototypes takes place after a great deal of planning. Once the circuit and/or system has been designed it needs to be tested. This can be done digitally on simulation software but should always be physically tested using a prototyping board such as breadboard. Once the circuit is confirmed to work it can then be made on a PCB.

As covered in Chapter 51, PCB construction either uses **through-hole** components or **surface mount technology** (SMT) components. Many hybrid PCBs use a combination of the two.

PCB mounting methods

When the PCB is completed it needs to be held securely in position so that it can withstand any forces and stresses in use. The PCB will also need to be connected to any input and output devices. Common ways to hold a PCB in place include **PCB pillars**, which are plastic, or metal supports that attach to the PCB and the casing. Alternatively, PCBs can be held securely between two channels. These are often grooves routed in to the casing or plastic channels bonded to the casing walls.

To ensure all connections to a circuit board are robust a number of **cable management** techniques can be used. **Sleeving** can be used to slide over exposed cables or wires. Sleeving comes in a variety of diameters and can be used to encapsulate many separate wires. **Heat shrink** varieties are available and will tighten around cables creating a tight and water-resistant fit. **Cable ties** and other forms of ties are used to ensure **looms** of cables stay together and thus aids the routing of cables around a system. This can be seen in the internal view of the PC below. Other forms of cable management include **spiral wrap**, which helps to keep wire looms together.

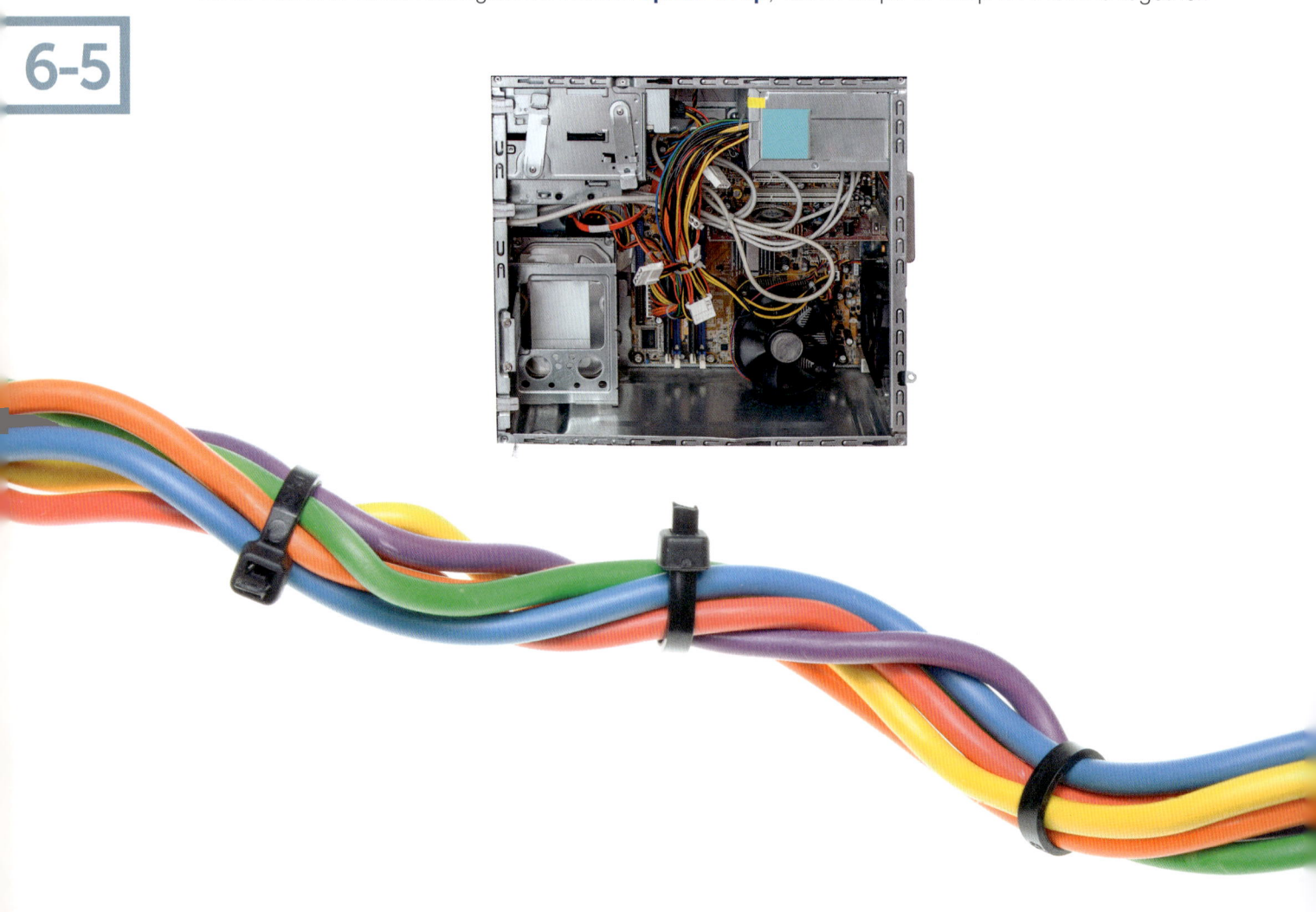

Shaping

When products are manufactured the materials used need to be shaped using any number of different techniques and processes. The rest of this chapter looks at the types of processes that you need to know about.

Shaping processes fall in to two main categories:

Wasting is the term used to remove material involving processes like drilling, sawing and abrading.

Addition is the term used for constructing or fabricating a product or prototype using jointing, bonding and forming methods, where materials are added together.

Drilling

When drilling PCBs, very small drill bits are required and it is much easier to use a specialist drill as it assists with accuracy. The drill bits required to drill the holes in PCBs are often 1mm to 1.5mm diameter. Some chucks on normal drills struggle to hold a regular twist drill of this size. A special tool called a pin chuck can be used to create a better grip, or specialist drill bits can be obtained that have thicker shanks.

Drilling a hole into plastics for casing **fabrication** requires careful speed control. Large diameter drill bits require a slower speed than narrow ones to avoid overheating and the potential for the plastic to melt. The feed rate is another factor to consider – too much pressure can cause plastics to crack.

A pillar drill is good for accuracy and is powerful enough to drill larger holes in thicker materials. A cordless drill is very adaptable and usually has variable speeds.

Name	Characteristics	Image	Name	Characteristics	Image
Twist drill bit	General purpose drill bit, also used on plastic, metal and wood		Hole saw	Used to cut large holes. They can easily overheat due to fast peripheral speed	
Countersink bit	Used to ensure countersunk screw heads are flush with the surface		PCB drill bits	Very small drill bits for drilling copper-clad plastic board, fitted to a shank for ease of mounting	

Q2 What is the most essential piece of PPE to be worn when using a drill?

Cutting and sawing PCBs

The best way to cut a PCB is to use a specialist **guillotine**. The blade is contained behind a transparent plastic guard. The PCB can be marked out clearly and cut to the line accurately. This should be completed before soldering any components. When cutting PCBs to size, consider the most economical way to cut the shape you require to avoid waste. Guillotines will only cut straight lines so certain saws can be used to cut curves if required.

Soldering

Soldering is used to connect two or more contacts so that electricity can flow between components. In industry, soldering is mainly done automatically; however, you will need to learn how to manually solder your own PCBs. Most solder designed for school soldering contains flux which assists the solder to flow around a joint. Soldering techniques and PCB population is covered in Chapter 52.

Hand soldering a printed circuit board

Automated printed circuit board construction

Machinery

A number of machines can be used to assist in the production of PCBs. The circuit boards are made using one of two main methods. They can either be etched using a solution that dissolves away the copper from the surface of the PCB or it can be physically cut away using a CNC mill or routers. These methods are covered in Chapter 52.

Digital design and manufacture

PCB design is not easy and various digital tools exist to help make accurate planning and layout possible. Software such as Circuit Wizard and Yenka allow circuits to be drawn, simulated, tested and laid out as a PCB enabling a mask to be printed for PCB etching or for outputting to a PCB engraver.

Other digital design software allows housings for PCBs to be created in 3D. Software such as SketchUp, Autodesk® Inventor and TinkerCAD, to name a small selection, enable designs to be fully rendered to simulate the real product but also have the ability to output files to 3D printers, CNC mills, lathes and routers, assisting manufacture. Additionally, 2D software like 2D Design and CorelDRAW can be used with laser cutters and vinyl cutters to plan 2D layouts.

CNC laser cutting

Laser cutters are one of the most accurate ways to cut many different plastics. The laser itself can follow a design to a very fine tolerance, but they must be set-up correctly.

Lasers cut using a combination of speed and power to control the cut. The deepest cut would be on the slowest speed at the highest power and the lightest engraving would require the fastest speed and the least power. It is important to select the correct settings for the type and thickness of material and the type of cut or engraving required.

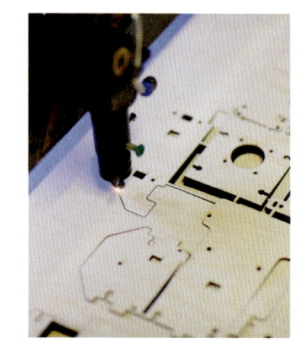

> **Q3** A material is being engraved using a laser cutter. The settings read 100% power and 100% speed. Which setting would you change in order to make a deeper engraving?

Vacuum forming

Vacuum-formed products include many casings for electronic products. A sheet of thermoplastic is heated and pressed onto the former (mould) by atmospheric pressure, as the vacuum reduces the pressure below the softened thermoplastic. The plastic takes on the shape of the mould, then cools and sets in position before the mould is removed.

HIPS (high impact polystyrene) is the most commonly used plastic to vacuum form within schools. In industry, polyester PETG, ABS and acrylic are also used.

To ensure a good product is made, the mould must:

- have a positive draft angle > 3° to ensure easy removal of the material from the mould
- avoid undercuts that would make removal of the mould impossible
- not have too deep a profile so that the plastic is drawn too thin and could easily burst
- have vent holes drilled to avoid air pockets where there are dips in the profile
- have corners and edges rounded with a small radius to aid removal
- have a smooth finish so as not to adhere to the hot plastic – a release agent can be applied to the mould to assist removal

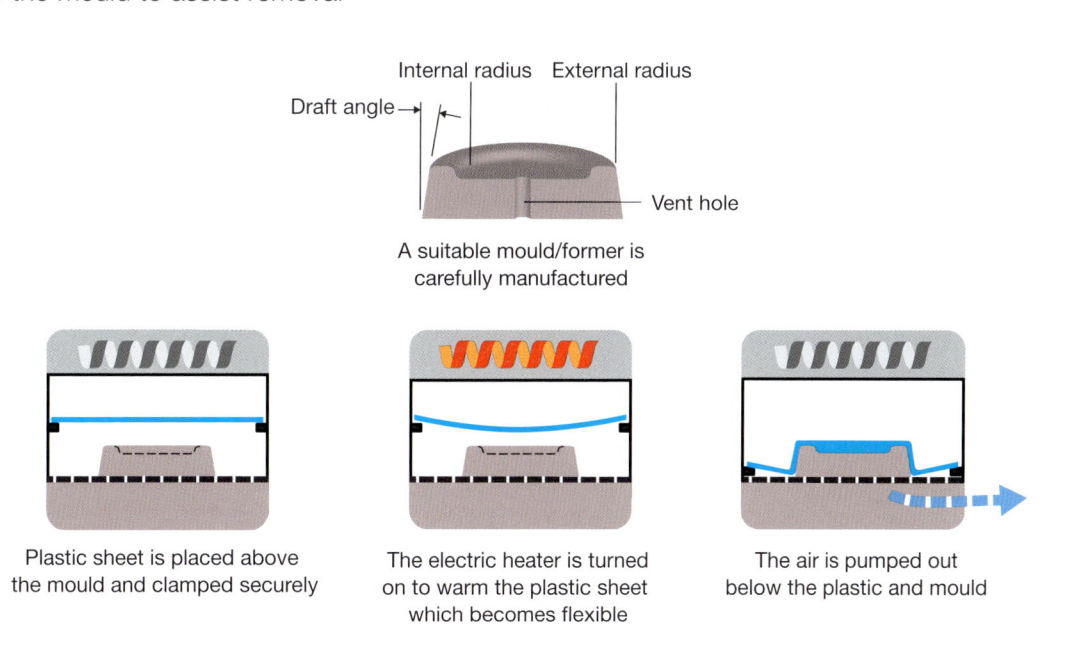

A suitable mould/former is carefully manufactured

Plastic sheet is placed above the mould and clamped securely

The electric heater is turned on to warm the plastic sheet which becomes flexible

The air is pumped out below the plastic and mould

> **Q4** On the sketched former shown, what features would you add or change to make it perform its job more efficiently?

3D printing

3D printing enables physical objects to be formed from reels of thermoplastics. 3D printers use special CAD files, usually in STL or VRML format, and converts them into a series of coordinates that the printer will follow, building up the image in layers.

There are different types of 3D printers available, including the following:

- Stereolithography (SL) involves using lasers to part cure the printed shape from a bath of liquid resin. This is an expensive but very accurate method.
- Digital light processing (DLP) is similar to stereolithography but uses a powerful light source rather than a laser.
- Laser sintering uses a powdered material instead of a resin bath. The solid shape is created as the heat from the laser fuses and solidifies the powder.
- An extrusion method also known as Fused Deposition Modelling (FDM) is the most popular in schools and involves melting a plastic filament with the heated extrusion head.

The most common technology in schools are single-head printers that use reels of printable plastic filament. ABS and PLA are usually used in FDM style printers and come in pre-coloured cartridges. New and interesting materials are frequently being developed which allow for printing in wood, steel and brass effect. Soft rubbery materials are also becoming available, making prototype products even more realistic.

Very complex shapes can be 3D printed and some filament printers can print in more than one colour. Dry powder printers can even print in full colour.

3D printers can print other materials besides plastics, including metals, paper, ceramics and even food. 3D bio-printing is also being developed, meaning that in the future we may be able to successfully print replacement body parts.

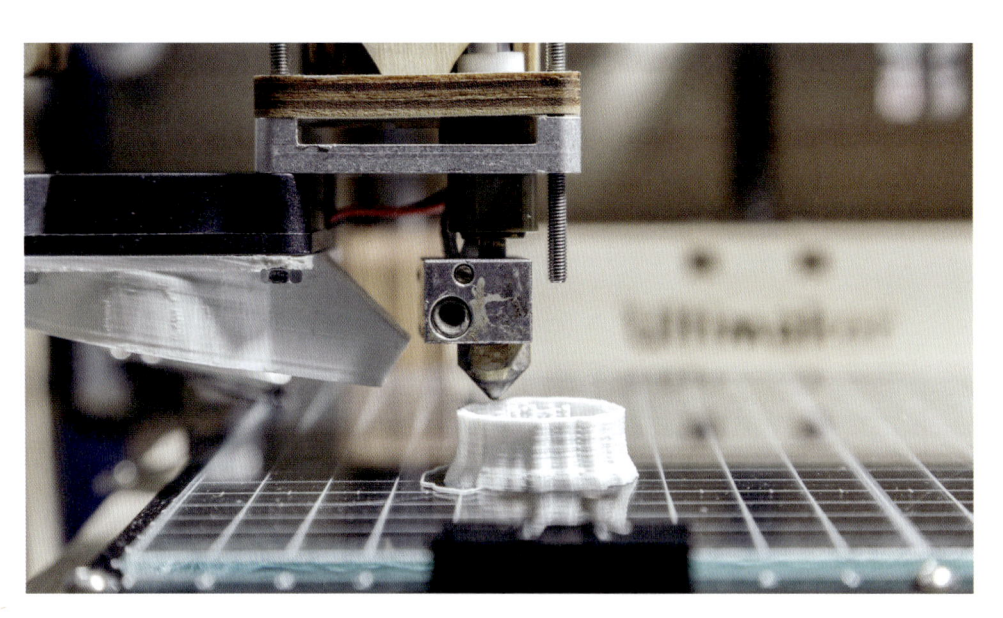

Fused deposit modelling

Q5 Why are 3D printers so useful for creating prototypes and scale models?

Chapter 54 – Material treatments and finishes

Objectives

- Evaluate a range of surface finishes and treatments for electronic products and components

Surface finishes and treatments

A number of specialist treatments and finishes are on offer, depending on the desired finish required. Some spray-on products are solvent-based and are not very environmentally friendly, as they may contain high levels of **volatile organic compounds** (VOCs). This means that they give off fumes that are considered hazardous to health and should be used according to the manufacturer's instructions, normally in a well ventilated area with a mask being worn. Water-based products are becoming more readily available which are kinder to the environment and should be used where possible.

Metal plating

Metal plating is a common technique used to enhance the functionality and performance of electronic connections. Gold is most commonly used to plate connectors however other metals are used. Gold is a metal that resists oxidising and tarnishing giving a very reliable connection over a long time. Silver and copper are also excellent conductors but prone to oxidising, so a thin layer of plated gold enhances connections using these metals.

PVC covered cable with a gold-plated audio connector

Insulating coatings

Coating and coverings can be used for insulating components, devices and casings for either functionality and/or safety reasons. The most common covering is PVC as it is robust, flexible and resistant to water and heat. Other coverings include silicone rubber which gives the cable greater flexibility and even better heat protection (often found on soldering irons) and cotton covered cable which can he found on heating appliances such as irons. The cotton protects the cable from melting given accidental contact with a heating element.

Sometimes electronic products with metal cases are lined to avoid short circuiting. Different self-adhesive polymers can be used for this purpose. PVC insulation tape is common, as is PVC shielding, which can be slid on to bare wires and connections. Another form of shielding is called heat shrink. This, as the name suggests, tightens around an electrical connection when heated up, protecting the joint, creating a water resistant seal if required.

PCBs can be protected from premature oxidation by spraying with PCB lacquer or conformal coating. These are a polymer-based transparent spray that coat a PCB and protect it from dust, chemicals and excessive temperature fluctuations.

Resistor colour code

The coloured bands that are used to identify the resistance values of resistors are added to ensure that they can be easily and correctly identified. The Resistor colour code, covered in Chapter 50, allows simple visual identification which would be impossible to see if numbers were used. There is an additional band added to the resistance value bands which specifically relates to the tolerance of the resistor.

Finishes applied to cases

Aluminium is a popular material for use in electronic and mechanical products. It is a very lightweight metal compared to steel and it offers a high strength-to-weight ratio.

Aluminium does not corrode, but it does oxidise over time, giving it a dull finish. To enhance some of its aesthetic and functional properties it can be **anodised** using an electrochemical process which bonds an outer surface onto the aluminium.

The anodic oxide layer, that forms on the aluminium when it is anodised, has the following benefits:

- It is an electrical insulator
- It can be dyed a variety of colours
- It has increased resistance to wear
- It can give improved lubrication or adhesion

The aluminium is first prepared by cleaning. It is then chemically etched for a matt finish, or chemically brightened for a smooth finish before being anodised to form the aluminium oxide layer. It is dyed to the required colour and finally sealed to stop the oxide layer from being porous and to prevent colour fade.

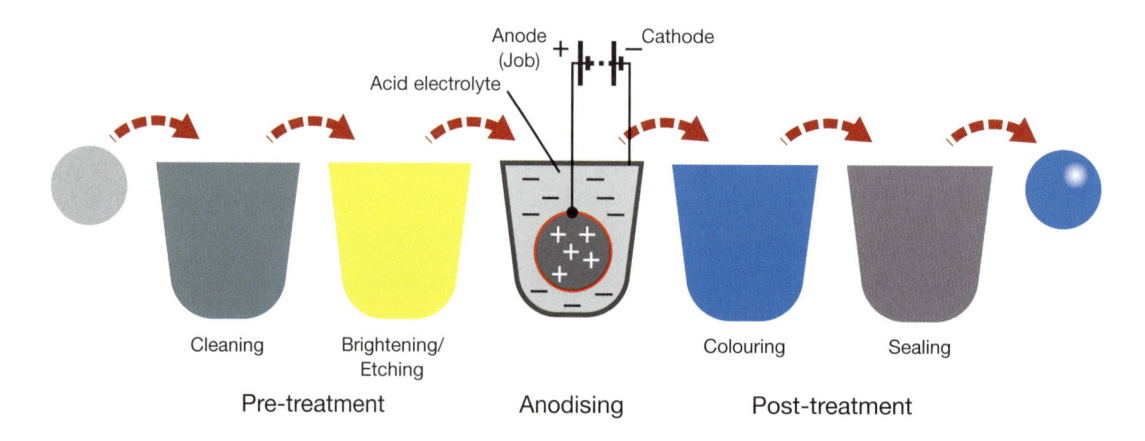

The anodising process

Painting and screen printing

A relatively simple way to apply an aesthetic finish to a case is to hand or spray paint it. Spray painting gives a better finish as you do not see the brush marks, however care needs to be taken in the preparation and application, making sure correct PPE is adhered to and that work areas are well ventilated due to the potentially high VOCs associated with solvent based paints

Screen printing is an alternative painting process which can be used on a wide range of substrates and offers a very professional finish. It is time consuming and therefore suited to one-off and batch production. The screen consists of a very fine mesh fabric stretched across a frame and fixed in place. The mesh is first coated with photo emulsion and once that has dried, a silhouette of the artwork to be printed is laid onto the screen as a mask. This is often done using a printed transparency. Light is shone onto the screen; this fixes the photo emulsion that is left exposed, then the mask is removed, and the un-exposed photo emulsion is washed away.

A different screen has to be made for each different colour and jigs are often used to help align the screens for printing. To make a print, the screen is laid on top of the substrate, ink is applied at the top of the screen and pulled across the screen using a squeegee. The ink is transferred to the casing through the porous parts on the screen. Screens can be washed and reused.

Automated screen printing machine drawing ink across a product casing

Exercises

1. This question is about social and ecological impact.
   (a) Explain what an ecological footprint measures. [2]
   (b) Explain what the social footprint of a company covers [2]

2. Name a composite material used to make printed circuit boards. [1]

3. Explain **one** advantage of using stock materials and components giving a suitable example in your answer. [3]

4. Explain how ribs are used to reinforce polymer casings used for electronic products giving a suitable example for this technique in your answer. [2]

5. Describe **two** different ways that circuit boards can be constructed. [4]

6. Study the circuit board pictured below and describe **two** features that make it suitable for mass production. [4]

7. Describe **two** ways that cable management can be improved in an electronic product. [4]

8. A printed circuit board is 300mm long by 225mm wide.
   Calculate the area of the PCB in cm^2. [2]

9. Discuss the advantages and disadvantages of surface mount technology compared to through hole components for use in batch produced printed circuit boards. [6]

10. When selecting materials for the manufacture of a product, designers should consider the sustainability and recyclability of any materials used.

    Discuss the use of printed circuit boards and electronic components in relation to their sustainability in manufacture, in use and end of life. [6]

Section 6-6
Textiles

In this section:

Chapter 55	Sources, origins and sustainability	288
Chapter 56	Physical and working properties	295
Chapter 57	Selection of materials	300
Chapter 58	Stock forms, planning and production methods	304
Chapter 59	Material processing	309
Chapter 60	Surface treatments and finishing	316
Exercises		321

Chapter 55 – Sources, origins and sustainability

Objectives

- Explain where textiles come from and how they are obtained from animal, vegetable and synthetic sources
- Be aware of the social and ecological footprint of textiles

Raw materials for textiles

Textiles can be made from either natural or synthetic fibres, but frequently the two are combined to produce **blended fabrics** that have improved functionality. Most textiles are constructed from fibres that have been spun into yarns before they are woven or knitted into a flat, sheet material known as fabric or cloth. Some fibres are randomly entangled to form a non-woven material, such as felt. Animal skins and some solid synthetic materials are not woven. (See Chapter 19 for more detail.)

It is estimated that clothing (a large portion of the textiles industry as a whole) contributes more to climate change than the aviation and shipping industry combined. The social and ecological footprint of a textile or textiles product is affected by the raw materials used, their geographical origin, how they are processed, transported, manufactured, packaged, used and disposed of.

> **Q1** Make a list of the specific raw materials from which textiles can be obtained.

Animal sources

Animal fibres and skin can be processed into textiles. Fibres are spun into yarns and skins are treated to create hides. Wool fibres are obtained from a variety of animals (refer to Chapter 19 for more information on wool) and silk comes from the cocoon of the silkworm.

Name	Appearance	Image	Characteristics	Example uses
Silk	Very fine natural protein fibre from the cocoon of the silkworm. The thread has a natural shine due to its triangular structure and readily takes dye. A watered effect, called moiré, is often seen on silk.		Produces fine, strong and lustrous fabrics that drape well. Very soft and fine finish, gentle on skin, can feel cool in summer yet warm in winter. Absorbent, strong when dry (weaker when wet), tricky to wash, can crease easily and is usually expensive	Luxury clothing including nightwear and underwear, soft furnishings, bed sheets, silk paintings and wall hangings

> **Q2** Name some animals, other than sheep, that are farmed for their wool.

> **Q3** What properties of silk make it suitable for luxury items of clothing?

Synthetic sources

Synthetic threads come from chemical sources. Most are made from petroleum based products including polyester, acrylic (see Chapter 19 for more information) as well as nylon (polyamide) and Lycra® (elastane). Aramids are modified polyamide fibres used for very strong and heat resistant materials such as Kevlar® and Nomex®. Some synthetic fibres are manufactured from wood pulp and cotton linters (a by-product of cotton manufacture). These are used to make **regenerated cellulosic** materials including viscose, acetate and Tencel®.

Name	Appearance	Image	Characteristics	Example uses
Regenerated cellulosic: Viscose, acetate, Tencel®	Can be manufactured to mimic the appearance of natural fabrics such as cotton and silk		Commonly referred to as rayon. Softwood wood pulp is dissolved in caustic soda and the resulting solution is extruded into fibres which are used to make yarns and fabrics. Low-cost, creases easily, weak when wet. Must be ironed at low temperature to prevent melting	Clothing, underwear, bathrobes, bedding
Polyamide (Nylon)	A very versatile fibre, woven into many different forms including rip-stop. Easily coloured. Extrusions can be manufactured to mimic different types of natural fibre		Good strength, hard wearing, non-absorbent, machine washes well, easily and frequently blended	Clothing, ropes and webbings, parachutes and sports material. Used as a tough thread on garments
Elastane (LYCRA®)	Smooth to touch with a sheen and easily takes colour. Also known as Spandex (an anagram of expands).		Added to fabric to enhance working properties, particularly to add stretch. Returns back to shape without sagging. Allows freedom of movement, quick drying, holds colour well, machine washable. Easy to care for, durable and tear-resistant. Commonly blended with other fibres	Sportswear, exercise clothing, swimsuits, hosiery, general clothing, surgical and muscular supports

Q4 Explain what happens to synthetic fibre clothing if it is sent to landfill and not recycled.

Vegetable sources

Many of the fibres used in the manufacture of cloth come from renewable plant sources. The most common are cotton and flax, which is made into linen (cotton is covered in detail in Chapter 19). Other vegetable-based sources include jute, hemp and coir which is made from coconut fibres.

Name	Appearance	Image	Characteristics	Example uses
Linen	Cellulose fibres are extracted from the stems and roots of fast-growing flax plants; then combed and spun into yarn. Fibres give a smooth, lustrous look or a coarse aesthetic depending on the spinning process used.		Durable, strong, absorbent fabric with hypoallergenic properties. Low elasticity and abrasion resistance. More expensive than cotton due to the labour intensive manufacturing process	Clothing, upholstery, bed linen, curtains, wall coverings

Textile origins

The raw materials for textiles are sourced from all over the world. Textiles farmed from animal and plant sources rely on certain **climatic conditions** which affect the geographical locations they can be sourced from. **Geology** affects where oil for synthetic fabrics are sourced; when oil reserves were formed millions of years ago, **offshore** environments provided the ideal location: densely populated with marine life with oxygen-free conditions on the sea bed.

Social factors, such as labour costs and political issues, including trade laws, make certain locations more favourable than others. Ancient trade routes, such as the Silk Road, were based on the silk trade. The Silk Road (which was actually made up of several different routes) ran from China in the East to Europe in the West. This provided a lucrative network for commodity and cultural exchange.

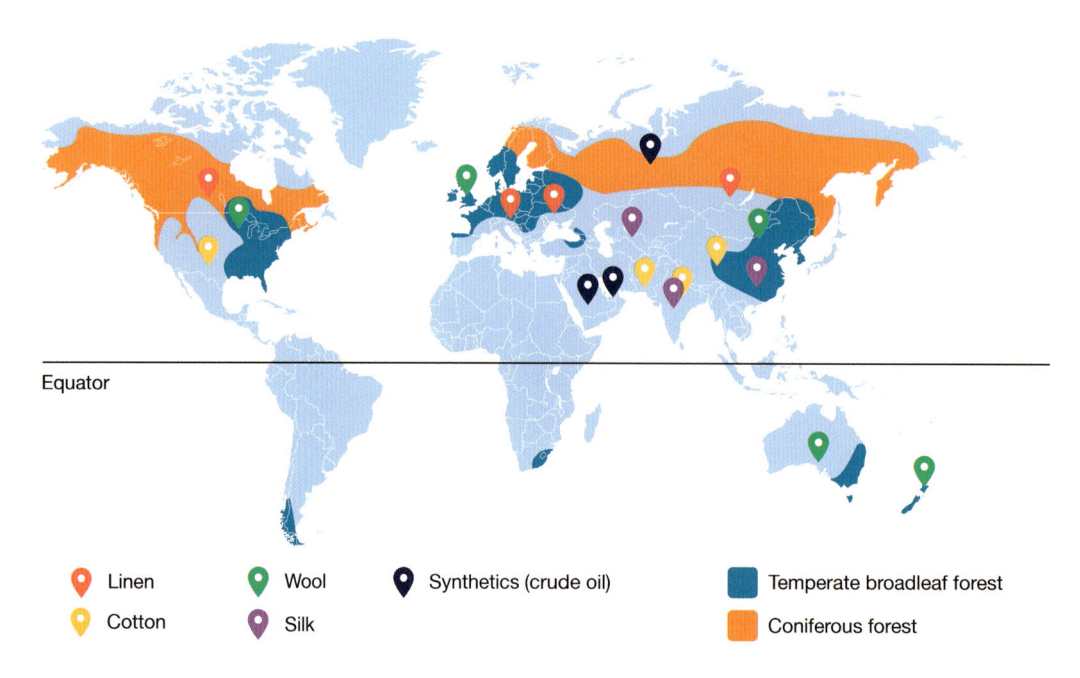

- Linen
- Cotton
- Wool
- Silk
- Synthetics (crude oil)
- Temperate broadleaf forest
- Coniferous forest

Linen – Flax for linen is grown in Russia, Canada, Ukraine and Europe

Cotton – Cotton plantations are largely in China, India, the USA and Pakistan

Silk – Silk fibres come from the cocoons of silkworms farmed in China, India and Uzbekistan

Wool – Sheep wool, which makes up the vast majority of the wool market, is farmed in Australia, New Zealand, China, the USA and the UK

Softwood pulp – Spruce, pine and hemlock trees from alpine forests provide the cellulose and wood pulp required for acetate

Hardwood pulp – Oak and birch trees grown in deciduous forests in Europe produce the hardwood pulp needed for Lyocell™

Synthetics – Oil reserves deep underground in Russia, United Arab Emirates (UAE) and Saudi Arabia provide oil for synthetic fabrics

> **Q5** Explain how local climate affects the types of crops that can be grown.

Ecological and social footprint

Designers and manufacturers have a responsibility to reduce the negative social and ecological impact of the materials and products they design and make.

Many different factors affect the **ecological footprint** of textiles and textile products:

- The properties of the raw material itself
- The distance travelled to convert raw materials and bring products to market
- The infrastructure needed to farm and extract raw materials
- The treatments and processes applied to fibres, yarns and fabrics
- The impact of extraction, farming and material production on local communities
- The detergents, water and energy used to clean products while in use
- How materials are used and disposed of

A **social footprint** is a measure of the impact that a company's social policies have on its employees, partners or subcontractors and on society as a whole. Companies have an obligation to protect the environment by reducing their ecological footprint wherever possible, but they also have a duty to consider the effect that company policies have on all those affected. For example:

- Is there a flexible hours policy for parents who need to pick up children from school?
- Is the company understanding when a parent has to stay at home because a child is sick?
- Is the health and safety of all employees a primary concern?
- Are employees being paid a fair wage?
- Are there appropriate training schemes for employees?
- Are promising employees sponsored through University?
- Does the company contribute anything to the local community?

Most developed societies have a set of rules that govern working conditions for employees, but many countries do not protect their workers to the same extent. Much of the planet's workforce has little or no protection against their employers; they can be paid very low wages and have to work excessively long hours in poor conditions. One of the biggest problems workers face is the lack of health and safety provision to protect them from danger whilst at work. This may include unsafe levels of light or dust, inadequate personal protective equipment PPE, poorly maintained machinery and the structural integrity of buildings.

To understand the overall social and environmental impact of a product, it's useful to conduct a **life cycle analysis (LCA)**. See Chapter 7 for more information.

The Rana Plaza textile factory collapsed in Bangladesh (2013) in which 1,129 people died

> **Q6** As a consumer, how can you support more ethical business practices?

Oil exploration and extraction

Synthetic fabrics are made from oil extracted from deep below the surface of the Earth. While synthetic fibres have many favourable properties such as colour fastness, strength and durability, they are made from a finite resource and do not biodegrade. In addition, the infrastructure and energy required to extract crude oil is detrimental to wildlife and natural habitats and causes pollution.

Deforestation

Plant-based textiles are grown on farmland which requires vast areas of land. Swathes of forests are felled to make space for the farmland itself, as well as for the associated infrastructure, such as roads and facilities for storage and processing. Various environmental issues are associated with deforestation including **soil erosion**, **flash flooding** and loss of **natural habitats**. **Farming** in itself, particularly cotton farming, uses a huge amount of water as well as **agrochemicals** such as pesticides, herbicides and fertilisers. This results in pollution of the water table.

> **Q7** Other than loss of habitat, state **two** other problems caused by deforestation.

Product miles

Every mile a material or component takes to bring a product from raw materials to the consumer and on to disposal contributes to **product miles**. Product miles require energy, usually obtained from burning fossil fuels. More product miles mean a larger ecological footprint. In the textiles industry, labour is usually outsourced to developing countries where labour costs are low. This keeps product costs down but dramatically increases product miles.

There is a growing movement among British consumers to buy British products whenever possible. This helps to reduce product miles and **CO_2 emissions**. When ordering products, it is worth finding out where they will be dispatched from so as to avoid excessive miles. The transportation of products overland or by sea is much better for the environment than by air. Buying locally also helps to support jobs and increases investment in the local economy.

Harris Tweed has been woven for centuries in the Outer Hebrides, Scotland

> **Q8** Explain why buying local produce is considered worthwhile.

Pollution

Solvents released during textile production and operations such as dry-cleaning cause pollution. Processes such as calendering, heat setting, drying and curing produce emissions as textiles containing lubricants and plasticisers are exposed to heat. Dust and lint produced during the processing of fibres, as well as by spinning, napping and carpet shearing, can cause respiratory problems if not carefully extracted from the atmosphere.

Detergents, heavy metals used in dyes, chemicals such as bleach and formaldehyde, (used in textiles production) as well as agrochemicals used in farming, make their way into waterways, causing **oceanic pollution** and damaging wildlife. Plastic clothes tags and **packaging** are particularly dangerous to marine life – as plastic does not degrade, many sea creatures and birds ingest plastic pieces, which can cause death from intestinal blockages and poisoning.

Plastic tagging barbs, used on apparel, toys and soft furnishings, can make their way into the oceans

New innovations in textile processing allow chemicals and water to be reused in a **closed-loop system**. Water-free dye, vegetable dyes and eco-friendly detergents reduce toxic by-products. The growing popularity in organic materials, such as organic cotton also helps reduce the ecological footprint.

Packaging, branding and trends

The rise of low cost, mass produced products has led to **consumerism** and a culture of 'fast-fashion' and a **throw away culture** where products, particularly clothing, are viewed almost as disposable items. The average piece of clothing in the UK lasts for as little as 3.3 years before being disposed of or passed on. Product packaging is designed to protect and promote products. While protection of the product is essential, products are often overpackaged to give a sense of added value. This uses unnecessary resources and produces toxic waste streams. Customers are often willing to pay more for products that are branded with a logo they recognise. Promotional messages on packaging and clever branding also encourages consumerism.

Sustainability

Designers, manufacturers and consumers can make ethically responsible decisions to make the textile industry more sustainable. Almost all textiles are recyclable or biodegradable. Some textiles are reused in crafting activities such as appliqué and patchwork quilting or simply altered, reshaped or repaired.

Washing at lower temperatures and with less water, natural drying as opposed to tumble drying and ironing less reduces the impact of textiles. Selecting materials with a smaller ecological footprint can also help. The greatest environmental impact of textiles in terms of carbon is the extraction of fibres via oil or agriculture. Flax farming for linen production, however, requires no irrigation or chemicals. The whole flax plant is used so there's very little waste.

Many people give unwanted items to charity shops or, if the items are of a certain standard, they can be sold in vintage shops or online.

When items are no longer fit for purpose they can be recycled. They can be turned into cleaning cloths and rags used in industry or they are processed into fibres and made into various products such as insulation, yarn and even paper.

> **Q9** Why is donating useable clothes to charity shops more environmentally friendly than recycling them into recycled yarn?

Case study: Cotton T-Shirt

Cotton is used in about 40% of the world's clothing e.g. jeans, shirts and even nappies. It takes about 220g of cotton to make the average cotton t-shirt. As a renewable resource, you might assume that the environmental impact would be low. In fact, there are many environmental consequences to cotton production. The cotton may have been grown and harvested in the USA, transported to China, Pakistan or India for manufacturing and then transported back for sale in Western markets so the number of product miles is high.

Cotton itself is farmed on land which could otherwise provide natural habitats for wildlife. It's a thirsty crop – it's estimated that 2,700 litres of water is needed to produce enough cotton to make one t-shirt. Rivers are often diverted to service cotton fields which disrupts natural habitats and the agrochemicals used to increase the yield of cotton plants cause pollution. Various chemical finishes and surface treatments required to convert raw cotton into fabric produce toxic by-products. Product packaging requires materials and energy and produces waste which must be recycled or disposed of in landfill. The water, energy and detergents used to wash, dry and iron cotton during its use causes perhaps the greatest ecological impact. At the end of a t-shirt's life it is up to the consumer to dispose of the product responsibly. Textile products, particularly garments, are often donated to charity for reuse, alternatively the fabric can be recycled. Many textiles inevitably make their way into landfill.

Chapter 56 – Physical and working properties

Objectives

- Describe the physical characteristics and working properties of different textiles and textile constructions
- Demonstrate an awareness of the influence of forces and stresses on textiles
- Describe a range of reinforcement and stiffening techniques

Textile properties

The physical and working properties of textiles change depending on various factors such as the raw fibre used, how fibres are blended, the construction technique, the treatments and finishes applied as well as the way a product is constructed. By applying the information regarding the different types of textiles covered in Chapters 19 and 55 you will be able to work out which materials you might use for a given task.

Most textiles will absorb water, however the speed at which they dry varies considerably. Some manufactured fabrics are designed to repel moisture and some can even breathe, allowing vapour to escape through the fabric, to keep the wearer dry inside the garment. Most natural fibres tend to absorb moisture more readily and take longer to dry than synthetic fibres.

To enhance the functional and aesthetic properties of textiles, many different chemicals and compounds can be added. Pigments and dyes are added to change the colour; chemicals and other compounds are added to decrease water absorption, repel insects, add UV protection or to decrease flexibility for example. Products can be reinforced and stiffened in various ways to help resist the forces acting upon them.

To select the best possible materials for any given product, designers and manufacturers must be aware of the physical characteristics and working properties of a wide range of materials.

> **Q1** Make a list of the different ways textiles are used in our daily lives and in different industries.

Physical characteristics and working properties

Textiles have a range of different **physical characteristics** that make them suitable for different uses.

- **Allergenic** – Describes materials that cause allergic reactions due to their chemical make-up, texture or finish
- **Texture** – Describes how a textile feels to the touch
- **Density** – Describes the relationship between mass and volume

Natural fibres like cotton are considered **hypoallergenic** and **breathable** which makes them ideal for use in baby clothes as they are less likely to irritate sensitive skin. **Filament** fibres such as silk are prized for their smooth, lustrous texture whereas short **staple** fibres like wool give a fluffier texture.

The **construction** of a textile often has the greatest effect on its density, however, different types of fibre affect density too. For example, angora fibres from rabbits are hollow and so less dense compared to sheep wool fibres.

Chapter 56 **Physical and working properties**   295

> **Q2** How could the texture of a fabric be affected by fabric construction?

Working properties describe the way a material responds to external stimuli.

- **Tensile strength** – the amount of load a material can withstand when being pulled in opposite directions
- **Breathability** – how well moisture or water vapour flows through a material
- **Absorbency** – the tendency to attract or take on an element, usually a liquid such as water or moisture, but could include light or heat
- **Electrical conductivity** – the ability of a material to conduct electricity
- **Thermal conductivity** – the ability of a material to conduct heat

Properties such as elasticity, resilience and durability are covered in Chapter 19.

> **Q3** Why would a dense fabric with a fluffy texture be ideal for insulating heat?

> **Q4** Conductive thread can carry an electrical current. Suggest an application for such a material.

Construction techniques

There are many different types of weave. The most common are **plain** and **twill weave** (see Chapter 19). Other types of woven fabric construction are **satin weave** and **pile** fabrics.

Satin weave

Satin weaves are constructed with either the warp or weft threads dominating the surface with **floating yarns** that overlay four yarns at a time.

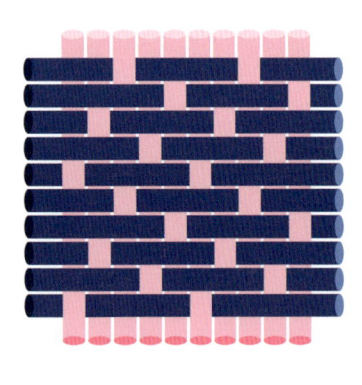

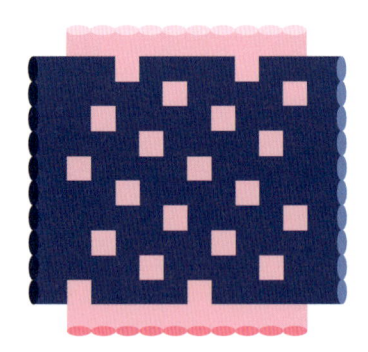

Weave   *Fabric*

The unbroken yarns on the surface give a glossy texture and different coloured yarns can be used to make a pattern. Satin weave fabrics drape nicely and have a lustrous aesthetic ideal for ribbons, curtains and fabrics for formal dress.

Jacquard is a textile which uses satin weave to create fabrics with a repeated or complex pattern. Special programmable looms are used to make the patterns. Traditionally, punched card was used to raise and lower different warp yarns on the loom as the weft yarns were passed from right to left. Nowadays, looms are programmed by computers.

Punched card used to control Jacquard looms and the resultant patterned Jacquard fabric

The weave produces a heavily textured and often dense fabric ideal for curtains and upholstery. Jacquard is durable, heavy and drapes well, but frays easily and can be expensive to produce.

Pile fabrics

Textiles constructed with pile weave produce materials with a variety of different physical and working properties depending on the raw materials used and the length and structure of the pile. Towels, fake fur and velvet are all pile fabrics.

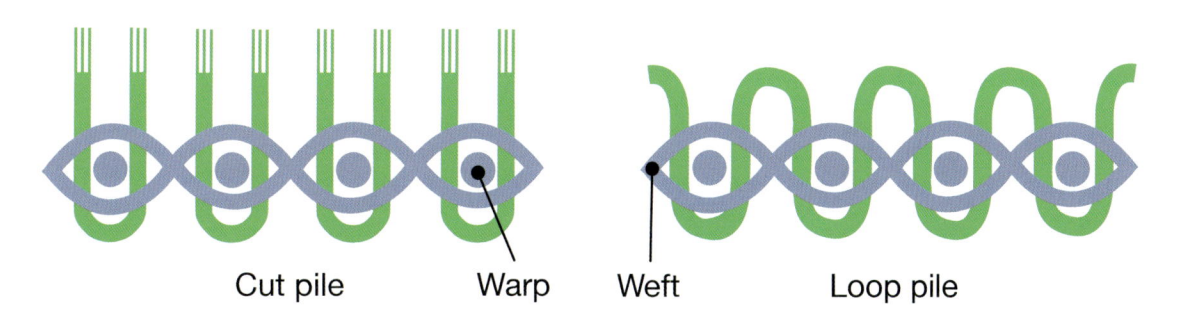

Cut pile   Warp   Weft   Loop pile

They are constructed with densely packed, upright yarns which are held in a woven foundation. In **cut pile** fabrics, such as velvet and fake fur, the upright yarns are trimmed. The upright yarns on **loop pile** fabrics, such as towelling, are continuous.

Long pile fabrics, such as fake fur have longer upright yarns which give a shaggy texture. In **short pile** fabrics, like velvet, the upright strands are trimmed short to give a **nap** to the fabric. Pile fabrics are dense, drape well and offer good heat insulation. Loop pile fabrics made from cotton and linen are much more absorbent than those made from synthetic fabrics.

> **Q5** Compare the construction and materials used to make velvet compared to those used to make towelling.

Forces and stresses

All materials, structures and products have to withstand stress as certain forces are applied to them when they are in use. The ability to withstand stress is what allows them to perform their functions successfully.

Chapter 56 **Physical and working properties**   297

Tension Compression Shear Flexibility

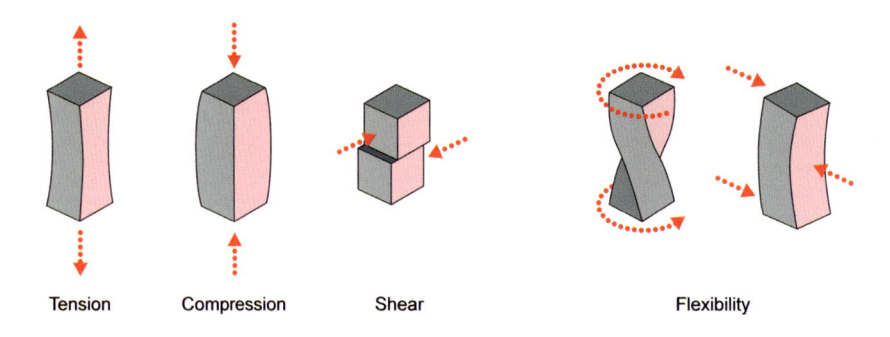

- **Tension** – Materials with high tensile strength resist pulling forces
- **Compression** – Materials with high compressive strength are resilient and resist crushing forces
- **Shear** – Materials that can resist two forces working against each other along an axis
- **Flexibility** – Flexible materials recover their shape after a bending or twisting force

The properties of a textile, and various reinforcement and stiffening techniques, can be used to resist forces acting on a product during use. For example, materials with high elasticity prevent sagging in areas of extreme flex such as knees and ankles on figure-hugging garments. Materials and construction methods used in mattresses and upholstered furniture are resilient and designed to resist compressive forces. Rivets used on jeans protect against shear forces.

> **Q6** What forces are zips and buttons designed to resist?

> **Q7** What happens to a material if it is subjected to greater tensile forces than it can bear?

It is useful to understand the **natural forces** acting within a fibre. These forces give the fibre its shape and also affect its properties. Silk fibres are long and have a triangular end profile which makes them naturally straight, shiny and strong. Conversely, wool fibres from sheep are short and crimped. This makes them lack lustre and more prone to deforming but increases their thermal insulation properties and makes them more elastic. Synthetic fibres can be manufactured to mimic these different fibre shapes to take on the properties of natural fibres.

Reinforcement and stiffening techniques

The properties and characteristics of different textiles help resist forces and stresses. Various construction, fabrication, assembly and manufacturing techniques can provide additional stiffness and reinforcement to give extra resistance to everyday forces acting on a textile or textile product.

Ribs and **boning** were first made from whale bone and used in crinolines and corsets. Nowadays, metals and plastic components are used. They give structure to a garment by incorporating a kind of skeleton into a textile product. Ribs and bones reduce flexibility. In fact, ribs and boning are so effective at giving structure to a garment that corsets could be done up so tightly that they restricted breathing, causing the user to faint!

Laminating involves bonding two or more materials to improve a product's strength, stability, aesthetics and even its **flexibility**. Bonding a polymer-based layer to a fabric makes it waterproof, more resistant to wear and tear as well as wipe clean; all while maintaining the original aesthetic of the base fabric. Interfacing, commonly used on shirt cuffs and collars, may be fused or stitched to a fabric to add stiffness and rigidity. A baseball cap, for example, uses a heavyweight interfacing to keep the peak rigid, as opposed to a collar which would need greater flexibility and would require a much lighter weight interfacing.

> **Q8** Interfacing is used only in specific areas of a shirt. Apart from the collar and cuffs, where might it be used and what is its purpose?

Protective clothing and extreme sportswear are designed to give maximum protection to the user while allowing freedom of movement. Embedding composites into the structure of a garment helps reinforce areas where impact and wear and tear are likely to occur.

D30 is one composite commonly used in protective clothing – while it's extremely tough, it's also fairly lightweight and flexible, making it comfortable to wear.

> **Q9** What parts of a motorcyclist's leathers would benefit from embedded composites?

Stay stitching is a sewing technique designed to resist forces during product construction and assembly, and is commonly added to curved parts of a pattern piece, such as a neckline or armholes. A row of straight stitches is added just inside the seam allowance to resist tension and compression forces which can cause the fabric to fray and lose its shape.

Denim jeans and jackets have small metal rivets in specific places such as around the pockets. Areas where a lot of fabric needs to be stitched together require greater strength and rivets increase tear resistance. Rivets also mean the material can cope with the added forces caused by the user constantly taking items in and out of the pocket. Rivets have since become a popular design feature. Additional layers or rows of stitching are often added to vulnerable areas such as belt loops and seams.

> **Q10** What type of strengthening, apart from rivets, can be applied to the seams of a pair of jeans?

Chapter 57 – Selection of materials

Objectives

- Explain the different factors that influence the selection of textiles
- Be aware of how environmental, cultural and ethical issues affect material choices

Material selection

Textiles are incredibly versatile. They are flexible and lightweight, may be opaque or transparent, permeable or impermeable. Colours, patterns and motifs can be added with dyes, print and through weaving. Embossing, heat treatments and construction methods have a dramatic effect on texture.

Designers have a wide range of options and different factors to consider when selecting materials for a given product including:

Aesthetics	Cost	Weight
Size of product	Size of material available	Desired properties
Where it will be used	Required finish	Workability
Stability	Availability	How long it is to last
Environmental issues	Sustainability	Social influences

Q1 What factors would need to be considered when designing a disposable overall for surgical procedures?

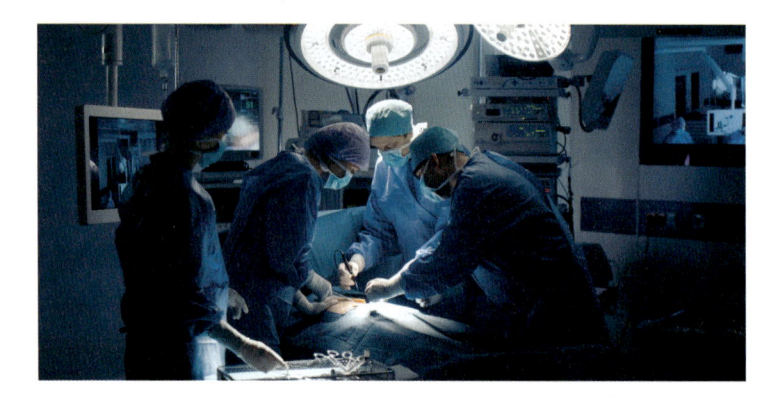

Aesthetic factors

The aesthetic qualities of a textile include **form**, **colour**, **texture**, **lustre**, **sheen** and **shine**. Most fabrics are designed to **drape** in fluid forms while others are more structural. Different forms are achieved through construction and reinforcement techniques like knitting, crochet, ribs and boning, lamination and weaving as well as heat treatments and embossing.

Colour is commonly added with dyes and pigments. Polymer-based textiles are difficult to dye - their colour is dictated by the pigment used during the manufacture of the synthetic fibres. This makes them **colourfast** – they hold their colour well. Fabrics made from natural fibres accept dye more readily and so can be dyed at any stage of production (as fibres, yarns, fabrics or final products). Dyes can be applied uniformly to the whole product or in a more artistic fashion, for example using resist dying techniques (covered in Chapter 60).

Different **textures** can be created in many ways, through fabric construction, yarn weight, processing and surface finishing treatments. Yarn made from short **staple fibres**, such as wool and cotton, gives a soft and fuzzy texture compared to long **filaments** from silk or synthetic fibres which are lustrous and smooth. Staple fibres like mohair (from goats) and angora (from rabbits) are so fine that they give a fuzzy 'halo' effect.

Hat made from mohair with a fuzzy halo texture

Lustrous fabrics can be achieved through fibre selection as well as construction techniques. For example, satin weave produces a shinier fabric than plain weave or knitting. Finishing processes, such as hot calendering, give a polished effect (refer to Chapter 60 for more information on finishing techniques).

Environmental factors

In our fast-fashion culture, many textile products, particularly clothing, are only used a few times before they fall out of favour and are disposed of. This increases demand on raw materials for new products and produces levels of waste that are unsustainable. There are, however, a variety of ways to dispose of textiles products in a responsible way. Donating unwanted items to charity means products can be reused, either by local markets or those in developing countries. Reusing products requires no energy for reprocessing and so is the most environmental method of disposal.

Textiles are fairly easy to recycle. The recycling process involves the donation, collection, sorting and processing of textiles which are subsequently transported to end users of used garments, rags or other recovered materials. Materials for recycling come from two primary sources: post-consumer (garments, vehicle upholstery, household items) and pre-consumer (scrap by-products from yarn and fabric manufacture). Donation of post-consumer waste is supported by charities. Textile products that are not suitable for reuse are graded and baled then sold by weight for reprocessing.

Bales of used textiles at wholesaler ready for recycling

Unlike metals, the process of recycling textiles degrades the raw material as different fabrics and fibres are blended. However, recycling textiles reduces demand on raw materials, requires less energy and water to process, and avoids the use of chemicals and dyes required to extract/farm and process virgin materials. Textile recycling diverts waste from landfill and reduces pollution. There are many applications for recycled textiles.

Upcycling is a current trend which celebrates used retro and vintage products and reworks them into new products. Reclaiming materials in this way requires very little energy, water or chemicals and gives a new lease of life to products that would otherwise have been disposed of.

Q2 What are the advantages and limitations of upcycling?

Availability factors

When planning the design and manufacture of a product, you should know the types, shapes, sizes and weights of standard stock materials. The majority of products can be made from **stock materials** but some require **specialist materials** that are created for a specific product.

Stock materials for textiles are mass-produced and include rolls of fabric, spools of yarn and hanks of wool (see Chapter 58 for more detail on stock forms). Using stock forms offers several advantages to the manufacturer:

- Materials can be purchased repeatedly
- Repeat purchases will be consistent in terms of colour, quality and size
- Identical/similar products will be available from a range of different suppliers
- Cost of stock materials is lower than that of specialist materials due to economies of scale

Specialist materials are those which are commissioned or developed for a particular purpose or product. Specialist textiles may be required by fashion houses for a limited edition product or for a high performance technical application. The production run for specialist textiles is short and the set-up costs for manufacture will be reflected in the cost of the final material. The exclusivity of specialist materials, as well as the research and development necessary to bring them to market, make them more expensive.

Cost factors

Materials are often selected based on their cost. Higher quality materials demand a higher price - they may use higher grade raw materials, take longer to manufacture or require specialist skills to make them. **Treatments** and **finishing processes**, such as fire proofing and water proofing, add to the cost of a material as they require more time and resources to manufacture.

Locally manufactured products may demand a higher price due to higher labour costs, however, transporting materials around the globe also incurs costs. The more complex a supply chain and the greater the distance travelled by materials and components, the higher the likely cost.

> **Q3** What ethical issues are associated with textile manufacture in developing countries?

Social, cultural and ethical factors

Our traditions, cultural beliefs and values influence textile selection. Traditional dress uses particular colours, patterns and techniques to celebrate ancestral backgrounds. **Fashions** and **trends** dictate the popularity of different textile products in terms of aesthetics and material types.

Textiles can be controversial too. For example, vegans refuse food and materials derived from animal products so use of wool, silk, fur or leather would not be appropriate.

Colours, symbols and language carry different significance and meanings in different cultures. Careful market research is necessary to avoid offence and help ensure that a product will be popular with the intended user group.

The Massai people of Kenya use intricate beadwork to denote their ages, status and identity

Traditional dress is often referenced by the fashion industry. The Massai people have trademarked their fashion and beadwork to prevent fashion houses using their designs without permission.

Customers are increasingly concerned with the provenance of the products they use. Ethical factors, such as fair pay and working conditions for those who make the products we use, are playing a greater part in the decisions we make as consumers. This puts pressure on manufacturers and designers to adopt more ethical business practices.

> **Q4** What clothes would you wear to represent your culture or heritage?

Our consumer society has given rise to built-in obsolescence. This is when products are designed to have a limited life span due to their quality, the components used or indeed their aesthetic. In textiles, **built-in obsolescence** is linked to fast-fashion where low-cost, mass produced clothing is made, used and disposed of quickly as trends change. Built-in obsolescence is considered unethical as it encourages consumerism and puts unnecessary pressure on our natural resources.

Chapter 58 – Stock forms, planning and production methods

Objectives

- Identify a range of different stock forms
- Describe the characteristics of the different scales of production
- Explain how different manufacturing processes and techniques are used in different scales of production

Stock forms

Most textiles come in a range of standard sizes. Stock forms allow manufacturers and designers to specify different types, weights and sizes to select the best materials for a given product.

When ordering textiles, you should ensure you have the correct measurements to hand. Standard practice is to use length x width for fabrics. Other factors include fabric weight, thickness and transparency.

Fabrics are mostly available by the roll and are cut to length as required. Rolls come in widths of 90, 137 and 154cm and are usually bought by the linear metre. Commonly used fabrics are often available in various widths; some more bespoke fabrics may only be available in one width.

Wider rolls are necessary for larger garment sizes and can help reduce the number of seams needed to assemble a product. Upholstery foam is sold in blocks which is cut to size to fit different products.

Denier is used in hosiery and shapewear to describe the fineness of the fibre used to create a fabric. Denier describes the mass in grams per 9000m of a given fibre. This is based on a natural measurement: a 9000m strand of silk weighs 1 gram, a single stand of silk is about 1 denier. The higher the denier, the thicker the fabric.

> **Q1** How does denier effect thermal conductivity and opacity?

Fabric **weight** may refer to the mass of a fabric, which is measured in **grams per square metre (GSM)**. Fabric weight changes depending on the fabric construction, type of fibre used and the finishes applied. A lightweight fabric like chiffon is typically between 30-150 GSM, medium weight fabrics such as denim are about 150-350 GSM and a heavyweight fabric is about 350 GSM or more e.g. PVC.

Weight can also refer to the construction of the fabric. **Single weight** fabric has a right-side and a wrong-side i.e. a side which is designed to be seen and one that is designed for the inside of a product. Single weight jersey is a knitted fabric used for t-shirts. It's cheap, comfortable and lightweight but is prone to curling at the edges. **Double weight** fabric is woven or knitted to make two smooth surfaces. This construction is heavier and durable but more expensive. Double weight woven fabric can have identical surfaces or contrasting patterns on the face and back.

Confusingly, **yarn weight** does not refer to the mass of a yarn, but its thickness. The finest yarns are used to make lace. If you look closely at the construction of a sock or t-shirt you will see that the jersey is knitted from very thin, lightweight yarn. Medium and heavy weight yarns are used in knitted gloves, scarves and jumpers.

Different **laminates** are classified as stock forms. Laminated fabrics vary enormously from high performance Kevlar and Gore-Tex®, to PVC-backed fabrics or faux leather.

Scales of production

Products are manufactured in different volumes to meet consumer demand. The number of products being made determines the level of production required. There are no definitive quantities that make an item suitable for one type of production rather than another, but there are a few principles that make selecting the appropriate production method easier to understand.

The scales of production you need to know about are:

- **One-off production** – One unit is tailor-made to suit the needs of a specific client
- **Batch production** – Products made in small batches to meet seasonal or sporadic demand
- **Mass production** – High-volume production required to meet demands of the mass-market
- **Continuous production** – Non-stop production required to meet constant demand

Textiles is one of the few remaining industries which still calls for a great deal of handmade manufacturing processes, even at high volumes. This is owing to the complexity of the processes needed to assemble a textile product.

One-off production and prototypes

Items suitable for **one-off**, bespoke or tailor-made production include made-to-measure products such as suits, wedding dresses and curtains. Production requires highly skilled craftspeople, is labour intensive, time consuming and usually results in a more expensive product. Higher value is associated with one-off products as they are designed exactly to a client's specification. Designers and manufacturers often work closely with their clients to deliver the desired outcome.

When products are being developed, designers will make a **prototype**. These are one-off versions of a product and are used to test out ideas and to receive feedback from user groups and potential clients. Many products made for theatre and television are one-off products. A GCSE project will be a prototype and hence a one-off product.

> **Q2** One-off products are usually much more expensive than mass-produced goods. Using an example of a particular item, suggest reasons why a customer might ask a designer or manufacturer to create a one-off product for them.

Batch production

Batch production is used when a certain number of identical products are required. This is known as a **batch**, as they will all have been produced together. One batch could contain a large or small number of products.

Batch production methods tend to use higher levels of automation than one-off production, but also have a high level of flexibility to meet changing demands. Machines may be specifically set up to perform certain tasks and **templates**, **jigs**, **patterns**, **moulds** and **formers** are used to save time and ensure parts are identical. Usually, once a batch has been produced some or all of the processes will be altered to produce the next batch. This may be as simple as changing the colour or size of a product for the next batch, or it may involve making a totally different product.

Batch production still uses some highly skilled labour. However, as some of the tasks are more repetitive, small production lines and semi-skilled workers may be employed. Expensive specialist tools and equipment are frequently needed to produce batches of products and initial set-up costs can be high. The more products being made, the cheaper the overall unit cost of each item. Products associated with batch production include seasonal, limited edition or novelty products.

The **lead times** on batch produced products are fairly short allowing manufacturers to respond to market demand quickly.

> **Q3** Explain what is meant by lead time.

Mass production

Mass-produced products tend to be items that are in constant use and where the design does not change significantly. Due to the large number of units produced and sold, high set-up costs can be justified and the products can still be sold at an affordable price for the mass market.

When large numbers of products are required, the best way to produce them is to set up a dedicated production line that does not need to change. This way their manufacture can be highly automated and use as little skilled labour as possible. Where manual workers are needed, the tasks tend to be simple and repetitive. Production lines need to have some highly skilled technicians to keep them running efficiently, as any downtime could be very costly.

Continuous production

Continuous production is very similar to mass production although the products tend to be made to create stock or standard material forms (primary processing) before final processing or assembling elsewhere. The factory will operate up to 24 hours a day 7 days a week. Staff are mainly low-skilled and operate the factory in shifts. The products made rely on the highest levels of automation and this type of factory normally makes a very limited range of products. This saves any potential changes to the production line, avoiding any downtime. This scale of production is the least labour intensive and produces products with the lowest unit costs. Continuous production is suitable for products that are in constant demand, such as medical textiles and nappies.

With the introduction of digital techniques such as CNC embroidery, laser cutting and digital printing, a number of products that are **customised** and **personalised** for consumers blur the lines between one-off and other levels of production. Having your name engraved on something does not make the product a one-off. One-off products are not available for anyone other than the original client or purchaser.

> **Q4** Suggest a suitable scale of production for each of the following: Halloween costume, wet wipes, ceremonial dress, football socks.

Production processes

There are various means of cutting, shaping and processing materials. You should consider the scale of production when selecting manufacturing processes to ensure production is efficient, consistent and accurate.

A decent pair of tailor's **shears** are an essential element to any sewing kit – they are versatile and give a crisp edge to cut fabric. **Stamps** are used like a biscuit cutter to cut the shape of a pattern piece repeatedly for batch production as they ensure that each piece is identical. Higher levels of production call for higher levels of automation – CNC devices such as **laser cutters** can be used to cut elements designed on a computer.

Manufactured fibres such as Lyocell™ and polymer-based fibres are **extruded** in long filaments before being spun into yarn for fabrics. Synthetic fabrics are prone to fraying but a **heated element** such as a **soldering iron** can be used to cut fabric, melting and fusing all the way along the cut to prevent fraying. Soldering irons are also used to create decorative cut-aways in fabrics.

Quantity production

When making more than one product, consistency of quality, size and performance between products is key.

Templates, **jigs**, and **patterns** can have reference points and markers to show the number of parts to be cut as well as the grain direction and the face and back side of the fabric. They are used to ensure repetitive accuracy when marking out, cutting out or processing materials. These are reusable aids that are produced to save time and effort when manufacturing multiple copies of a product or component. They are often used in **batch** production.

Processes controlled by **computer-aided manufacture (CAM)** are highly accurate, easily editable, fast and efficient. Machines can run 24/7 and do not suffer from fatigue in the way that a human workforce does. In textile production, CAM may be used to control a range of processes including laser cutting, weaving, knitting and embroidery. Computer-aided design programs are used to create **lay plans** to minimise waste.

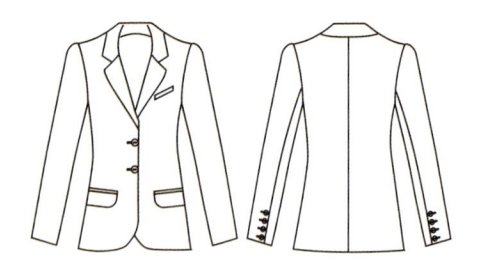

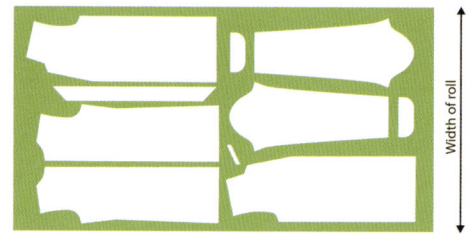

Lay plans help to minimise the amount of wasted fabric

Tolerance

Tolerance is the amount of error that is allowed for a given task. It is often thought of as a measurement that is plus or minus (±) a specific distance e.g. ±1mm. As well as distance it can also apply to the weight of fabric or the strength of a seam in a test.

During a making activity, it may not be possible to achieve 100% accuracy. Therefore, an appropriate degree of tolerance needs to be considered for a given product, material or component. This could vary from a fraction of a millimetre to a few millimetres. A narrower tolerance is usually required for very technical elements, for example, the lining up of a repeat pattern in a garment. For other parts where less accuracy is required, a larger tolerance may be acceptable.

In industry generally, the narrower the level of tolerance required, the more an item will cost to produce. It is simply more time-consuming and therefore more expensive to make products very accurately. However, well-made products tend to work more effectively and last longer, so may in the end be better value for money.

Quality control

When textile products are made, checking that they are being produced correctly is an essential stage. This is known as quality control (QC) and is vital to ensure dimensional and visual accuracy are consistent.

One of the main areas for quality control within textiles is checking a repeating print against an original sample. This ensures it repeats correctly both vertically and horizontally. A garment, like a dress or a jacket, visually hops from front left panel, to front right panel, to sleeve, to back right panel and so on. It is not always possible to get everything to align perfectly but it should look as good as possible. The sample garment will be made to a strict set of guidelines set by the designer's specification. Any imperfections will be rejected if they fall outside a certain tolerance.

Mismatched fabric pattern alignment

> **Q5** If you were joining a left and right panel made from a fabric that had a horizontal repeat pattern of 150mm, what would be the maximum allowance you would need on each side in order to guarantee alignment?

Chapter 59 – Material processing

Objectives

- Describe and evaluate a variety of tools and techniques used to manufacture textiles and textile products

Specialist tools, equipment, techniques and processes

A number of specialist processing techniques are used to manipulate textiles. The colour, texture, shape and drape of a product will depend on what processing has taken place. This section looks at common forms of textile manipulation.

Hand tools and machinery

Tools and techniques vary depending on the material being used and the quantity required. Common cutting tools are shown in the table.

Name	Image	Uses	Name	Image	Uses
Shears or tailors shears		Used to cut fabrics. The long blades help make cutting straight lines easier and faster	Pinking shears		Used to cut material prone to fraying. The zigzag edge can also be used as a decorative finish
Rotary cutting wheel		Cuts accurate lines and curves on multiple layers of fabric	Embroidery scissors		Small bladed scissors for delicate work and cutting threads
Seam ripper		Sharp internal blade between two prongs used to unpick seams	Thread snips		Multi-purpose mini shears that can be used as embroidery scissors or seam rippers
Textile band saw		Fast and efficient method to cut multiple layers of cloth in one pass. Used in commercial settings	Electric rotary cutting wheel		Speeds up the process of cutting textiles. Used in commercial settings
Tailors chalk		Marks out fabric	Tracing wheel and carbon paper		Used to trace a pattern onto materials
Pins		Holds patterns in place during marking out and cutting	Measuring tape		Measuring straight lines or curved shapes accurately

French curve		Used to draft patterns and make alterations	Fade away pens		Fabric markers that fade away in 48 hours
Sewing machine		Used for machine sewing in multiple stitch styles, widths and lengths	Overlocker		Used for finishing edges to prevent fraying. Binds with a 2, 3 or 4 thread stitch and cuts simultaneously

Q1 State **two** additional health and safety concerns when using electric cutting tools over manual ones.

Q2 How do pinking shears reduce the chance of a material from fraying?

Digital design and manufacture

Digital design and manufacture has improved the quality, consistency and efficiency of production and manufacturing. The ability to use computer-aided design (CAD) software and computer-aided manufacturing (CAM) machines is now an expectation for anyone entering the industry.

CAD is used in a variety of ways in the textiles industry, for example to design prints, visualise garments and generate layplans to reduce waste and make best use of materials. CAM machines associated with the textiles industry include laser cutters, plotters, embroidery machines, digital printing and knitting and weaving machines.

Commercial weaving involves the production of modern textiles produced on large scale industrial looms which are computer controlled. The automation allows the fabric designs to be created in special CAD software. This not only controls the loom, but allows weave **simulations** to be run in order to test manufacturability or try out alternative colour schemes and weave patterns before prototype production begins. At this stage it is easy to correct mistakes before full production starts.

Industrial looms can take a very long time to set up but once running they can produce fabrics very quickly and accurately.

Shaping techniques

Sewing is perhaps the most essential skill to learn when manipulating the shape of textiles. Some sewing techniques can be quite complicated and require lots of practice. Sewing can be performed by hand or with a machine. Some very delicate and fine work can only be completed by hand which can be labour intensive. Heat treatments, reinforcement and stiffening techniques also affect the shape of a product.

Adding and reducing fullness

Pleating is a method of folding fabric by doubling it back on itself and securing it in place. Pleats can be ironed or heat-pressed to create a permanent crease so that the material hangs in a particular way or they can be left to fall naturally giving the garment a softer more flowing appearance.

There are many different types of pleat and each has a different effect on the aesthetic, form and movement of a product. For example, **godet** pleats, are formed by adding triangular panels to give a flaring effect. Pleating can be used in specific areas in a garment to enhance aesthetics and functionality. Pleating can create space for ease of movement, create strength in areas of stress or add weight for warmth.

> **Q3** A traditional Scottish kilt for the average man uses about 8 metres of material. What factors do you think justify this amount of material being used?

Gathering is a technique used to shorten a piece of material which gives the impression of fullness through ruffling or bunching. It gives a similar effect to pleating but usually with a more flexible and less formal effect. It is frequently used in curtains and on upholstered items and interior furnishing; it is also used in country and bohemian style clothing. It is quite a simple technique and can often be found in many traditional clothing items from around the world.

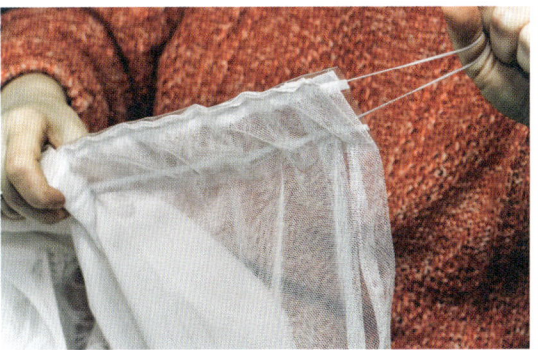

Gathering uses one or more rows of running stitch (other stitches can be used, especially by machines) along the length of the section of material to be gathered.

The thickness of the material and the size of the individual gathers required will govern the spacing and length of the running stitch. Larger stitch length and spacing will create bigger gathers. Shirring elastic can be used to gather fabric which creates both fullness and stretch. Once the gathered material is spaced as required, it can be sewn onto another piece of material, such as a waist band, so that it stays in position.

> **Q4** Why is gathering such a popular technique used in curtain making?

Under stitching adds a line of stitching to linings or facings to stop them from sliding out from the inside of a garment – often used at the neckline.

Additional shaping techniques are described in the grid below:

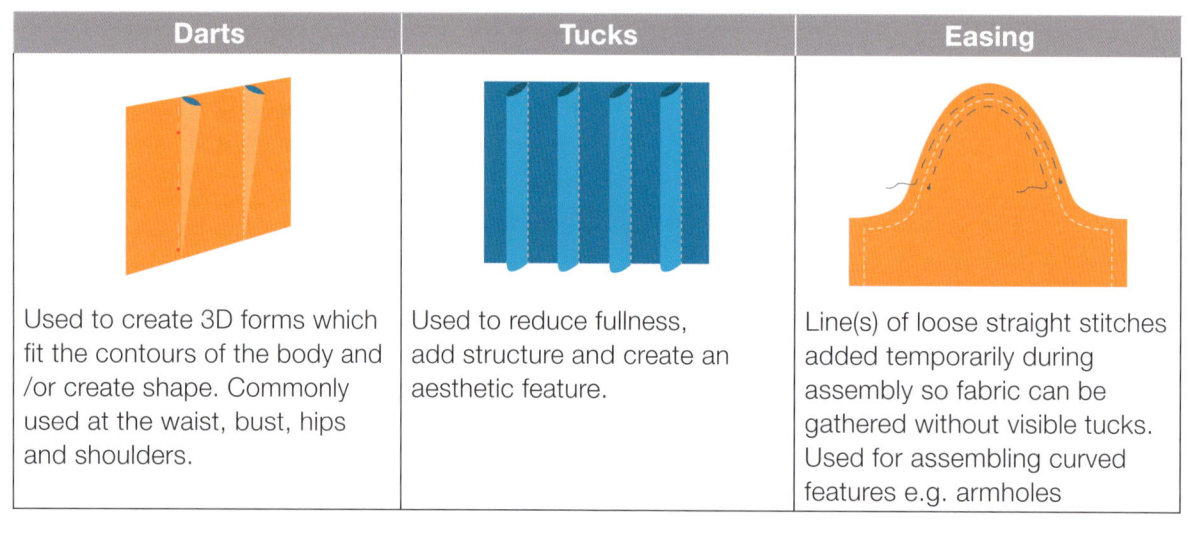

Darts	Tucks	Easing
Used to create 3D forms which fit the contours of the body and /or create shape. Commonly used at the waist, bust, hips and shoulders.	Used to reduce fullness, add structure and create an aesthetic feature.	Line(s) of loose straight stitches added temporarily during assembly so fabric can be gathered without visible tucks. Used for assembling curved features e.g. armholes

Woven and non-woven fabrics can be **moulded** into 3D forms using steam, heat or adhesive. Polymer-based textiles can be formed by heating the fabric to just below the melting point of the thermoplastic fibre, forming, then allowing the fabric to cool. This method can be used to create textures and elastic fabrics. Milliners use water, steam and heat to form and drape felt.

Adding structure

Interfacing is used to create stiffer, more rigid elements to a garment (see Chapter 56). Different weights of interfacing are more rigid than others. Collars and cuffs, for example, need more structure than most other parts of a garment.

Highly structured garments such as bodices, corsets, bras and crinolines (in times gone by) use **boning** to add rigidity and shape to garments. Boning is usually incorporated into seams. Strips of boning are used to create an internal structure, like a skeleton, which fabric can hang from.

Crinoline used to give shape to the skirt of a period costume

Fabricating, constructing and assembling

Textile products are assembled using various techniques. Some are addition techniques which join materials and components where as others are wastage techniques which remove material.

> **Q5** Consider the last textile product you made and list the fabrication and construction techniques you used to make it.

Draping to create forms

There are two methods of forming items of clothing by draping and they differ considerably. The first uses the natural drape of a fabric when hung over a model or a dress form (tailor's dummy) to create a garment. A draper has a skilled role in the fashion industry and is able to see and feel the way a particular fabric falls in order to create the balance between aesthetics and wearability. Fabric is often cut and positioned on the **bias** during drape forming to make the most of the drape of the fabric. This can improve the way a garment moves, as well as the way it fits around the body. Making garments that are cut on the bias is more costly as more material has to be wasted. This technique is often used when making bespoke items such as ball gowns, wedding dresses and suits.

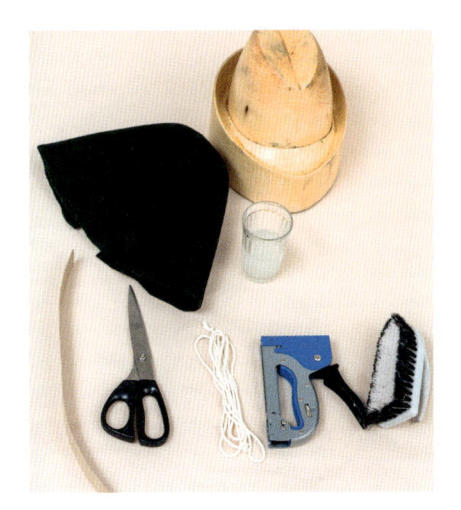

The second method refers to the forming of **felt products**, particularly hats, over a former. Felt has no natural drape when it is dry, but when it is soaked in hot water it can be stretched over a former with relative ease. Care must be taken not to damage the felt, which is very delicate whilst wet. The warm and wet felt is slowly stretched and pinned or tied into its final position and left to dry. As it dries the felt attempts to shrink around the shape of the former and sets. Complex patterns can be formed. Once the felt is dry it can be trimmed and finished as required.

> **Q6** Why do you think felt in particular is able to morph to the shape of the former so easily?

Seams

Seams are used to join pattern pieces together. Plain seams are the fastest and easiest way to create a seam and are the basis for many other types of seam. Other seams are more decorative, can provide housing for boning, hide raw edges and add functionality.

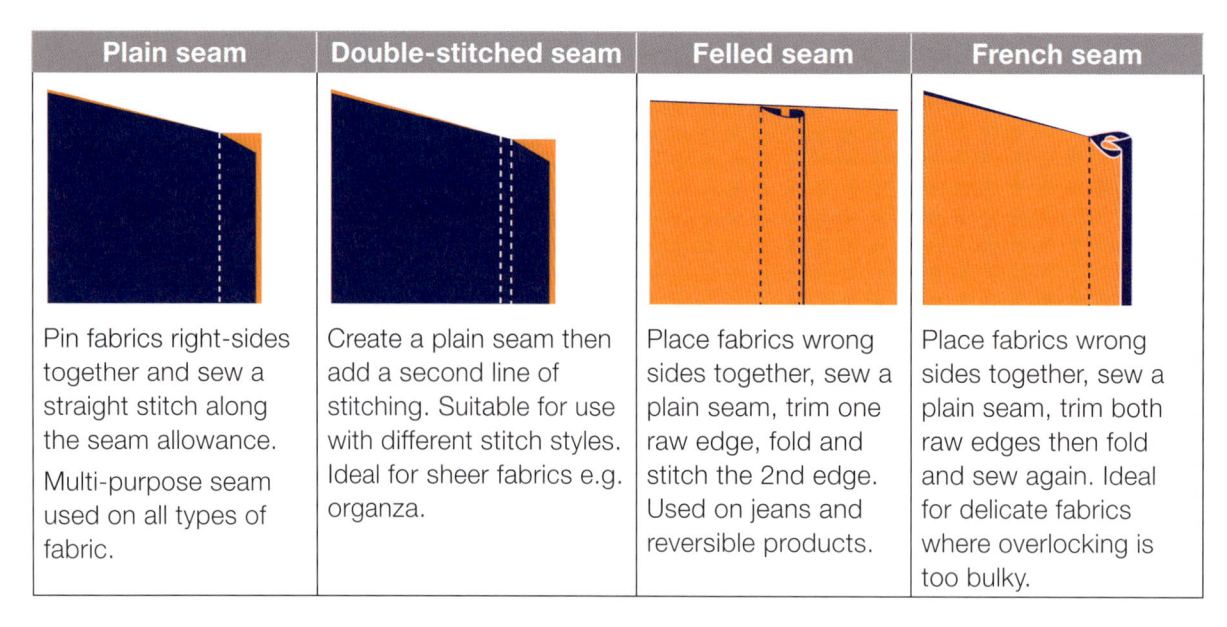

Plain seam	Double-stitched seam	Felled seam	French seam
Pin fabrics right-sides together and sew a straight stitch along the seam allowance. Multi-purpose seam used on all types of fabric.	Create a plain seam then add a second line of stitching. Suitable for use with different stitch styles. Ideal for sheer fabrics e.g. organza.	Place fabrics wrong sides together, sew a plain seam, trim one raw edge, fold and stitch the 2nd edge. Used on jeans and reversible products.	Place fabrics wrong sides together, sew a plain seam, trim both raw edges then fold and sew again. Ideal for delicate fabrics where overlocking is too bulky.

Topstitching is often incorporated into seams and contrasting thread colours can be used to add an aesthetic accent to a product. Sandy-coloured topstitching is an iconic aspect of the seams on jeans.

> **Q7** What does the term topstitching mean?

Fully waterproof products call for **sealed seams**. While waterproof fabrics may be impermeable, their surface is punctured during product assembly allowing water to seep in at the seams. Nylon tape laminated to a thin heavy-duty rubber is bonded to the inside of seams on waterproof jackets, tents and trousers to create a sealed or taped seam.

Finishing raw edges

Hems are a way of finishing the edges of a textile product to prevent the fabric from fraying. Felt, other non-woven and some laminated fabrics do not require edge finishing but all other woven or knitted fabrics will fray unless the edges are finished in some way.

One of the most common and straightforward ways of creating a hem is to turn the raw edge under then press and sew it in place. Using pinking shears or a **zig-zag** stitch is one of the fastest most versatile methods of hemming, but delicate fabrics may need a lighter touch. **Rolled** hems are ideal for lightweight fabrics but the most common hemming method is to fold, press and sew hems into place. **Bound** hems are created by stitching a separate fabric tape around the raw edge and topstitching it in place – this method is used on towels.

Blind hemming and **invisible stitching** are used when the hem must not be visible. The hem is sewn, by hand or machine, with only a few stitches catching the front of the fabric to hold the hem. A specialist machine foot and stitch style are required for blind hemming or the process can be done by hand. Commonly used on blinds and garments, especially formal garments made from silky fabric.

Bonded hems are created with **hemming tape**. Hemming tape is a web of heat activated adhesive that, when sandwiched between two layers of fabric under heat and pressure, will fuse the layers together. Bonding hems in this way is a fast but less durable method used on low-cost and utility garments such as school uniforms.

Overlocking

The overlock stitch is created with a special sewing machine called an **overlocker**. It's a quick way to achieve a durable edge, hem or seam as it can cut, finish and join in one operation. Overlockers, or sergers, can be set up with 2, 3 or 4 threads – the two-thread set-up is for neatening without adding too much bulk or weight, a 4-thread set-up gives maximum strength.

Components

You need to be familiar with a variety of different components that are used in textiles. Some of the most common textile components are listed below.

Name	Image	Characteristics	Name	Image	Characteristics
Button		A small fastener sewn to the fabric, made from various materials such as plastic, wood and metal	Eyelet		Used to strengthen holes for receiving lacing or attachment by a cord or hook
Velcro® Hook and loop		Velcro is a trade name for a hook and loop fastener, the two parts quickly attach and release	Press-stud		A secure button like fastener made from metal. Special pliers are used to attach the stud
Hook and eye		Simple fastener sewn on to garments. Often used on lingerie items and at the top of a zip e.g. the necks of dresses	Zip		Cloth fastener sewn into garments and textile products. Interlocking teeth secure sides together
Buckle		A strap and metal hasp are used to form an adjustable fastening, often with a leather or firm fabric strap	Toggle		A plastic or wooden toggle is fed through a loop attached to a garment. A robust fastener often used on coats

Chapter 60 – Surface treatments and finishing

Objectives

- Evaluate a range of surface finishes and treatments for textiles and textile products

Textile surface treatments and finishes

Many modern textiles are given a surface finish so that they perform more efficiently. The reasons for applying a finish fall into two main areas; aesthetics and functionality.

Aesthetics can mean manipulating the surface of the fabric to:

- make the surface very smooth to improve sheen and lustre
- add decoration and colour
- change the texture

Functionality can mean:

- resistance to water, staining and shrinking
- making it easier to care for
- flame retardancy
- improving the ability to retain heat more efficiently
- adding smart finishes such as insect repellent and anti-bacterial properties

Decorative finishing techniques

A number of specialist techniques are used to decorate textiles. Decorative techniques are often combined to achieve the desired visual effect and texture.

One of the oldest techniques for decorating textiles is silk painting. Various fabric paints and pens are available on the market today but the art of silk painting was a job for highly skilled artisans. First used in Asia, paintings were created freehand or with a latex substance called gutta, to act as a resist. Traditional works depict portraits and landscapes, modern fabric paintings have a more varied and contemporary aesthetic.

Japanese 18th century silk painting

Batik and resist dying

Resist dying techniques use various methods to prevent dye from reaching certain areas of the fabric. In **mechanical resist** techniques the fabric is bound so tightly that dye cannot permeate the fabric in certain areas. Other methods of resist dying use wax, stencils and chemical treatments.

Batik uses hot wax or paraffin to mask the area that is decorated therefore resisting absorption from the dyeing process which follows. Firstly, a pattern is drawn on, or applied to the material. This can be printed or hand drawn. Sometimes it is coloured so that it remains there permanently, but it can also be made to wash away leaving no mark. Secondly, molten wax is then applied. A tjanting (or canting) tool or a brush is used for hand drawn designs. A printing block known as a cap may be used for larger, more repetitive designs and batch produced items. As the wax is applied it soaks into the fabric and sets in position.

Lastly, the material is dyed with the desired colour. The material is then boiled to remove the wax and finally, the material is ready. This process can be repeated. additional colours can be added on top of /overlapping previous colours as well as on to clear sections.

Q1 What factors make batik dyeing techniques a labour intensive process?

Laminating

Some technical textiles are available where two or more layers of the same or different fabrics are bonded together, usually to improve its physical properties. The different layers, sometimes known as ply, can be sewn together or bonded using heat or adhesive.

Gore-tex® is an example of a technical textile that has many layers, each doing a different job. See Chapter 12 for more detail on how Gore-Tex® works.

PVC fabrics, such as faux leather are also laminated. They have a water resistant plastic layer bonded to a fabric lining material so that it is softer and more comfortable for the wearer. It also makes the cloth stiffer as unlined PVC can be too flexible for some applications. Lamination is classified as a chemical treatment. Other chemical treatments are covered later in this section.

Quilting and patchwork

Quilting is a traditional technique which has differing methods of construction around the world, but it usually consists of a decorative top layer with a plain backing sandwiching thicker material between them. The layers are all sewn together to make a quilt. The thicker middle layer is often made from wadding (known as batting) and is used to add thickness, weight and thermal insulation.

The decorative top layer is the most interesting and many traditional techniques, patterns and textures exist around the world, such as **patchwork**. Patchworks are created by recycling sections of material which can include sentimental family hand-me-downs. Quilts, in particular, are a form of textile that can become an heirloom item.

Q2 Why is quilting an ideal technique for using scrap and recycled textiles?

Other techniques you should be familiar with include:

Appliqué	Couching	Embroidery
Fabric shapes cut out and layered then bonded and/or stitched in place, usually with a zigzag stitch.	A thick thread or cord is laid on fabric along a seam with hand or zigzag stitching to hold it in place. Commonly combined with patchwork.	Densely stitched thread used to embellish fabric. Can be made by hand or using CAD/CAM.

Printing

There are various commercial textile printing techniques available. These include roller printing, using metal plates to transfer images on to the fabric, screen printing to push coloured inks onto fabric through special fabric screens and digital printing. Digital printing uses CAD and CAM to create very complex images.

Digital printing is becoming much more commercially viable. Historically it has been seen as a very expensive process, but as technology has improved and equipment costs have lowered, it is becoming more accessible. Digital printing allows a full colour range to be applied to the fabric as it uses inkjet technology to combine the dyes at the print head.

Other benefits of digital printing include a reduction in water and chemical consumption. There is also less waste produced. Prototyping is a very quick and simple way of testing different patterns and colourways. There is effectively no maximum length of run as the printable fabric is available on very long rolls.

Chemical finishes and treatments

Chemical treatments are used to change the aesthetics, function and structure of a textile. For example, easy-care, shrink resist and stain resist treatments make products easier to wash and clean. Most fabrics are porous but can be coated, sprayed or washed to resist water. Synthetic fabrics are prone to generating electrostatic charge through friction, like a balloon being rubbed on your hair. **Anti-static** agents prevent the build-up of electrostatic charge and prevent clothes from clinging.

As with any treatment, there are pros and cons. For example, **bleaching** removes stains and gives a uniform base for dyes and printing, however, it also weakens the fabric. Coatings such as paint-on and spray-on products are generally solvent based and not very environmentally friendly as they can contain high levels of volatile organic compounds (VOCs).

Most homes are furnished with textile-based products such as carpets and curtains and we cover ourselves with clothes which all have the potential to burn. In order to reduce fabric combustion and potential fire hazards, **flame retardants** are used.

Strict guidelines govern the manufacture and treatment of fabrics used for tents, toys, upholstery and nightclothes. Look out for attached labels explaining fire precautions.

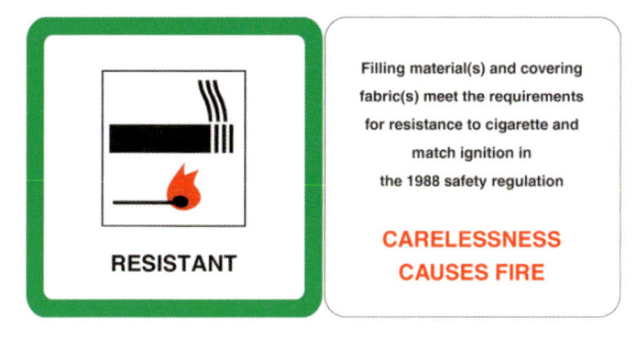

Flame retardants are designed to produce a chemical reaction that slows down and even stops ignition taking place. The two types of flame retardants used on textiles are **halogenated** flame retardants which reduce the amount of fuel available to combust and **phosphorus** flame retardants which form a 'charred' carbonaceous layer also reducing the available fuel.

> **Q3** Why do you think nightclothes are specifically covered by flammability guidelines?

Carbonising and **mercerising** are two of the first processes to be performed on natural fibres and fabrics. Newly constructed fabric, also known as **greige**, is littered with tiny fragments of plant which cannot be removed by physical means. Carbonising involves passing the fabric through sulphuric acid, heating then rinsing to remove excess cellulose matter. Mercerising is used to relax the helix shape of cellulose fibres such as cotton. The process involves soaking the fabric in caustic acid under tension. This turns the helix shape into cylindrical, more lustrous fibres which are less prone to shrinking. The caustic soda breaks down the cell walls which improves the fabric's ability to accept dyes.

Physical finishes and treatments

These treatments use physical movement to change the look, feel and handle of a fabric. Many of these treatments were originally carried out by hand but are now executed by machines as part of a production line.

Calendering involves passing fabric through a series of rollers to create shiny, smooth or embossed surface. **Singeing** and **desizing** are often carried out in sequence. Greige is passed through a naked flame at high speed to remove excess fibres from the surface to give a smoother finish. The desizing process passes fabric through water or an enzyme or chemical solution to remove excess starch. This makes the fabric less stiff, improving drape.

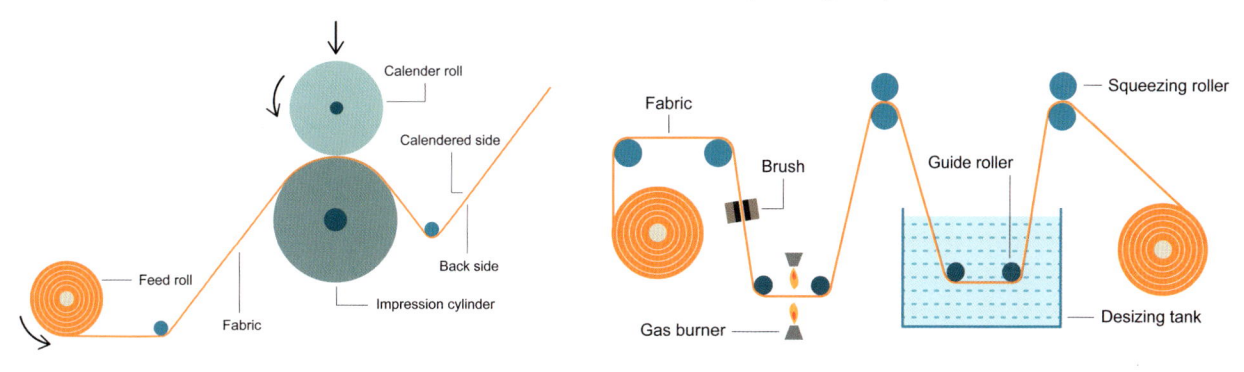

Calendering

Singeing and desizing

Chapter 60 **Surface treatments and finishing** 319

During fabric construction the warp and weft yarns become misaligned, stretched and shrunk. **Tentering** and **heat setting** are used to realign the yarns and pull fabrics to the correct width. Tentering involves hooking both edges of a fabric roll on to tenter hooks and gradually pulling the fabric to the required width. Heat setting exploits the thermoplastic properties of polymer-based synthetic yarns. In this process the fabric is heated to close to its softening point during tentering.

The soft, fuzzy brushed effect on suede and synthetic fleece is known as the **nap**. This texture is created through **raising** and/or **emerising** which both involve pulling the fabric over abrasive rollers. Emerising pulls the fabric over rollers covered in emery paper, whereas raising uses wire brushes.

Freshly made fabric can have a loose structure which limits its use. Agitating the fabric tightens up its structure which makes it easier to work with and of a more consistent quality. This process is achieved through **milling** and **fulling** or **'walking'**. Traditionally, the fulling process involved immersing fabric in urine (a natural detergent) and walking on it or beating it with clubs. Fulling was carried out manually by slaves before the process was mechanised using mills. These days, machines and alternative detergents are used.

Biological finishes and treatments

Biological processes use enzymes to modify the appearance and properties of a textile. Using enzyme solutions as opposed to chemicals dramatically reduces the environmental impact of textile production. **Biostoning** uses enzymes to affect the dye in fabric to create a stonewashed effect without the use of chemicals and pumice stones. **Biopolishing** uses enzymes to remove excess fibres and achieve a smooth, glossy appearance on cotton.

Smart finishes and treatments

Smart materials are those which change properties based on an external stimulus, such as a change in temperature or moisture. Smart materials can be applied to fabrics as coatings, pigments or additives to create smart textiles. **Thermochromic** fabric changes colour in response to heat whereas photochromic pigment changes colour in response to UV light. Both these smart materials are commonly used for novelty aesthetic purposes but **photochromic** materials are also used to indicate exposure to the sun to prevent skin damage.

Electrochromic materials change colour in response to an electrical current. These can be woven into textiles to create a futuristic look as well as used in displays and medical applications. **Solvation chromism** is colour change in response to moisture levels – commonly used in nappies to indicate when the nappy is full.

Microencapsulation traps liquid or solid substances within the fibres of the material. When microencapsulated textiles are rubbed or in some applications, heated, the walls of the fibres open up allowing the encapsulated substance to be released. Uses for this technology include insect-repellent clothing, where insecticide is slowly released, **anti-bacterial** clothing for sports and medical applications and phase-change micro-encapsulation (PCM) which enables textiles to regulate the wearer's body temperature.

Microencapsulation is also used for trapping thermochromic dyes used in colour-changing clothing.

> **Q4** Some microencapsulated clothing products lose their effectiveness after a number of washes. Why do you think this is the case?

Exercises

1. This question is about regenerated cellulosic fibres.
   (a) State the raw materials of regenerated cellulosic fibres. [1]
   (b) Explain how regenerated cellulosic fibres are processed. [2]

2. This question is about social and ecological impact.
   (a) Explain what an ecological footprint measures. [2]
   (b) Explain what the social footprint of a company measures. [2]

3. Give **two** effects of deforestation on the environment. [2]

4. Explain what is meant by the term 'product miles'. [2]

5. Describe how embedded composites help to reinforce extreme sportswear. [2]

6. Explain **two** advantages of using stock materials. [4]

7. Four different types of forces are tension, compression, shear and flexibility. Which is the primary force involved in each of the following scenarios? Explain each of your answers.
   (a) A hammock. [3]
   (b) Eyelets on a shoe. [3]
   (c) An upholstered footstool. [3]
   (d) A swimsuit. [3]

8. This question is about stiffening and reinforcement.
   (a) Explain what is meant by laminating a product, giving an example. [3]
   (b) Describe how ribs and boning are used to reinforce products and give a suitable application for this technique. [3]

9. This question is about scales of production.
   (a) Explain the term 'one off production' and give an example of a suitable product. [3]
   (b) Explain the term 'batch production' and give an example of a suitable product. [3]
   (c) Explain the term 'mass production' and give an example of a suitable product. [3]
   (d) Explain the term 'continuous production' and give an example of a suitable product. [3]

10. Which **one** of the following best describes the process of carbonising? [1]
    ☐ Used to stretch fabric to a standard width
    ☐ Used to remove fragments of cellulose material from natural fabrics
    ☐ Used to relax the helical shape of cotton fibres
    ☐ Used to remove excess starch from fabric

Notes

Index

0-9
3D
 drawing 115
 printing 240, 281
7000 series aluminium 159, 161

A
ABS 225
accelerometer 30
acrylic 86, 89, 252
adhesives
 metals 179
 polymers 247
 timbers 145
aesthetic factors
 metals 160
 papers and boards 192
 polymers 227
 systems 259
 textiles 300
 timber 129
agro-textiles 55
Alessi 106
alloys 82
aluminium 82, 154
 anodising 182, 284
annealing 163
annotation 113
Apple 106
applique 318
apprenticeships 14
architrave 135
automation 3
availability
 metals 161
 papers and boards 194
 polymers 229
 systems 263
 textiles 302
 timbers 131

B
bag press 138
balsa 94
batch production 21, 167
batik 316
batteries 44, 255
 alkaline 45
 disposal 46
 EU Battery Directive 255
 rechargeable 45
bauxite 154
beams 162
beech 94
belts 64
bespoke production 21
bevel gear 66

bias 313
binding 212
biofuel 43
Biopol 87, 228
biopolymers 219
blanking 174, 175
blow moulding 237
bluetooth 31
board 84
 manufactured 95
bonded fabric 91
bond paper 191
boning 312
 textiles 298
boxboard 84
Braille 215
brass 82
Brasso 249
brazing 176
breadboard 268
budget constraints 27
built-in obsolescence 255, 303
business
 funding 6
 privately owned 5
 start-up 6
buzzer 69

C
calendering 319
calico 90
CAM, (Computer-Aided Manufacturing) 138
cams 62
capacitor 265
carbon-fibre reinforced plastic 53
carbon footprint 32, 34
carbonising 319
carbon offsetting 35, 102
cartridge paper 83
carving 143
casting 167, 174
cast iron 81
cedar 95
cells. See batteries
children 14
chipboard 128
circuit board 268
CNC (Computer Numerical Control) 138
cold-formed rivet 176
collaboration 110
communication 31
communication technologies 253
components
 electrical 68
 programmable 70
 standardised 19
composite materials 52
compression
 of timber 128
computer aided design (CAD) 117

computer aided manufacture (CAM)
 metals 168
 polymers 240
 textiles 307
concrete 52
conductive fabrics 58
conductive inks 51
conductivity
 thermal 262
coniferous 93
construction
 textiles 55
consumer society 14
contact adhesives 247
continuous production 23
copier paper 83
copper 82, 154
corrugated board 84
corrugation 197
cotton 88
couching 318
counting 74
cracking 221
creasing 209
cross-section 165, 234
crowdfunding 5
culture 16, 100
current 263
 amp 266
cutting plotters 205

D
darts 312
data
 primary 109
 secondary 109
datum 136, 235
deciduous 93
deforestation 9, 123, 292
delay timer 73
demographic movement 4
denier 304
denim 90
depth stop 167
desertification 123
design
 decisions 26, 29
 developing ideas 112
 fixation 109, 111
 iterative 109
 proposal 26
 strategies 110
 systems thinking 111
 user-centred 110
desizing 319
die cutting 204
digital light processing 241
disabilities 15
domestic textiles 56
dowels 135
draping 313
drawing

assembly 117
exploded 116
orthographic 116
techniques 115
drop forging 168
Dura Vermeer 29
dynamic forces 157

E

easing 312
ecological footprint
    of systems 254
economic migration 4
edge staining 214
effort 60
elastane 289
electrical forces 158
embossing 197
    blind 215
    metals 175
    papers and boards 215
embroidery 318
emerging technologies 2
emery cloth 173
energy
    cost 47
    generation 39
    hydroelectric 42
    solar 42
    storage 44, 46
    tidal 40
    usage 35
    wind 41
engraving 246
enterprise 5
environment 8
environmental
    impact 33, 46
        of metals 155
        of papers and boards 188
        of polymers 221
        of systems 254
        of textiles 301
        of timbers 129
evaluation
    design proposal 26
evergreen trees 93
exploded drawing 116
extrusion 240

F

fabric
    pile 297
fabrics
    conductive 58
    fire resistant 58
fair trade 33
feedback loops 73
felt 91
ferrous metals 80, 81
fibres
    animal-based 89, 288
    plant-based 88
    synthetic 89, 289
    vegetable 289
finite resources 7, 9, 289
fire resistance
    fabrics 58
flat-pack furniture 140
floating yarns 296
flowchart 71
flow soldering 274
fluoroelastomer 225
flux 176
foil blocking 215
foil-lined board 191
folding 209
followers 62, 63
forces
    dynamic 157
    electrical 158
    metals 157
    papers and boards 195
    polymers 224
    static 157
    systems 260
    textiles 297
    timbers 133
forestry management 124
Forest Stewardship Council 6, 123
forging 167, 168
fossil fuels 40
fractional distillation 220
fuels
    biofuels 43
    fossil 40
    renewable 40
fulcrum 60
functionality
    of metals 162
fused deposition modelling 241
future scenarios 29

G

gathering 311
gauge 164, 233
gears 65
    bevel 66
    compound 65
    idler 66
    rack and pinion 66
genetic engineering 193
geo-textiles 56
glass reinforced plastic (GRP) 53
global warming 29, 31
godet pleats 311
go/no go fixture 137, 167
Gore-Tex 57
green design 102
gsm 199

H

hardening 163
hardwood 93, 127
Heatherwick Studio 108
heat transfer paper 191
hemming 314
high carbon steel 158
high impact polystyrene HIPS 86
hinges
    timber 147
holographic foil 215
human capability 103
hydroelectric 42

I

injection moulding 238
integrated circuits (IC) 70, 263
interfacing 299, 312
Internet of Things 18
ironmongery 147
iron ore 153
isometric projection 115
iterative design 109

J

jacquard 296
Joe Casely-Hayford 106
joining
    metals 175
    polymers 247
    textiles 313
    timbers 144
joints 144
just-in-time (JIT) 19

K

Kevlar 57
knock-down fittings (KDF) 146
knurling 172

L

labour 4, 32
laminating
    papers and boards 191, 196, 213
    polymers 244
    textiles 298, 317
    timber 128, 134
laser cutting 204, 246
laser sintering 241
lay plans 307
lead time 22, 28, 306
lean manufacturing 19
levers
    classification 60
    efficiency 61
Life Cycle Analysis (LCA) 12, 36
light dependent resistor (LDR) 67
light emitting diode (LED) 69
lignin 193
linear motion 59
line bending 239
linkages 62
    bell crank 62
    reverse motion 62

lithography 202
load 60
loops 73
low carbon steel 81
LunaTik 5
LYCRA 289

M

mahogany 94
manufacturing
    capabilities 28, 104
    timescale 27
manufactured board 95, 128
marking out
    metals 166
    papers and boards 208
    polymers 235
    textiles 309
    timbers 136
mass production 22
material
    composite 52, 260
    cost 104
    extraction 254
    modern 48
    piezoelectric 50
    properties 78
    robotic 54
    separation 12
    smart 48
    use 34
MDF 96
mechanical advantage (MA) 60
medical advances 30
mercerising 319
metal
    extraction 154
    ferrous 80
    non-ferrous 80
    refining 155
microcontroller 70, 258
microencapsulation 58, 320
microfibre 56
microns 199
microprocessor 258
migration 4, 16
mild steel 81
milling 173
mining
    environmental impacts 155
    surface 153
    underground 153
minorities 16
modelling
    3D 114
    frame 205
    intermediate 205
    test 205
modern materials 48
moisture
    sensor 257
motion
    linear 59
    oscillating 59
    reciprocating 59
    rotary 59
motor 259
moulding
    blow 237
    injection 238
    press 239
mouldings 135
moulds 169
movement 59

N

nails 146
nanomaterials 49
natural disaster 29
new technology 5, 15, 28
Nitinol 48
Nomex 58
non-ferrous metals 80, 81, 82
non-finite resources 7, 9
notching 210
not-for-profit organisation 6
nylon 289

O

oak 94
oblique projection 115
Ohm's Law 266
oil 149
one-off production 21
optic fibre 31
organisations
    not-for-profit 6
orthographic projection 116
oscillating motion 59
overlocking 315

P

packaging 12
paint 149
paper 83
paper engineering 209
patchwork 317
pattern 138, 167, 169
people 13
perforations 209
peripheral interface controllers 70
perspective drawing 115
PET 225
PHA 229
PHB 87, 228
photochromic glass 50
photocopying 203
photo etching 269
photo-resist PCB 269
PIC 258
pick and place 274
piezoelectric 50
    sensor 257
pig iron 154
pile 297
pine 95
Pixar 108
plating 283
pleating 311
ply 197
plywood 52, 96
polarity 67
pollution 11, 188
polyamide 289
polyester 89
    resin 86
polyhydroxy-butyrate 228
polymers
    biodegradable 87
    reinforced 54
    smart 30
    temperature responsive 51
    thermoforming 85, 86
    thermosetting 86
polystyrene 225, 252
    expanded 226
    extruded 226
    high-density 225
polyurethane 225
pop rivet 176
population 8, 31
population movement 16
Porsche 27
power. See energy
    battery 44
    electrical 44
    output 47
    portability 46
    powering systems 44
    storage 46
press moulding 239
primary data 109
printed circuit board 268
printing
    colour 201
    digital 203
    lithography 202
    offset 202
    screen 200, 285
    textiles 318
privately owned businesses 5
product
    analysis 105
    beneficiaries 32
production
    batch 21
    continuous 23
    lead time 22
    mass 22
    one-off 21
production aids
    metals 169
    papers and boards 206
    polymers 236
    textiles 307
    timbers 137

production techniques 19
product miles 292
programmable components 70
Programme for the Endorsement of Forest Certification (PEFC) 123
properties
   of metals 157
   of papers and boards 190
   of polymers 223
   of systems 257
   of textiles 295
   of timber 126
   physical 78
   working 78
prototype 305
pulleys 64
pulp 186
punch 174
punching 175
PVC 225

Q

quality control
   papers and boards 202
   metals 167
   polymers 235
   systems 274
   textiles 308
   timbers 137
quilting 317

R

rack and pinion 66
rare earth elements 252
Raymond Loewy 107
reactive glass 49
rechargeable batteries 45
reciprocating motion 59
recordings
   video and audio 114
recycling 102
   metals 156
   papers and boards 187
   polymers 222
   systems 255
   textiles 301
   tertiary 103
refining 220
   metals 155
regenerated cellulosic 289
reinforcing
   papers and boards 195
   polymers 231
   textiles 298
relay 258
remote working 17
renewable energy 40
repetitive timer 73
resistance
   ohm 266
resistor 69, 258, 261, 265

colour chart 261
parallel 267
series 267
resources
   finite 7, 9, 156
   natural 9
   non-finite 7, 9
responsible design 34
Restriction of Hazardous Substances 256
reuse 102
ribs 198, 261
   used in textiles 298
rigid polystyrene 225
rivets 175
rotary motion 59
rotary systems 62
routing 138

S

sanding 143
satin weave 296
scales of production 20
   metals 167
   papers and boards 207
   polymers 236
   systems 272
   textiles 305
   timbers 137
schematic diagram 72, 117
science parks 4
screen printing 200, 285
screws
   for metals 178
   for polymers 247
   for timbers 145
seams 313
seasoning 125
secondary data 109
sensor
   moisture 257
   piezoelectric 257
sewing 311
shape memory alloys (SMA) 48
shellac 149
shift patterns 17
signals
   digital and analogue 70
silk 288
singeing 319
sizing 186
sketching 112
slag 154
sliding bevel 136
smart
   materials 48
   polymers 30
smelting 154
social footprint
   metals 162
   papers and boards 184
   polymers 230

systems 253
textiles 291
timbers 132
society 17
   culture 16
   ethnic minorities 16
   segregation 16
softwood 93, 95, 127
soldering 177, 280, 271
solid white board 84
sources
   metals 153
   papers and boards 186
   polymers 219
   systems 254
   textiles 288, 290
   timbers 122
speaker 259
spelter 176
spot varnishing 213
staff
   apprentice 14
   highly-skilled 13
   labour 32
   wage 14
   working hours 17
stain 149
stainless steel 82
standardised design 19
start-up 6
static forces 157
stay stitching 299
steel
   high-carbon 158
   production 153
   tool 158
   tungsten 158
stencils 206
stereolithography 241
stitching 312
   under 312
stock forms
   metals 164
   papers and boards 198
   polymers 233
   systems 265
   textiles 304
   timbers 134
stripboard 269
Styrofoam 226
sub-assembly
   of metals 169
   of systems 275
   of timbers 139
sublimation paper 191
surface mining 153
surface-mount technology 264
sustainability 7
   metals 156
   papers and boards 187
   polymers 222
   systems 252
   textiles 294

timber 122
switches 67
   micro 257
   push to break (PTB) 68
   push to make (PTM) 68
   reed 258
   toggle 68
systems
   diagrams 117
   thinking 111

T

tapping 177
technical textiles 55
technology
   emerging 2
technology parks 4
tempering 163
template 138, 167, 169
tencel 289
tensol-12 247
tentering 320
Tesla 108
Tetra Pak 191, 214
textiles
   knitted 92
   sports 58
   technical 55
   woven and non-woven 89
thermistor 67
thermoforming polymers 85, 224
thermosetting polymers 85, 224
threading 177
through-hole components 264
tidal energy 40
timber conversion 124
timer 73
tin 154, 159
titanium 159
tolerance 235
   component 265
   metals 167
   papers and boards 202
   polymers 235
   systems 265
   textiles 308
   timbers 137
tool steel 158
tools
   metals 173
   papers and boards 208
   polymers 242
   systems 277
   textiles 309
   timbers 142
topstitching 314
tracing paper 83
transistor 68, 258
transportation 10
   costs 10
   product miles 10
travel 30

tucks 312
tungsten steel 158
turbines 39
   wind 41
turning 138, 143, 172

U

underground mining 153
unemployment 3
upcycling 103
   textiles 302
urea formaldehyde 86
urethane 225
UV varnishing 213

V

vacuum
   bag press 134
   forming 245
varnishing 149
   spot 213
velocity ratio (VR) 61
veneer 149
veneers 95
vernier calipers 136
Veroboard 269
Vertu 27
video conferencing 18
viscose, acetate 289
volatile organic compounds 181
voltage 263

W

wage levels 14
waste 11
   WEEE 11
wax 149
weave
   plain 90
   satin 296
   twill 90
weaving
   commercial 310
WEEE 11, 256
welding
   metals 168, 176
   polymers 238
wet and dry paper 173
wood joints 144
woodscrews 145
wool 89
workforce 13
   highly-skilled 13
   skill set 3
work hardening 163
working hours 17
woven textiles 89

Z

Zaha Hadid RA DBE 108

Edexcel GCSE 1DT0 (9-1) Specification map

Core content

New and emerging technologies

		Unit 1	Unit 2	Unit 3	Unit 4	Unit 5	Unit 6-1	Unit 6-2	Unit 6-3	Unit 6-4	Unit 6-5	Unit 6-6
1.1	Impact of new and emerging technologies	✓										

Informing design decisions

		Unit 1	Unit 2	Unit 3	Unit 4	Unit 5	Unit 6-1	Unit 6-2	Unit 6-3	Unit 6-4	Unit 6-5	Unit 6-6
1.2	Informing design decisions		✓									

Energy, materials, devices and systems

		Unit 1	Unit 2	Unit 3	Unit 4	Unit 5	Unit 6-1	Unit 6-2	Unit 6-3	Unit 6-4	Unit 6-5	Unit 6-6
1.3	How energy is generated and stored			✓								
1.4	Modern and smart materials			✓								
1.5	The functions of mechanical devices			✓								
1.6	Electronic systems			✓								
1.7	The use of programmable components			✓								

Material types, properties and structures

		Unit 1	Unit 2	Unit 3	Unit 4	Unit 5	Unit 6-1	Unit 6-2	Unit 6-3	Unit 6-4	Unit 6-5	Unit 6-6
1.8	Ferrous and non-ferrous metals				✓							
1.9	Papers and boards				✓							
1.10	Polymers				✓							
1.11	Textiles				✓							
1.12	Natural and manufactured timbers				✓							
1.13	Contextual practice				✓							

Designing principles

		Unit 1	Unit 2	Unit 3	Unit 4	Unit 5	Unit 6-1	Unit 6-2	Unit 6-3	Unit 6-4	Unit 6-5	Unit 6-6
1.14	Investigate social and economic challenges					✓						
1.15	Investigate the work of others					✓						
1.16	Avoiding design fixation					✓						
1.17	Developing design ideas					✓						

The content in each section of the textbook covers the same specification points as the corresponding downloadable teaching unit, e.g. Section 1 complements Unit 1.

Specialist material categories

		Unit 1	Unit 2	Unit 3	Unit 4	Unit 5	Unit 6-1	Unit 6-2	Unit 6-3	Unit 6-4	Unit 6-5	Unit 6-6
2.1	Design contexts											
2.2	Sources, origins and properties											
2.3	Influencing selection											
2.4	The impact of forces and stresses											
2.5	Stock forms, types and sizes											
2.6	Manufacturing processes											
2.7	Specialist tools, equipment and processes											
2.8	Surface treatments and finishes											

Materials covered in Units 6-1 – 6-6:

6-1 Timbers
6-2 Metals
6-3 Papers and boards
6-4 Polymers
6-5 Systems
6-6 Textiles

Edexcel GCSE Teaching Units

Exclusively for teachers

To accompany each section in the textbook, there is a series of teaching units for the new Pearson Edexcel 1DT0 (9-1) GCSE.

Each unit contains editable PPT and DOC format materials to enable effective delivery of the content with relevant and engaging examples for students.

There are worksheets and homework for each topic and an assessment test at the end of each unit with exam style questions.

Answers to all worksheets, homework tasks and the assessment are also included.

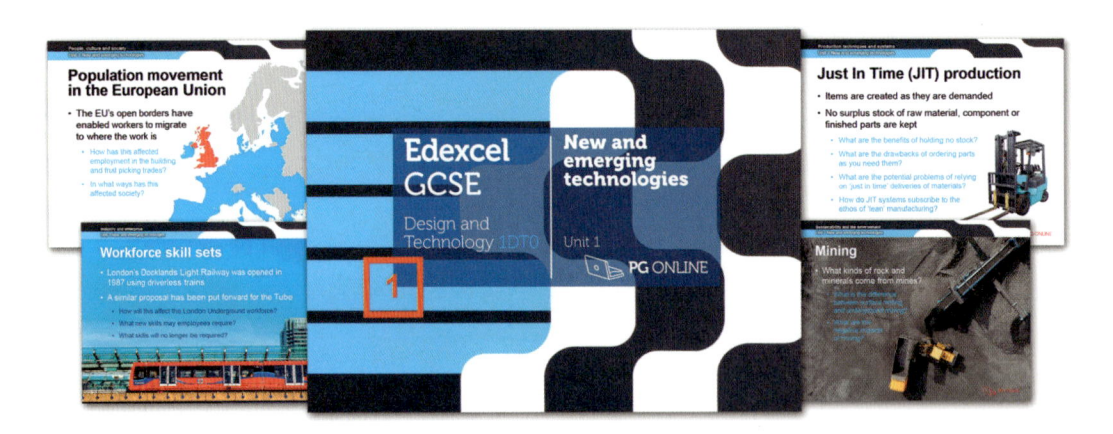

Unit 1 is free to registered teachers.

Downloadable Units to support the new Design and Technology 1DT0 Specification:

- Unit 1: New and emerging technologies
- Unit 2: Informing design decisions
- Unit 3: Energy, materials, devices and systems
- Unit 4: Materials types, properties and structures
- Unit 5: Designing principles
- Unit 6-1: Timbers
- Unit 6-2: Metals
- Unit 6-3: Papers and boards
- Unit 6-4: Polymers
- Unit 6-5: Systems
- Unit 6-6: Textiles

For more details on prices and discounts or to register your school:
visit www.pgonline.co.uk, email sales@pgonline.co.uk
or call 0845 840 0019.